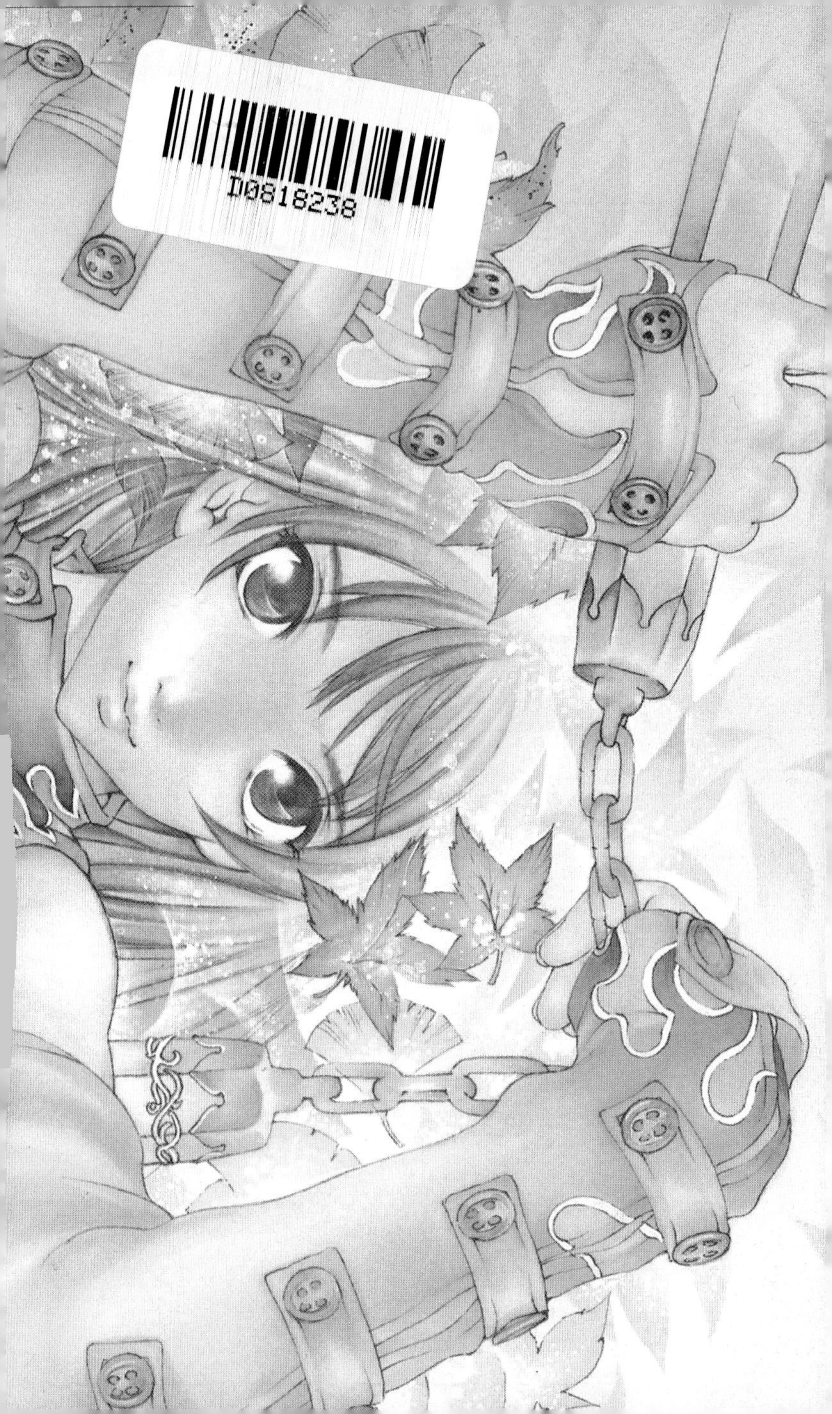

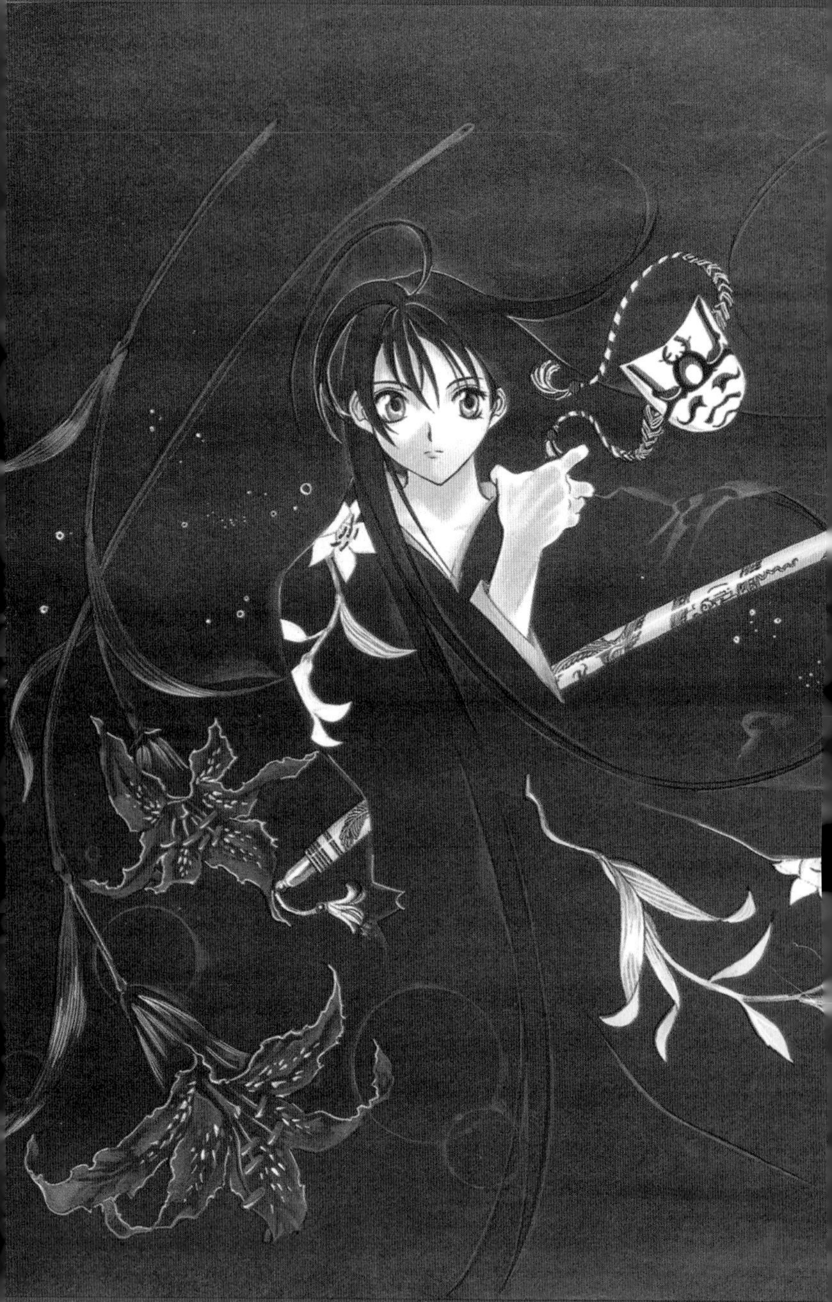

FIGHT:20

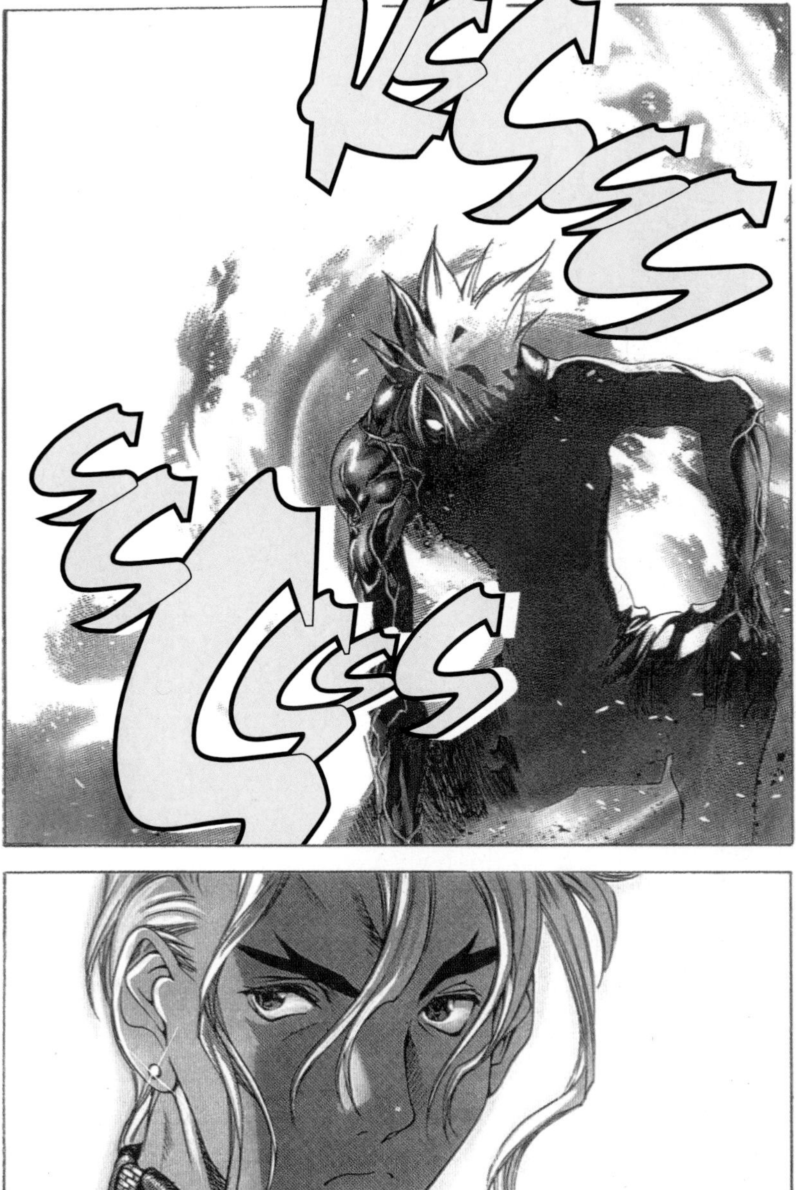

CONTENTS

4

GERMANY

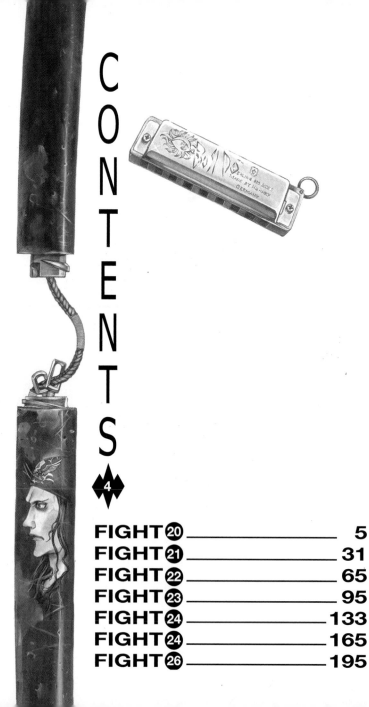

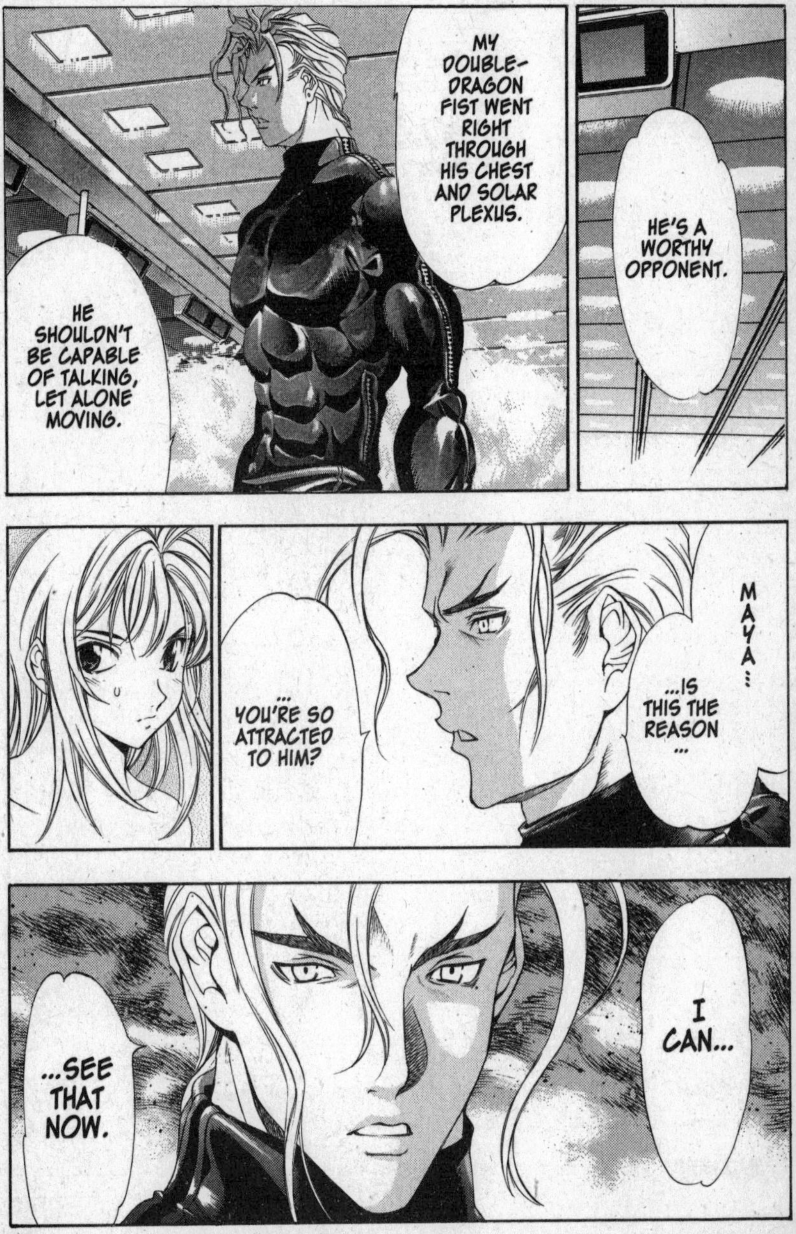
HE'S A WORTHY OPPONENT.
MY DOUBLE-DRAGON FIST WENT RIGHT THROUGH HIS CHEST AND SOLAR PLEXUS.
HE SHOULDN'T BE CAPABLE OF TALKING, LET ALONE MOVING.
MAYA...
...IS THIS THE REASON ...
... YOU'RE SO ATTRACTED TO HIM?
I CAN...
...SEE THAT NOW.

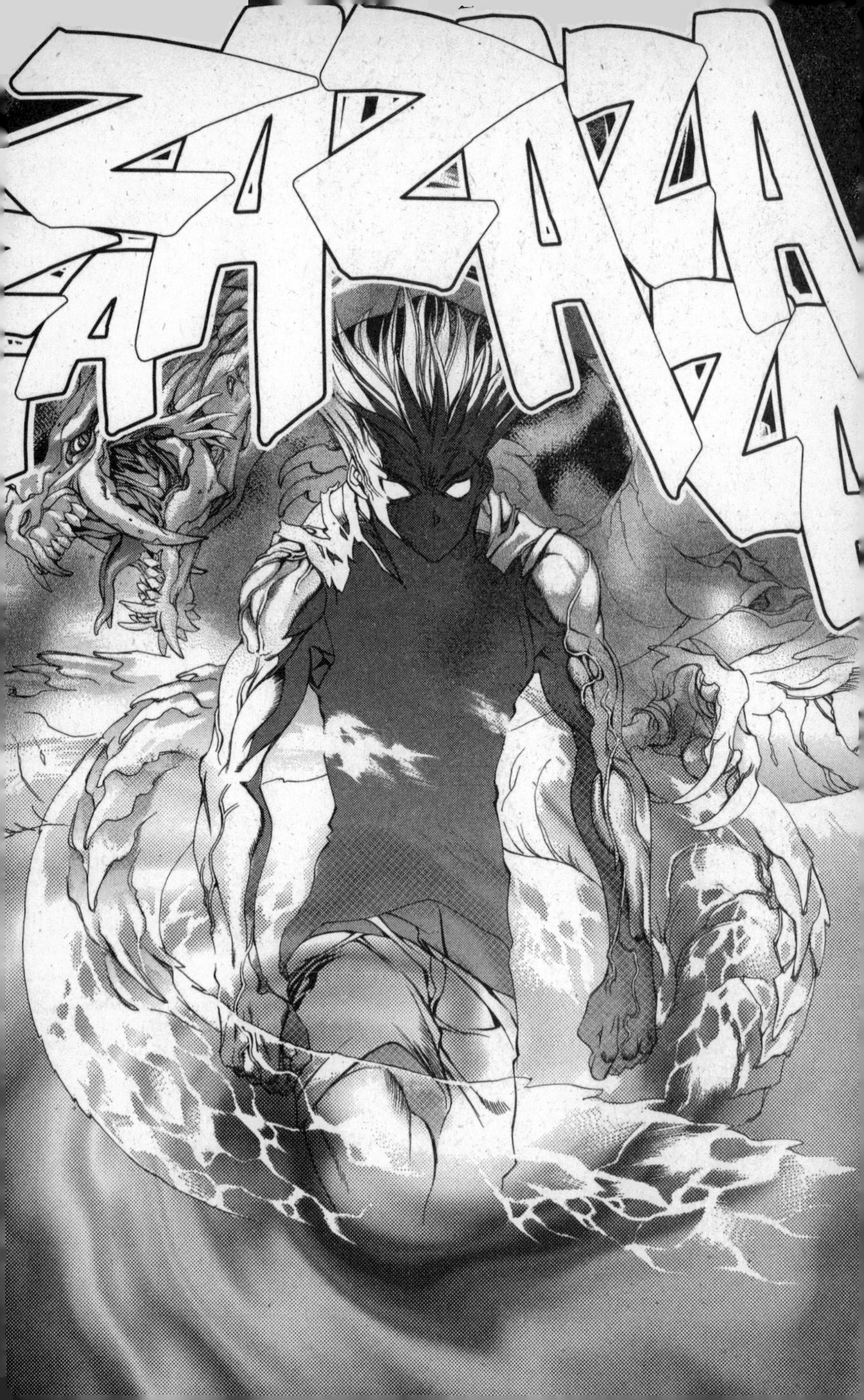
ZAZAZA

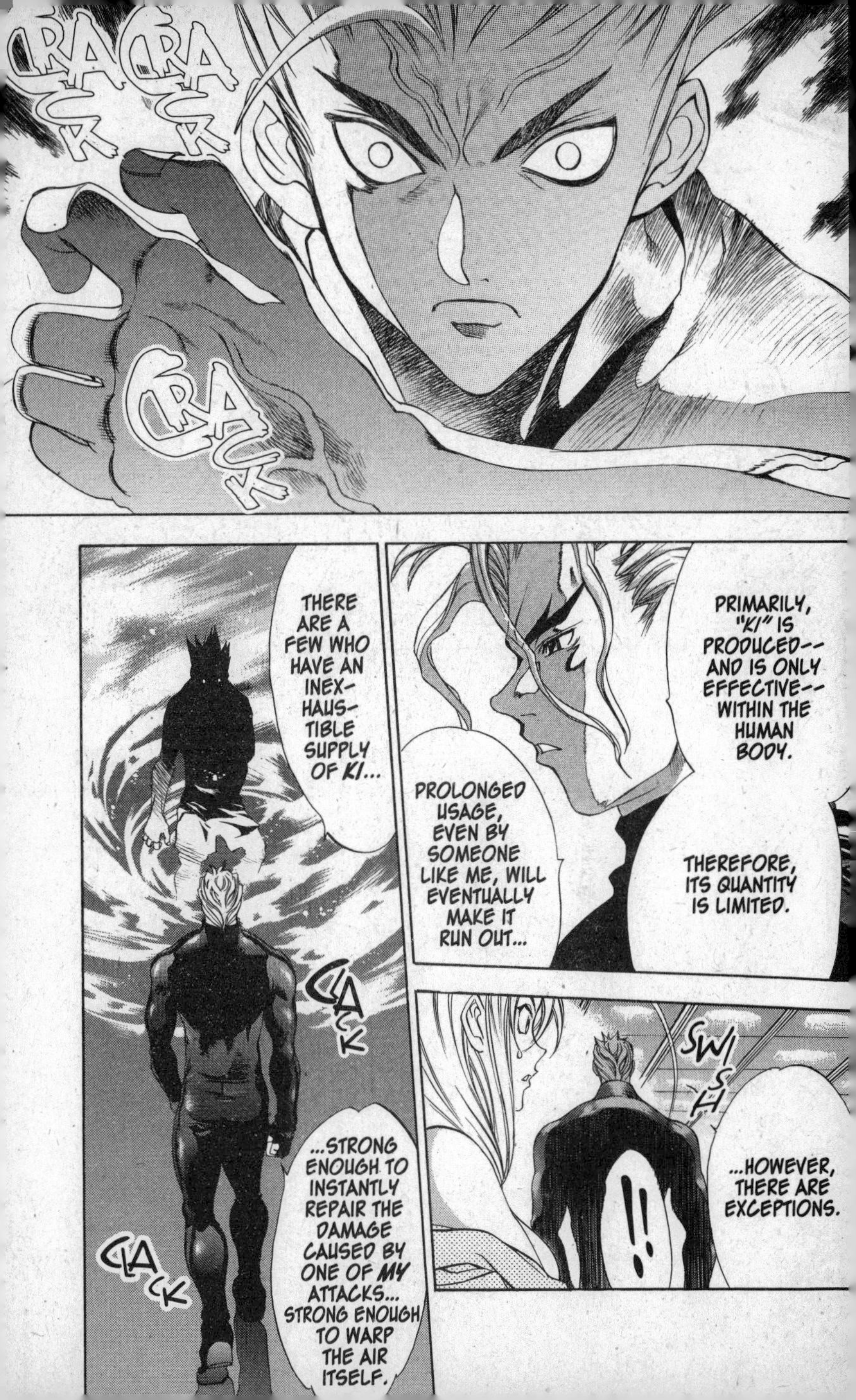

CRACK CRACK
CRACK
PRIMARILY, "KI" IS PRODUCED--AND IS ONLY EFFECTIVE--WITHIN THE HUMAN BODY.
THEREFORE, ITS QUANTITY IS LIMITED.
PROLONGED USAGE, EVEN BY SOMEONE LIKE ME, WILL EVENTUALLY MAKE IT RUN OUT...
SWISH
...HOWEVER, THERE ARE EXCEPTIONS.
!!
THERE ARE A FEW WHO HAVE AN INEXHAUSTIBLE SUPPLY OF *KI*...
CLACK
...STRONG ENOUGH TO INSTANTLY REPAIR THE DAMAGE CAUSED BY ONE OF *MY* ATTACKS... STRONG ENOUGH TO WARP THE AIR ITSELF.
CLACK

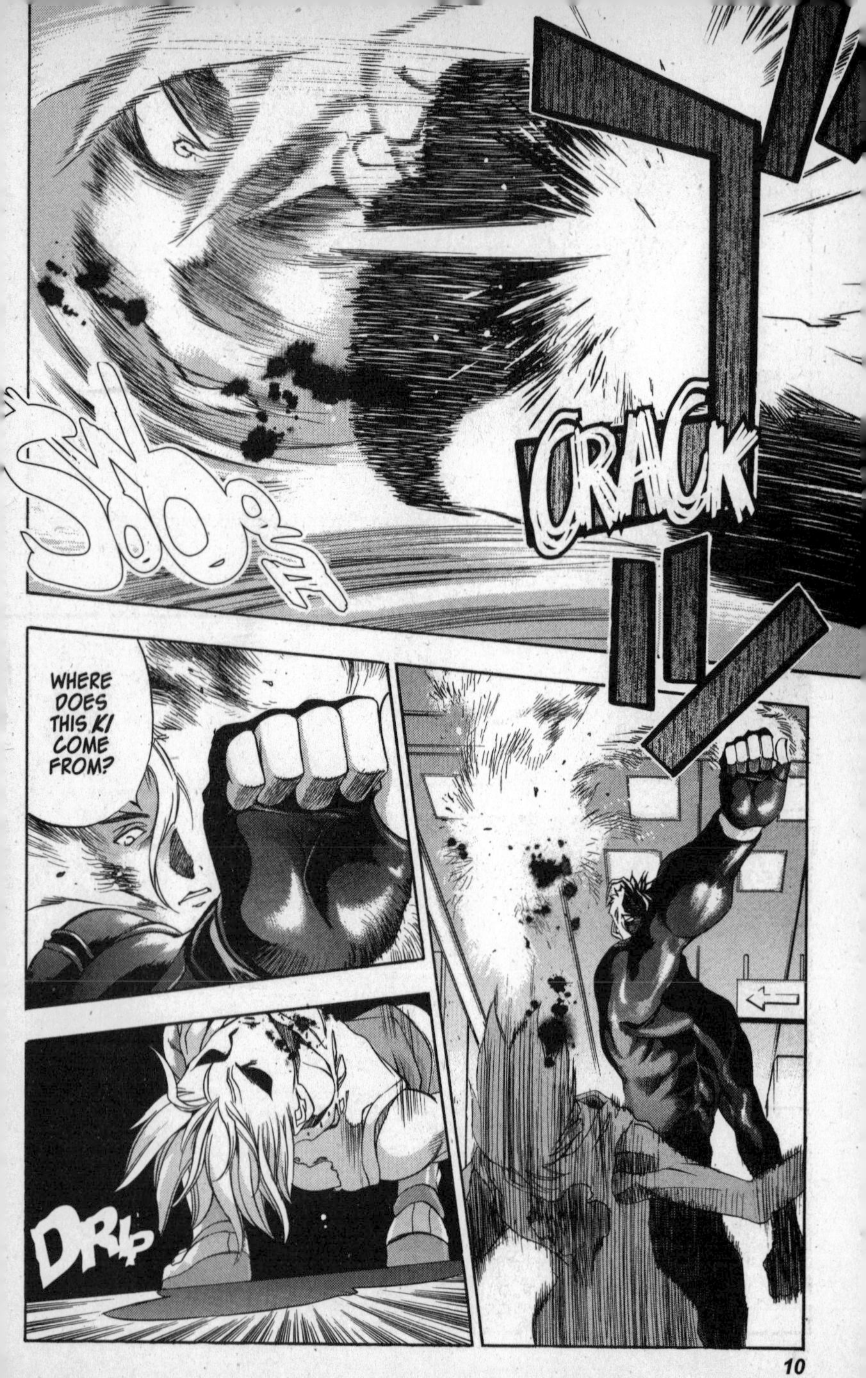
CRACK
SWOOSH
WHERE DOES THIS KI COME FROM?
DRIP

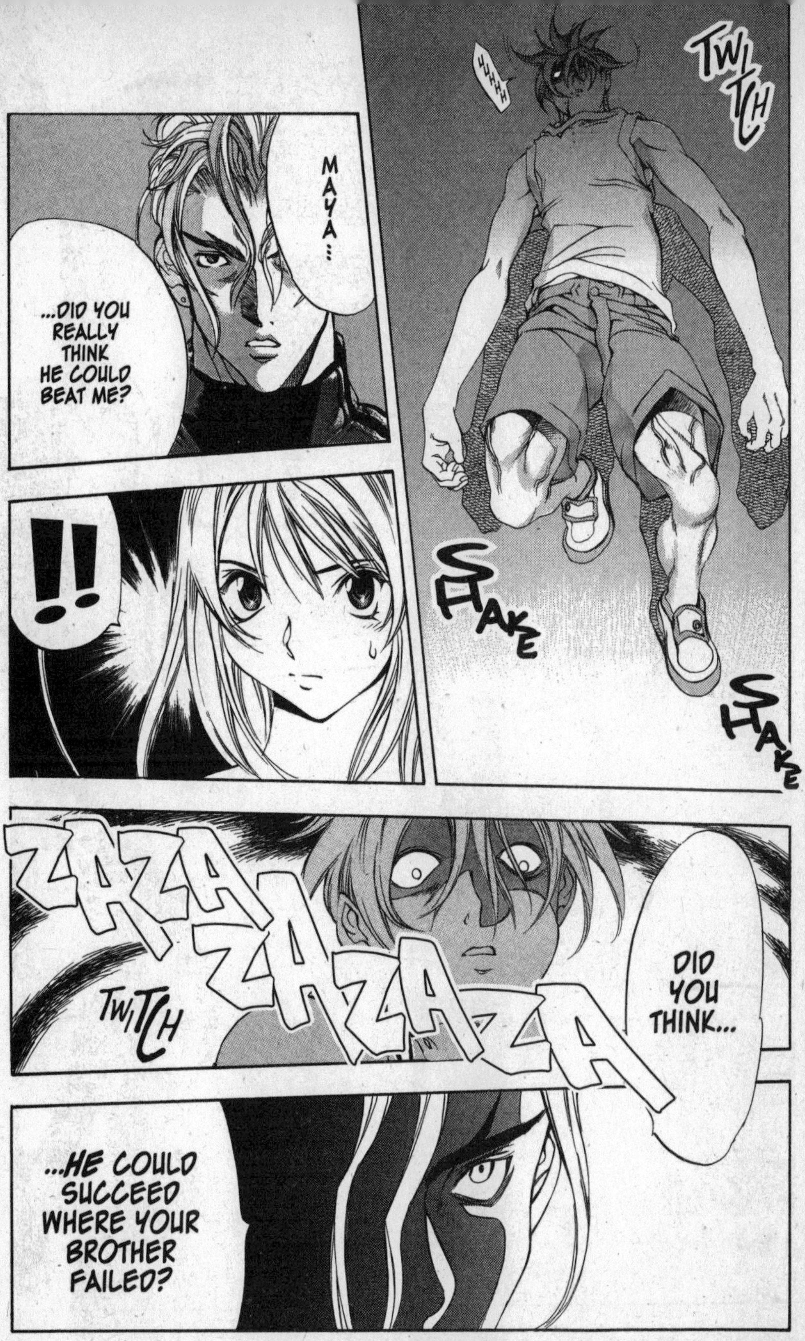
TWITCH
UUHHH
SHAKE
SHAKE
MAYA...
...DID YOU REALLY THINK HE COULD BEAT ME?
!!
DID YOU THINK...
TWITCH
ZAZAZAZAZAZA
...HE COULD SUCCEED WHERE YOUR BROTHER FAILED?

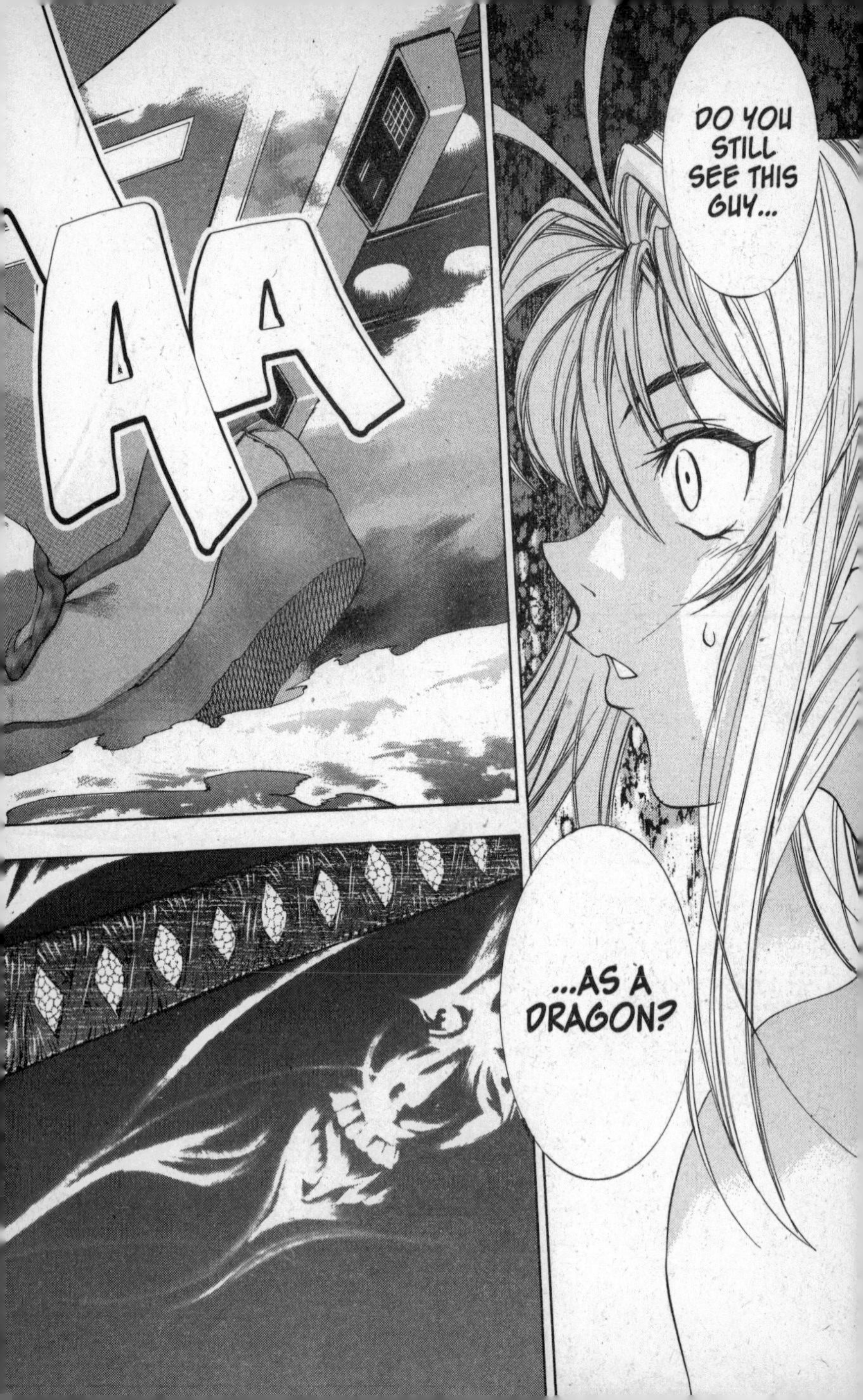
DO YOU STILL SEE THIS GUY...
...AS A DRAGON?
AA

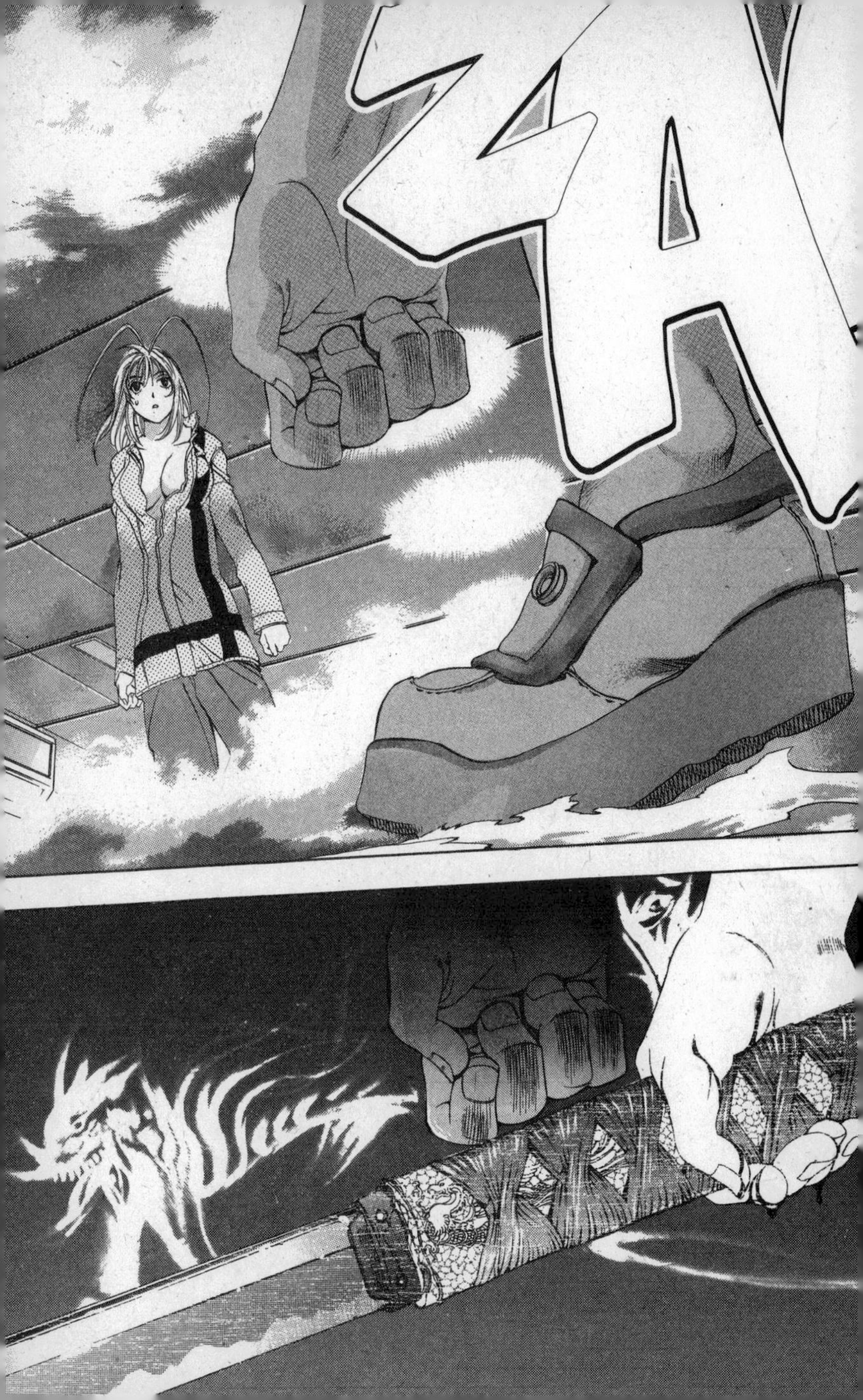
ZA

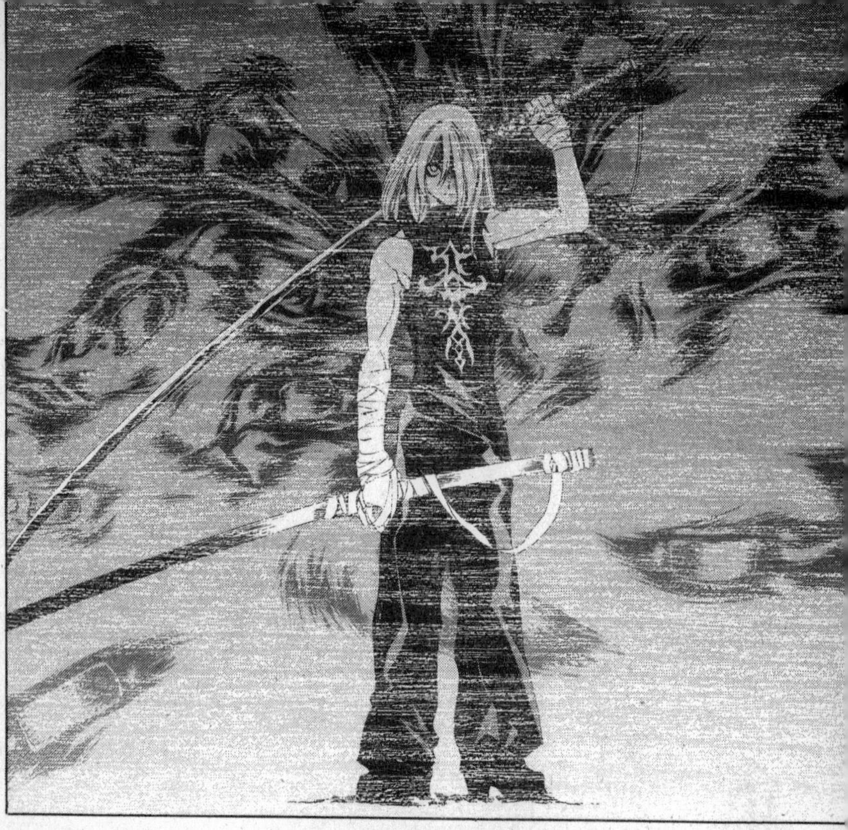

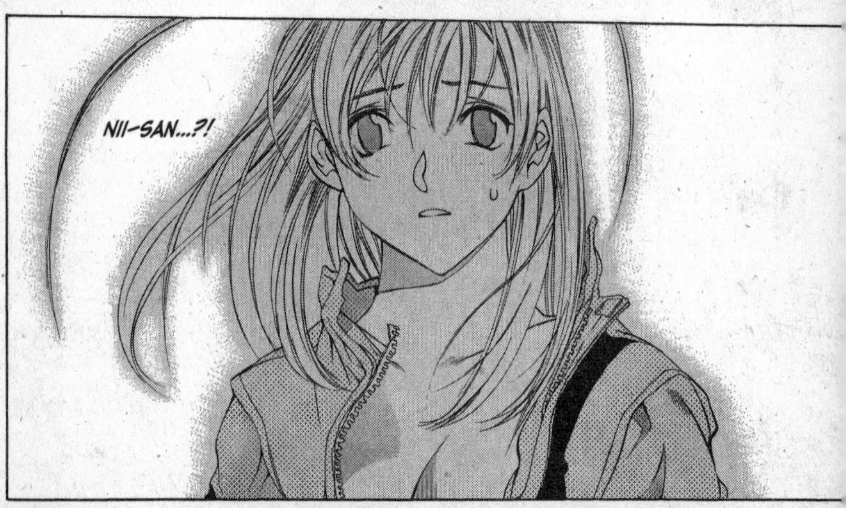
NII-SAN...?!

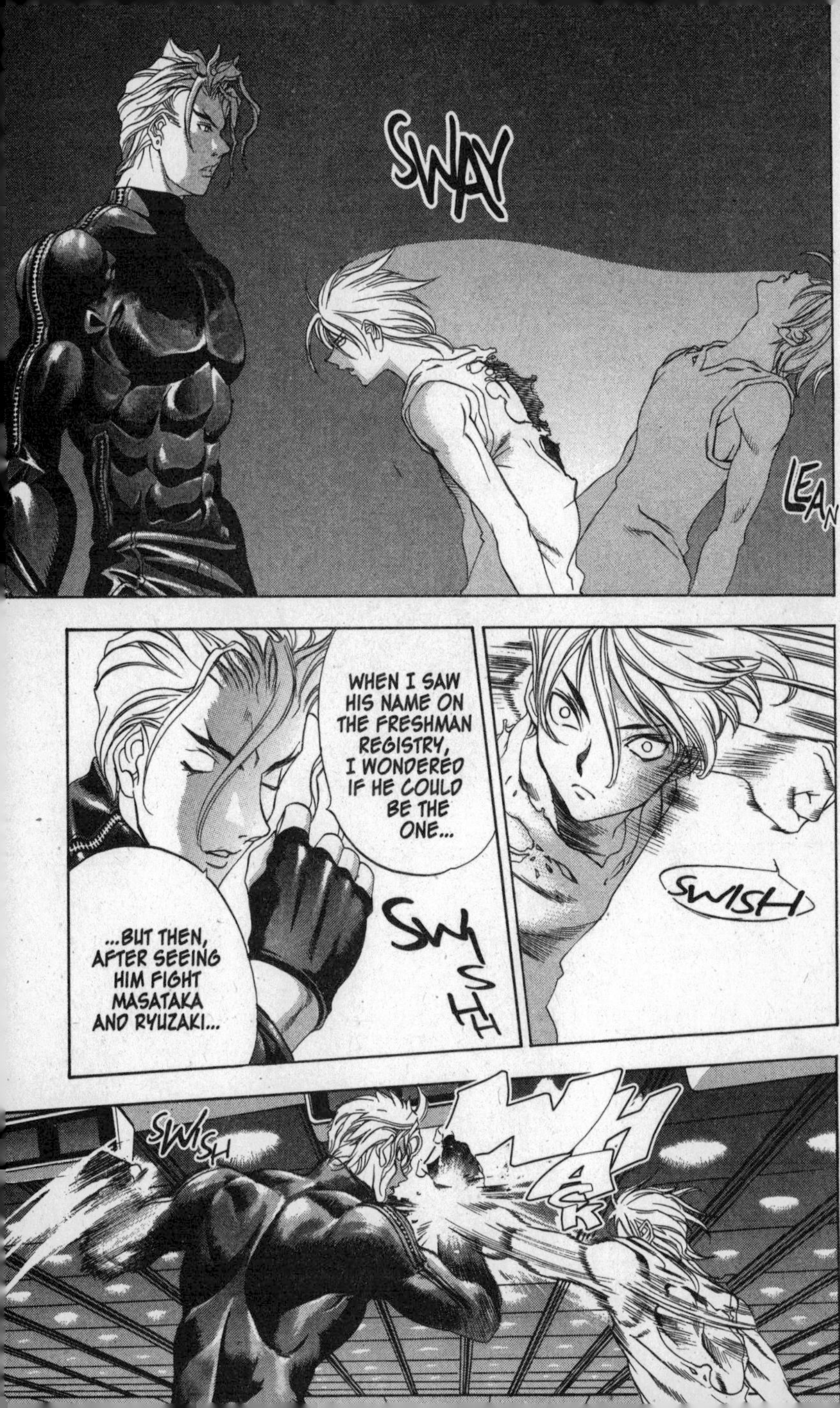
SWAY
LEAN
SWISH
WHEN I SAW HIS NAME ON THE FRESHMAN REGISTRY, I WONDERED IF HE COULD BE THE ONE...
...BUT THEN, AFTER SEEING HIM FIGHT MASATAKA AND RYUZAKI...
SWISHH
WHACK
SWISH

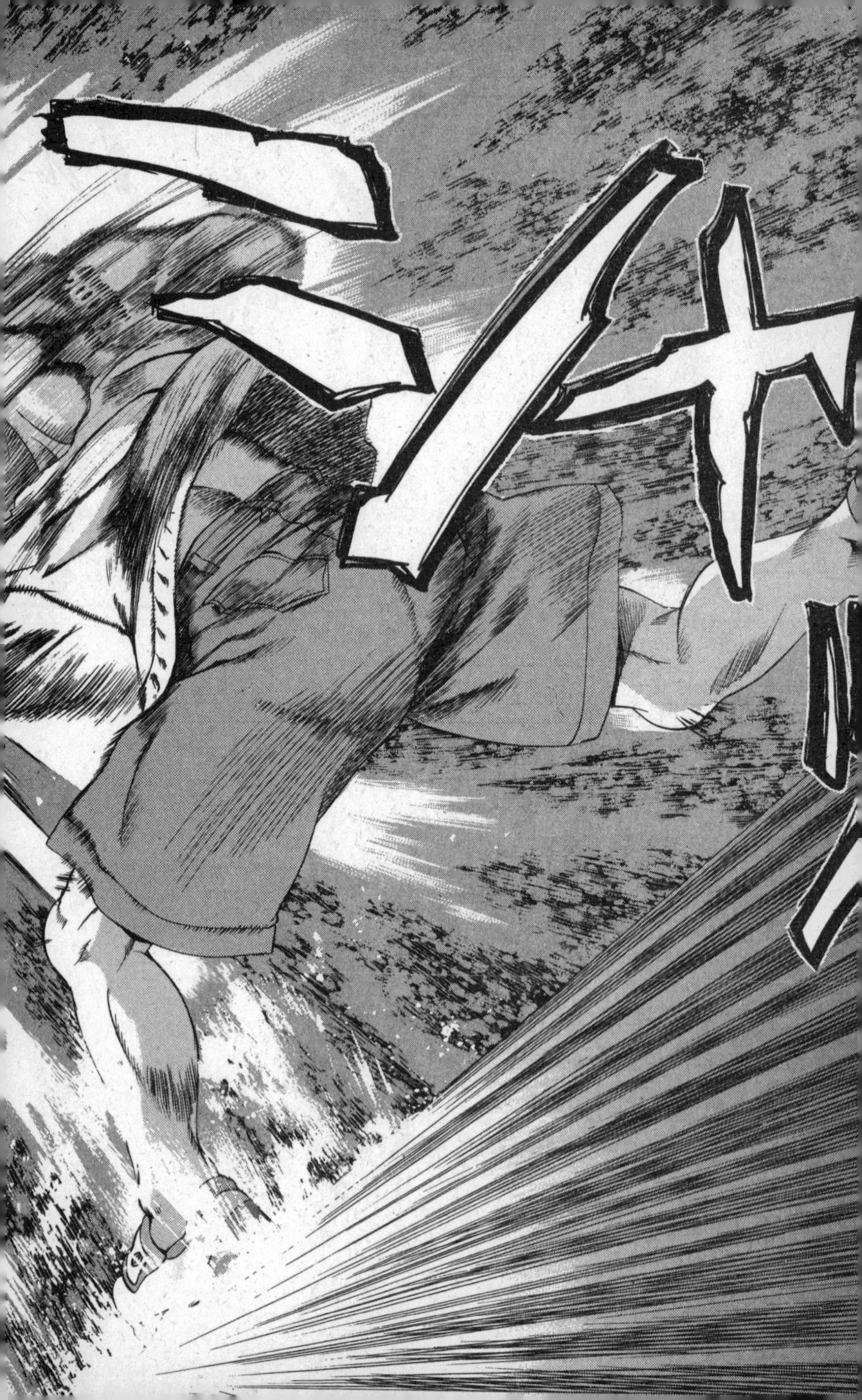

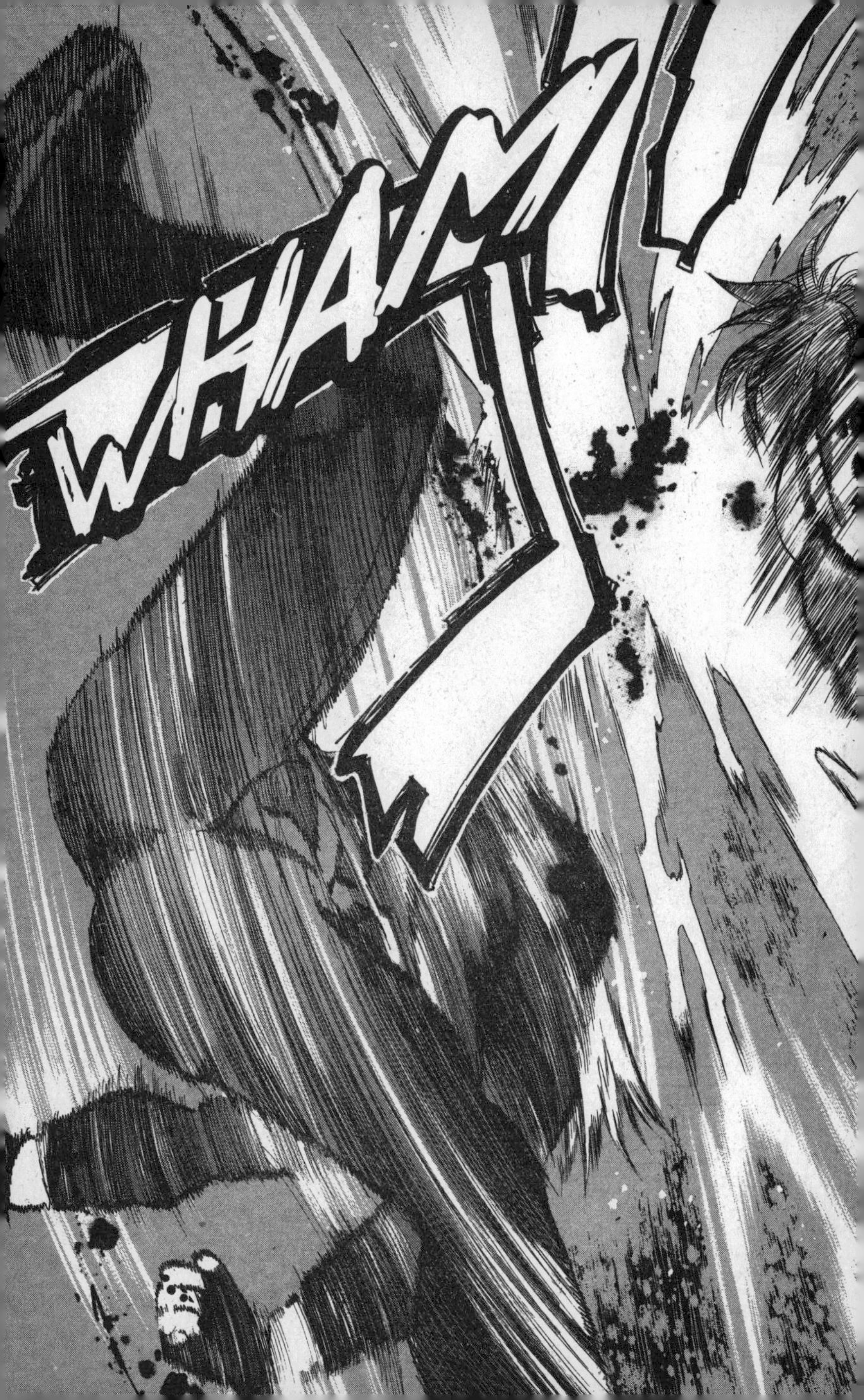
WHAM

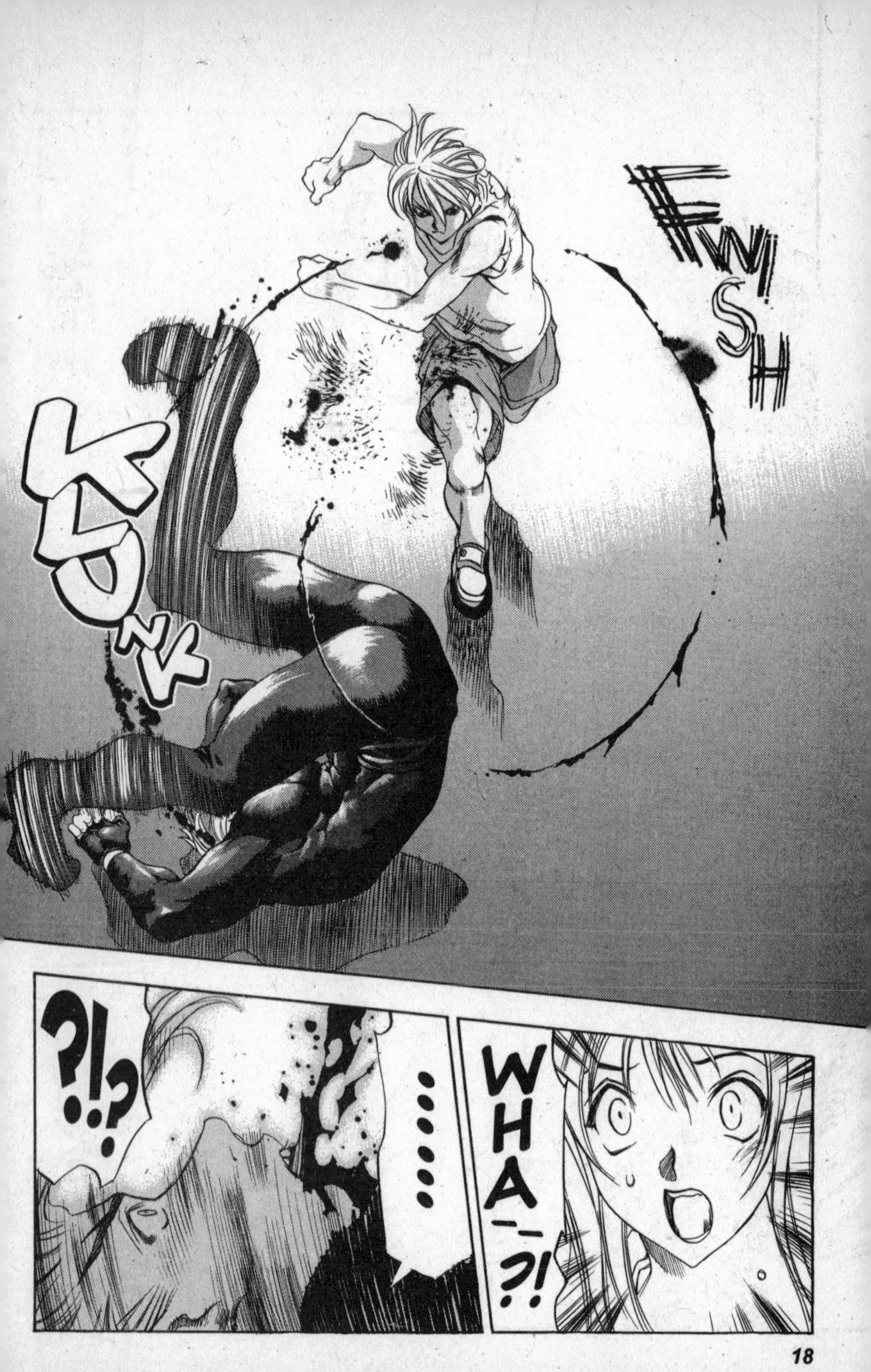
FWISH
KLONK
WHA--?!
......
?!?

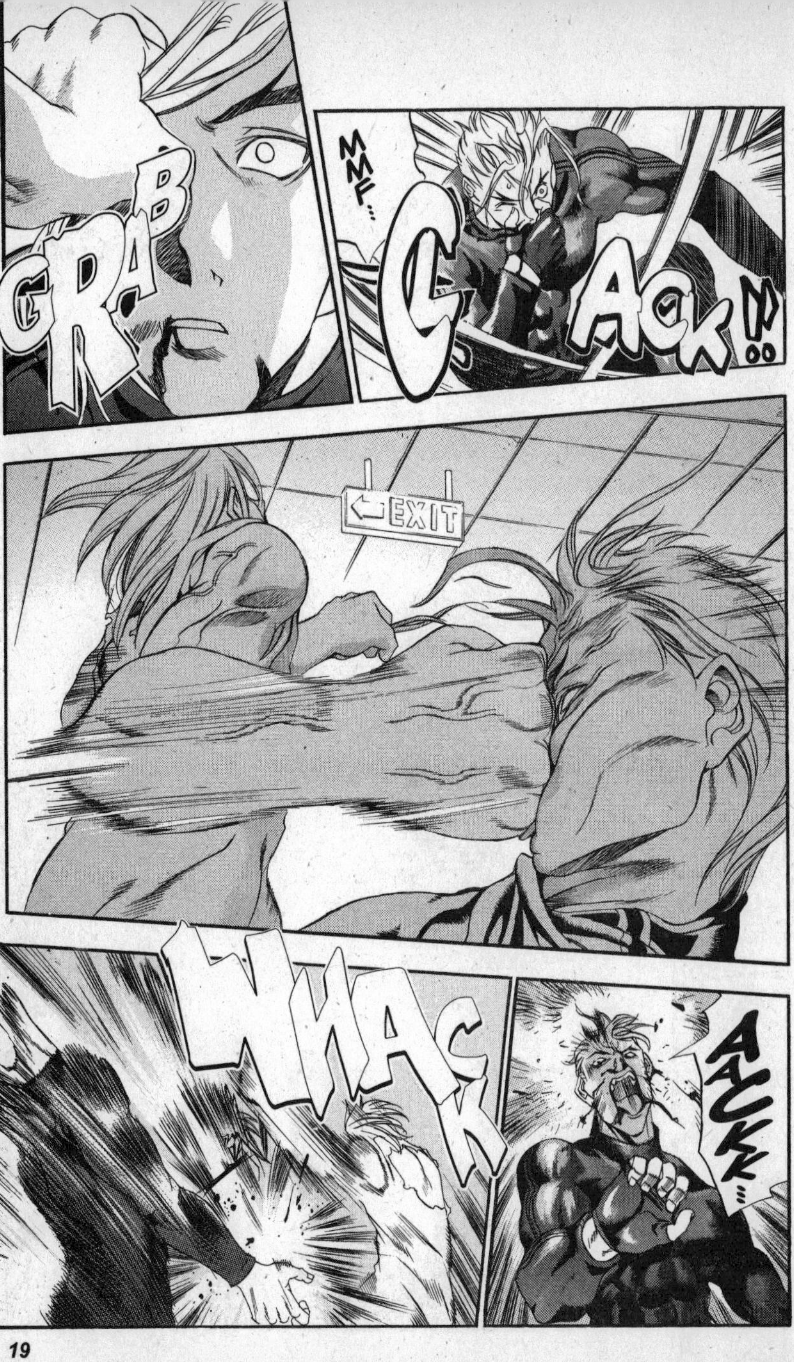
MMF...
CLACK!!
GRAB
EXIT
AACK...
WHACK

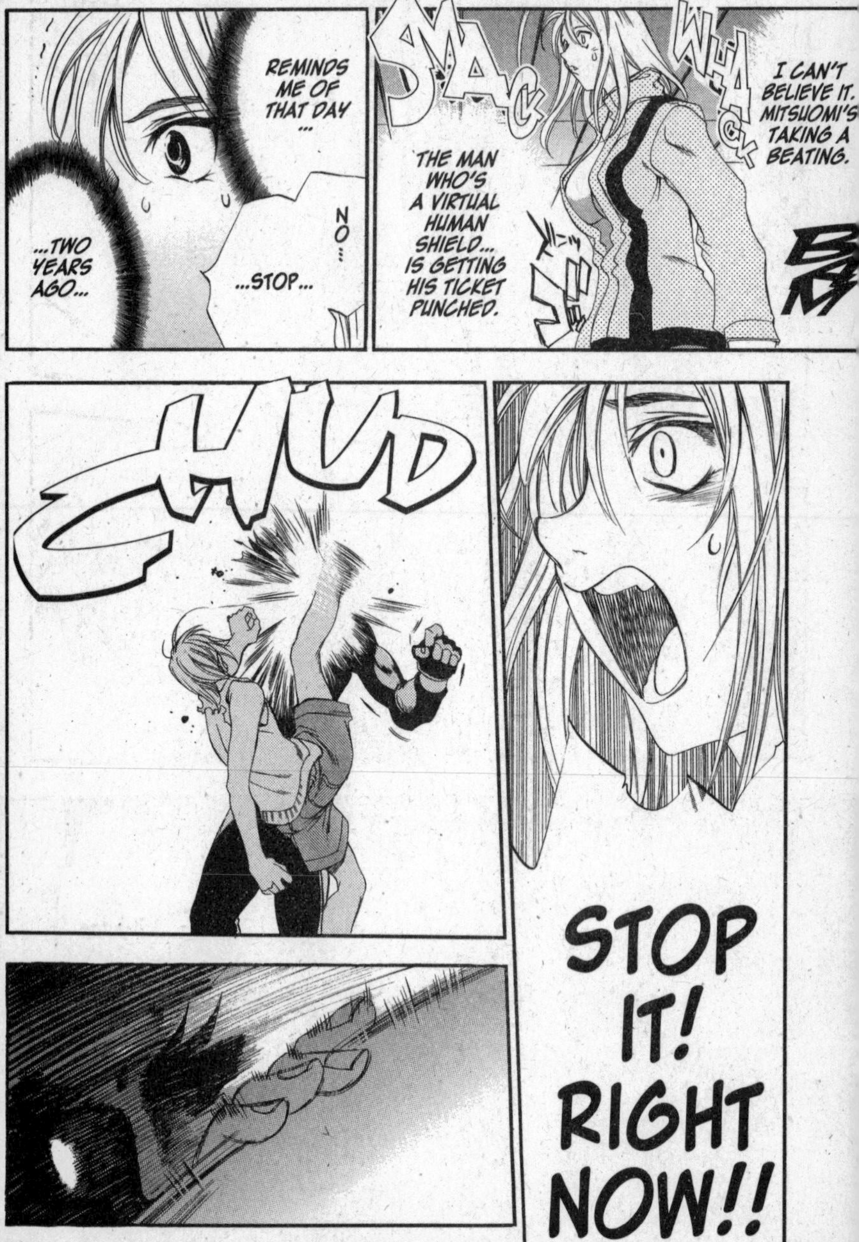
SMACK
WHACK
I CAN'T BELIEVE IT. MITSUOMI'S TAKING A BEATING.
THE MAN WHO'S A VIRTUAL HUMAN SHIELD... IS GETTING HIS TICKET PUNCHED.
REMINDS ME OF THAT DAY ...
NO...
...STOP...
...TWO YEARS AGO...
STOP IT! RIGHT NOW!!
THUD

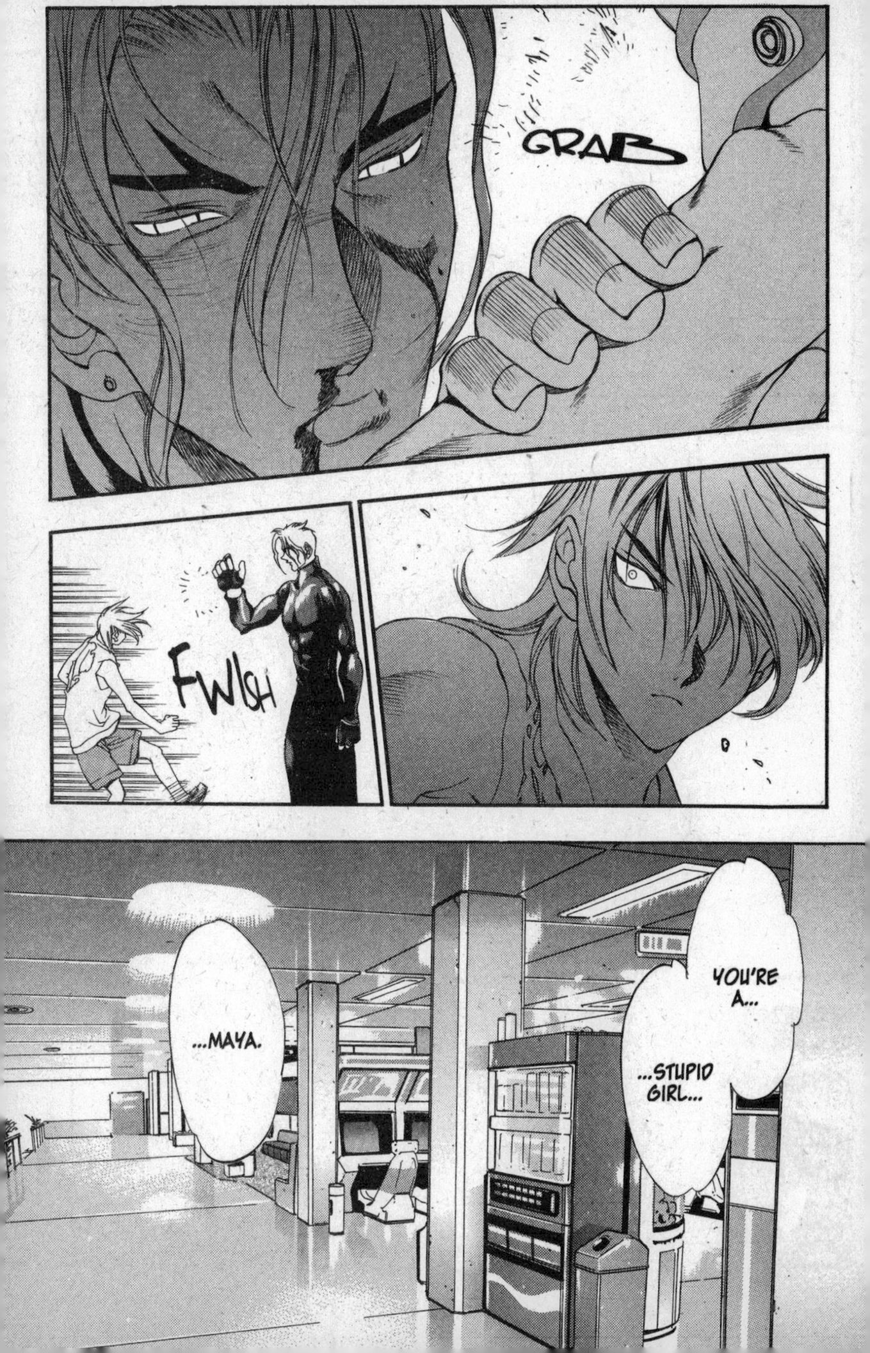
GRAB
FWISH
YOU'RE A...
...STUPID GIRL...
...MAYA.

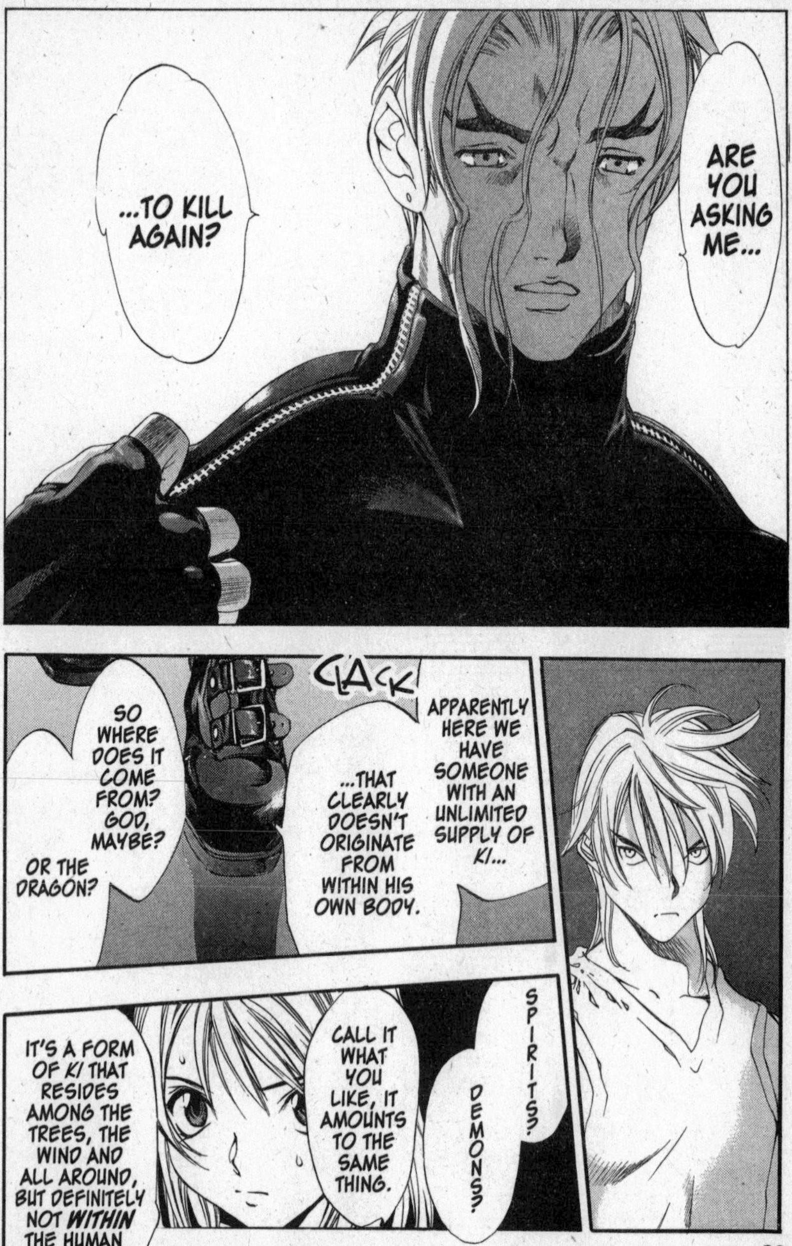
ARE YOU ASKING ME...
...TO KILL AGAIN?
CLACK
APPARENTLY HERE WE HAVE SOMEONE WITH AN UNLIMITED SUPPLY OF *KI*...
...THAT CLEARLY DOESN'T ORIGINATE FROM WITHIN HIS OWN BODY.
SO WHERE DOES IT COME FROM? GOD, MAYBE?
OR THE DRAGON?
SPIRITS?
DEMONS?
CALL IT WHAT YOU LIKE, IT AMOUNTS TO THE SAME THING.
IT'S A FORM OF *KI* THAT RESIDES AMONG THE TREES, THE WIND AND ALL AROUND, BUT DEFINITELY NOT ***WITHIN*** THE HUMAN BODY.

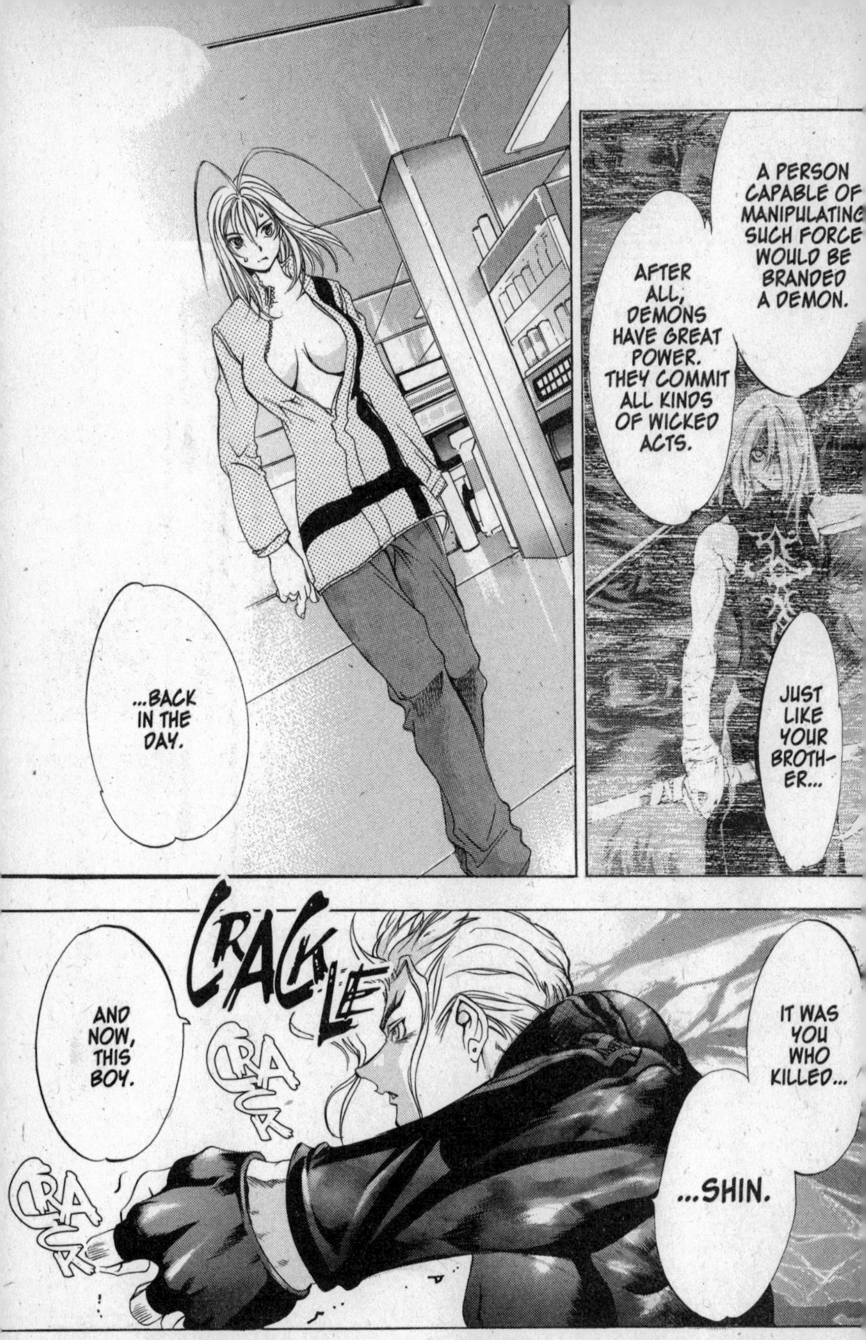
A PERSON CAPABLE OF MANIPULATING SUCH FORCE WOULD BE BRANDED A DEMON.
AFTER ALL, DEMONS HAVE GREAT POWER. THEY COMMIT ALL KINDS OF WICKED ACTS.
JUST LIKE YOUR BROTH-ER...
...BACK IN THE DAY.
IT WAS YOU WHO KILLED...
...SHIN.
CRACKLE
CRACK
AND NOW, THIS BOY.
CRACK

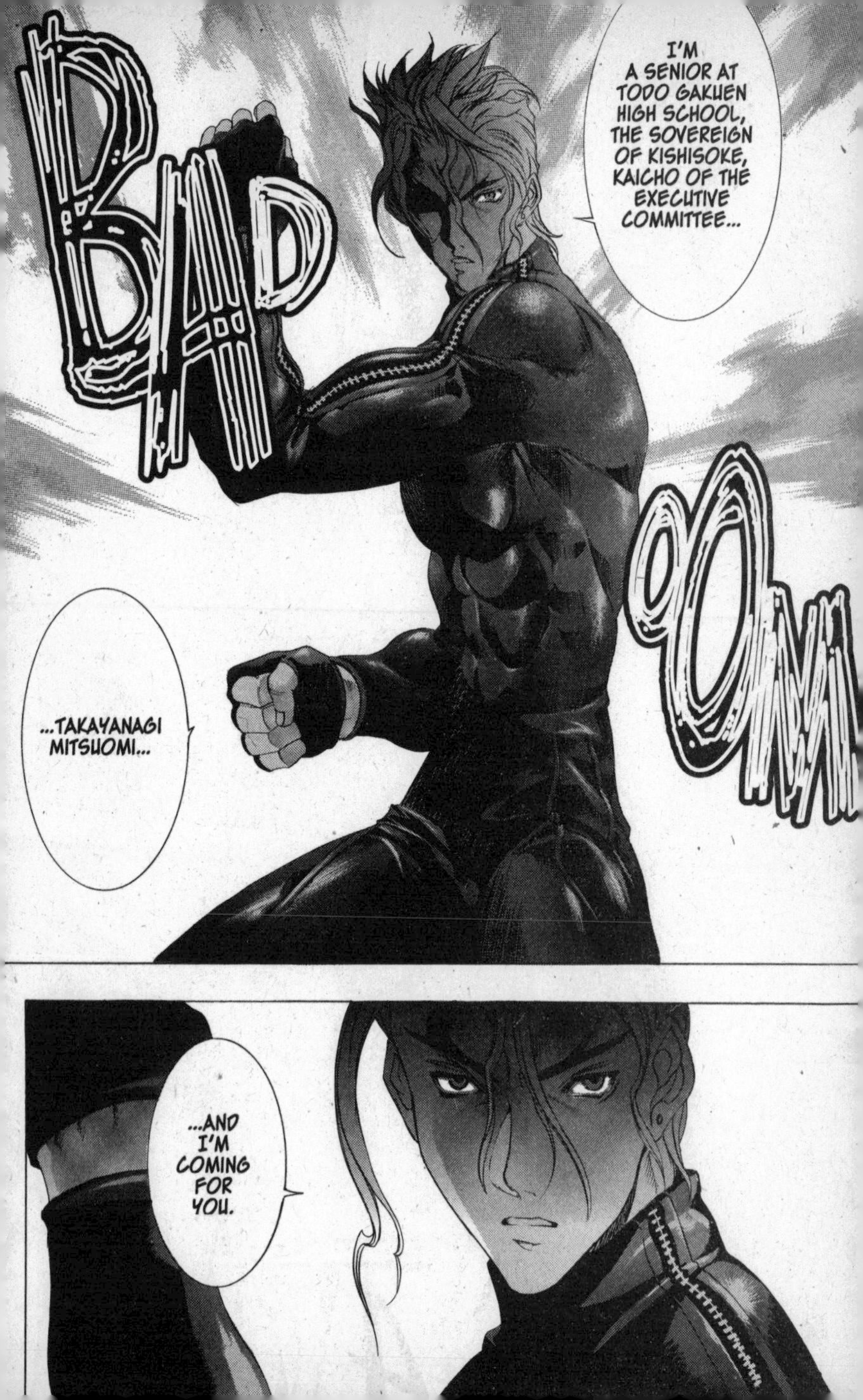
I'M A SENIOR AT TODO GAKUEN HIGH SCHOOL, THE SOVEREIGN OF KISHISOKE, KAICHO OF THE EXECUTIVE COMMITTEE...
BAP
OOM
...TAKAYANAGI MITSUOMI...
...AND I'M COMING FOR YOU.

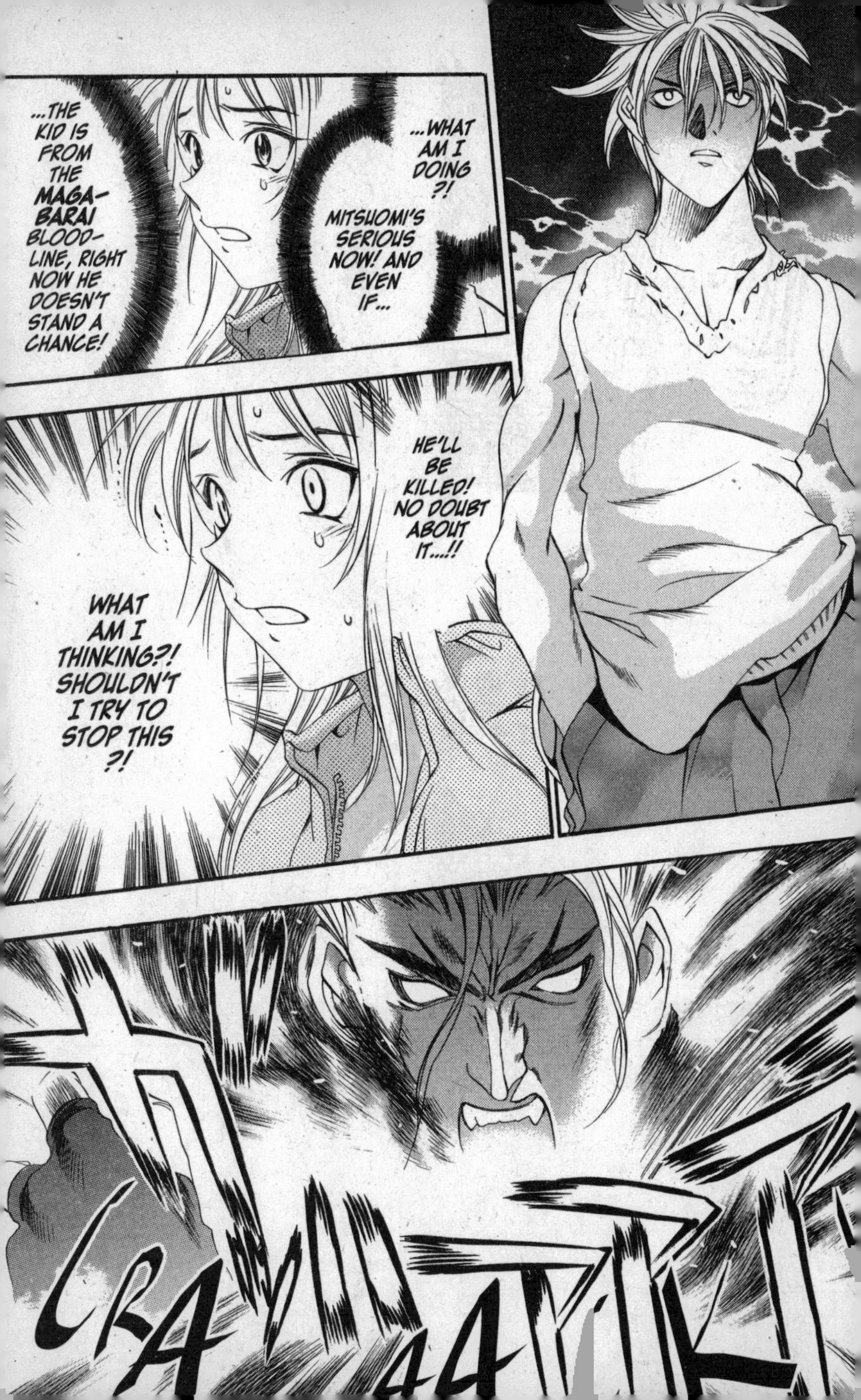
...WHAT AM I DOING?!
MITSUOMI'S SERIOUS NOW! AND EVEN IF...
...THE KID IS FROM THE MAGA-BARAI BLOODLINE, RIGHT NOW HE DOESN'T STAND A CHANCE!
HE'LL BE KILLED! NO DOUBT ABOUT IT...!!
WHAT AM I THINKING?! SHOULDN'T I TRY TO STOP THIS?!

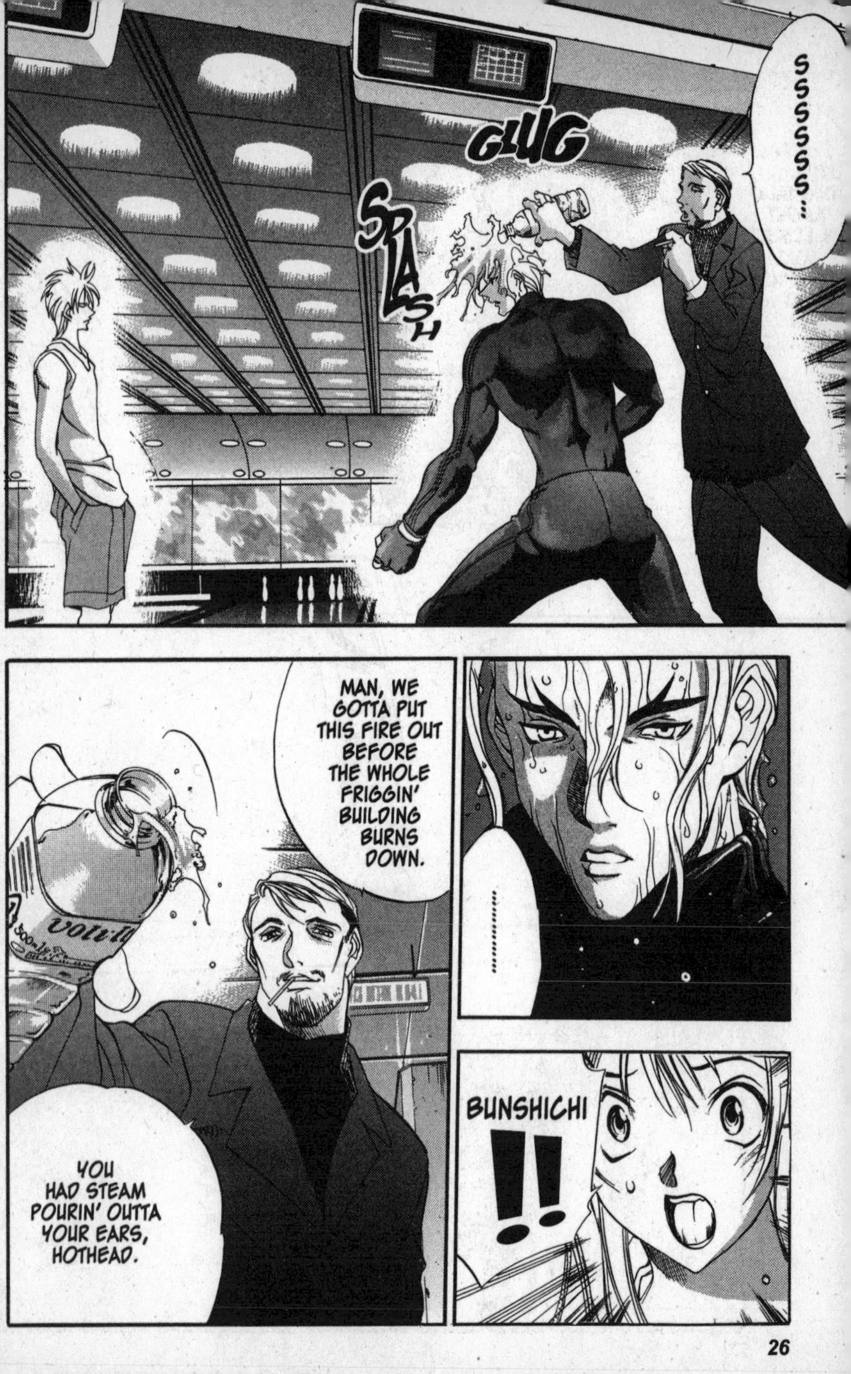
SSSSSS...
GLUG
SPLASH
......
BUNSHICHI !!
MAN, WE GOTTA PUT THIS FIRE OUT BEFORE THE WHOLE FRIGGIN' BUILDING BURNS DOWN.
YOU HAD STEAM POURIN' OUTTA YOUR EARS, HOTHEAD.

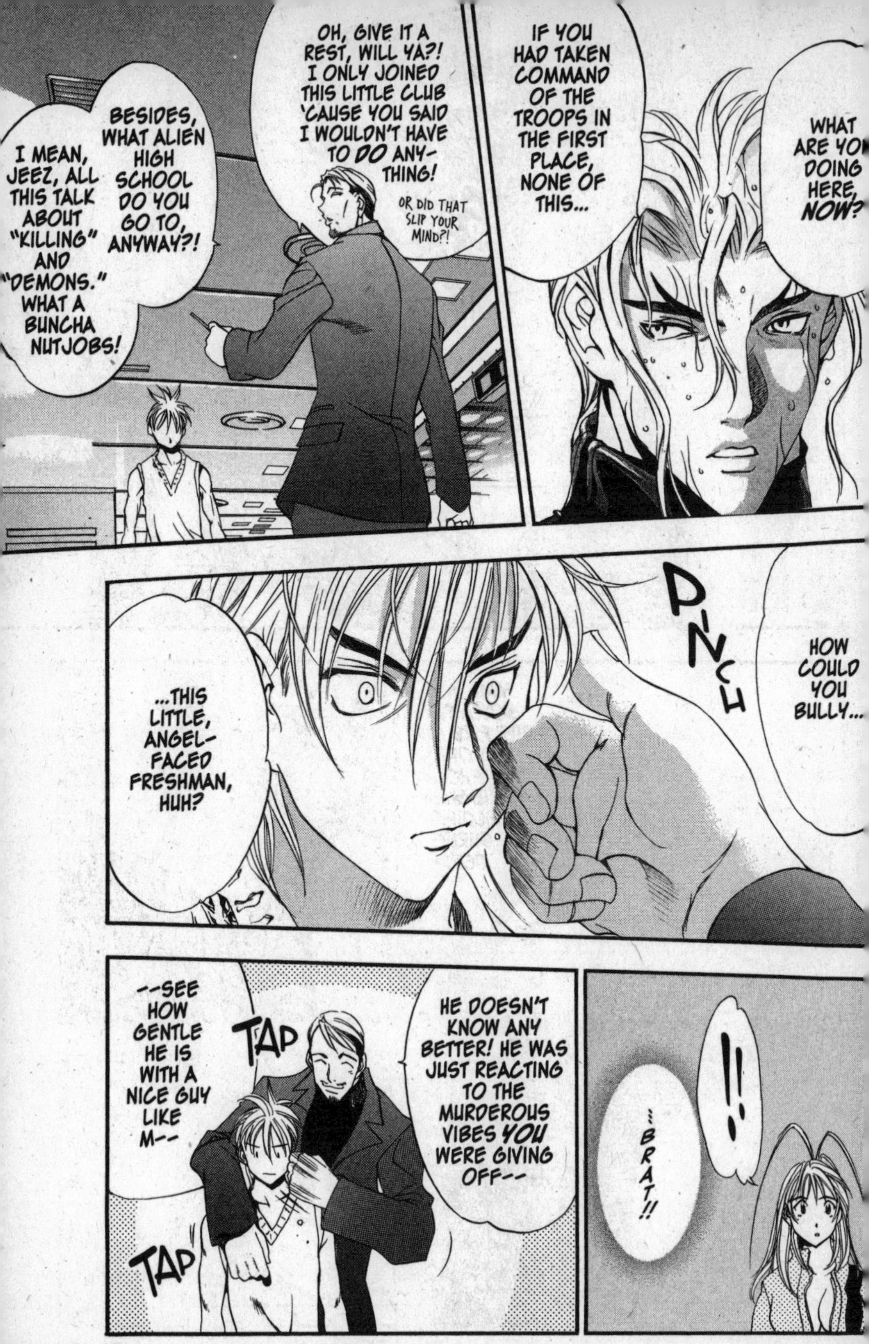
WHAT ARE YO DOING HERE, NOW?
IF YOU HAD TAKEN COMMAND OF THE TROOPS IN THE FIRST PLACE, NONE OF THIS...
OH, GIVE IT A REST, WILL YA?! I ONLY JOINED THIS LITTLE CLUB 'CAUSE YOU SAID I WOULDN'T HAVE TO DO ANY-THING!
OR DID THAT SLIP YOUR MIND?!
BESIDES, WHAT ALIEN HIGH SCHOOL DO YOU GO TO, ANYWAY?!
I MEAN, JEEZ, ALL THIS TALK ABOUT "KILLING" AND "DEMONS." WHAT A BUNCHA NUTJOBS!
PINCH
HOW COULD YOU BULLY...
...THIS LITTLE, ANGEL-FACED FRESHMAN, HUH?
!!
...BRAT!!
HE DOESN'T KNOW ANY BETTER! HE WAS JUST REACTING TO THE MURDEROUS VIBES YOU WERE GIVING OFF--
TAP
--SEE HOW GENTLE HE IS WITH A NICE GUY LIKE M--
TAP

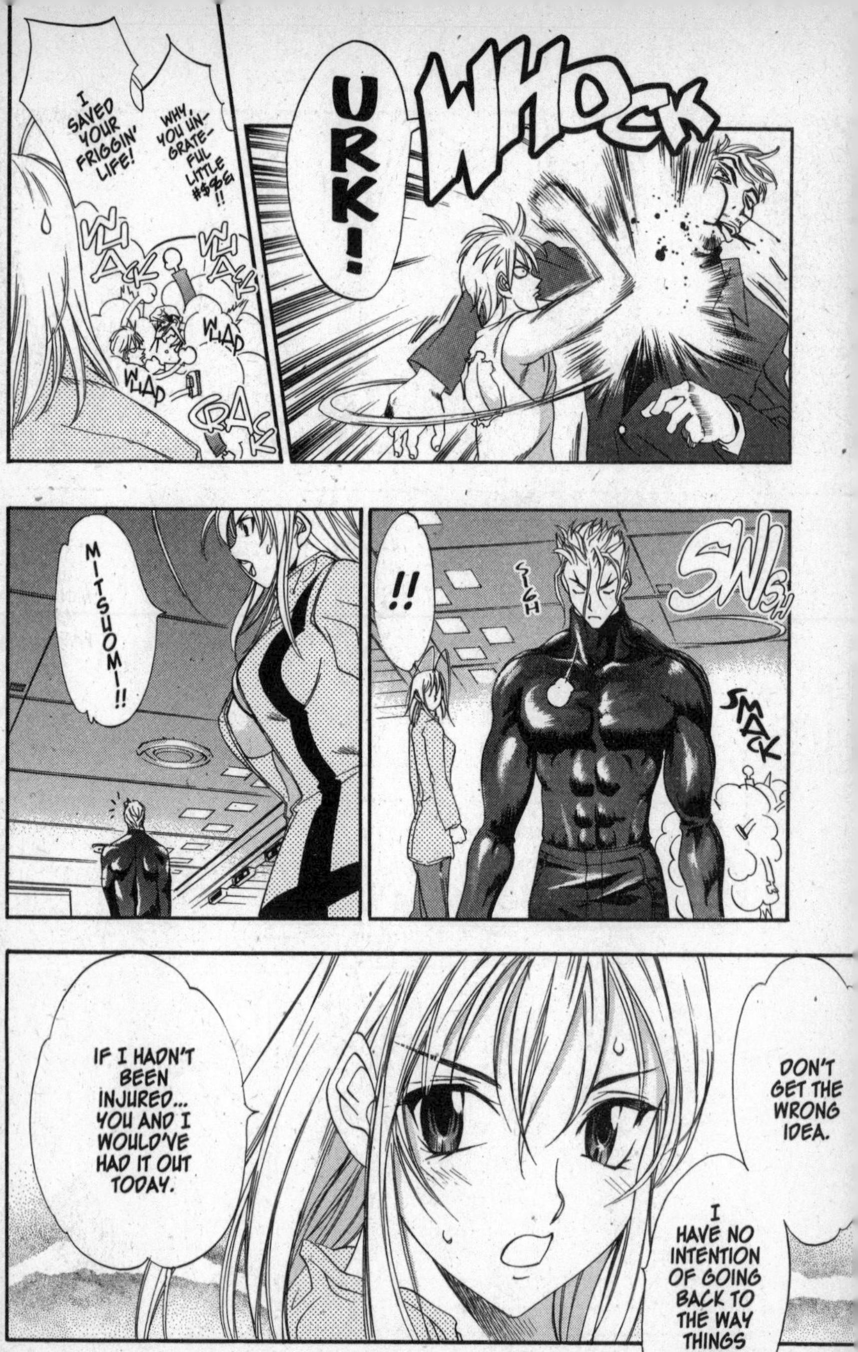
URK!
WHOCK
WHY, YOU UN-GRATE-FUL LITTLE #$%&!!
I SAVED YOUR FRIGGIN' LIFE!
WHACK
WHACK
WHAP
WHAP
CRACK
SWISH
SIGH
!!
SMACK
MITSUOMI!!
DON'T GET THE WRONG IDEA.
I HAVE NO INTENTION OF GOING BACK TO THE WAY THINGS WERE.
IF I HADN'T BEEN INJURED... YOU AND I WOULD'VE HAD IT OUT TODAY.

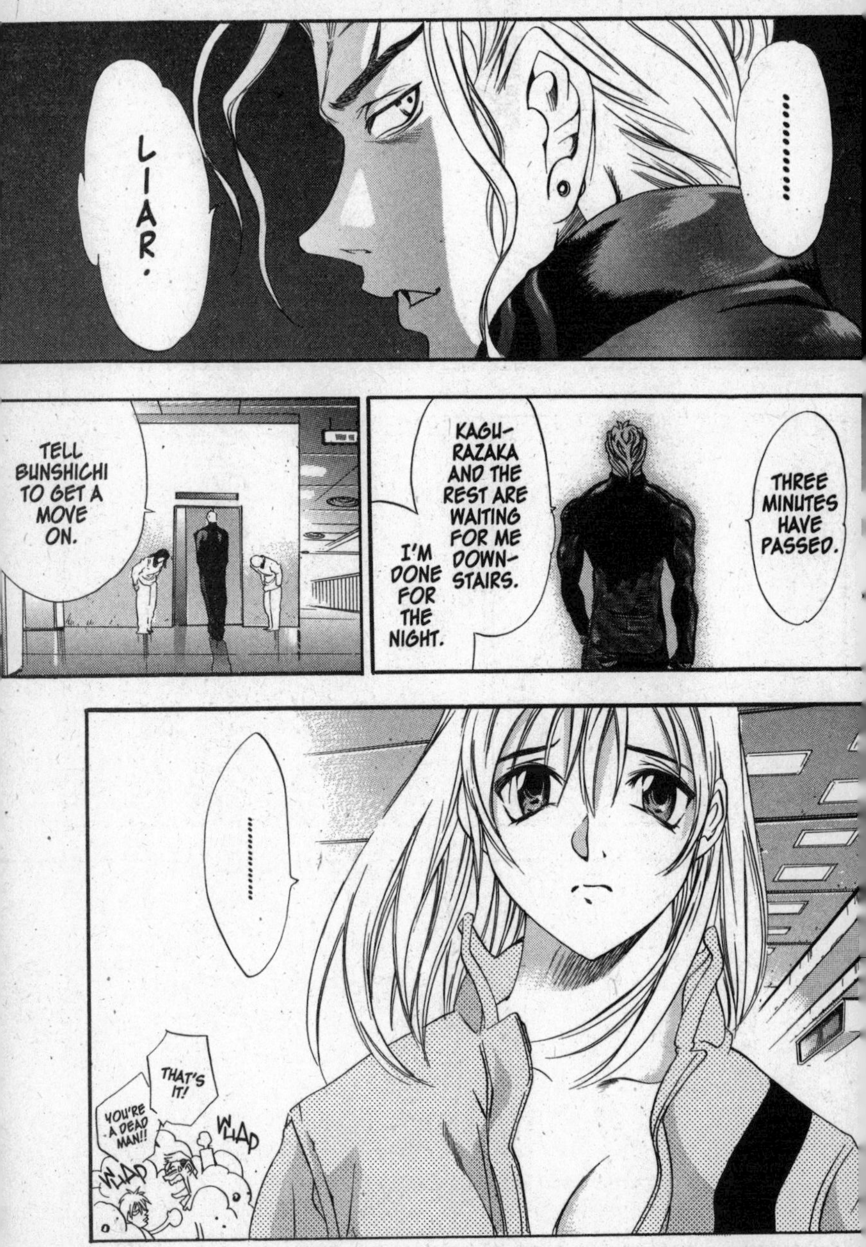
....
LIAR.
THREE MINUTES HAVE PASSED.
KAGU-RAZAKA AND THE REST ARE WAITING FOR ME DOWN-STAIRS.
I'M DONE FOR THE NIGHT.
TELL BUNSHICHI TO GET A MOVE ON.
....
THAT'S IT!
WHAP
YOU'RE A DEAD MAN!!
WHAP

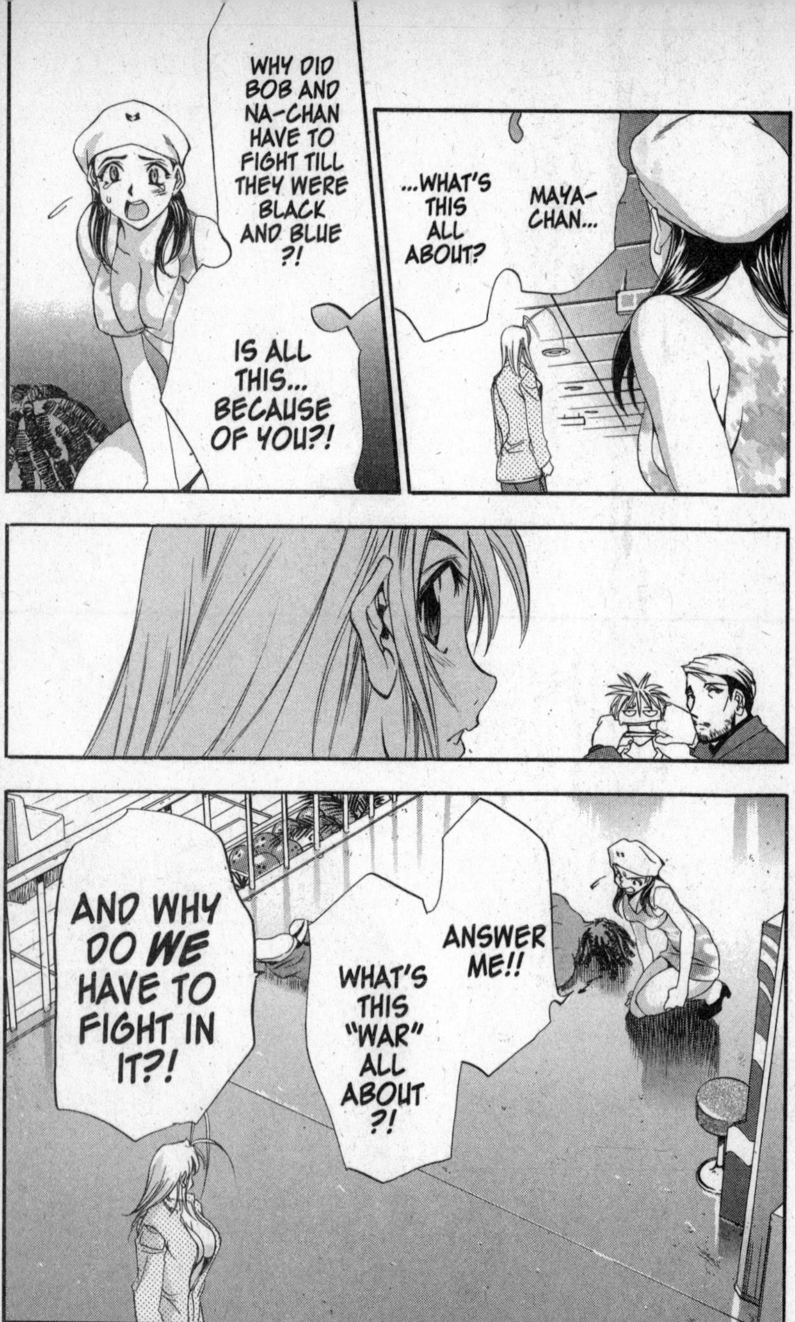
MAYA-CHAN...
...WHAT'S THIS ALL ABOUT?
WHY DID BOB AND NA-CHAN HAVE TO FIGHT TILL THEY WERE BLACK AND BLUE ?!
IS ALL THIS... BECAUSE OF YOU?!
ANSWER ME!!
WHAT'S THIS "WAR" ALL ABOUT ?!
AND WHY DO *WE* HAVE TO FIGHT IN IT?!

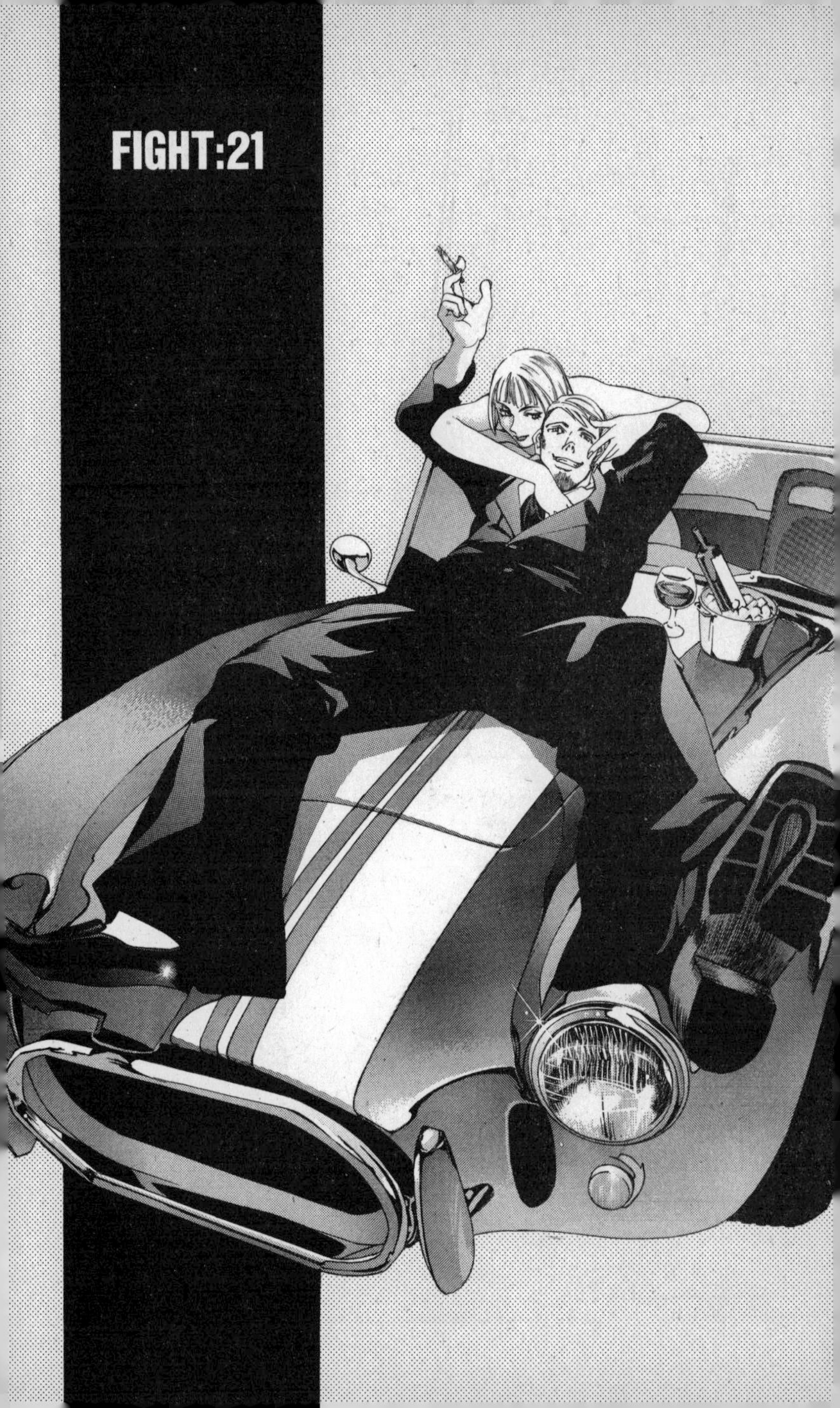
FIGHT:21

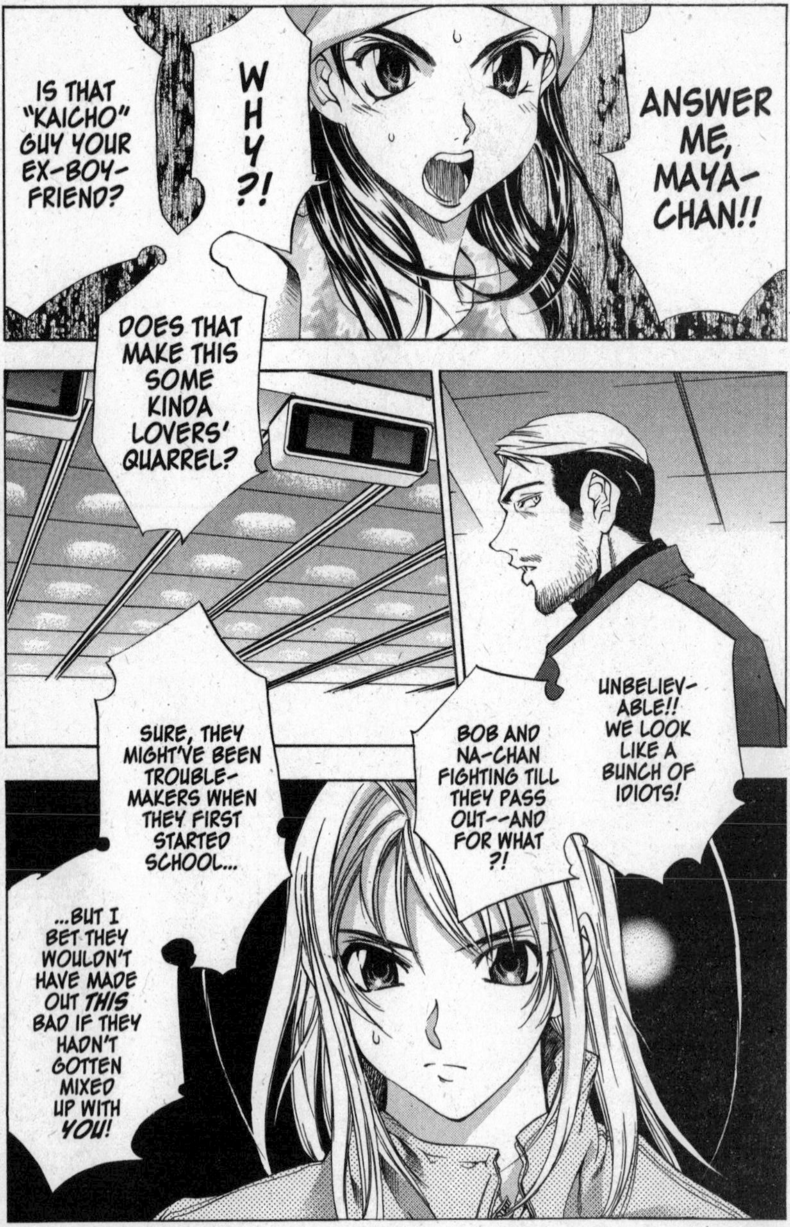
ANSWER ME, MAYA-CHAN!!
WHY?!
IS THAT "KAICHO" GUY YOUR EX-BOY-FRIEND?
DOES THAT MAKE THIS SOME KINDA LOVERS' QUARREL?
UNBELIEV-ABLE!! WE LOOK LIKE A BUNCH OF IDIOTS!
BOB AND NA-CHAN FIGHTING TILL THEY PASS OUT--AND FOR WHAT?!
SURE, THEY MIGHT'VE BEEN TROUBLE-MAKERS WHEN THEY FIRST STARTED SCHOOL...
...BUT I BET THEY WOULDN'T HAVE MADE OUT *THIS* BAD IF THEY HADN'T GOTTEN MIXED UP WITH *YOU*!

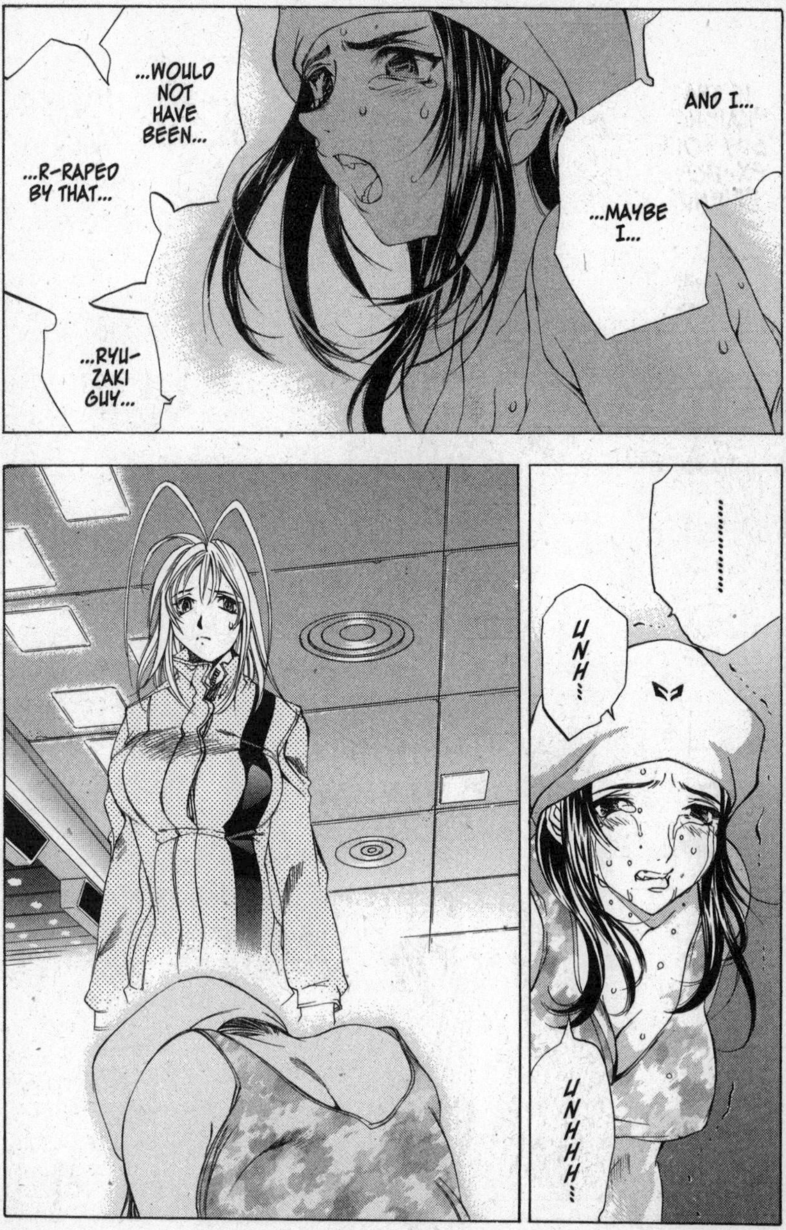
AND I...
...MAYBE I...
...WOULD NOT HAVE BEEN...
...R-RAPED BY THAT...
...RYU-ZAKI GUY...
......
UNH...
UNHHH...

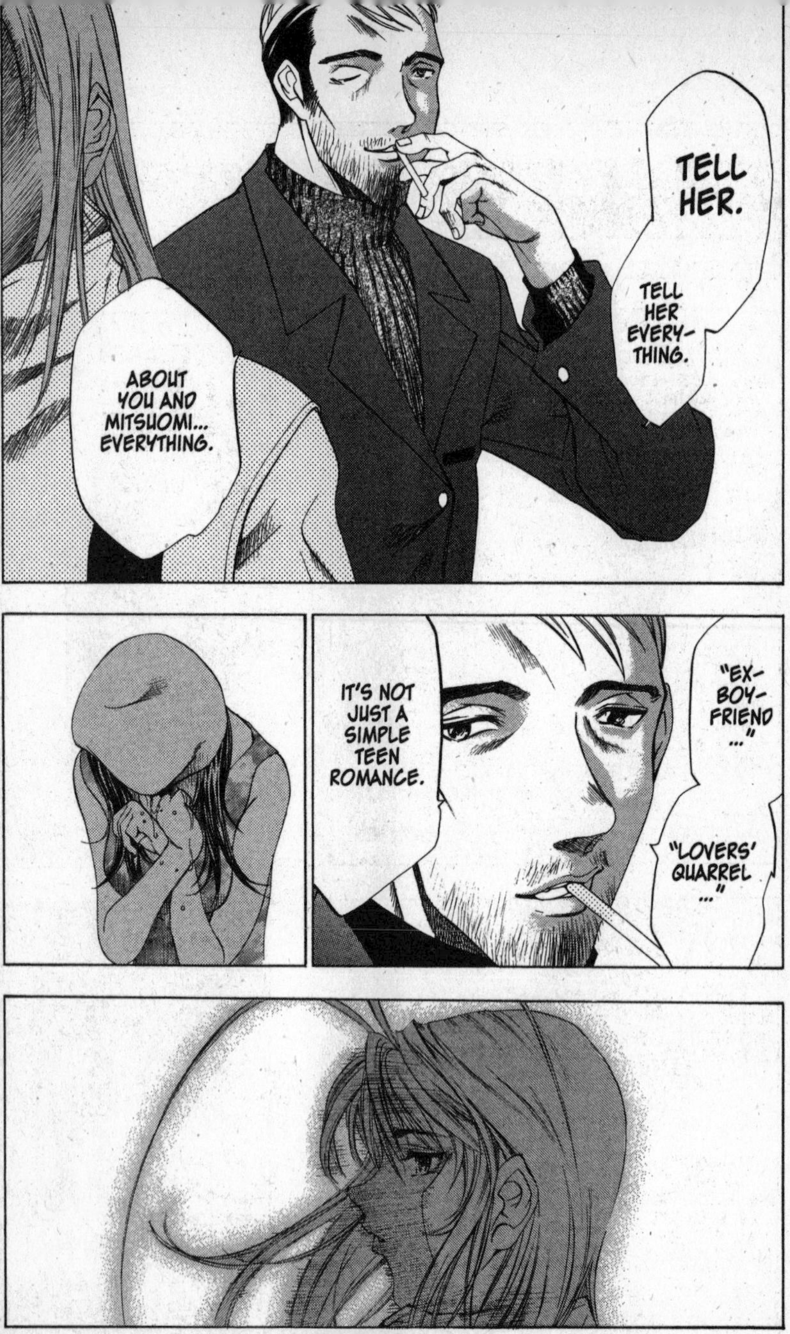
TELL HER.
TELL HER EVERY-THING.
ABOUT YOU AND MITSUOMI... EVERYTHING.
"EX-BOY-FRIEND..."
"LOVERS' QUARREL..."
IT'S NOT JUST A SIMPLE TEEN ROMANCE.

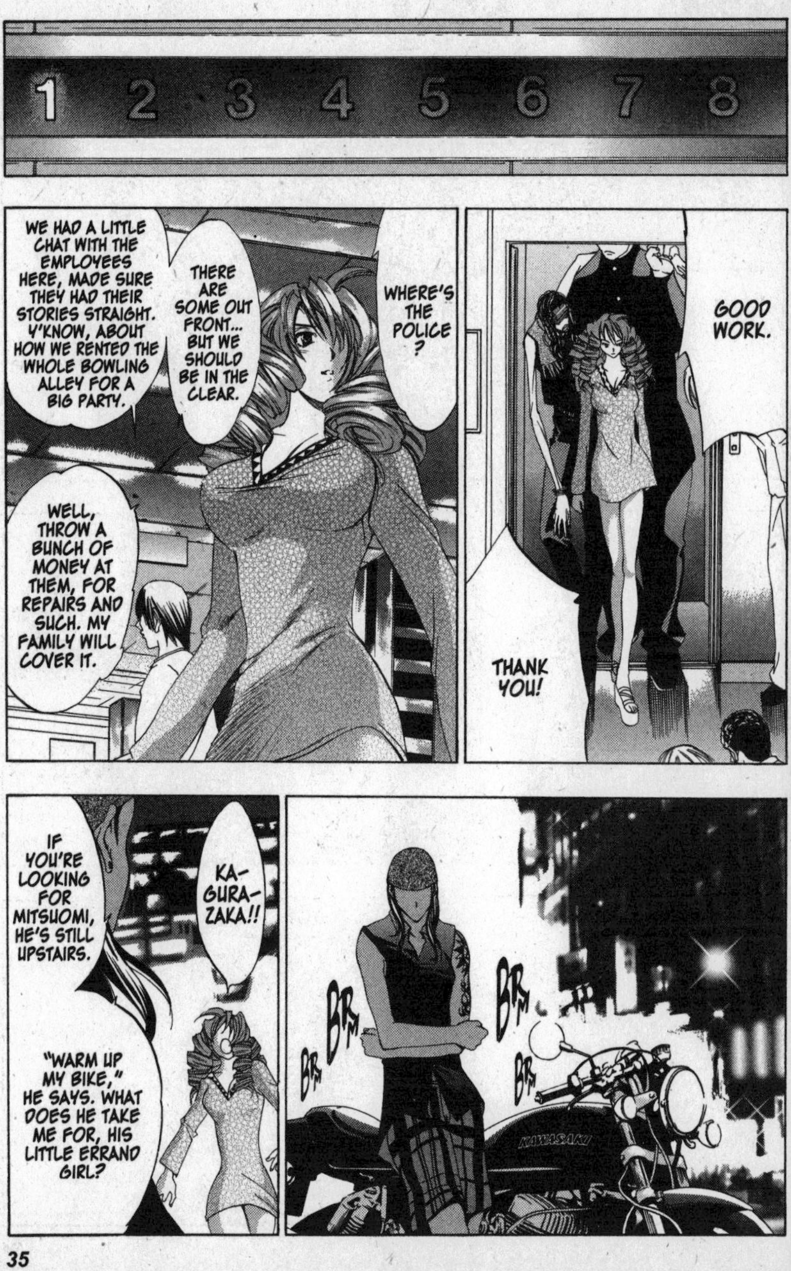
1 2 3 4 5 6 7 8
GOOD WORK.
THANK YOU!
WHERE'S THE POLICE?
THERE ARE SOME OUT FRONT... BUT WE SHOULD BE IN THE CLEAR.
WE HAD A LITTLE CHAT WITH THE EMPLOYEES HERE, MADE SURE THEY HAD THEIR STORIES STRAIGHT. Y'KNOW, ABOUT HOW WE RENTED THE WHOLE BOWLING ALLEY FOR A BIG PARTY.
WELL, THROW A BUNCH OF MONEY AT THEM, FOR REPAIRS AND SUCH. MY FAMILY WILL COVER IT.
BRM
BRM
BRM
BRM
KAWASAKI
KA-GURA-ZAKA!!
IF YOU'RE LOOKING FOR MITSUOMI, HE'S STILL UPSTAIRS.
"WARM UP MY BIKE," HE SAYS. WHAT DOES HE TAKE ME FOR, HIS LITTLE ERRAND GIRL?

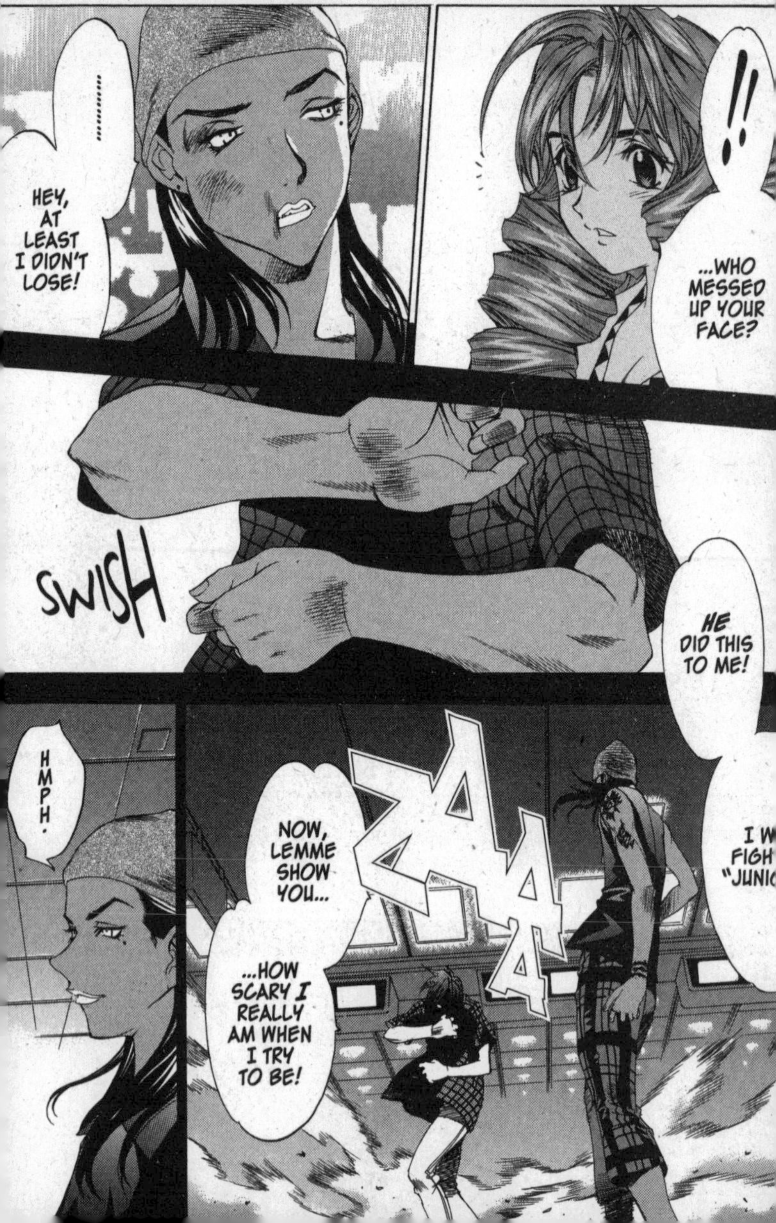
!!
...WHO MESSED UP YOUR FACE?
......
HEY, AT LEAST I DIDN'T LOSE!
HE DID THIS TO ME!
SWISH
NOW, LEMME SHOW YOU...
...HOW SCARY I REALLY AM WHEN I TRY TO BE!
HMPH.

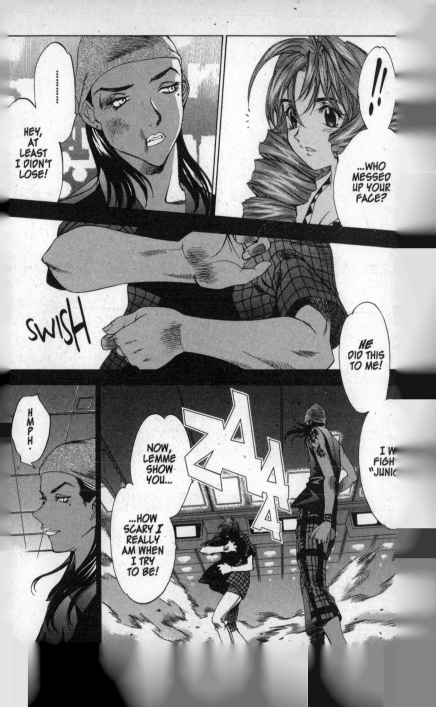

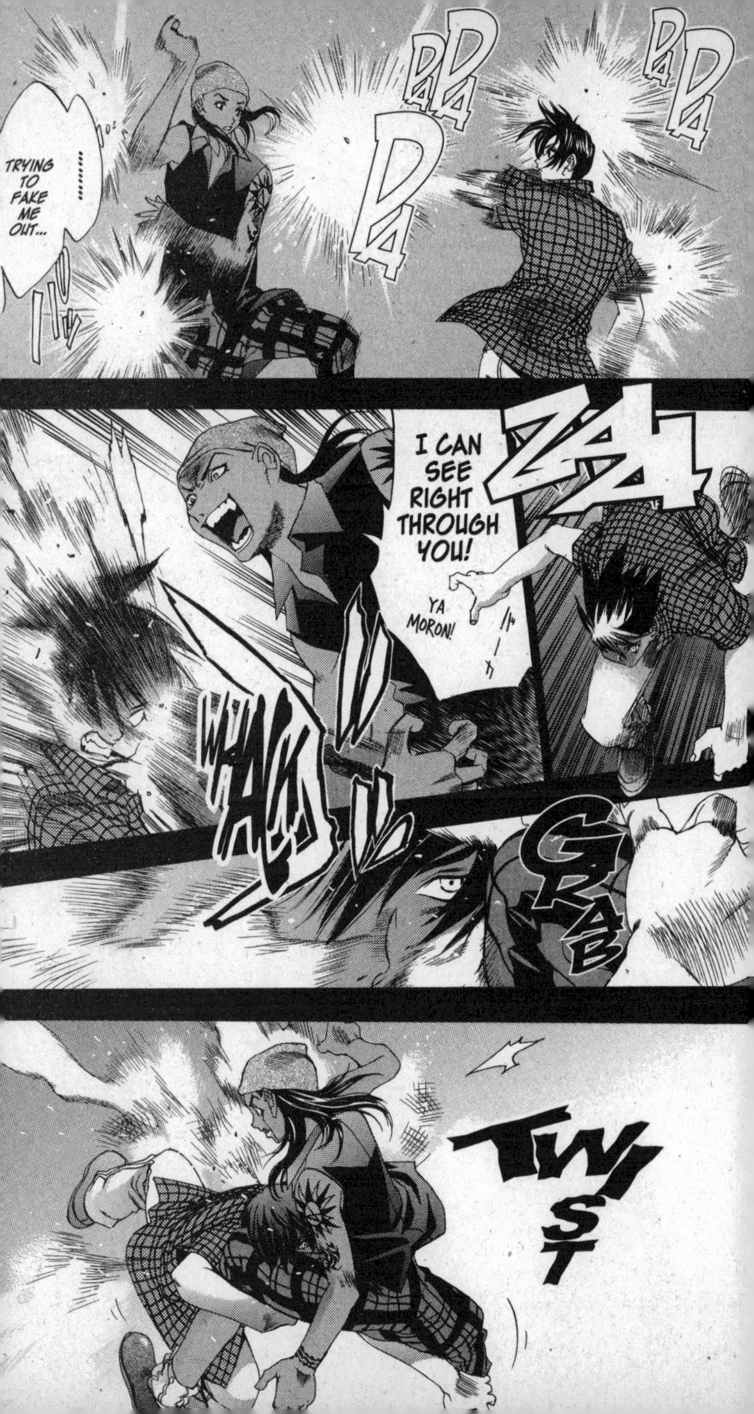
DADADA
DADA
DA
TRYING TO FAKE ME OUT...
I CAN SEE RIGHT THROUGH YOU!
YA MORON!
ZA
WHACK
GRAB
TWIST

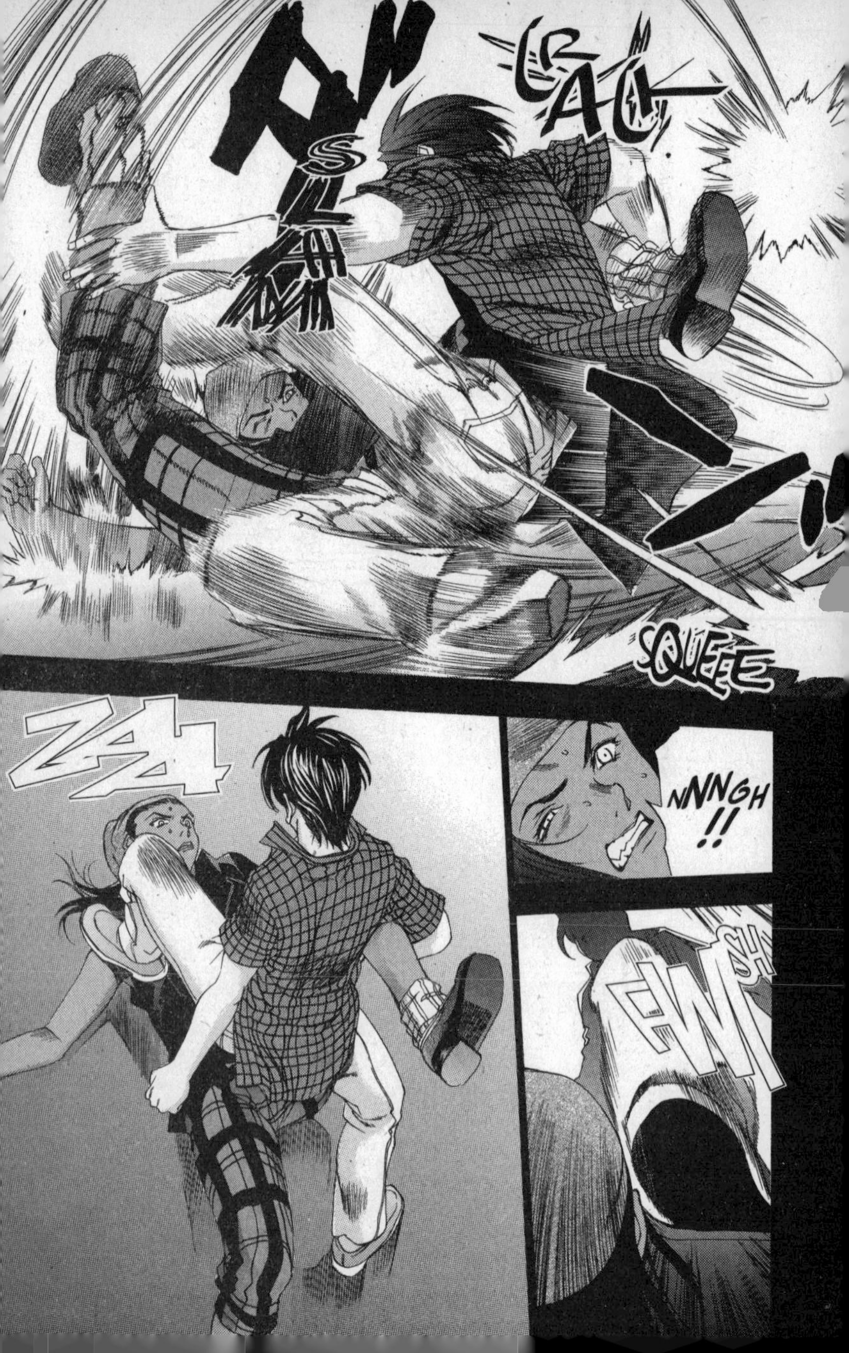
CRACK
SQUEEE
NNNGH !!

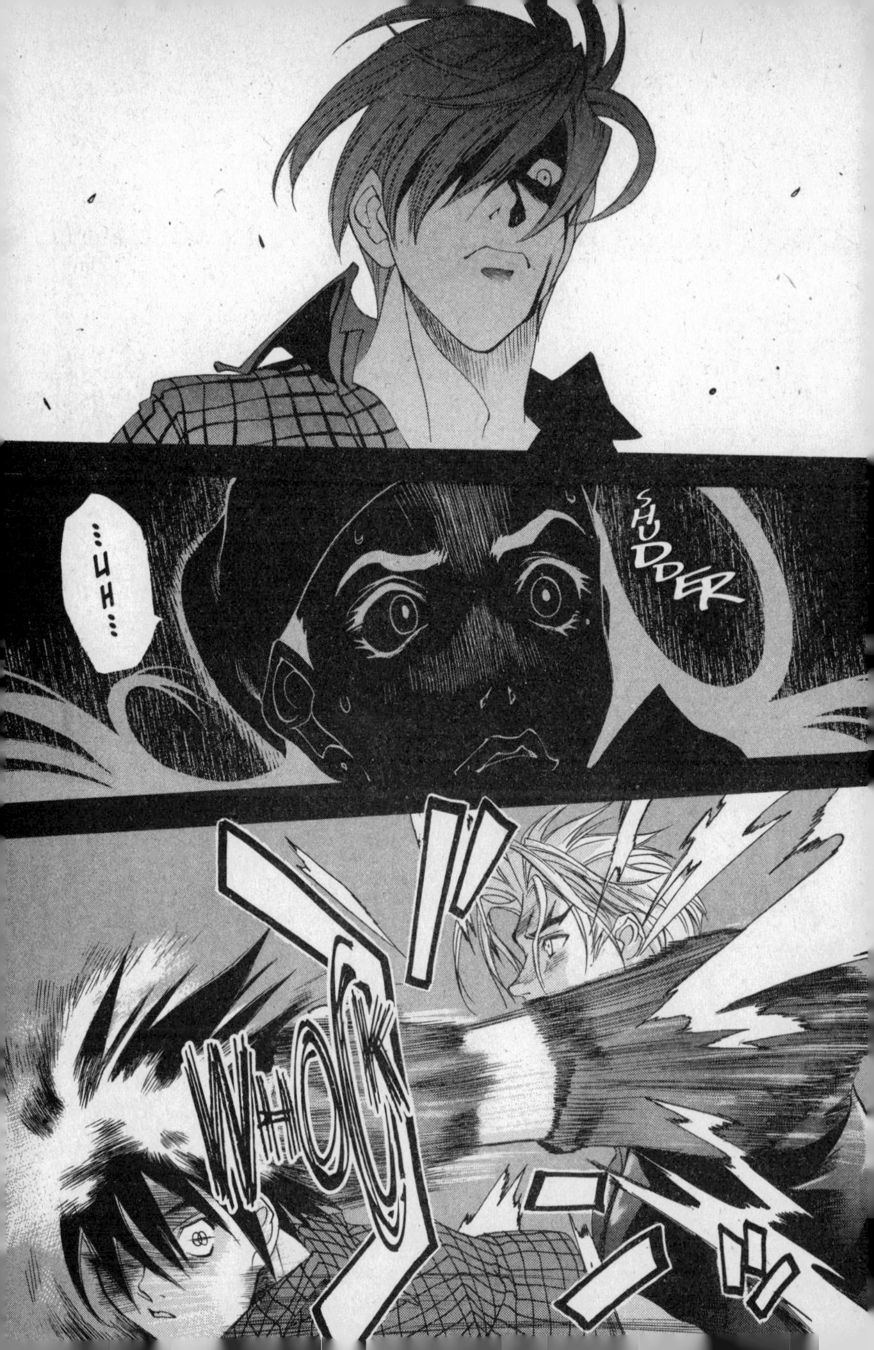
...UH...
SHUDDER
WHOOG

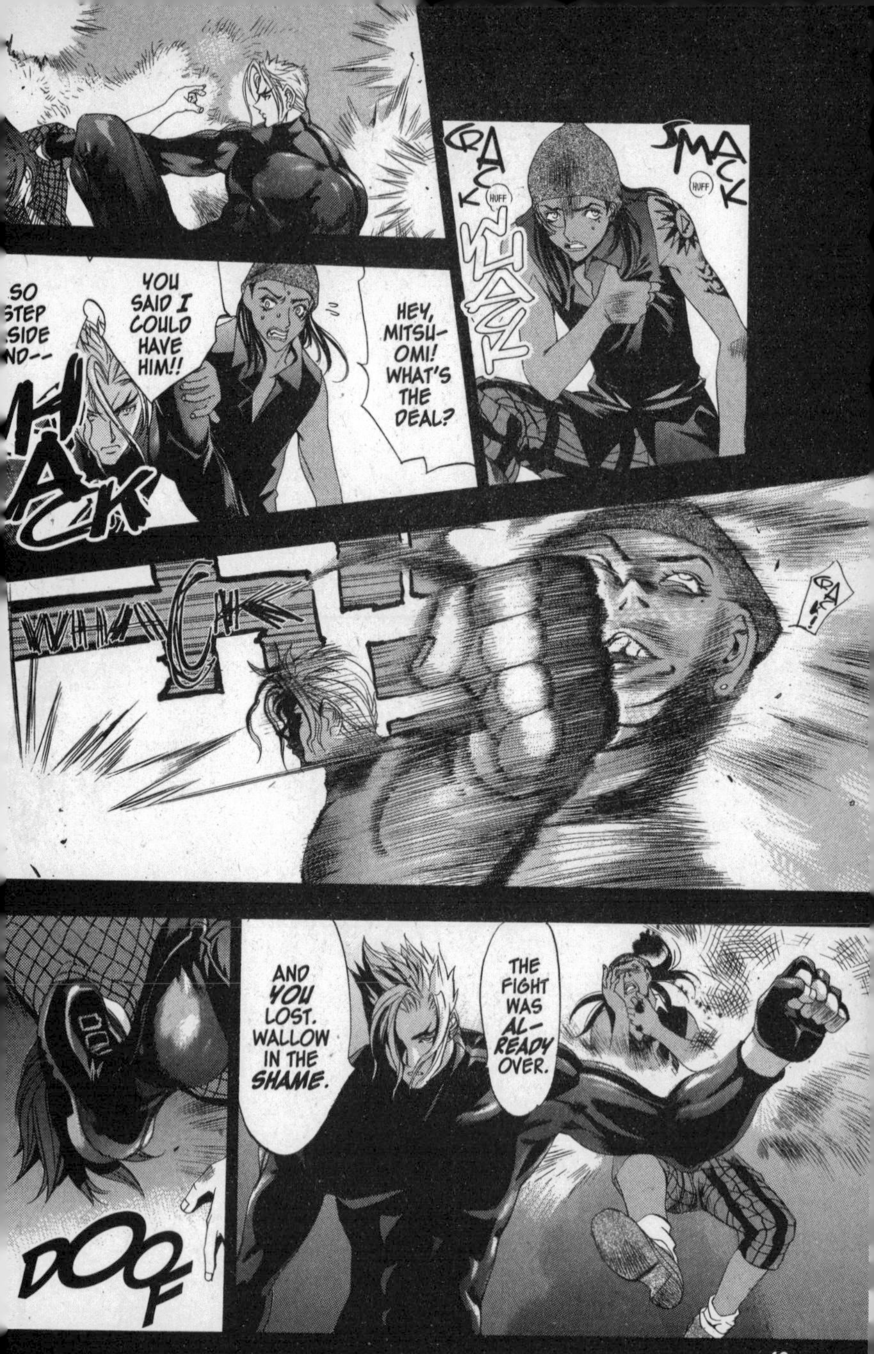
SMACK
HUFF
CRACK
HUFF
HEY, MITSU-OMI! WHAT'S THE DEAL?
YOU SAID I COULD HAVE HIM!!
SO STEP SIDE ND--
WHACK
CRACK!
THE FIGHT WAS AL-READY OVER.
AND YOU LOST. WALLOW IN THE SHAME.
DOOF

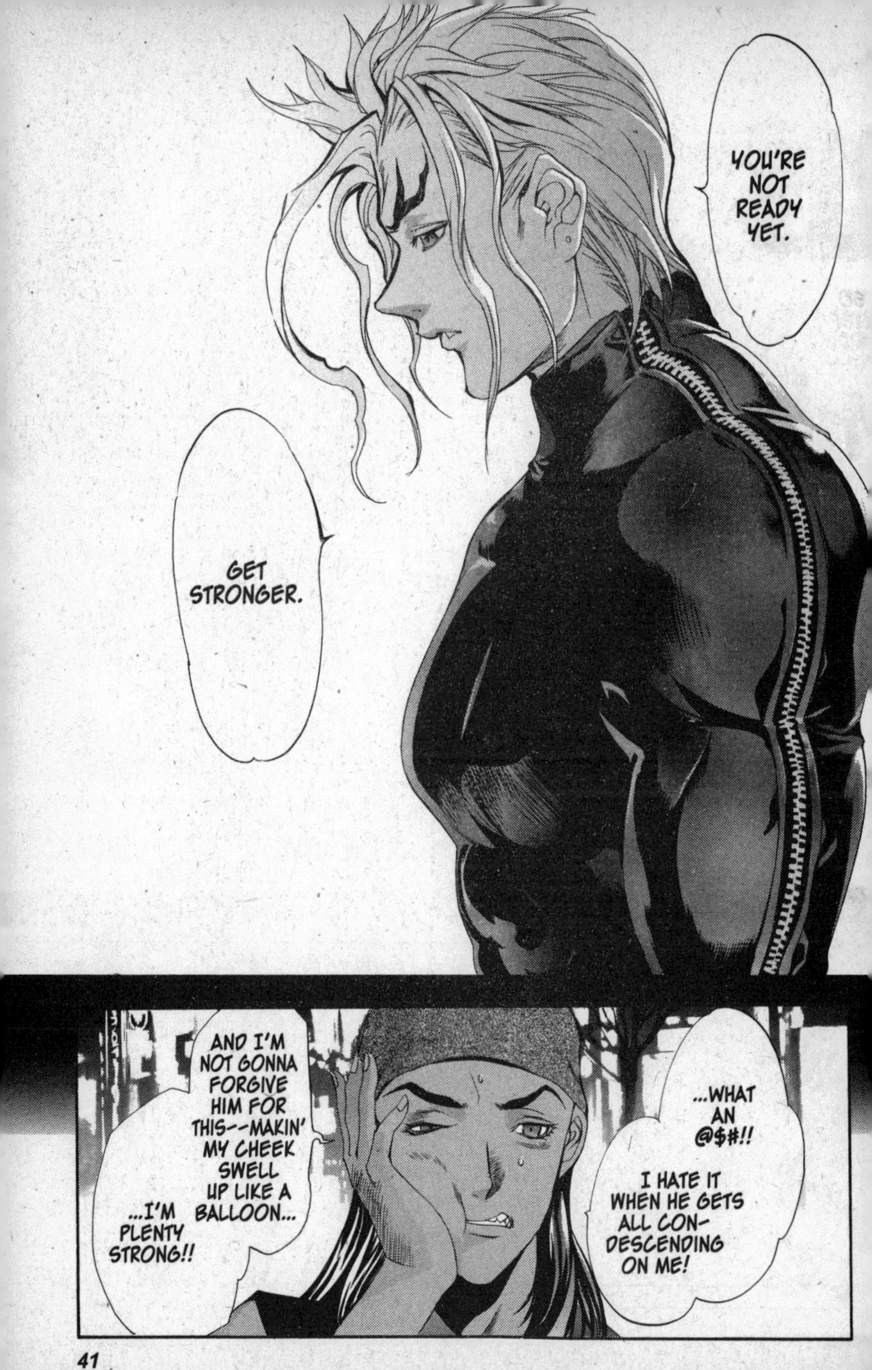
YOU'RE NOT READY YET.
GET STRONGER.
...WHAT AN @$#!!
I HATE IT WHEN HE GETS ALL CON-DESCENDING ON ME!
AND I'M NOT GONNA FORGIVE HIM FOR THIS--MAKIN' MY CHEEK SWELL UP LIKE A BALLOON...
...I'M PLENTY STRONG!!

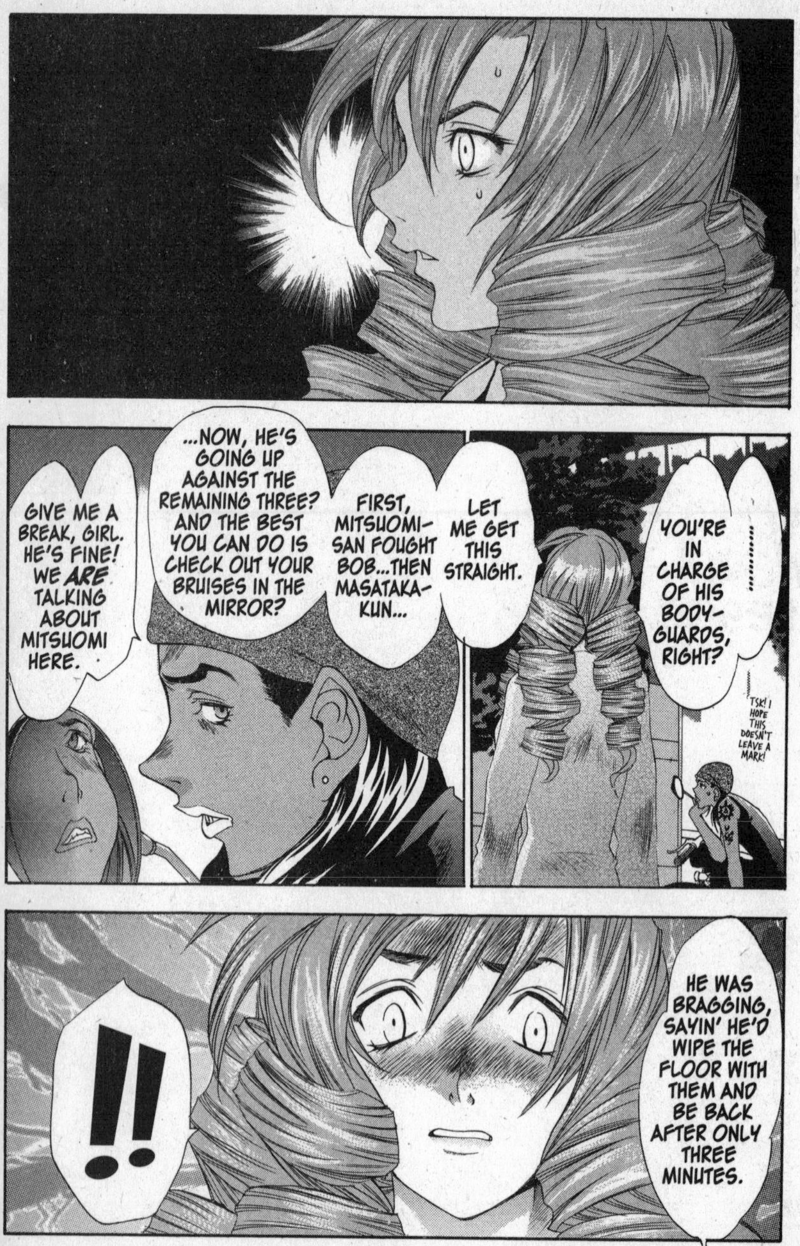
......
YOU'RE IN CHARGE OF HIS BODY-GUARDS, RIGHT?
TSK! I HOPE THIS DOESN'T LEAVE A MARK!
LET ME GET THIS STRAIGHT.
FIRST, MITSUOMI-SAN FOUGHT BOB...THEN MASATAKA-KUN...
...NOW, HE'S GOING UP AGAINST THE REMAINING THREE? AND THE BEST YOU CAN DO IS CHECK OUT YOUR BRUISES IN THE MIRROR?
GIVE ME A BREAK, GIRL. HE'S FINE! WE *ARE* TALKING ABOUT MITSUOMI HERE.
HE WAS BRAGGING, SAYIN' HE'D WIPE THE FLOOR WITH THEM AND BE BACK AFTER ONLY THREE MINUTES.
!!

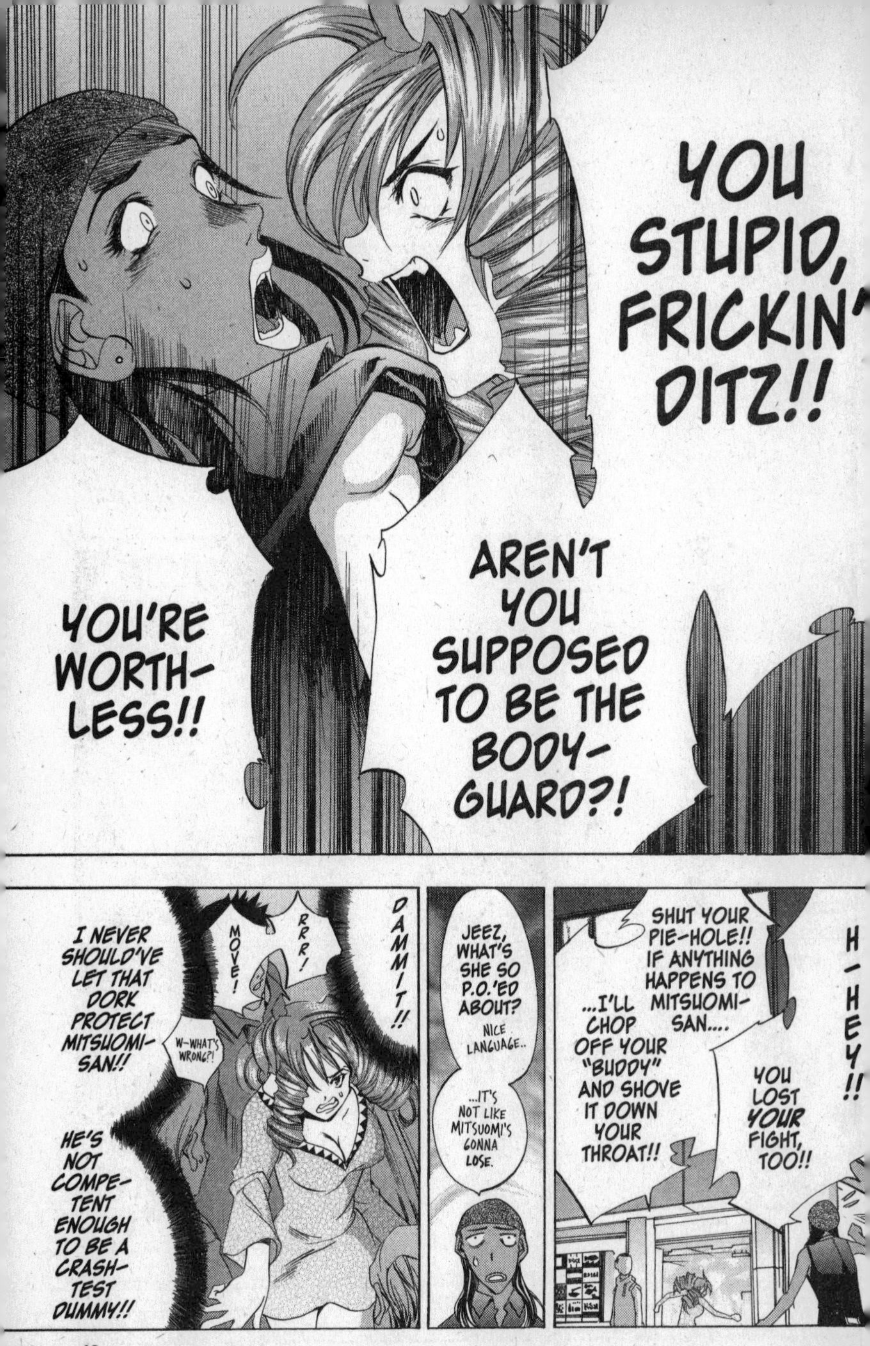
YOU STUPID, FRICKIN' DITZ!!
AREN'T YOU SUPPOSED TO BE THE BODY-GUARD?!
YOU'RE WORTH-LESS!!
H-HEY!!
SHUT YOUR PIE-HOLE!! IF ANYTHING HAPPENS TO MITSUOMI-SAN....
...I'LL CHOP OFF YOUR "BUDDY" AND SHOVE IT DOWN YOUR THROAT!!
YOU LOST YOUR FIGHT, TOO!!
JEEZ, WHAT'S SHE SO P.O.'ED ABOUT?
NICE LANGUAGE..
...IT'S NOT LIKE MITSUOMI'S GONNA LOSE.
DAMMIT!!
RRR!
MOVE!
I NEVER SHOULD'VE LET THAT DORK PROTECT MITSUOMI-SAN!!
W-WHAT'S WRONG?!
HE'S NOT COMPE-TENT ENOUGH TO BE A CRASH-TEST DUMMY!!

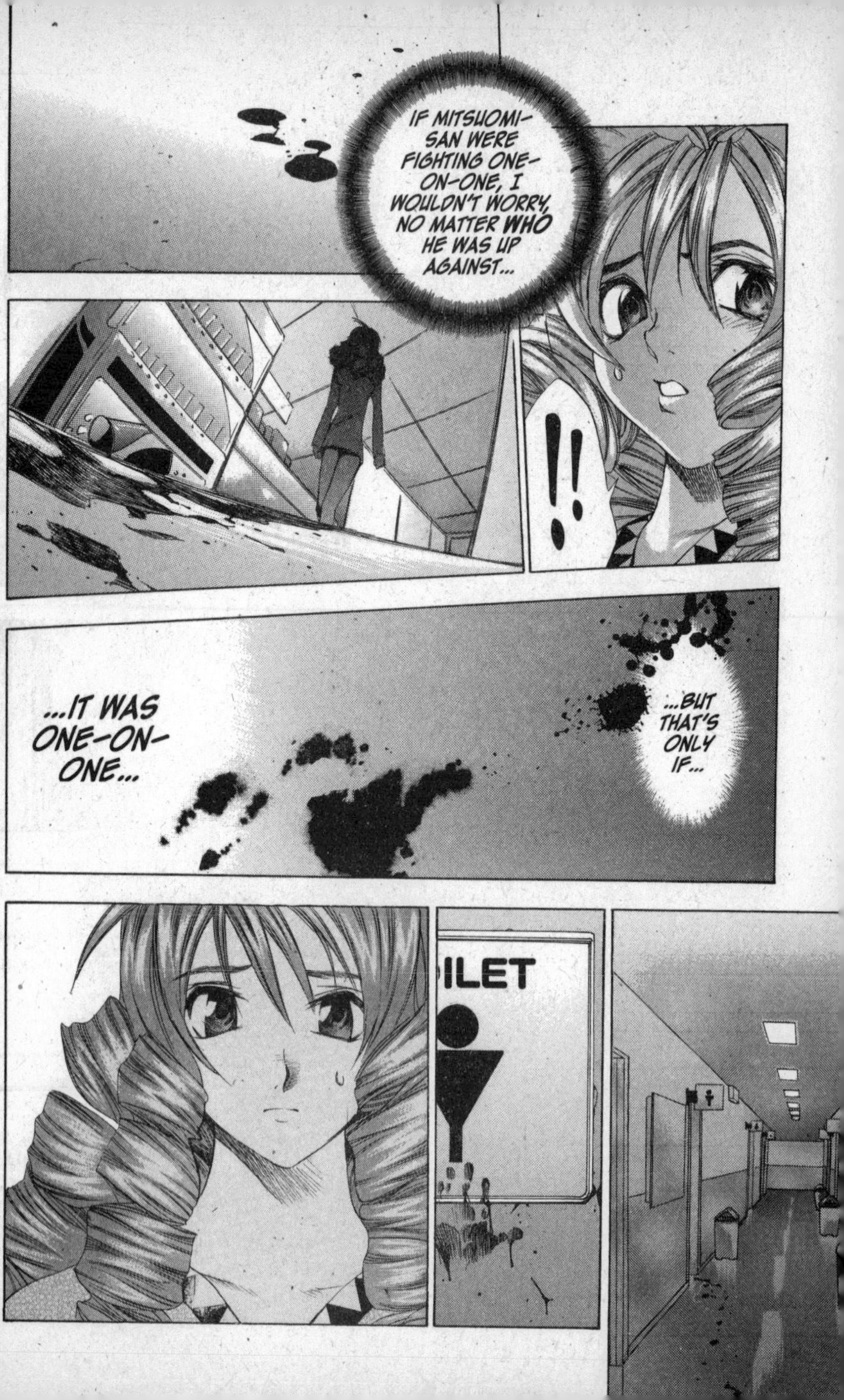
IF MITSUOMI-SAN WERE FIGHTING ONE-ON-ONE, I WOULDN'T WORRY, NO MATTER WHO HE WAS UP AGAINST...
!!
...BUT THAT'S ONLY IF...
...IT WAS ONE-ON-ONE...
ILET

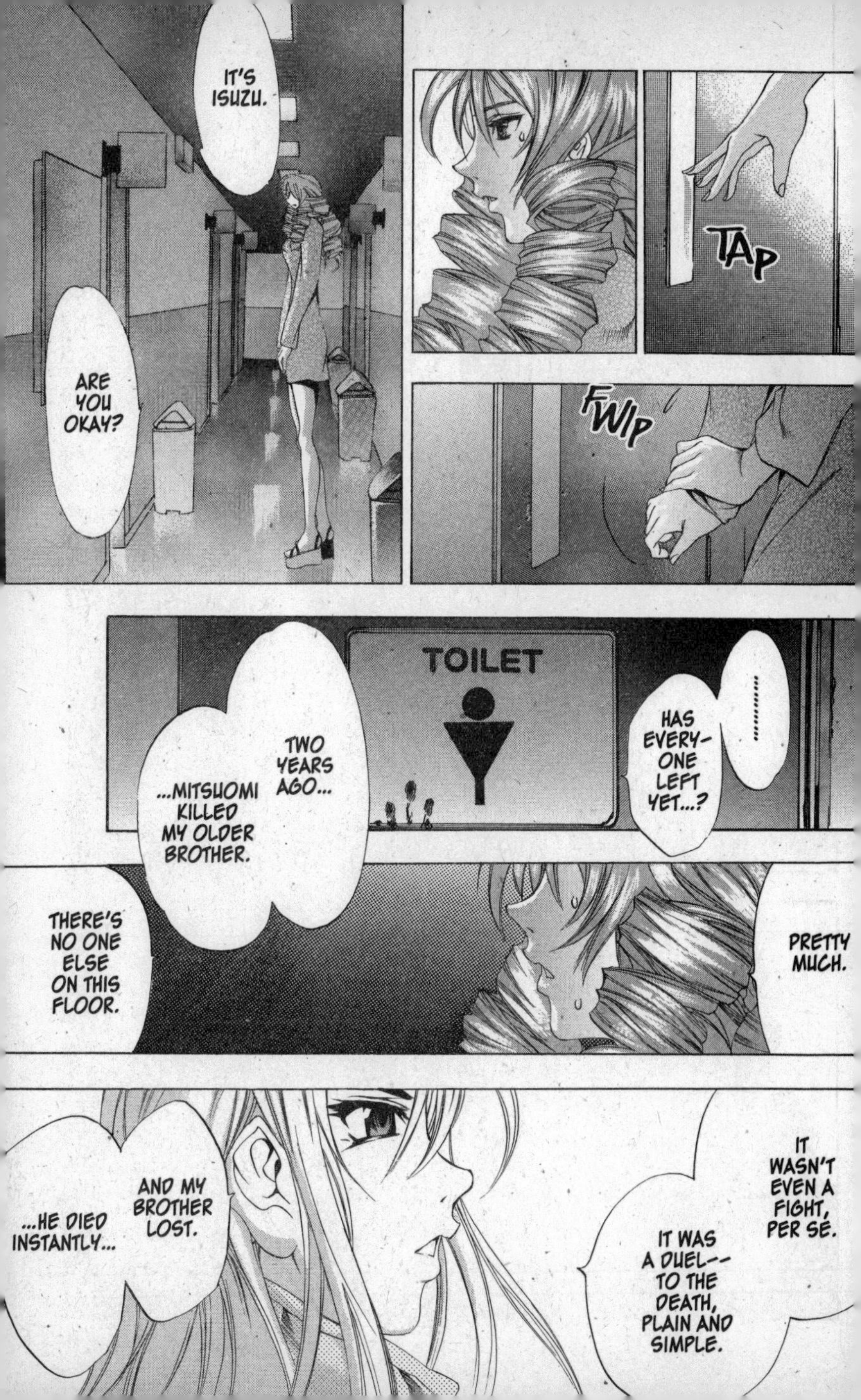
TAP
FWIP
IT'S ISUZU.
ARE YOU OKAY?
......
HAS EVERY-ONE LEFT YET...?
TOILET
TWO YEARS AGO...
...MITSUOMI KILLED MY OLDER BROTHER.
PRETTY MUCH.
THERE'S NO ONE ELSE ON THIS FLOOR.
IT WASN'T EVEN A FIGHT, PER SE.
IT WAS A DUEL--TO THE DEATH, PLAIN AND SIMPLE.
AND MY BROTHER LOST.
...HE DIED INSTANTLY...

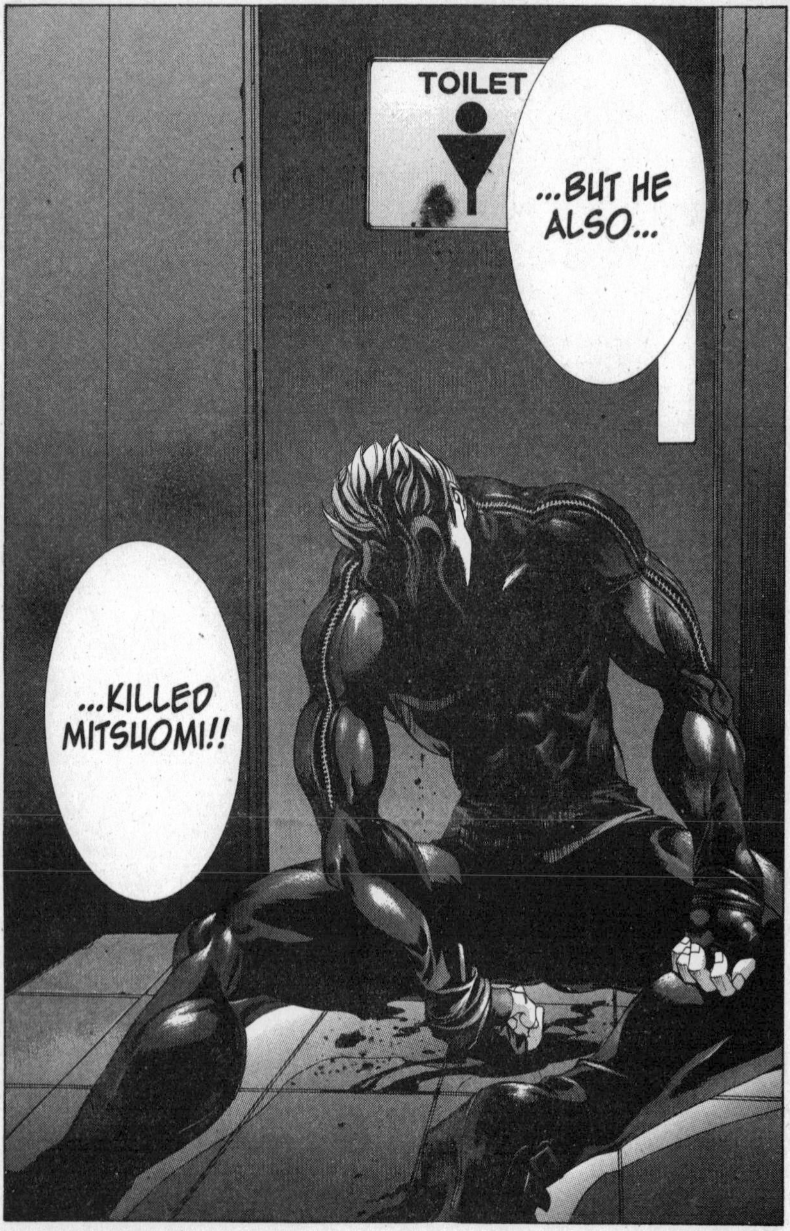
TOILET
...BUT HE ALSO...
...KILLED MITSUOMI!!

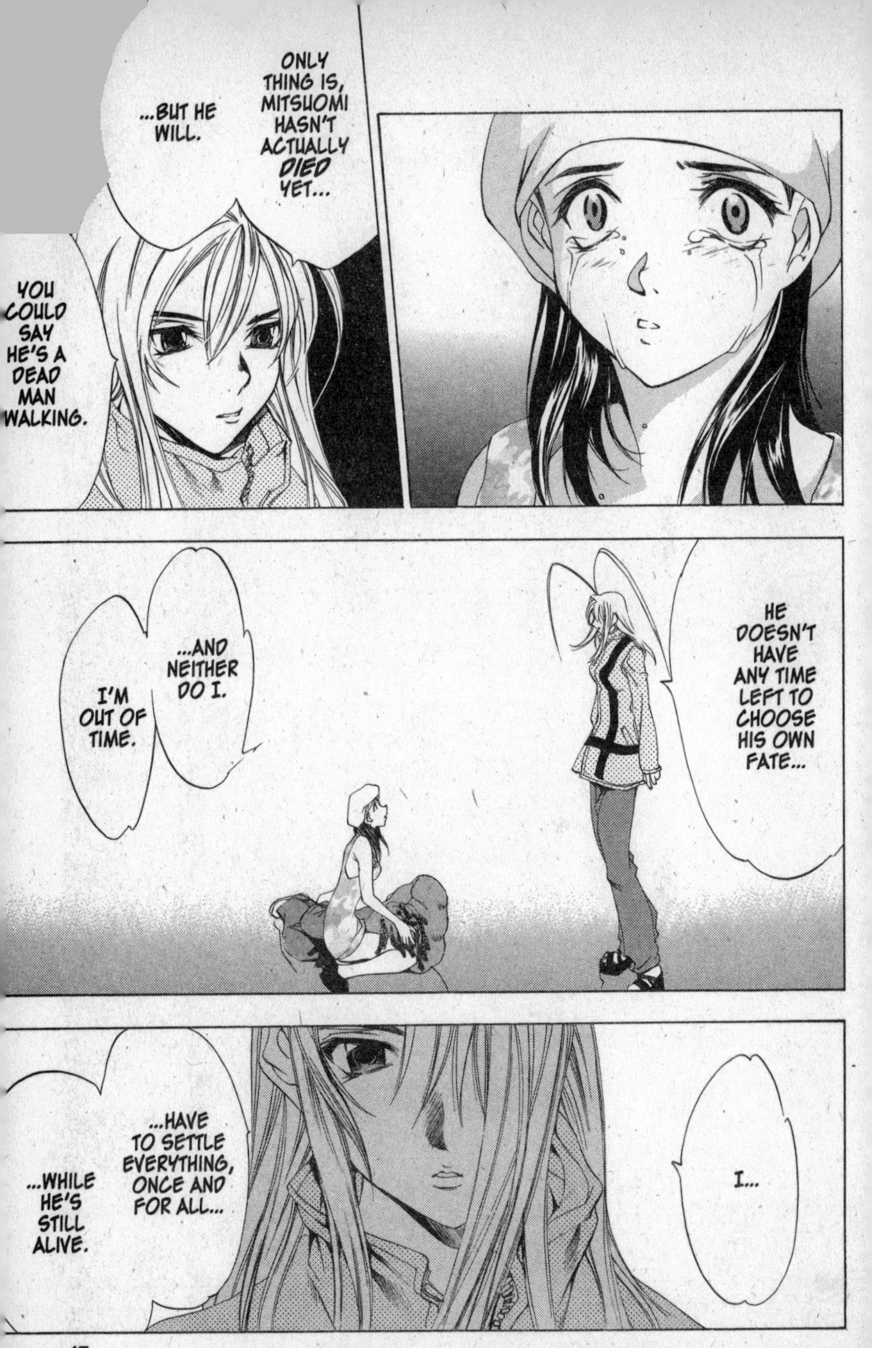
ONLY THING IS, MITSUOMI HASN'T ACTUALLY DIED YET...
...BUT HE WILL.
YOU COULD SAY HE'S A DEAD MAN WALKING.
HE DOESN'T HAVE ANY TIME LEFT TO CHOOSE HIS OWN FATE...
...AND NEITHER DO I.
I'M OUT OF TIME.
I...
...HAVE TO SETTLE EVERYTHING, ONCE AND FOR ALL...
...WHILE HE'S STILL ALIVE.

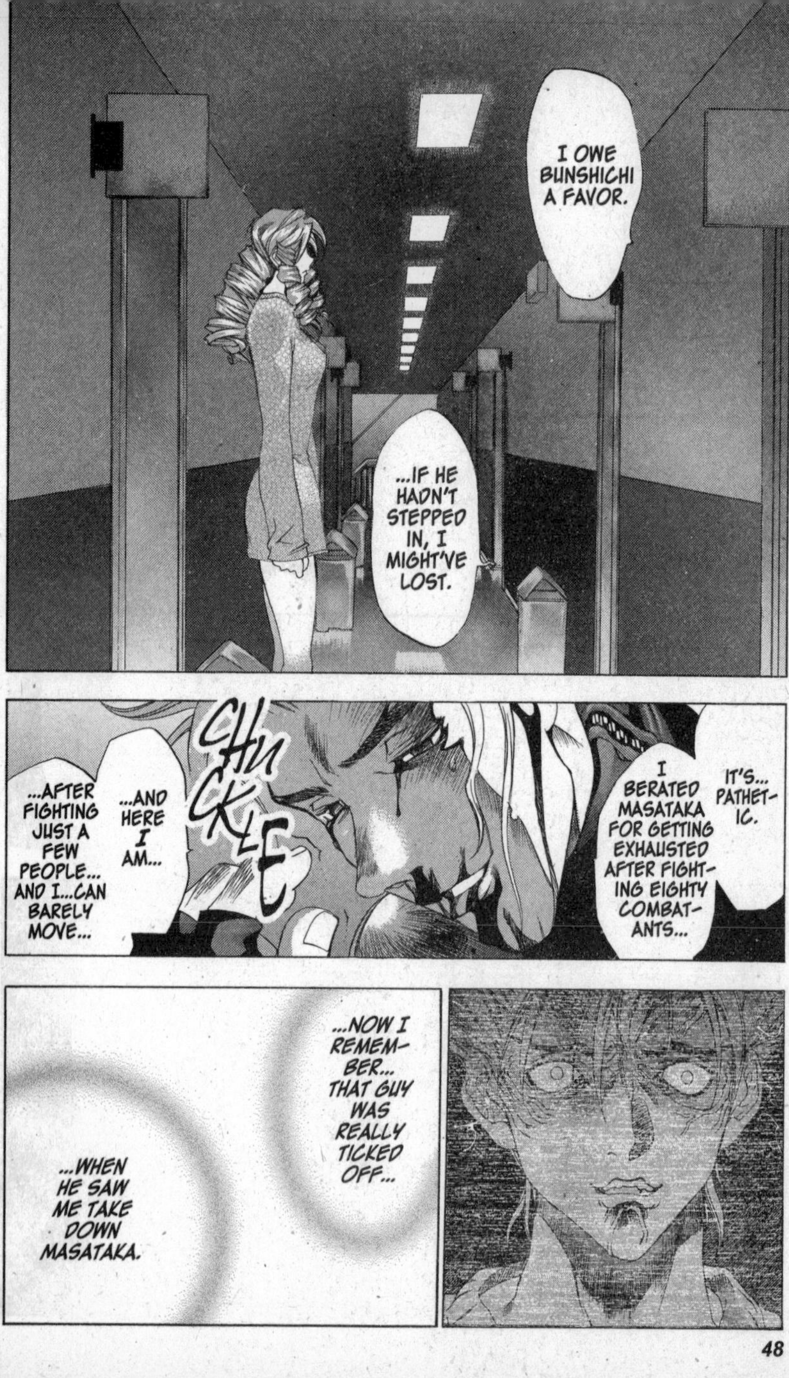
I OWE BUNSHICHI A FAVOR.
...IF HE HADN'T STEPPED IN, I MIGHT'VE LOST.
IT'S... PATHETIC.
I BERATED MASATAKA FOR GETTING EXHAUSTED AFTER FIGHTING EIGHTY COMBATANTS...
CHUCKLE
...AND HERE I AM...
...AFTER FIGHTING JUST A FEW PEOPLE... AND I...CAN BARELY MOVE...
...NOW I REMEMBER... THAT GUY WAS REALLY TICKED OFF...
...WHEN HE SAW ME TAKE DOWN MASATAKA.

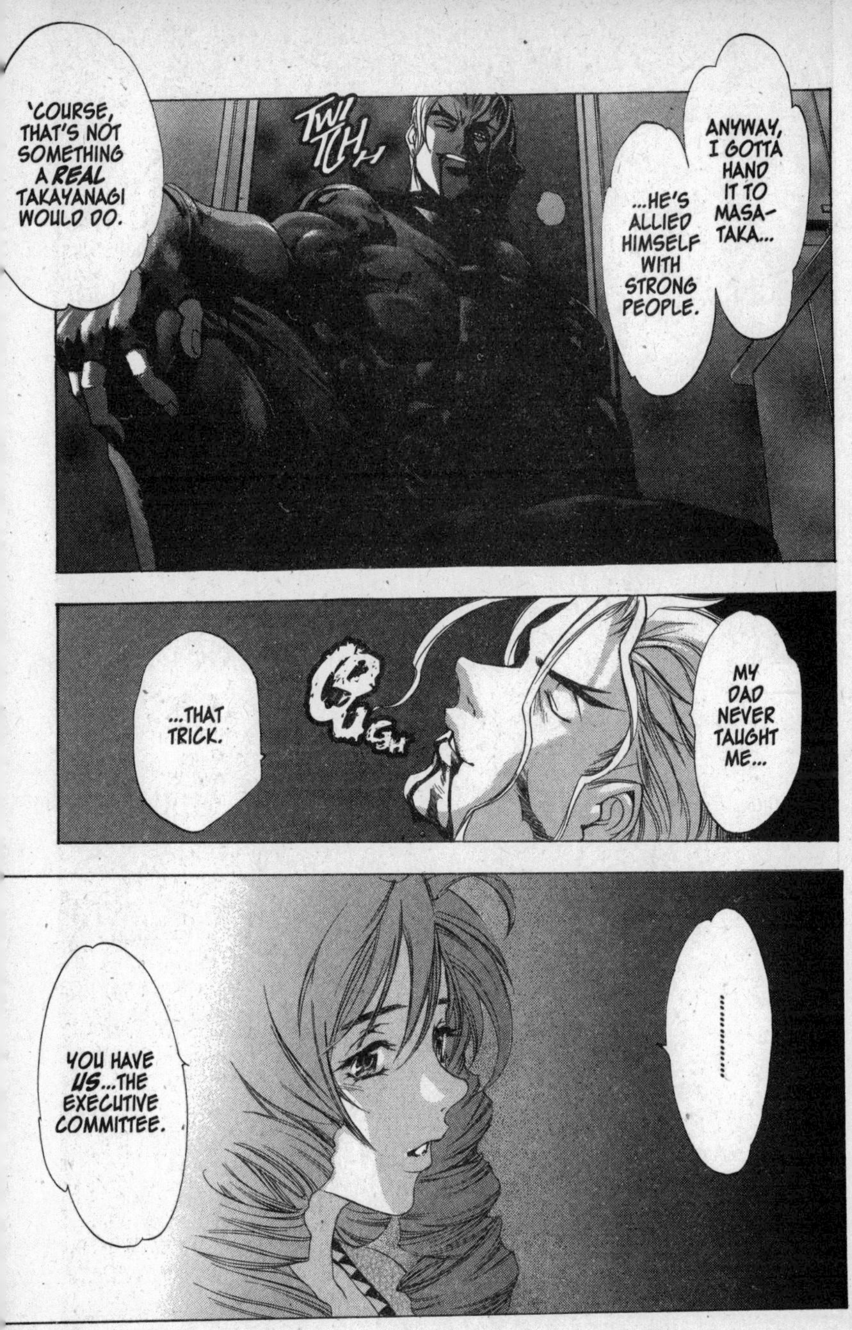
ANYWAY, I GOTTA HAND IT TO MASA-TAKA...
...HE'S ALLIED HIMSELF WITH STRONG PEOPLE.
TWITCH
'COURSE, THAT'S NOT SOMETHING A *REAL* TAKAYANAGI WOULD DO.
MY DAD NEVER TAUGHT ME...
GUGH
...THAT TRICK.
......
YOU HAVE *US*...THE EXECUTIVE COMMITTEE.

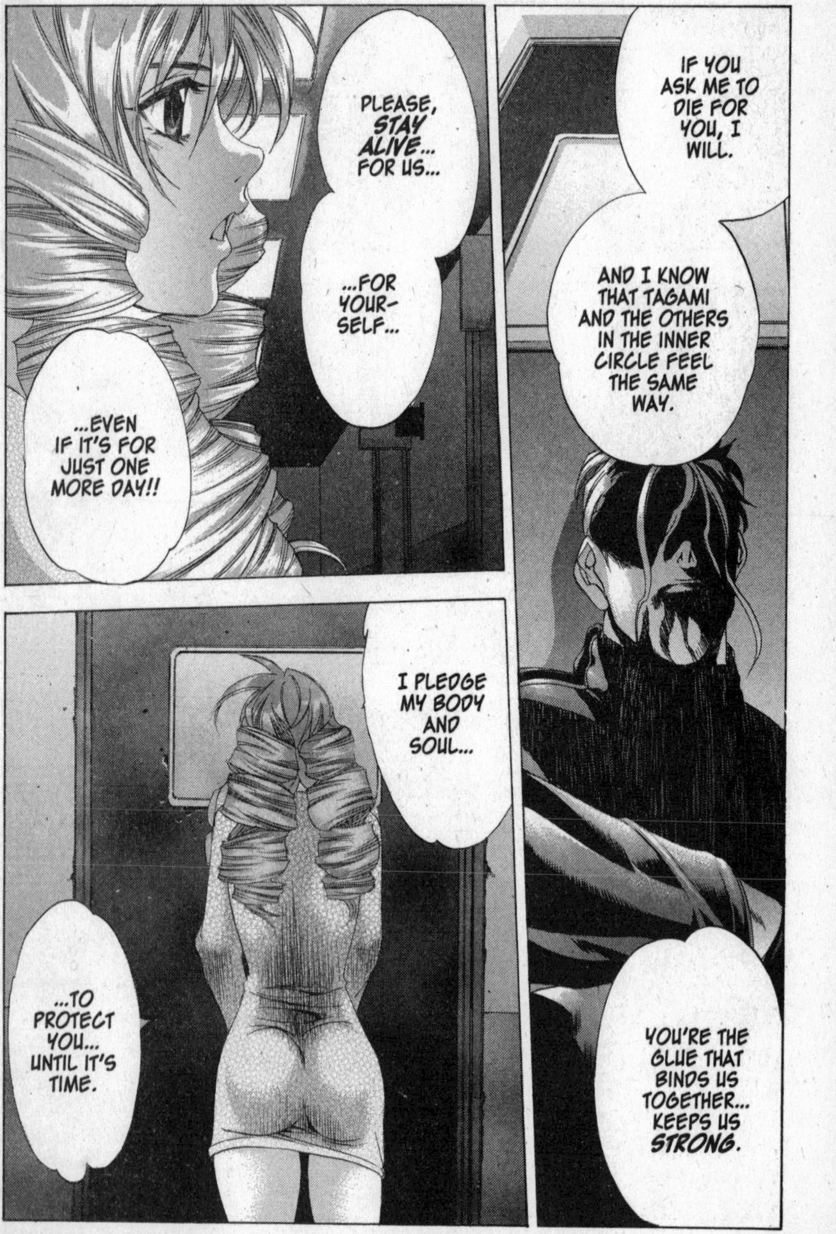
IF YOU ASK ME TO DIE FOR YOU, I WILL.
AND I KNOW THAT TAGAMI AND THE OTHERS IN THE INNER CIRCLE FEEL THE SAME WAY.
YOU'RE THE GLUE THAT BINDS US TOGETHER... KEEPS US STRONG.
PLEASE, STAY ALIVE... FOR US...
...FOR YOURSELF...
...EVEN IF IT'S FOR JUST ONE MORE DAY!!
I PLEDGE MY BODY AND SOUL...
...TO PROTECT YOU... UNTIL IT'S TIME.

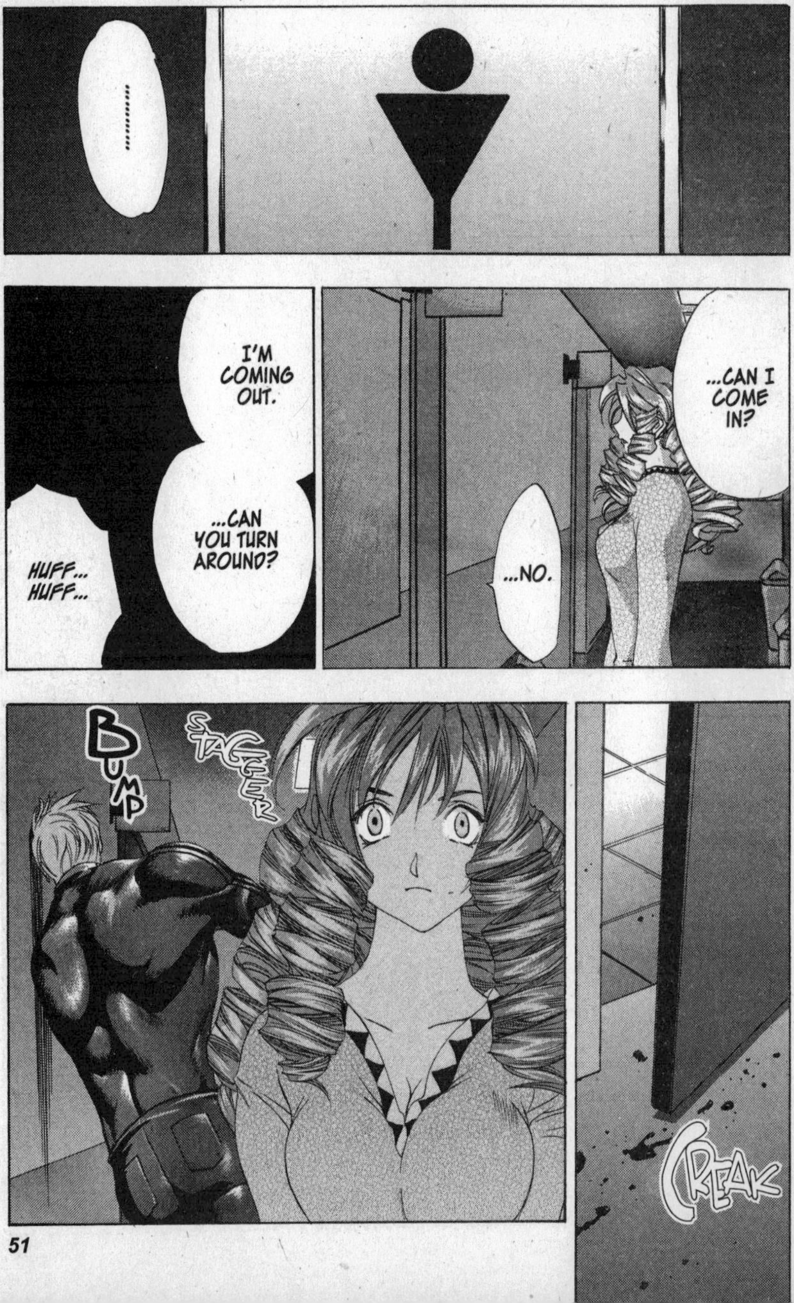
……
...CAN I COME IN?
...NO.
I'M COMING OUT.
...CAN YOU TURN AROUND?
HUFF... HUFF...
CREAK
STAGGER
BUMP

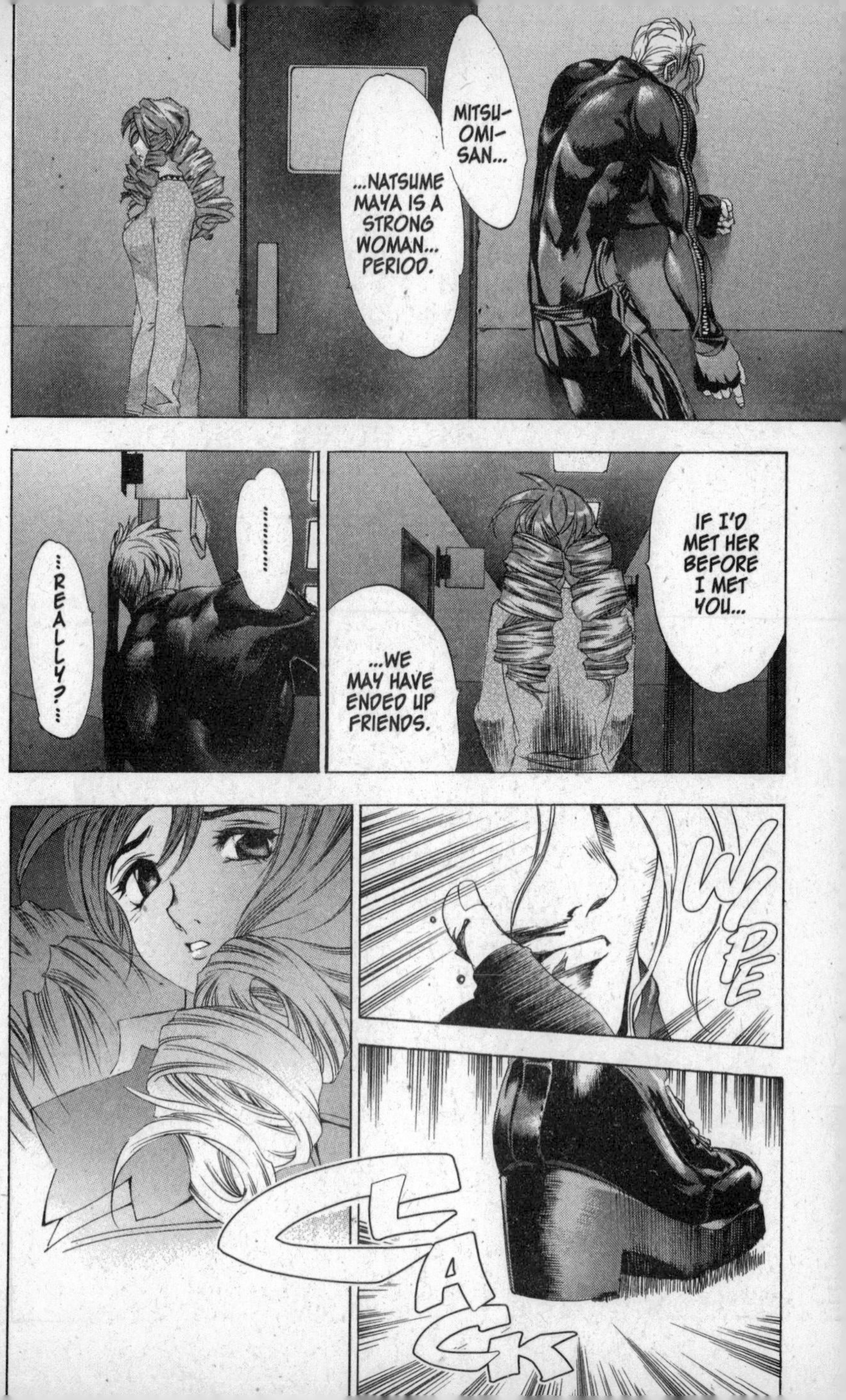
MITSU-OMI-SAN...
...NATSUME MAYA IS A STRONG WOMAN... PERIOD.
IF I'D MET HER BEFORE I MET YOU...
...WE MAY HAVE ENDED UP FRIENDS.
....
...REALLY?...
WIPE
CLACK

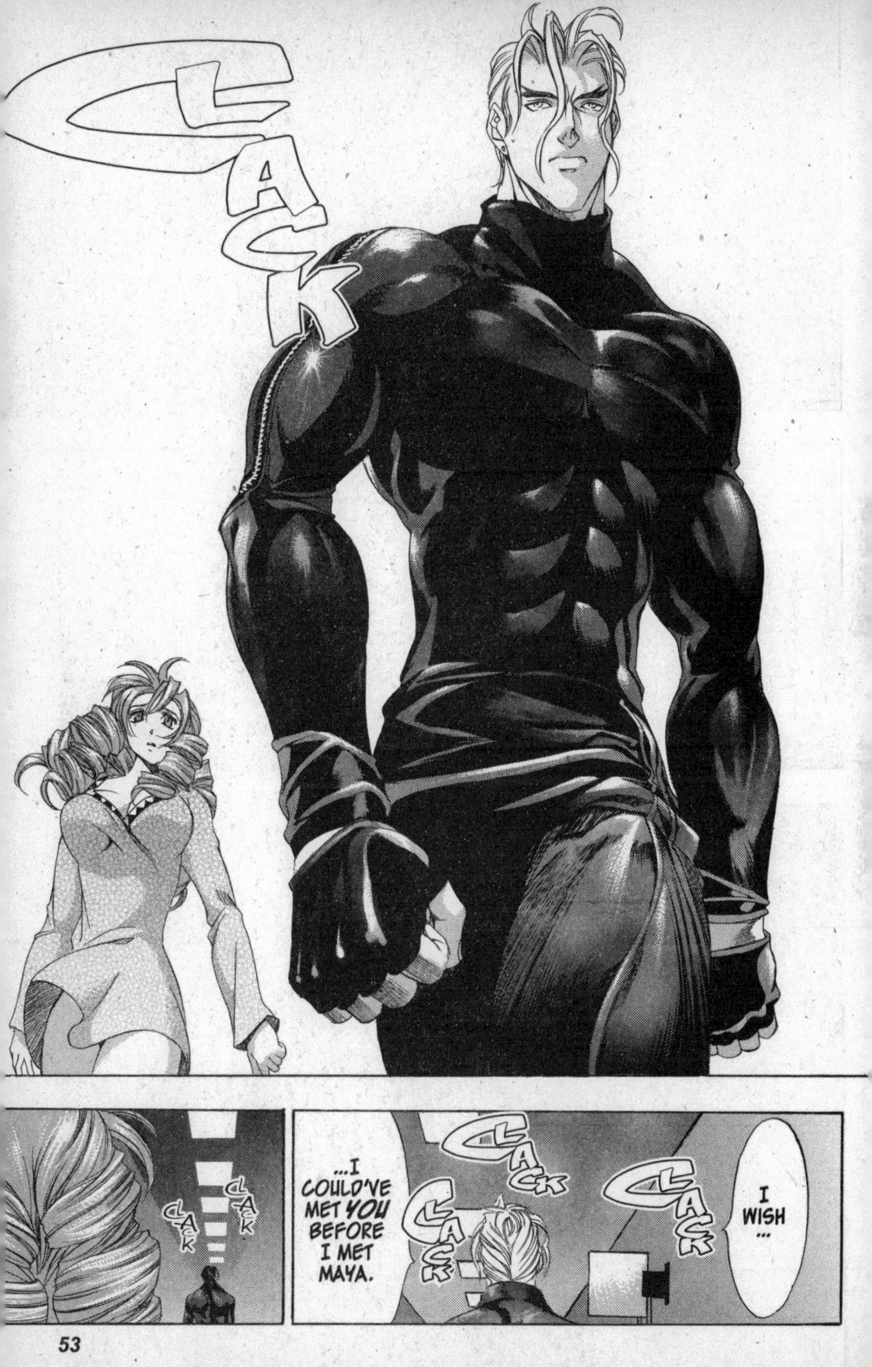
CLACK
I WISH ...
CLACK
CLACK
...I COULD'VE MET YOU BEFORE I MET MAYA.
CLACK
CLACK
CLACK

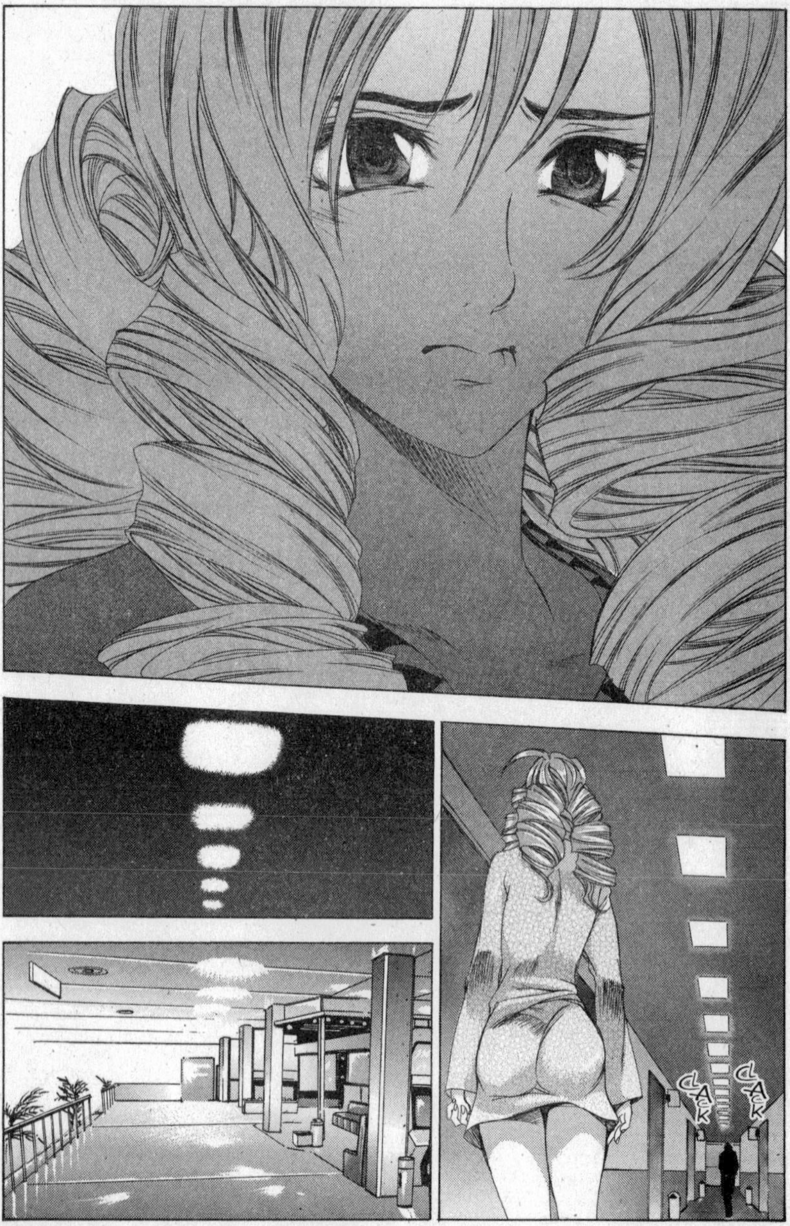
CLACK
CLACK

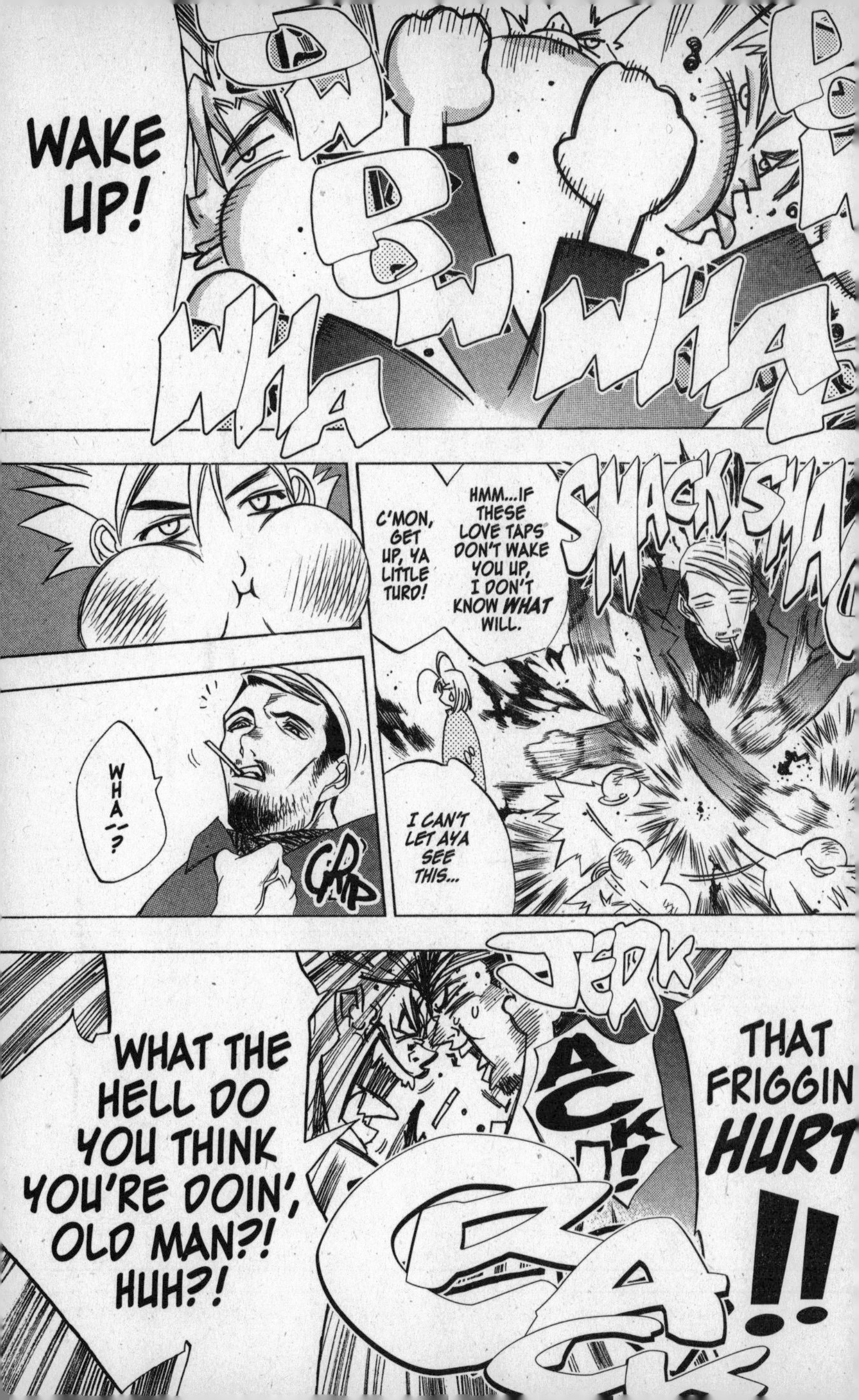
WHA WHA
WAKE UP!
SHACK SHA
HMM...IF THESE LOVE TAPS DON'T WAKE YOU UP, I DON'T KNOW WHAT WILL.
C'MON, GET UP, YA LITTLE TURD!
I CAN'T LET AYA SEE THIS...
WHA...?
GRIP
JERK
THAT FRIGGIN HURT!!
ACK
WHAT THE HELL DO YOU THINK YOU'RE DOIN', OLD MAN?! HUH?!

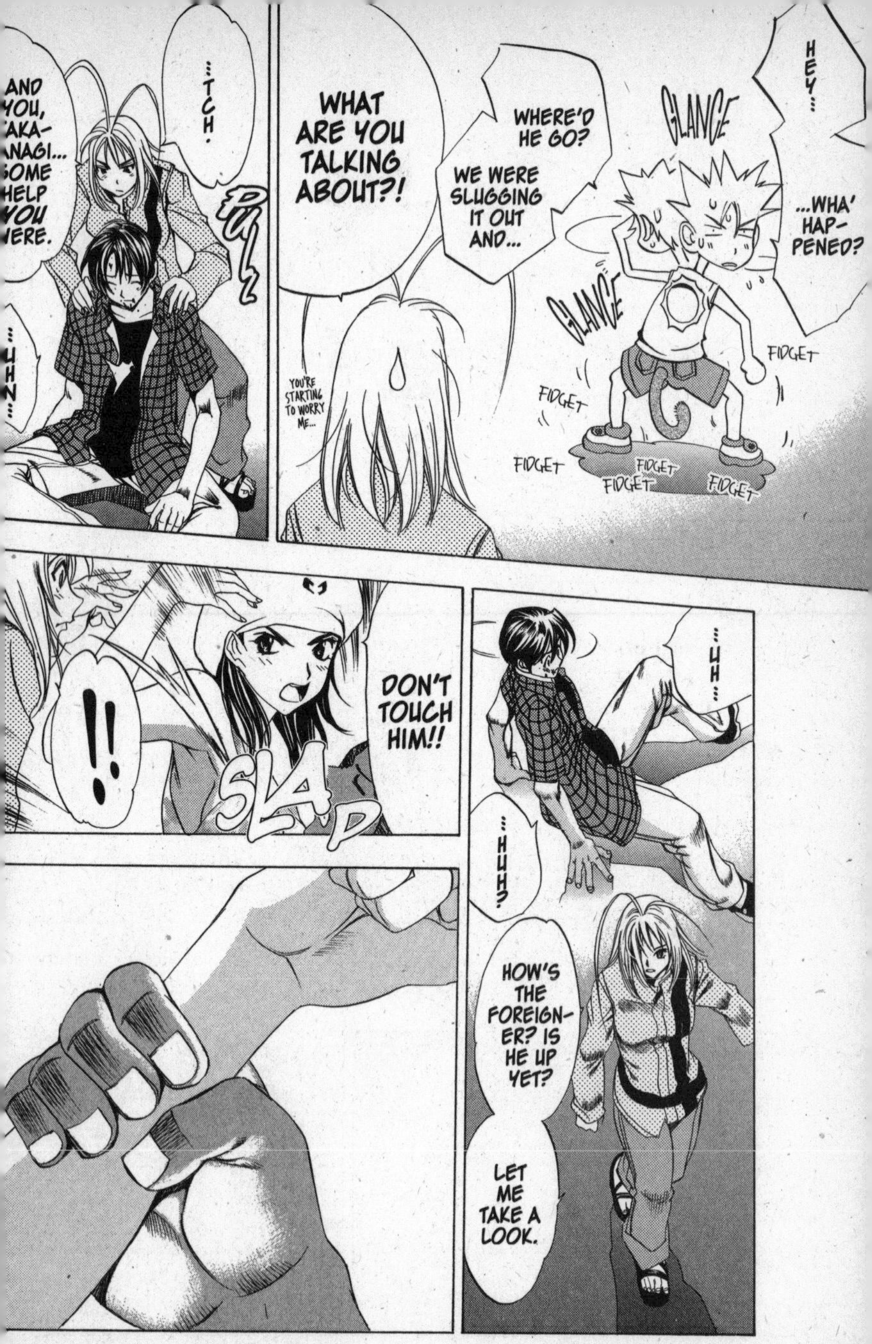
HEY...
...WHA' HAPPENED?
GLANCE
GLANCE
FIDGET
FIDGET
FIDGET
FIDGET
FIDGET
FIDGET
WHERE'D HE GO?
WE WERE SLUGGING IT OUT AND...
WHAT ARE YOU TALKING ABOUT?!
YOU'RE STARTING TO WORRY ME...
...TCH.
PULL
AND YOU, AKA-ANAGI... SOME HELP YOU WERE.
...UHN...
...UH...
...HUH?
HOW'S THE FOREIGNER? IS HE UP YET?
LET ME TAKE A LOOK.
DON'T TOUCH HIM!!
SLAP
!!

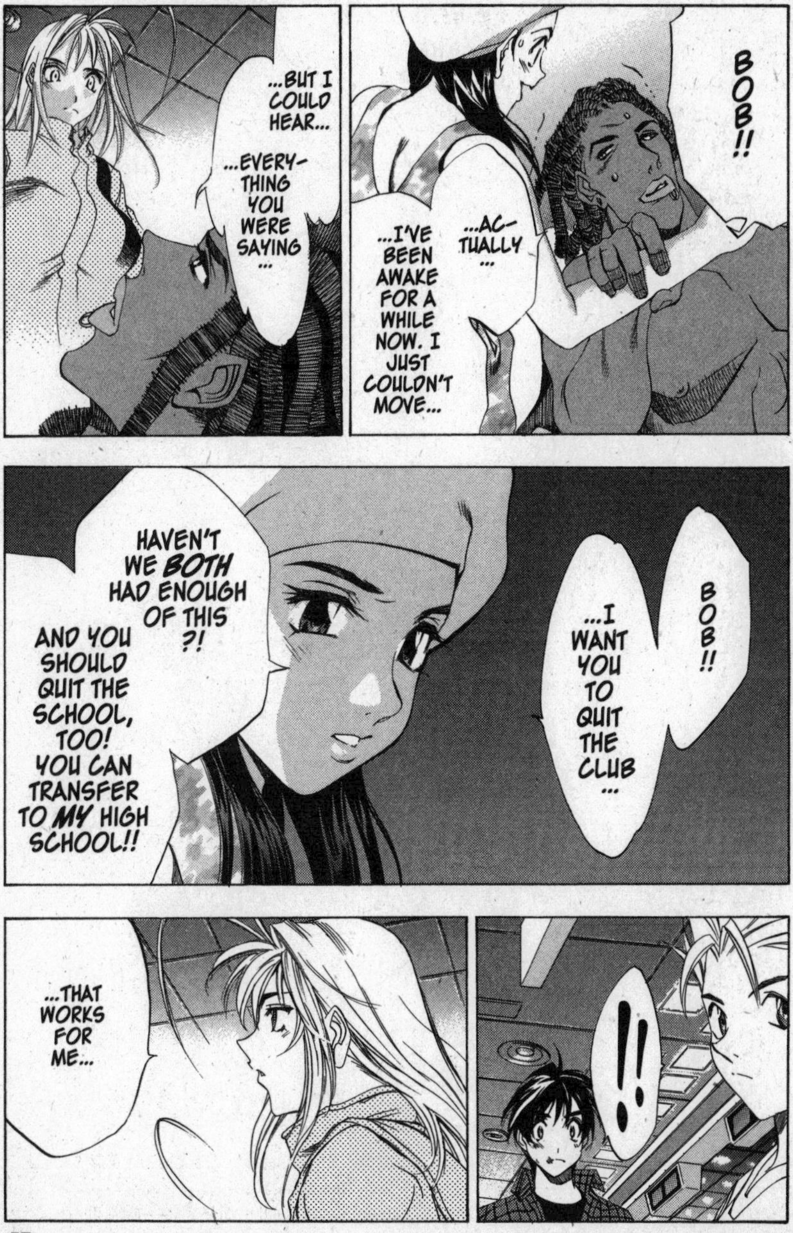
BOB!!
...ACTUALLY...
...I'VE BEEN AWAKE FOR A WHILE NOW. I JUST COULDN'T MOVE...
...BUT I COULD HEAR...
...EVERYTHING YOU WERE SAYING...
BOB!!
...I WANT YOU TO QUIT THE CLUB...
HAVEN'T WE **BOTH** HAD ENOUGH OF THIS?!
AND YOU SHOULD QUIT THE SCHOOL, TOO! YOU CAN TRANSFER TO **MY** HIGH SCHOOL!!
!!
...THAT WORKS FOR ME...

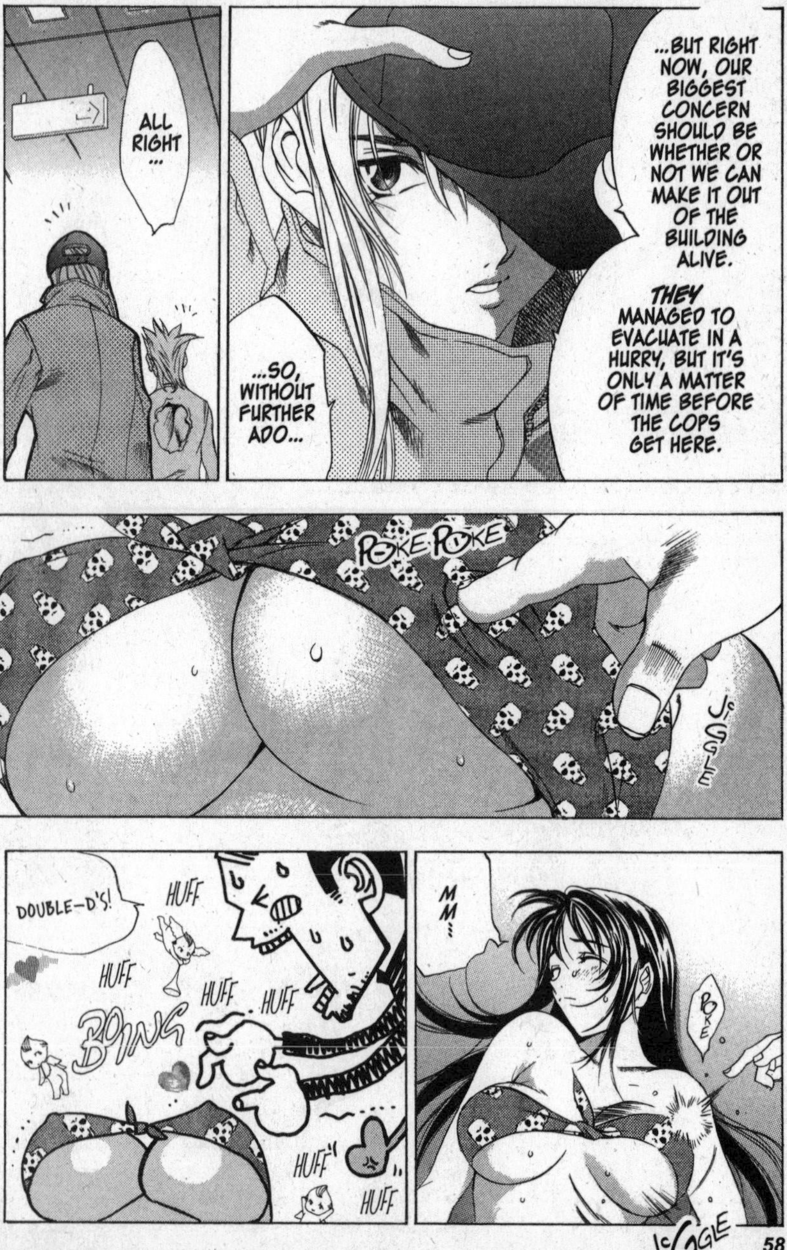
...BUT RIGHT NOW, OUR BIGGEST CONCERN SHOULD BE WHETHER OR NOT WE CAN MAKE IT OUT OF THE BUILDING ALIVE.
THEY MANAGED TO EVACUATE IN A HURRY, BUT IT'S ONLY A MATTER OF TIME BEFORE THE COPS GET HERE.
...SO, WITHOUT FURTHER ADO...
ALL RIGHT...
POKE POKE
JIGGLE
MM...
POKE
JIGGLE
DOUBLE-D'S!
HUFF
HUFF
HUFF
HUFF
BOING
HUFF
HUFF

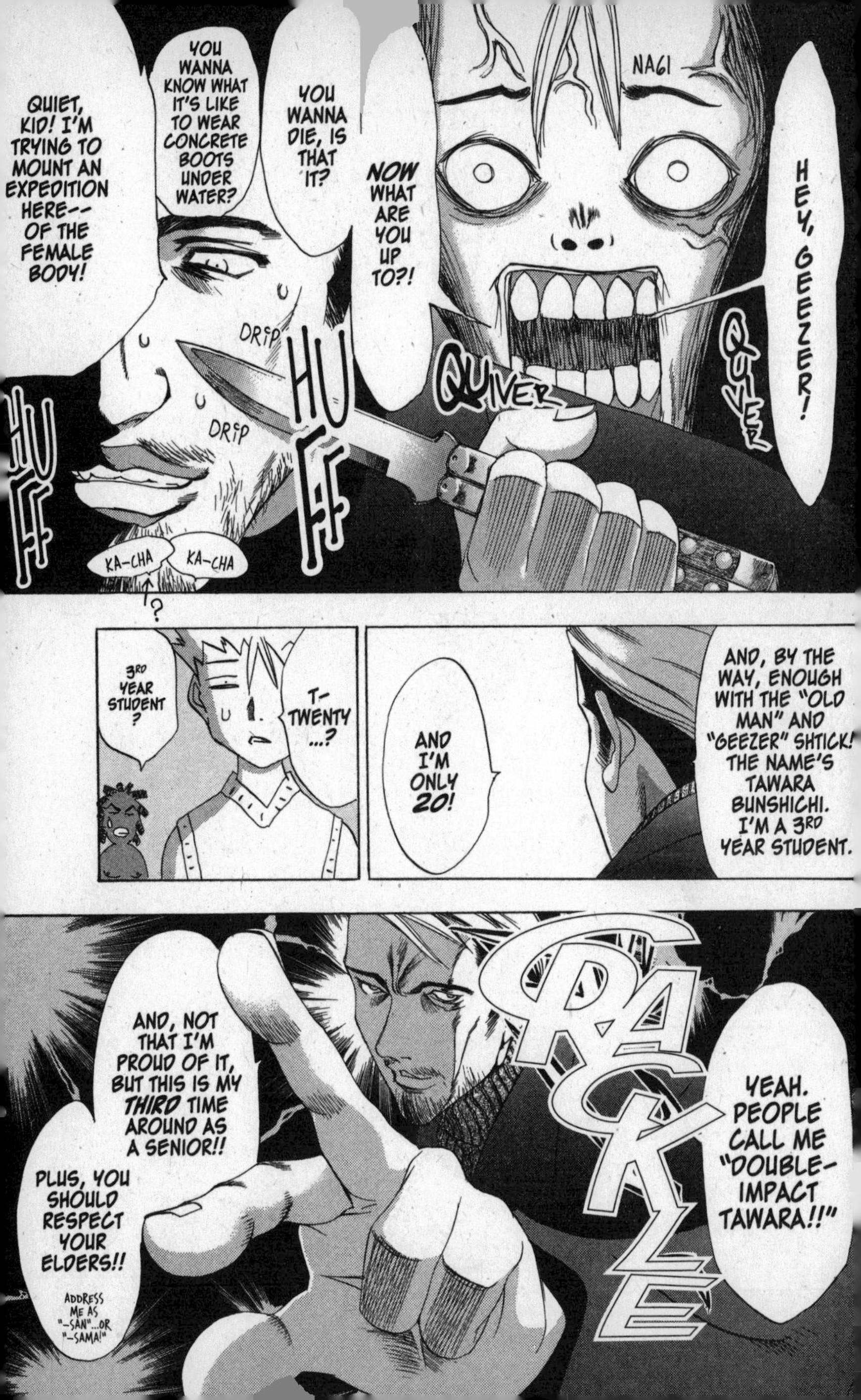
NAGI
HEY, GEEZER!
QUIVER
QUIVER
NOW WHAT ARE YOU UP TO?!
YOU WANNA DIE, IS THAT IT?
YOU WANNA KNOW WHAT IT'S LIKE TO WEAR CONCRETE BOOTS UNDER WATER?
QUIET, KID! I'M TRYING TO MOUNT AN EXPEDITION HERE--OF THE FEMALE BODY!
HUFF
DRIP
DRIP
HUFF
KA-CHA
KA-CHA
?
AND, BY THE WAY, ENOUGH WITH THE "OLD MAN" AND "GEEZER" SHTICK! THE NAME'S TAWARA BUNSHICHI. I'M A 3RD YEAR STUDENT.
AND I'M ONLY 20!
T-TWENTY ...?
3RD YEAR STUDENT?
YEAH. PEOPLE CALL ME "DOUBLE-IMPACT TAWARA!!"
CRACKLE
AND, NOT THAT I'M PROUD OF IT, BUT THIS IS MY THIRD TIME AROUND AS A SENIOR!!
PLUS, YOU SHOULD RESPECT YOUR ELDERS!!
ADDRESS ME AS "-SAN"...OR "-SAMA!"

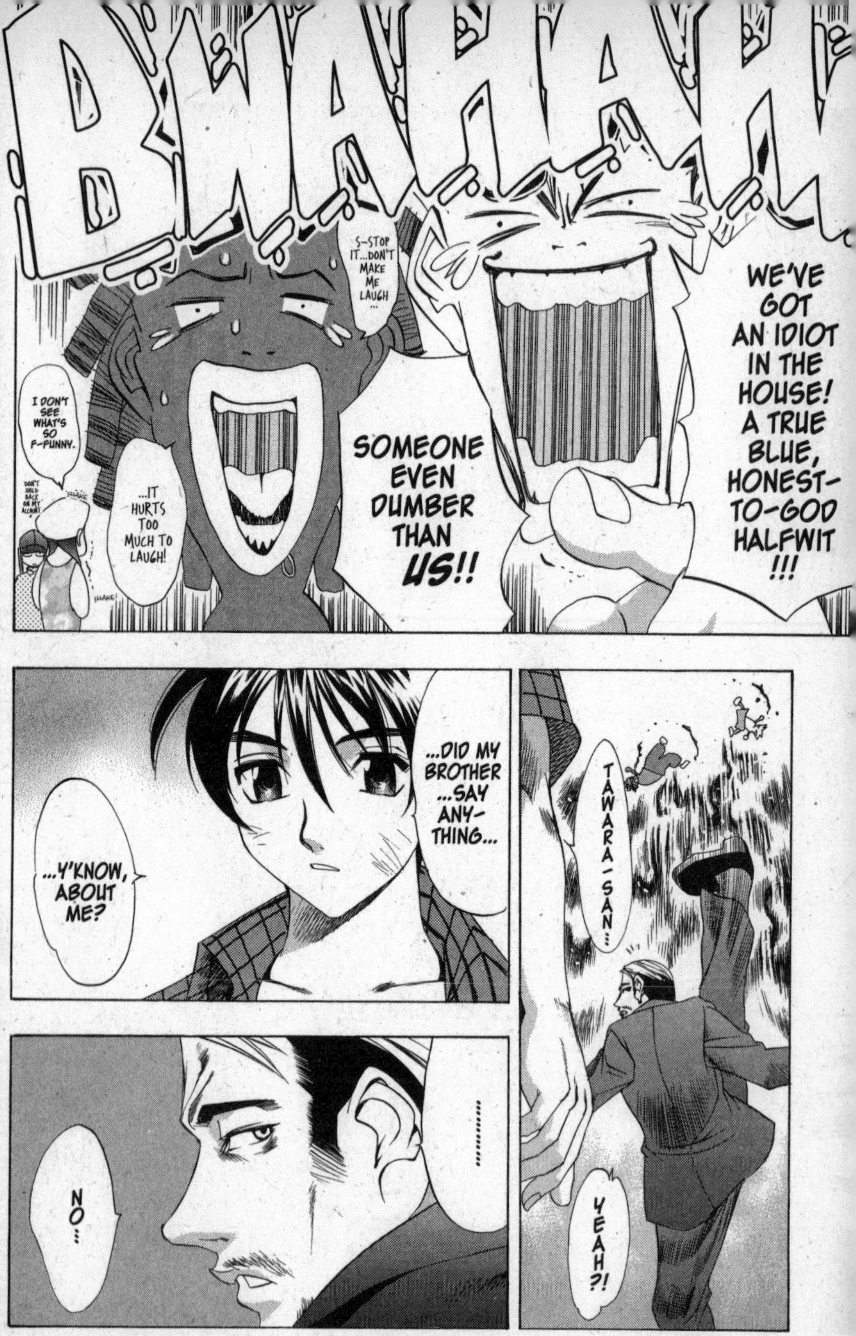
WE'VE GOT AN IDIOT IN THE HOUSE! A TRUE BLUE, HONEST-TO-GOD HALFWIT!!!
S-STOP IT...DON'T MAKE ME LAUGH...
SOMEONE EVEN DUMBER THAN US!!
...IT HURTS TOO MUCH TO LAUGH!
I DON'T SEE WHAT'S SO F-FUNNY.
DON'T HOLD BACK ON MY ACCOUNT.
SHAKE
SHAKE!
TAWARA-SAN...
YEAH?!
...DID MY BROTHER ...SAY ANYTHING...
...Y'KNOW, ABOUT ME?
......
NO...

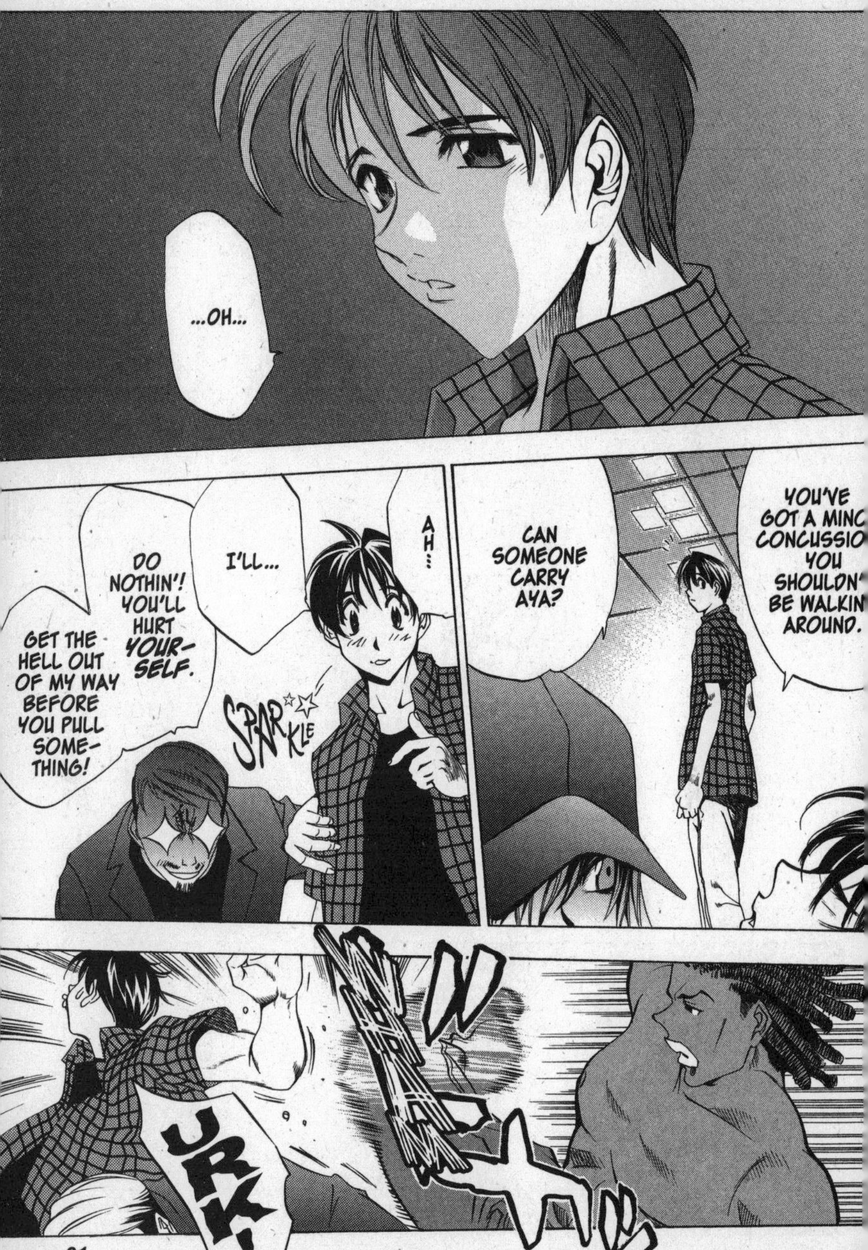
...OH...
YOU'VE GOT A MINC CONCUSSIO YOU SHOULDN' BE WALKIN AROUND.
CAN SOMEONE CARRY AYA?
AH...
I'LL...
DO NOTHIN'! YOU'LL HURT YOURSELF.
GET THE HELL OUT OF MY WAY BEFORE YOU PULL SOMETHING!
SPARKLE
URK!

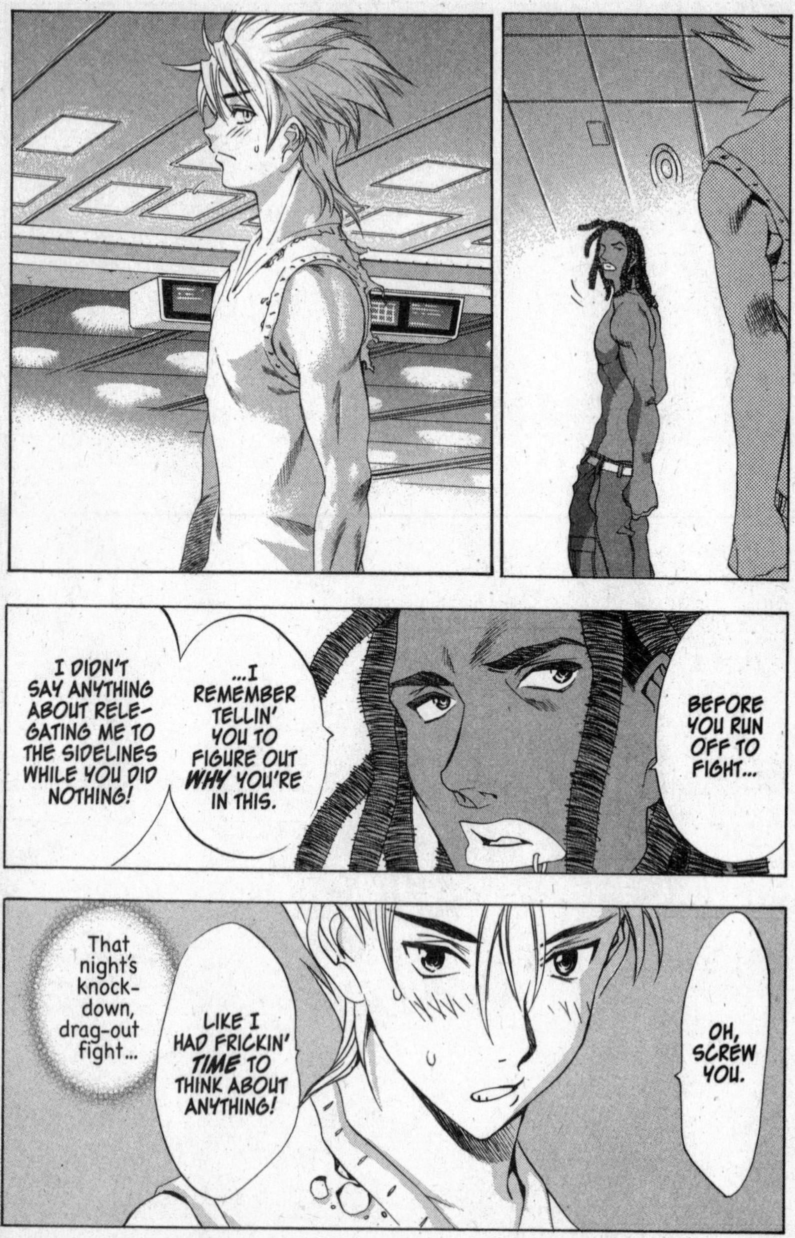
BEFORE YOU RUN OFF TO FIGHT...
...I REMEMBER TELLIN' YOU TO FIGURE OUT *WHY* YOU'RE IN THIS.
I DIDN'T SAY ANYTHING ABOUT RELE-GATING ME TO THE SIDELINES WHILE YOU DID NOTHING!
OH, SCREW YOU.
LIKE I HAD FRICKIN' *TIME* TO THINK ABOUT ANYTHING!
That night's knock-down, drag-out fight...

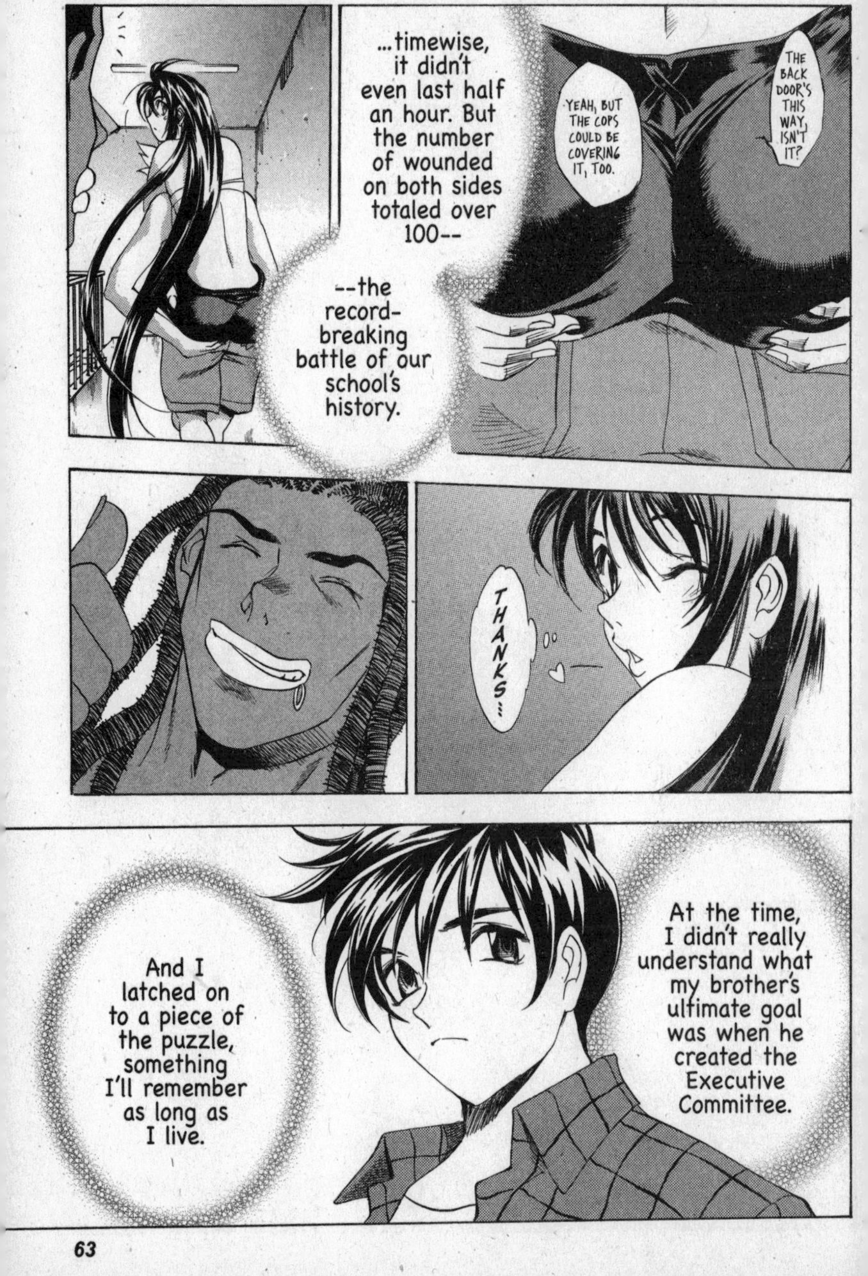
THE BACK DOOR'S THIS WAY, ISN'T IT?
YEAH, BUT THE COPS COULD BE COVERING IT, TOO.
...timewise, it didn't even last half an hour. But the number of wounded on both sides totaled over 100--
--the record-breaking battle of our school's history.
THANKS...
At the time, I didn't really understand what my brother's ultimate goal was when he created the Executive Committee.
And I latched on to a piece of the puzzle, something I'll remember as long as I live.

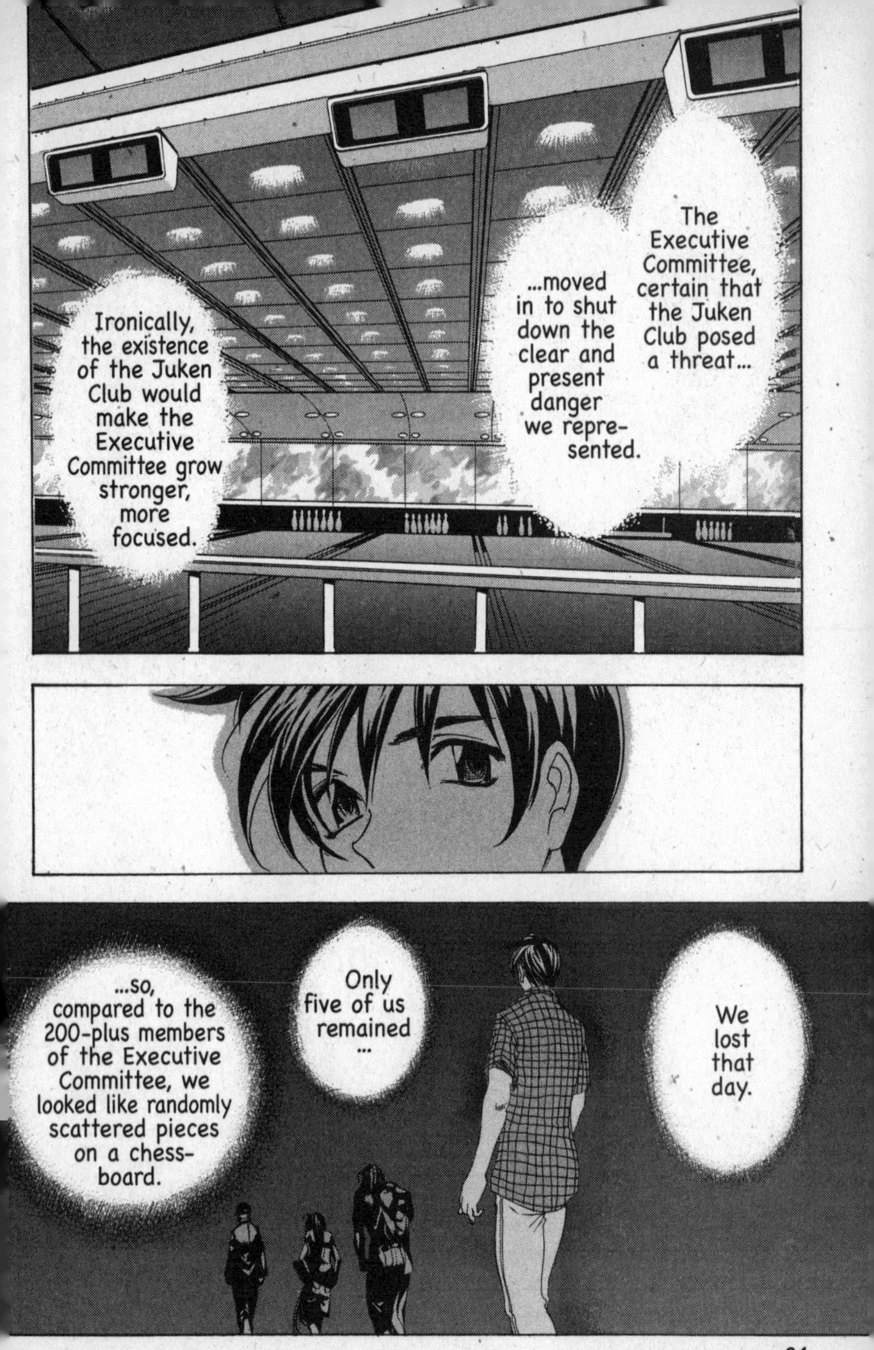
The Executive Committee, certain that the Juken Club posed a threat...
...moved in to shut down the clear and present danger we represented.
Ironically, the existence of the Juken Club would make the Executive Committee grow stronger, more focused.
We lost that day.
Only five of us remained ...
...so, compared to the 200-plus members of the Executive Committee, we looked like randomly scattered pieces on a chess-board.

FIGHT:22

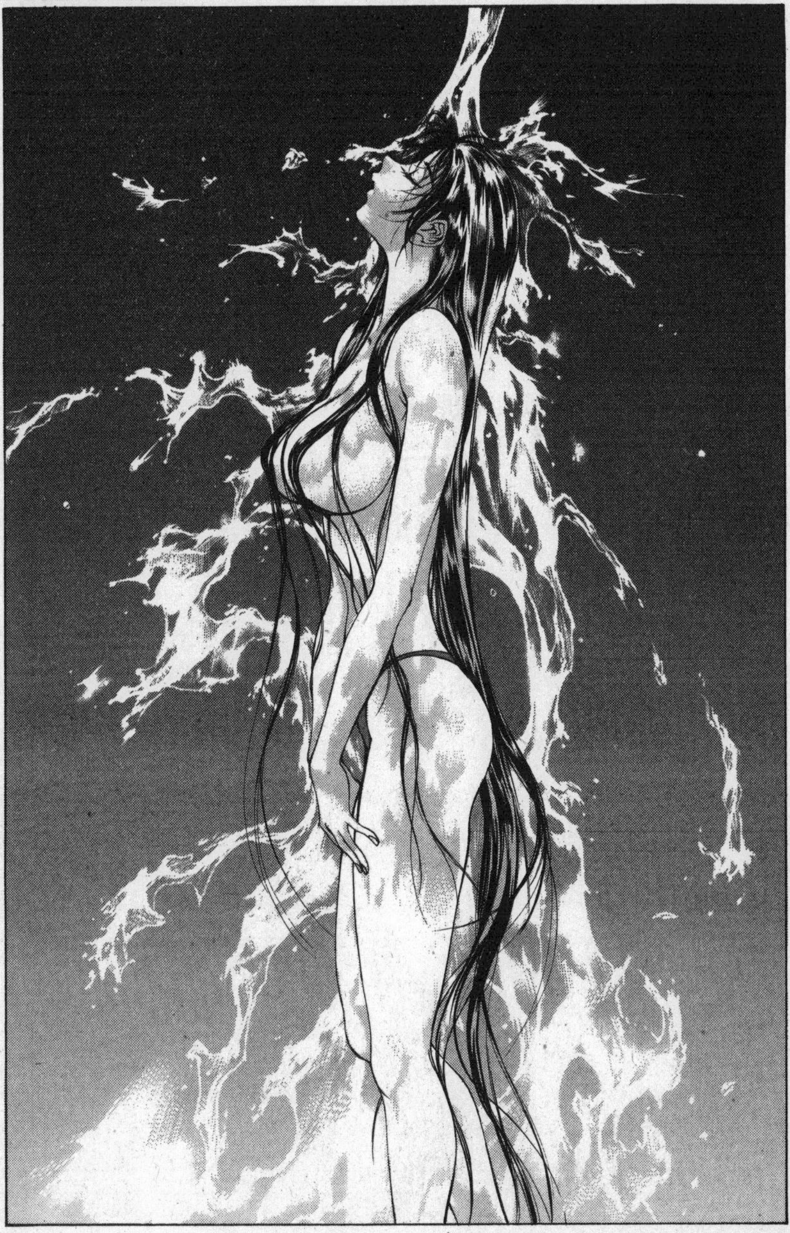

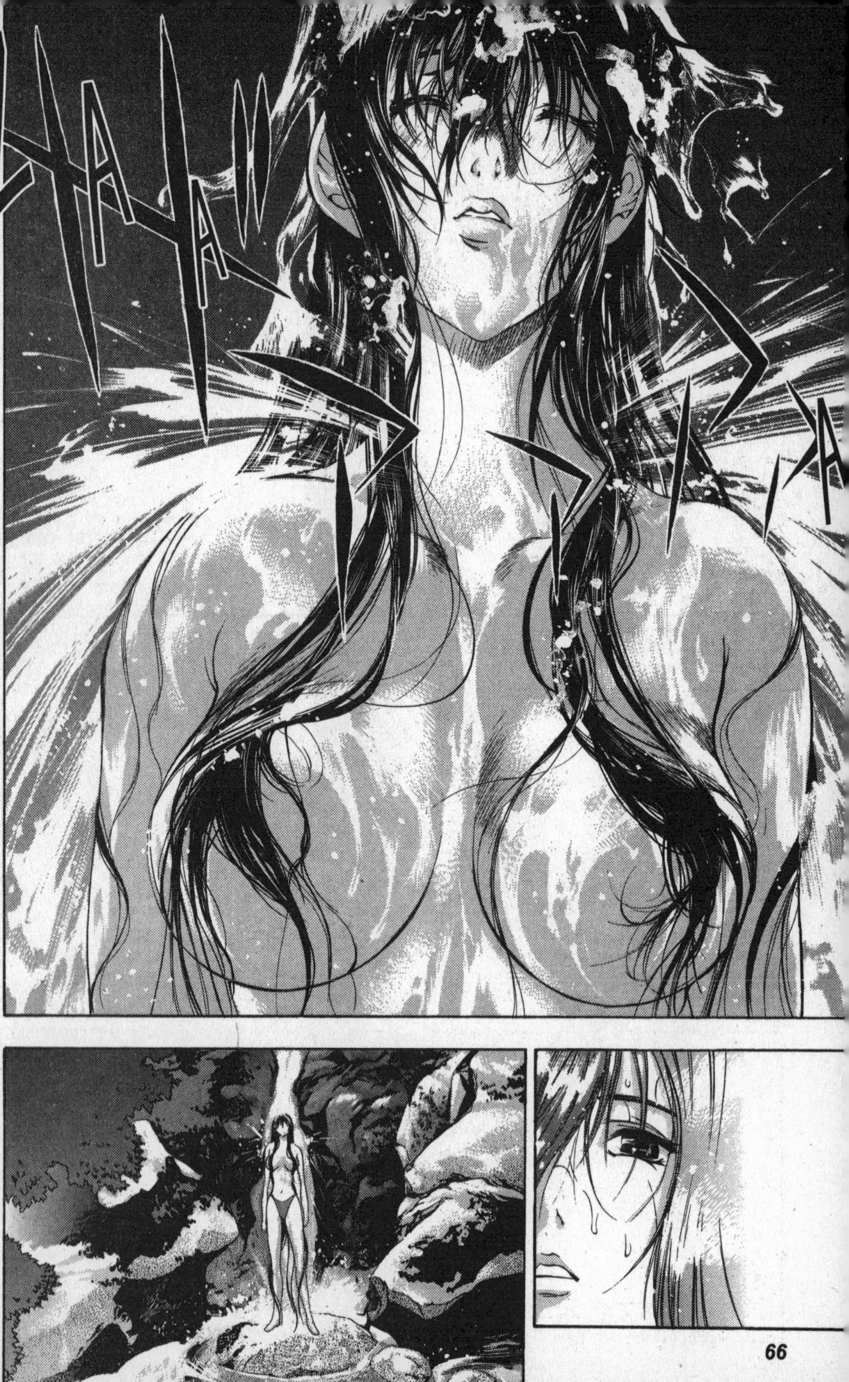

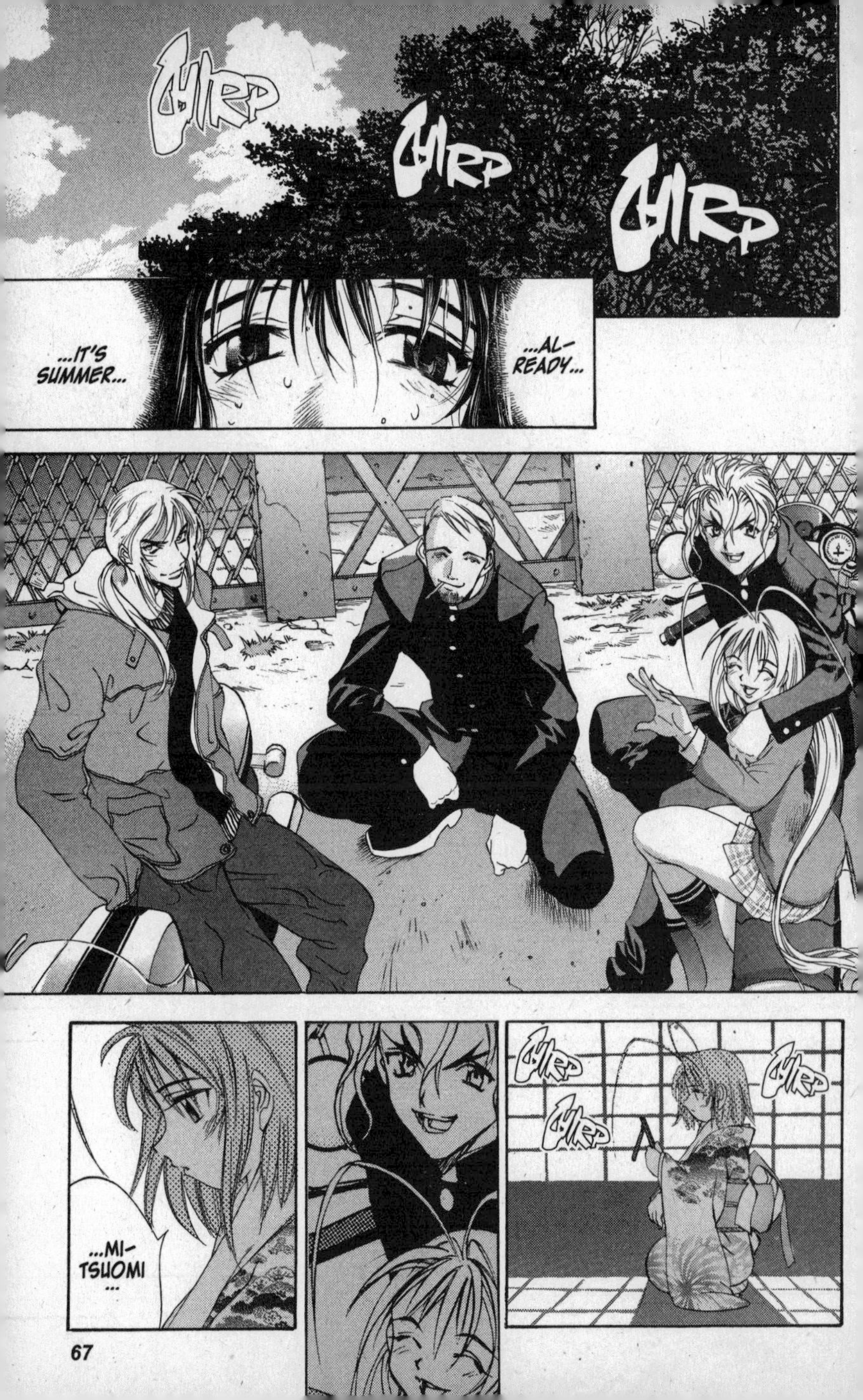

CHIRP
CHIRP
CHIRP
...AL-READY...
...IT'S SUMMER...
CHIRP
CHIRP
CHIRP
...MI-TSUOMI ...

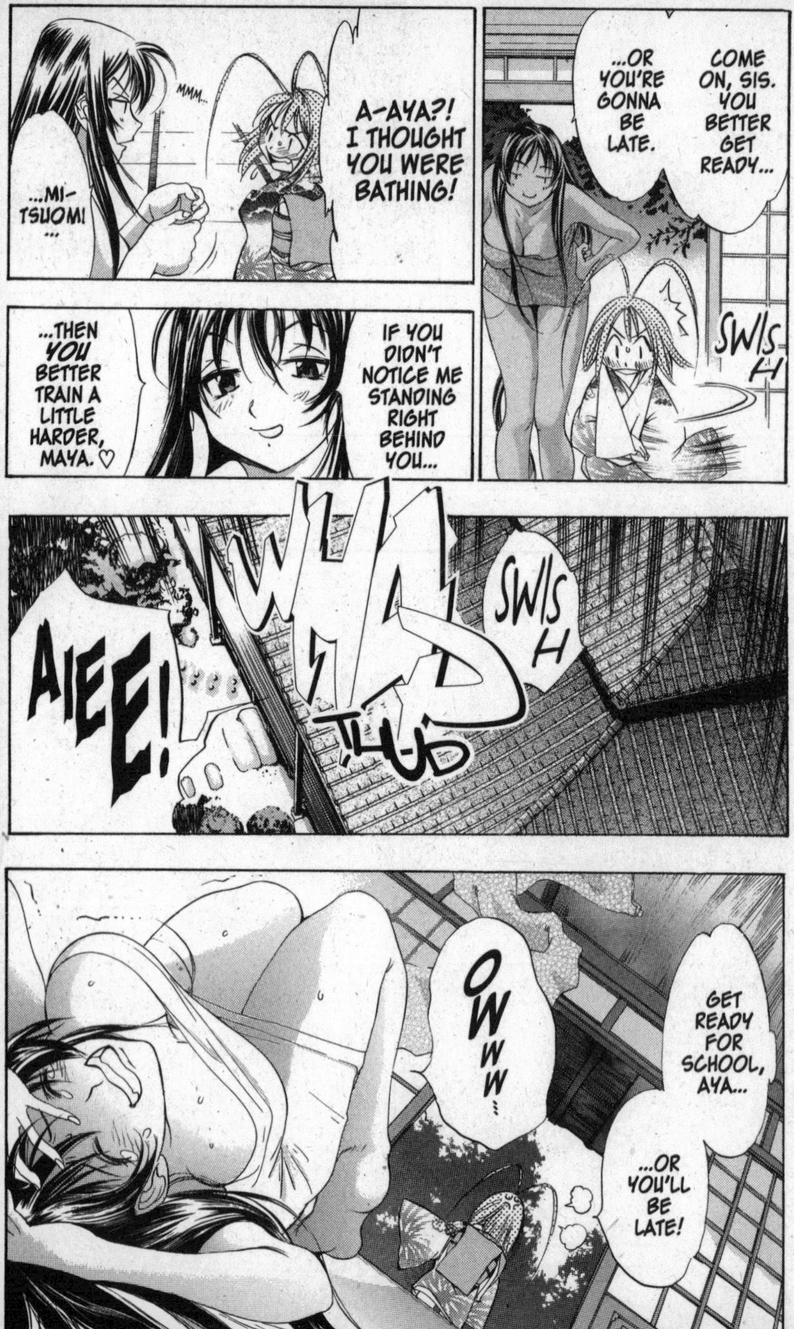
COME ON, SIS. YOU BETTER GET READY...
...OR YOU'RE GONNA BE LATE.
SWISH
A-AYA?! I THOUGHT YOU WERE BATHING!
MMM...
...MI-TSUOMI...
IF YOU DIDN'T NOTICE ME STANDING RIGHT BEHIND YOU...
...THEN YOU BETTER TRAIN A LITTLE HARDER, MAYA. ♡
SWISH
WHAP
THUD
AIEEE!
GET READY FOR SCHOOL, AYA...
...OR YOU'LL BE LATE!
OWWW...

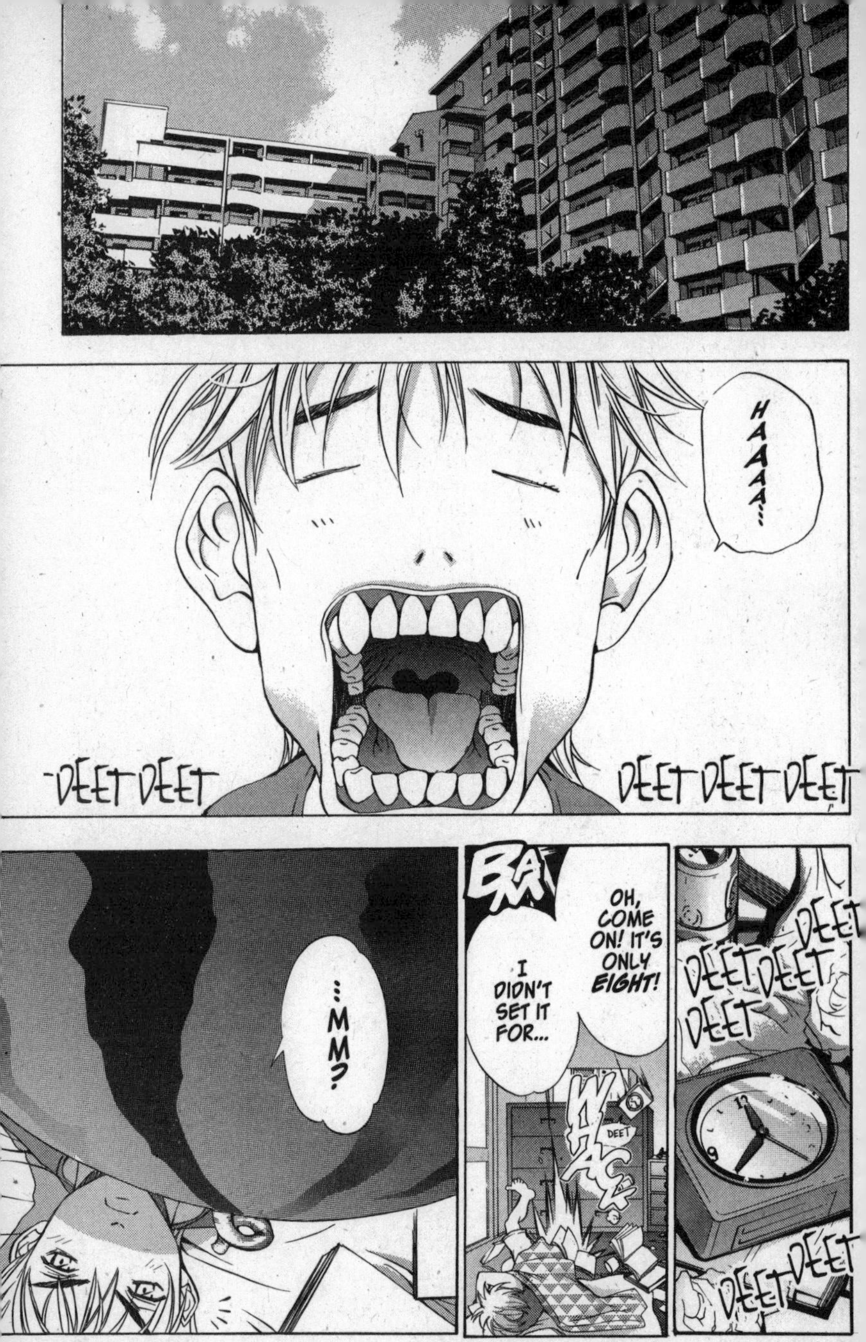
HAAAA...
DEET DEET DEET
DEET DEET
DEET DEET DEET DEET DEET
DEET DEET
BA
OH, COME ON! IT'S ONLY EIGHT!
I DIDN'T SET IT FOR...
WHACK
DEET
...MM?

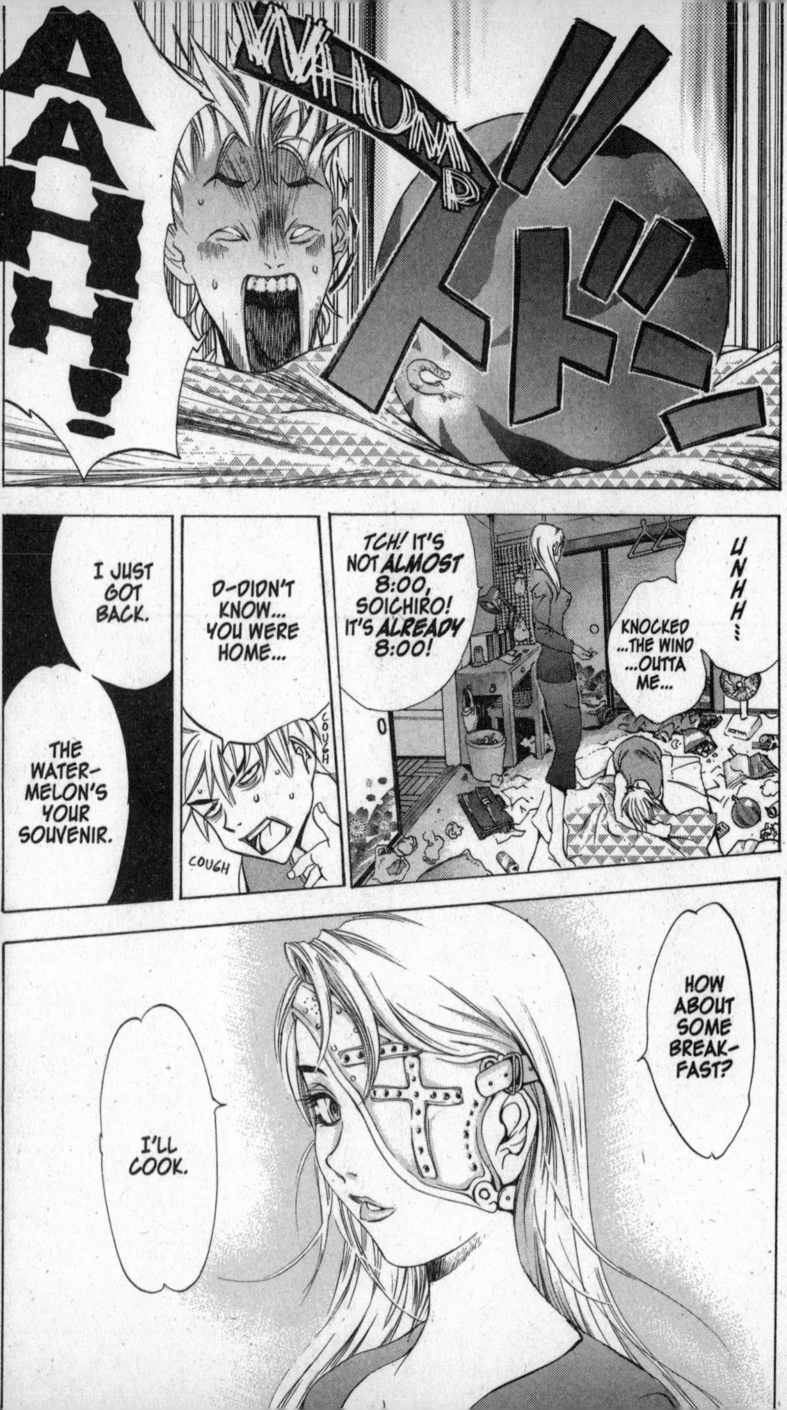
WHUMP
AAAH!
UNHH...
KNOCKED ...THE WIND ...OUTTA ME...
TCH! IT'S NOT ALMOST 8:00, SOICHIRO! IT'S ALREADY 8:00!
COUGH
D-DIDN'T KNOW... YOU WERE HOME...
COUGH
I JUST GOT BACK.
THE WATER-MELON'S YOUR SOUVENIR.
HOW ABOUT SOME BREAK-FAST?
I'LL COOK.

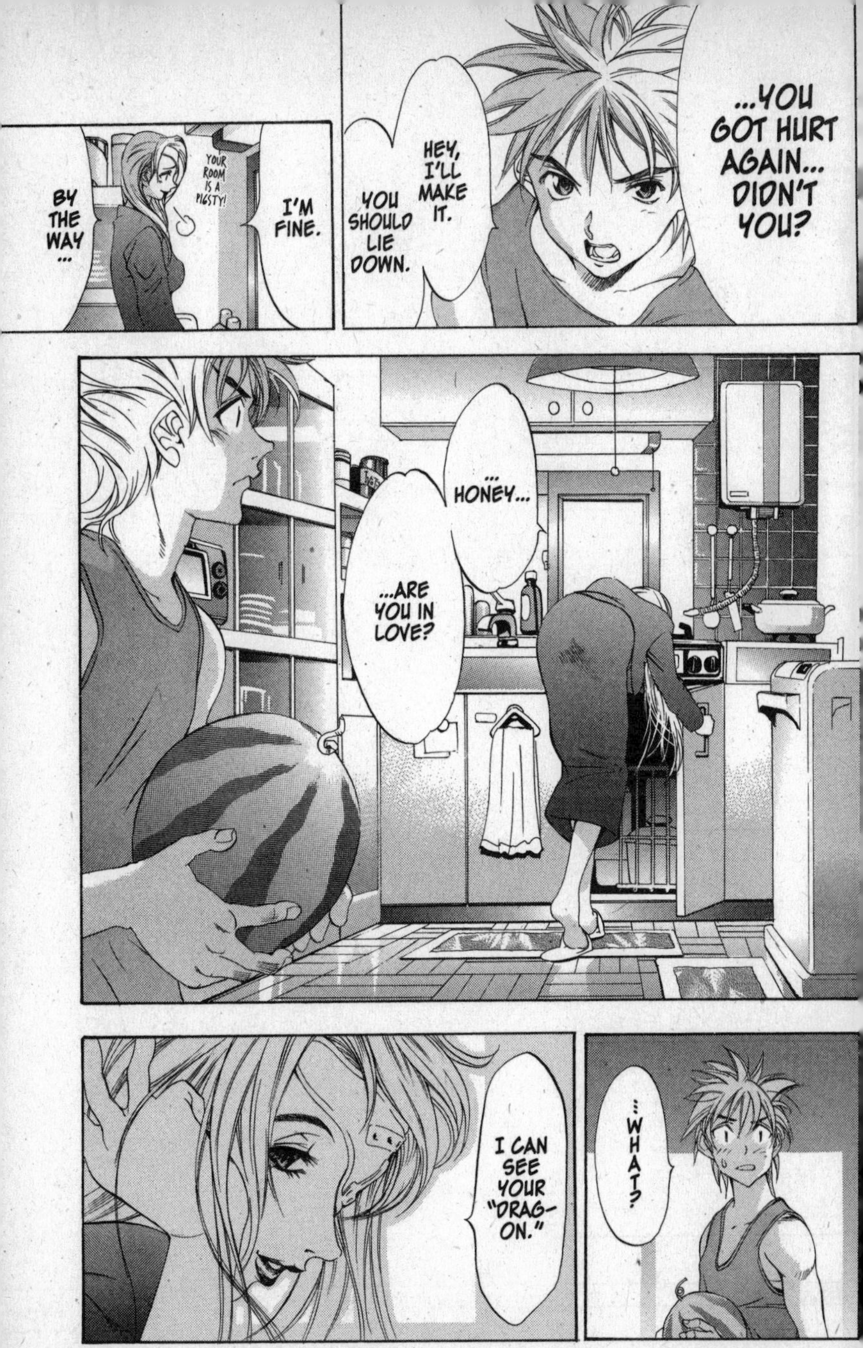
...YOU GOT HURT AGAIN... DIDN'T YOU?
HEY, I'LL MAKE IT.
YOU SHOULD LIE DOWN.
I'M FINE.
YOUR ROOM IS A PIGSTY!
BY THE WAY...
...HONEY...
...ARE YOU IN LOVE?
...WHAT?
I CAN SEE YOUR "DRAG-ON."

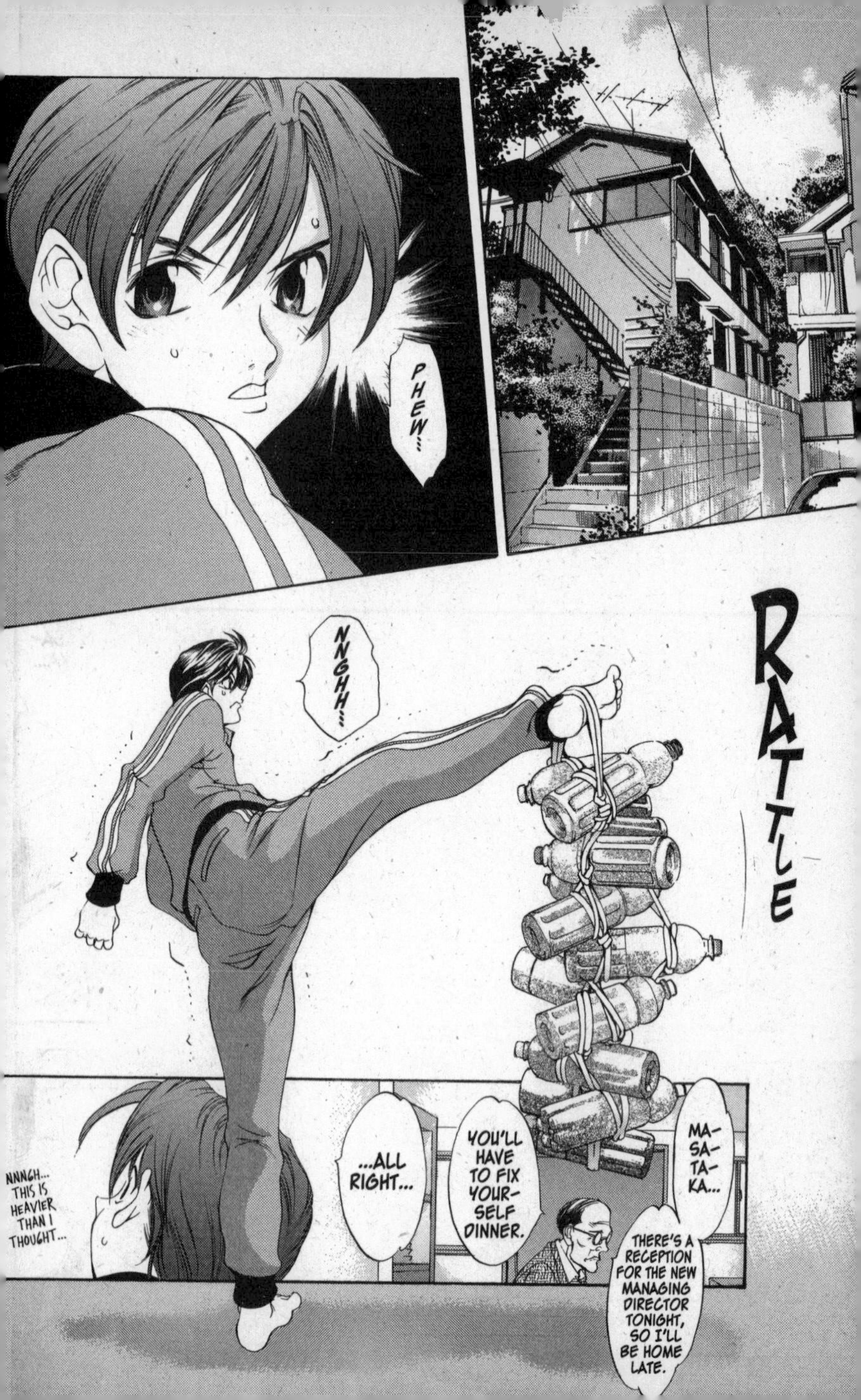
PHEW...
RATTLE
NNGHH...
MASATAKA...
THERE'S A RECEPTION FOR THE NEW MANAGING DIRECTOR TONIGHT, SO I'LL BE HOME LATE.
YOU'LL HAVE TO FIX YOURSELF DINNER.
...ALL RIGHT...
NNNGH... THIS IS HEAVIER THAN I THOUGHT...

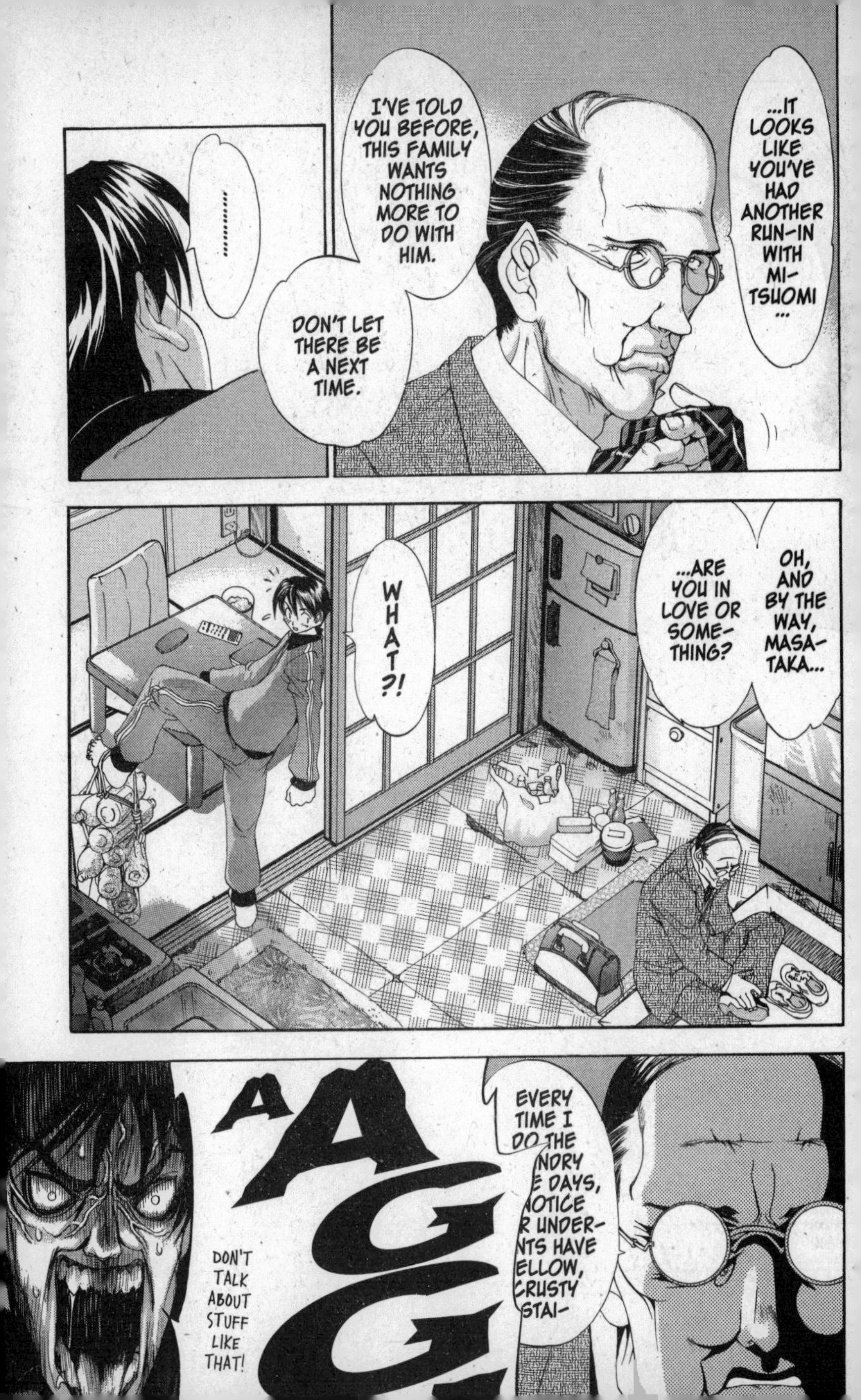
...IT LOOKS LIKE YOU'VE HAD ANOTHER RUN-IN WITH MI-TSUOMI...
I'VE TOLD YOU BEFORE, THIS FAMILY WANTS NOTHING MORE TO DO WITH HIM.
DON'T LET THERE BE A NEXT TIME.
......
OH, AND BY THE WAY, MASA-TAKA...
...ARE YOU IN LOVE OR SOME-THING?
WHAT?!
EVERY TIME I DO THE NDRY E DAYS, NOTICE R UNDER-NTS HAVE ELLOW, RUSTY STAI-
AAG
DON'T TALK ABOUT STUFF LIKE THAT!

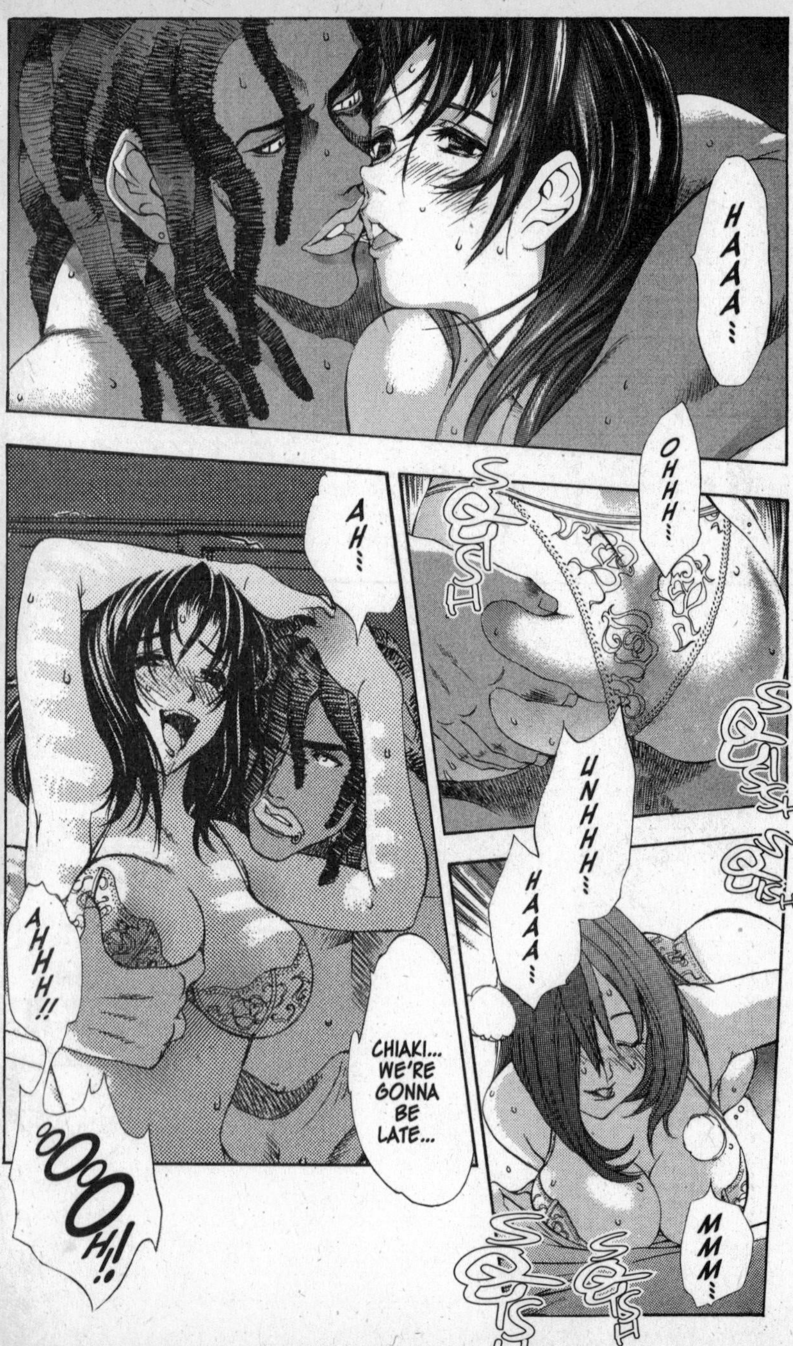
HAAAA...
OHHH...
SQUISH
UNHHHH...
SQUISH SQUISH
HAAAA...
MMM...
SQUISH SQUISH
AH...
AHHH!!
CHIAKI... WE'RE GONNA BE LATE...
OOOOH!!

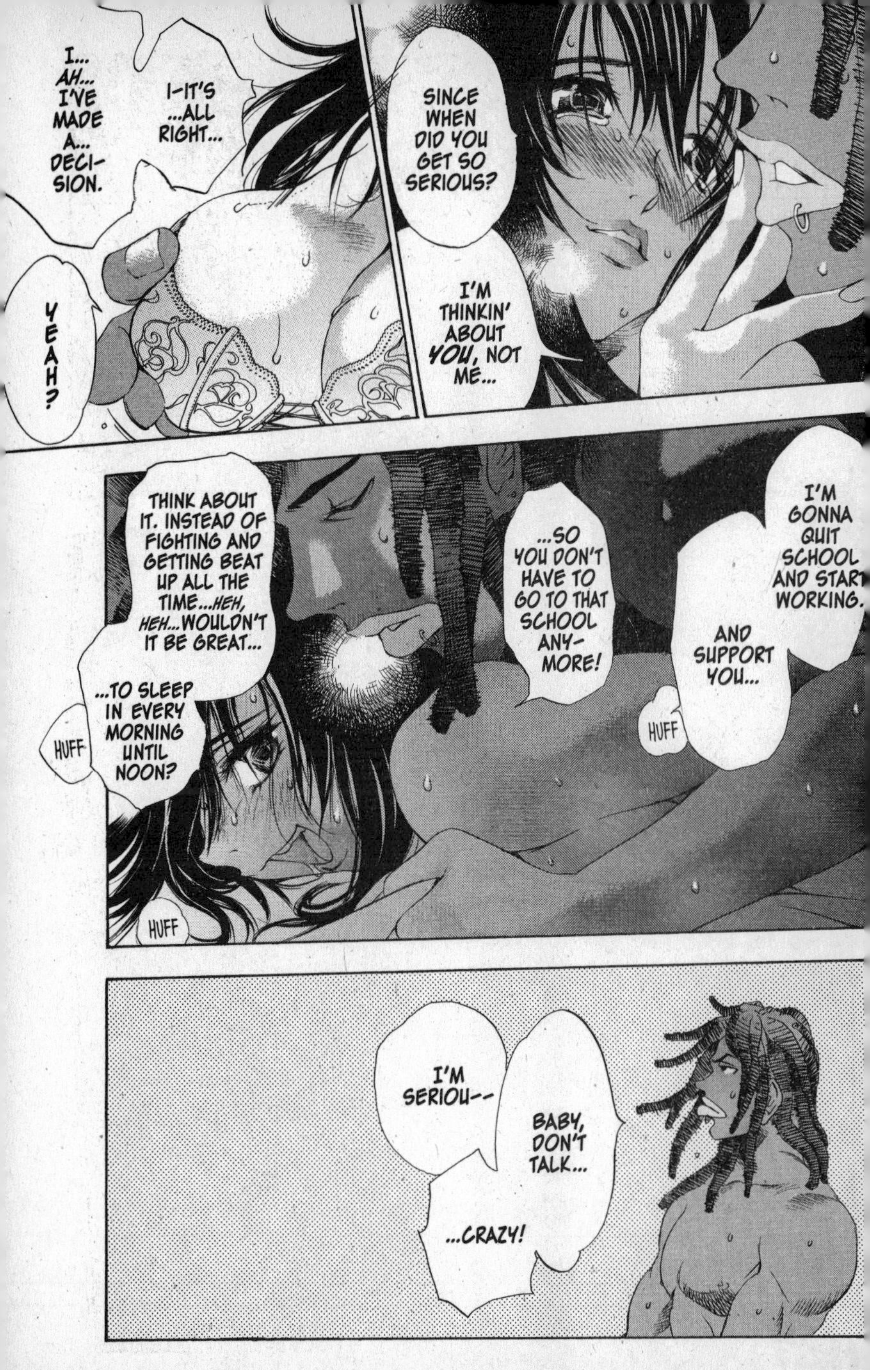
SINCE WHEN DID YOU GET SO SERIOUS?
I'M THINKIN' ABOUT *YOU*, NOT ME...
I-IT'S ...ALL RIGHT...
I... AH... I'VE MADE A... DECI-SION.
YEAH?
I'M GONNA QUIT SCHOOL AND START WORKING.
AND SUPPORT YOU...
HUFF
...SO YOU DON'T HAVE TO GO TO THAT SCHOOL ANY-MORE!
THINK ABOUT IT. INSTEAD OF FIGHTING AND GETTING BEAT UP ALL THE TIME...*HEH, HEH*...WOULDN'T IT BE GREAT...
...TO SLEEP IN EVERY MORNING UNTIL NOON?
HUFF
HUFF
I'M SERIOU--
BABY, DON'T TALK...
...CRAZY!

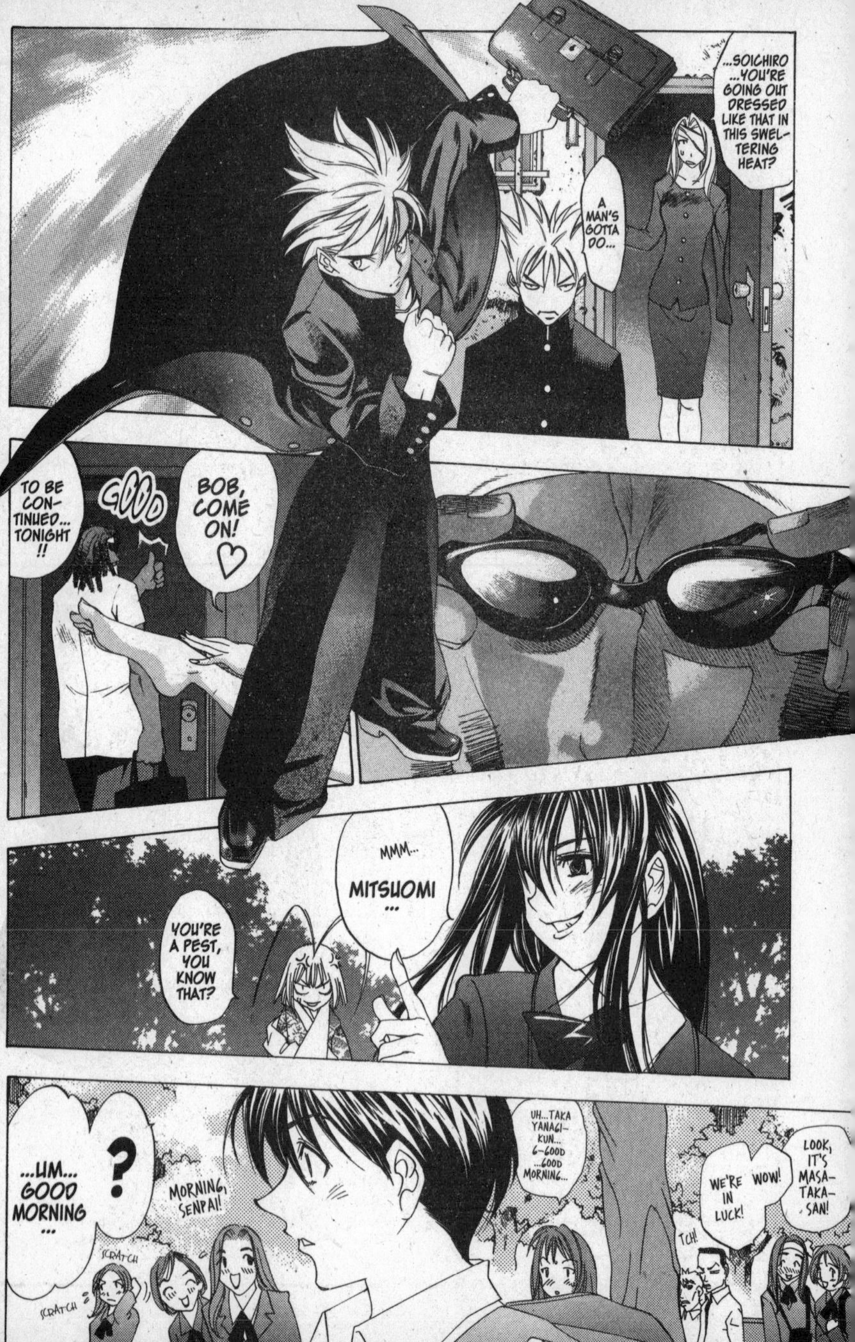
...SOICHIRO ...YOU'RE GOING OUT DRESSED LIKE THAT IN THIS SWEL-TERING HEAT?
A MAN'S GOTTA DO...
BOB, COME ON! ♡
GOOD
TO BE CON-TINUED... TONIGHT !!
MMM... MITSUOMI ...
YOU'RE A PEST, YOU KNOW THAT?
LOOK, IT'S MASA-TAKA-SAN!
WOW!
WE'RE IN LUCK!
TCH!
UH...TAKA YANAGI-KUN... G-GOOD ...GOOD MORNING...
MORNING, SENPAI!
?
...UM... GOOD MORNING ...
SCRATCH
SCRATCH

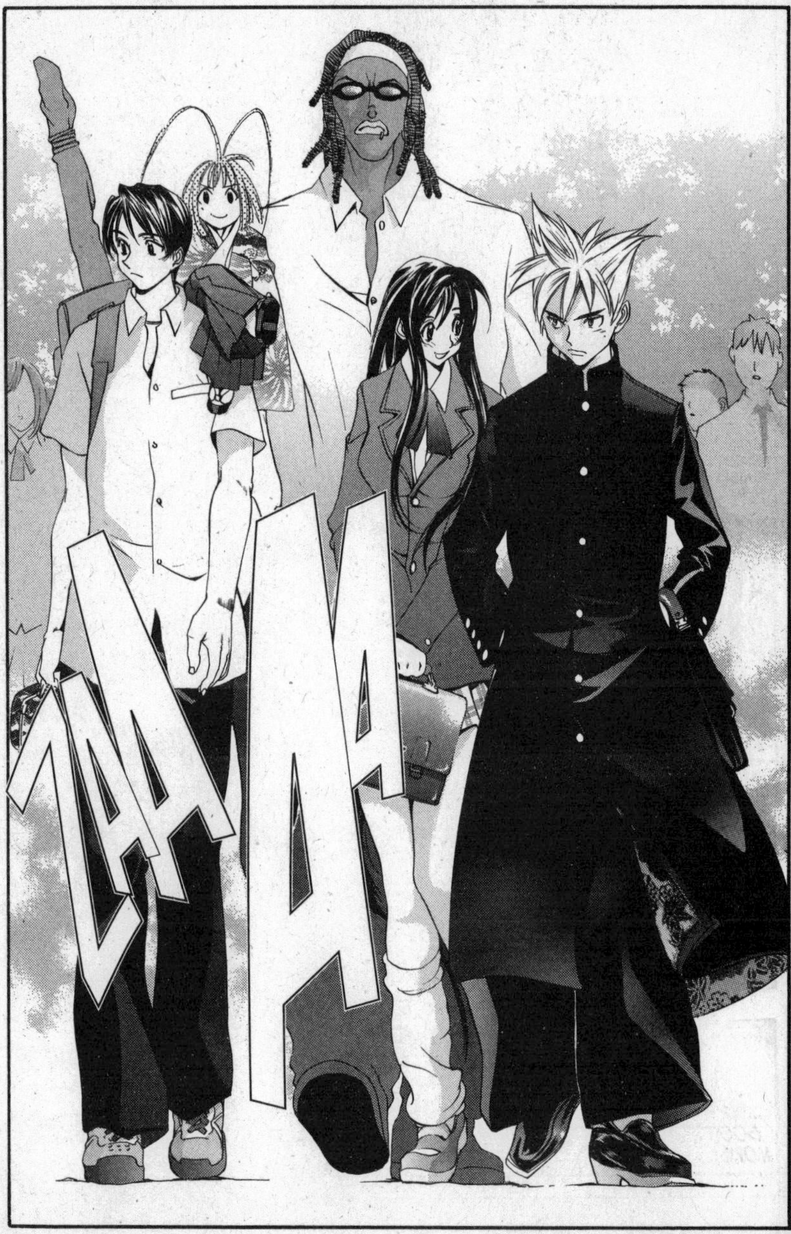
ZAAA

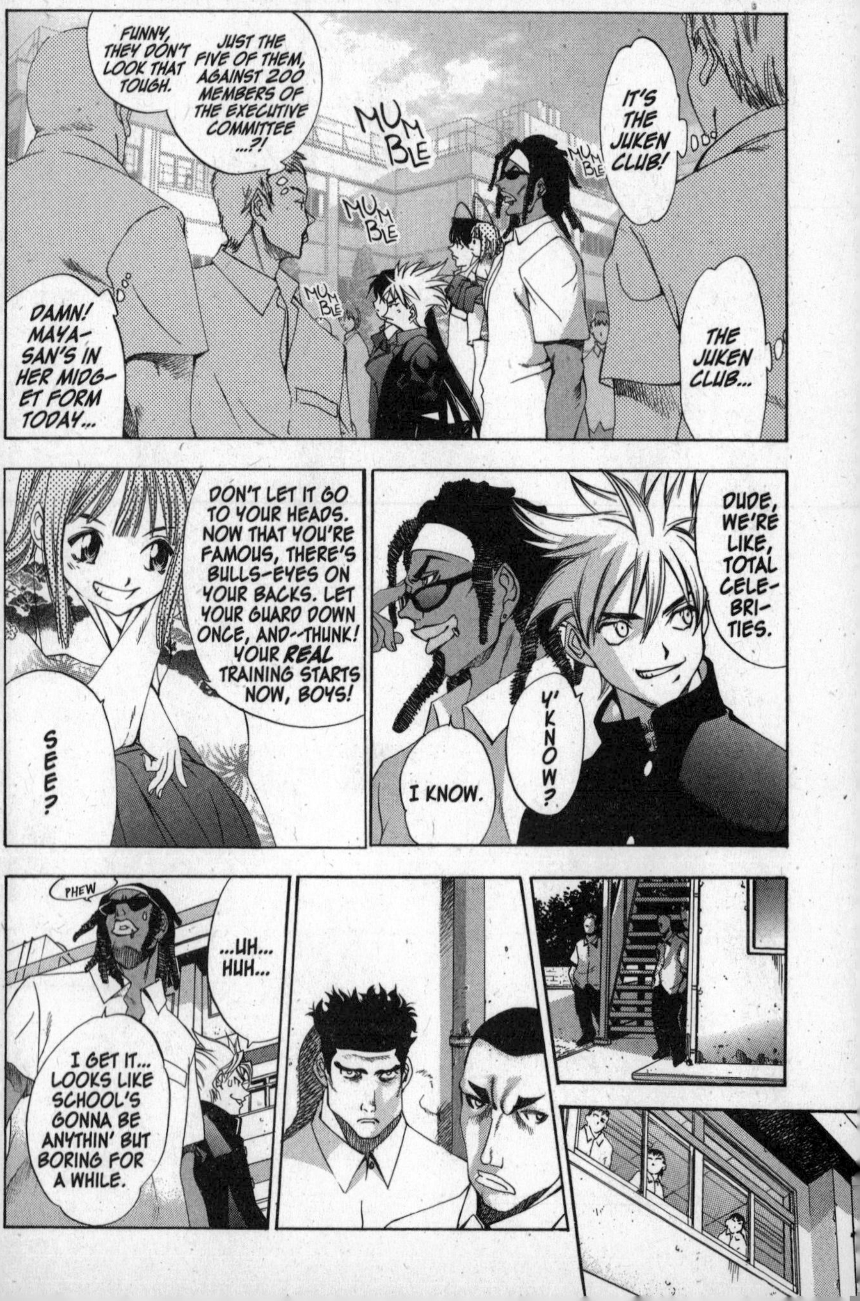
IT'S THE JUKEN CLUB!
THE JUKEN CLUB...
MUMBLE
MUMBLE
MUMBLE
MUMBLE
JUST THE FIVE OF THEM, AGAINST 200 MEMBERS OF THE EXECUTIVE COMMITTEE ...?!
FUNNY, THEY DON'T LOOK THAT TOUGH.
DAMN! MAYA-SAN'S IN HER MIDGET FORM TODAY...
DUDE, WE'RE LIKE, TOTAL CELEBRITIES.
Y'KNOW?
I KNOW.
DON'T LET IT GO TO YOUR HEADS. NOW THAT YOU'RE FAMOUS, THERE'S BULLS-EYES ON YOUR BACKS. LET YOUR GUARD DOWN ONCE, AND--THUNK! YOUR REAL TRAINING STARTS NOW, BOYS!
SEE?
...UH... HUH...
PHEW
I GET IT... LOOKS LIKE SCHOOL'S GONNA BE ANYTHIN' BUT BORING FOR A WHILE.

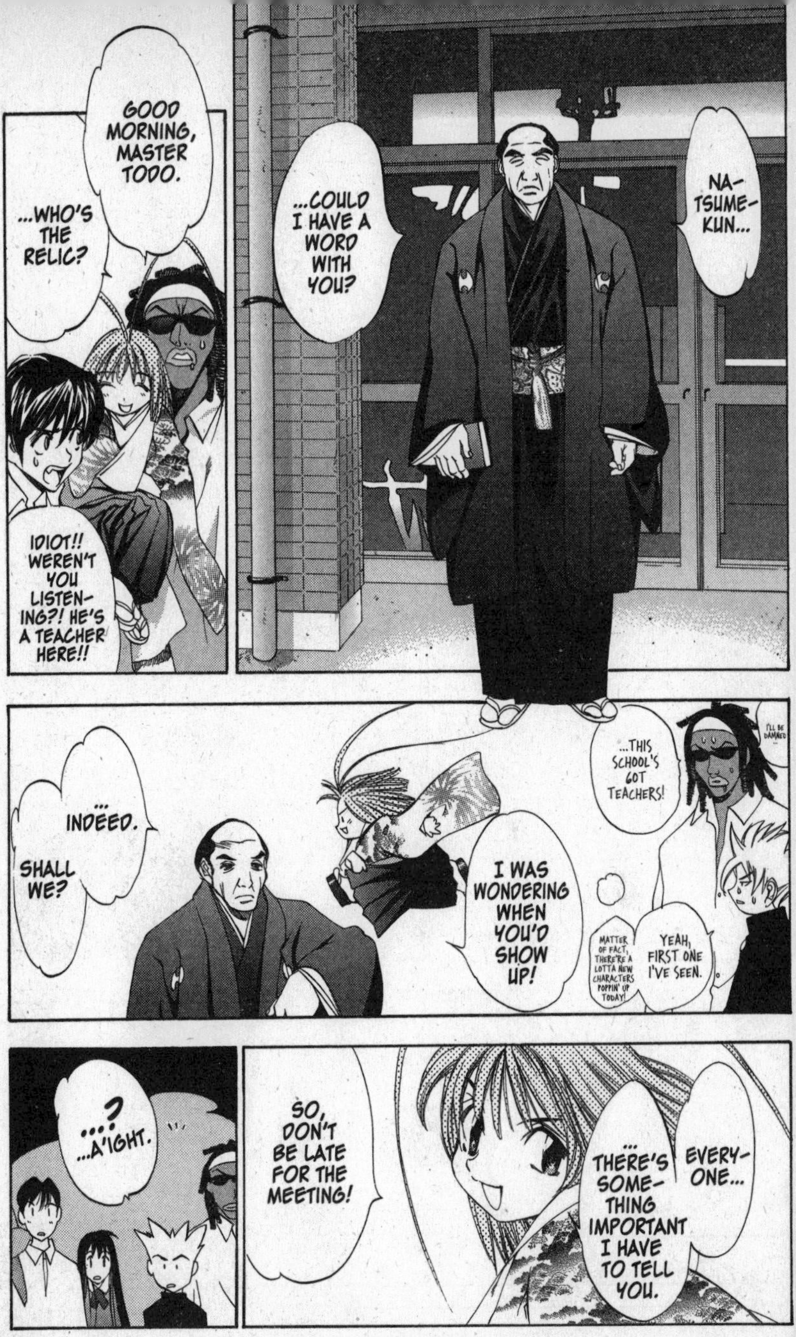
NA-TSUME-KUN...
...COULD I HAVE A WORD WITH YOU?
GOOD MORNING, MASTER TODO.
...WHO'S THE RELIC?
IDIOT!! WEREN'T YOU LISTEN-ING?! HE'S A TEACHER HERE!!
I'LL BE DAMNED...
...THIS SCHOOL'S GOT TEACHERS!
YEAH, FIRST ONE I'VE SEEN.
MATTER OF FACT, THERE'RE A LOTTA NEW CHARACTERS POPPIN' UP TODAY!
I WAS WONDERING WHEN YOU'D SHOW UP!
... INDEED.
SHALL WE?
EVERY-ONE...
... THERE'S SOME-THING IMPORTANT I HAVE TO TELL YOU.
SO, DON'T BE LATE FOR THE MEETING!
...?
...A'IGHT.

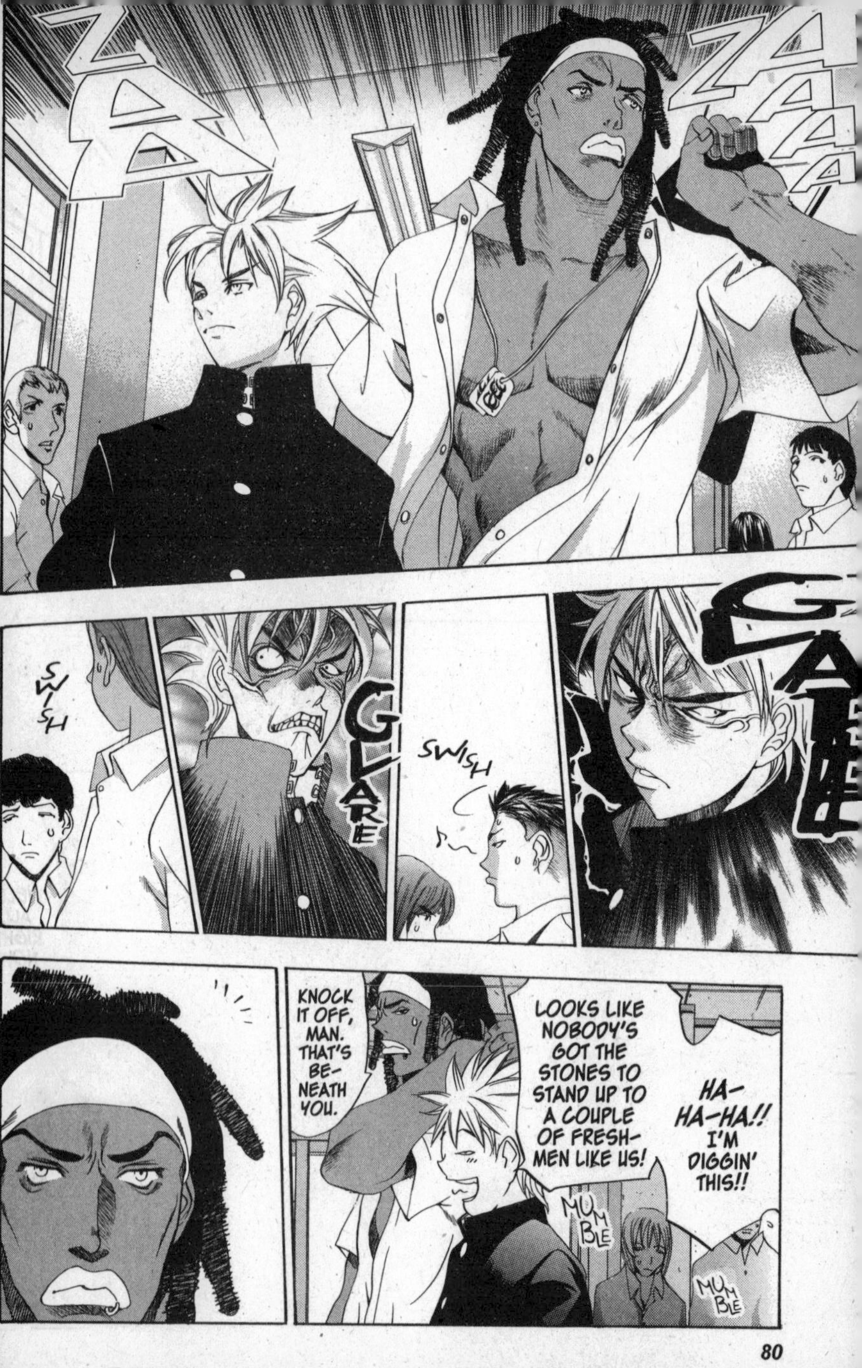
ZAAAA
ZA
GLARE
SWISH
GLARE
SWISH
HA-HA-HA!! I'M DIGGIN' THIS!!
LOOKS LIKE NOBODY'S GOT THE STONES TO STAND UP TO A COUPLE OF FRESH-MEN LIKE US!
KNOCK IT OFF, MAN. THAT'S BE-NEATH YOU.
MUMBLE
MUMBLE

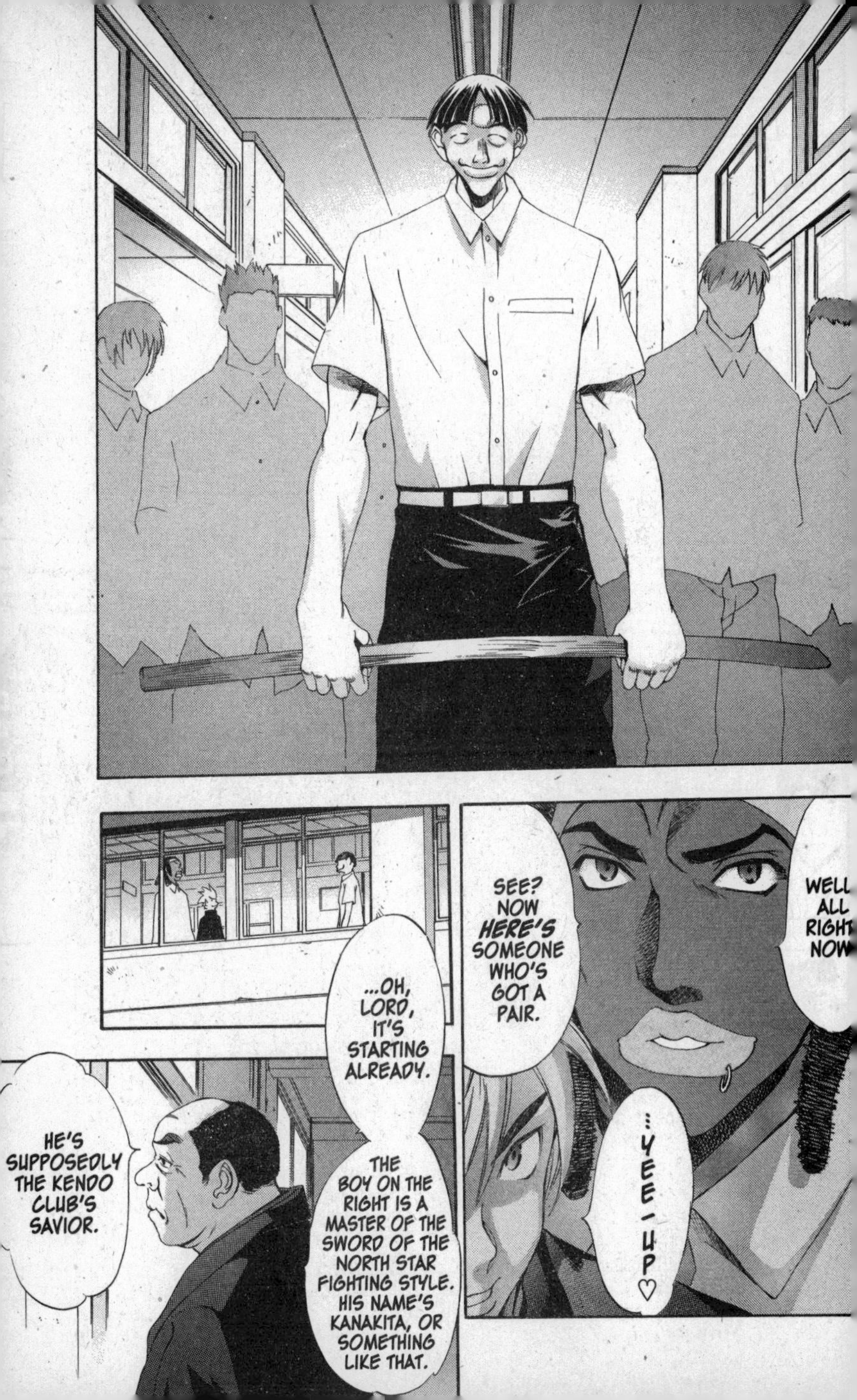
WELL ALL RIGHT NOW
SEE? NOW *HERE'S* SOMEONE WHO'S GOT A PAIR.
...YEE-UP♡
...OH, LORD, IT'S STARTING ALREADY.
THE BOY ON THE RIGHT IS A MASTER OF THE SWORD OF THE NORTH STAR FIGHTING STYLE. HIS NAME'S KANAKITA, OR SOMETHING LIKE THAT.
HE'S SUPPOSEDLY THE KENDO CLUB'S SAVIOR.

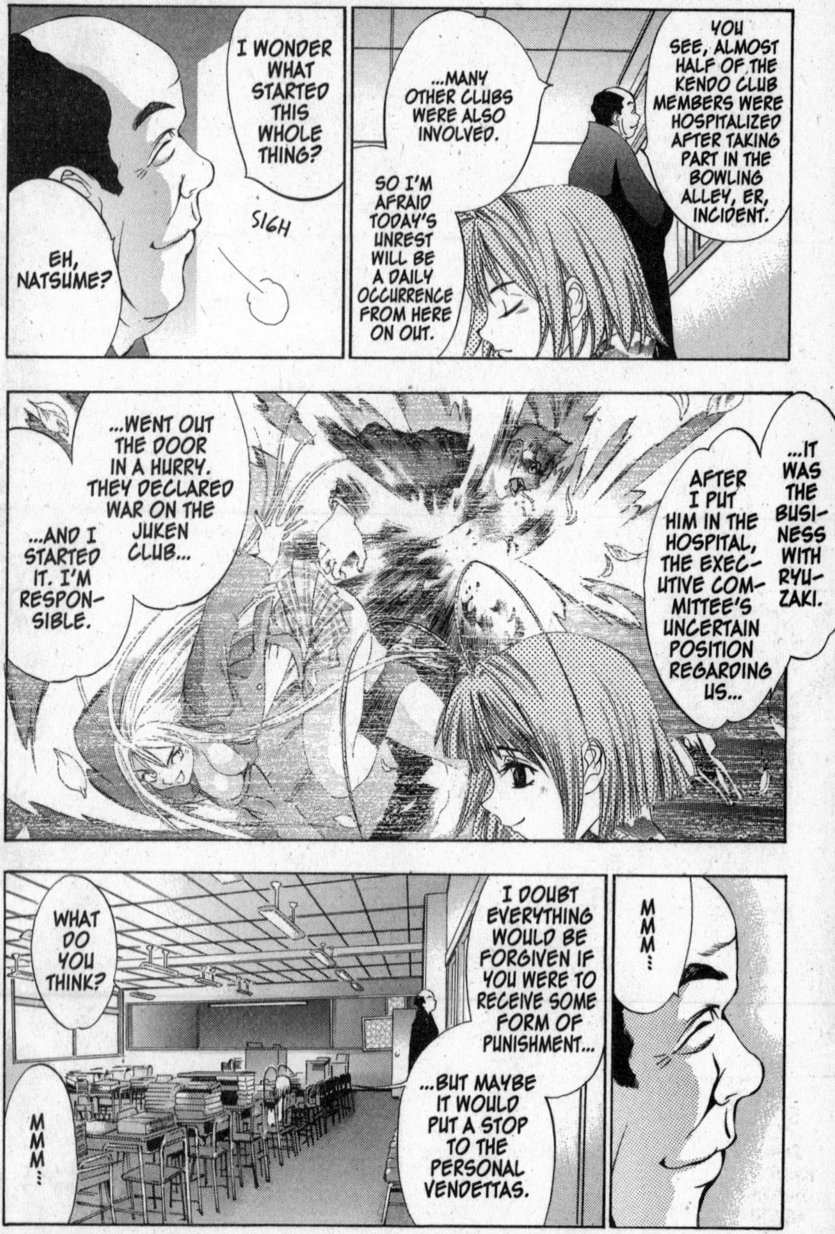
YOU SEE, ALMOST HALF OF THE KENDO CLUB MEMBERS WERE HOSPITALIZED AFTER TAKING PART IN THE BOWLING ALLEY, ER, INCIDENT.
...MANY OTHER CLUBS WERE ALSO INVOLVED.
SO I'M AFRAID TODAY'S UNREST WILL BE A DAILY OCCURRENCE FROM HERE ON OUT.
I WONDER WHAT STARTED THIS WHOLE THING?
SIGH
EH, NATSUME?
...IT WAS THE BUSINESS WITH RYUZAKI.
AFTER I PUT HIM IN THE HOSPITAL, THE EXECUTIVE COMMITTEE'S UNCERTAIN POSITION REGARDING US...
...WENT OUT THE DOOR IN A HURRY. THEY DECLARED WAR ON THE JUKEN CLUB...
...AND I STARTED IT. I'M RESPONSIBLE.
MMM...
I DOUBT EVERYTHING WOULD BE FORGIVEN IF YOU WERE TO RECEIVE SOME FORM OF PUNISHMENT...
...BUT MAYBE IT WOULD PUT A STOP TO THE PERSONAL VENDETTAS.
WHAT DO YOU THINK?
MMM...

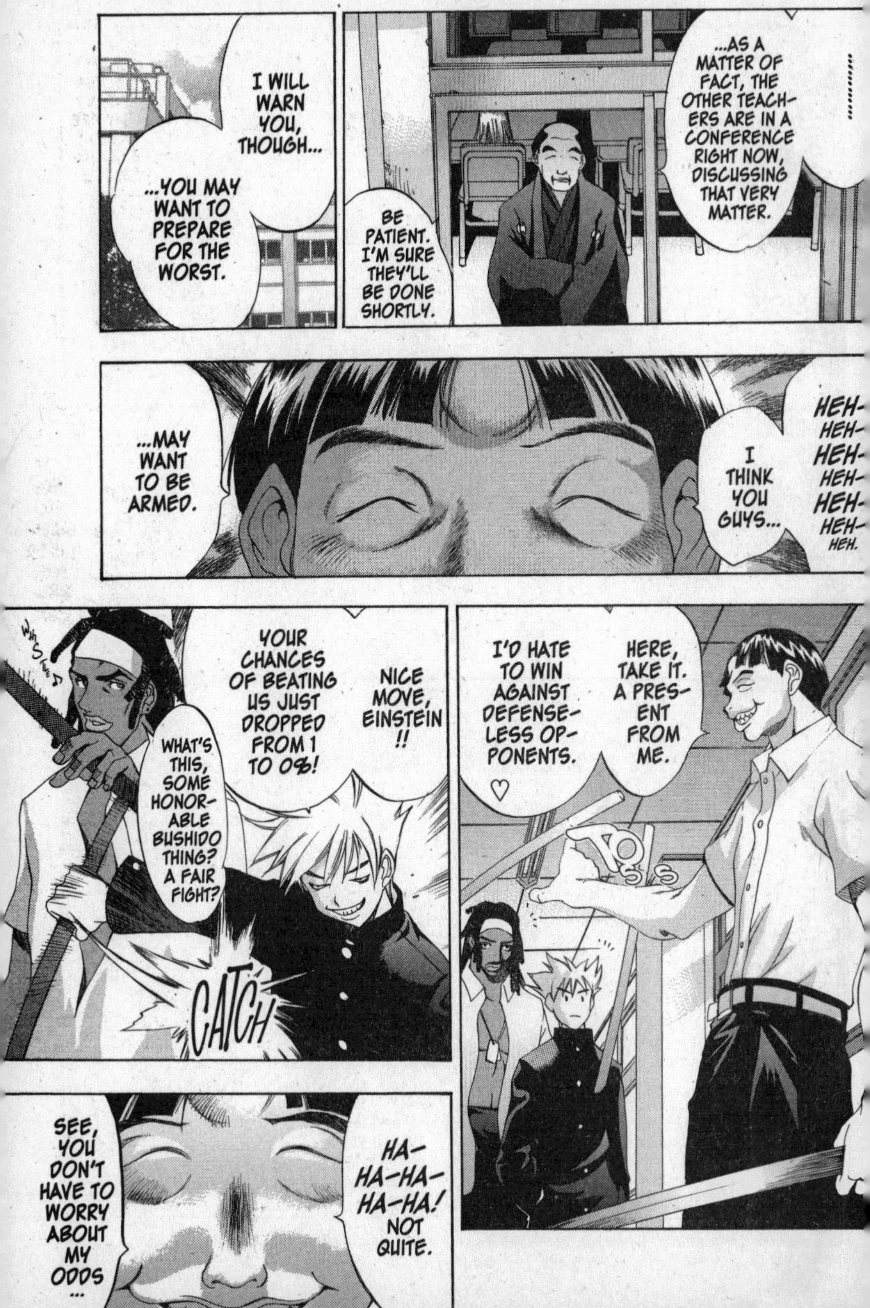
......
...AS A MATTER OF FACT, THE OTHER TEACHERS ARE IN A CONFERENCE RIGHT NOW, DISCUSSING THAT VERY MATTER.
BE PATIENT. I'M SURE THEY'LL BE DONE SHORTLY.
I WILL WARN YOU, THOUGH...
...YOU MAY WANT TO PREPARE FOR THE WORST.
HEH-HEH-HEH-HEH-HEH-HEH-HEH.
I THINK YOU GUYS...
...MAY WANT TO BE ARMED.
HERE, TAKE IT. A PRESENT FROM ME.
I'D HATE TO WIN AGAINST DEFENSELESS OPPONENTS. ♡
NICE MOVE, EINSTEIN!!
YOUR CHANCES OF BEATING US JUST DROPPED FROM 1 TO 0%!
WHAT'S THIS, SOME HONORABLE BUSHIDO THING? A FAIR FIGHT?
CATCH
HA-HA-HA-HA-HA! NOT QUITE.
SEE, YOU DON'T HAVE TO WORRY ABOUT MY ODDS...

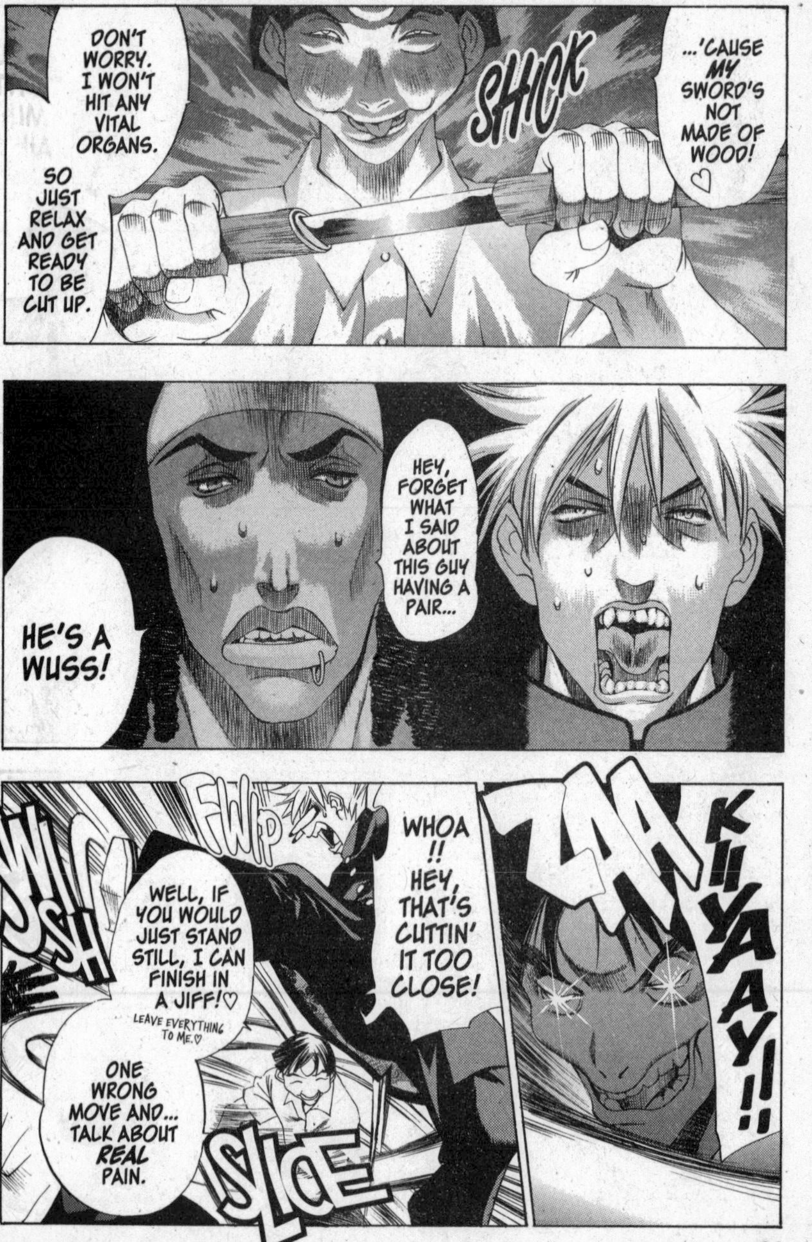
...'CAUSE MY SWORD'S NOT MADE OF WOOD! ♡
SHICK
DON'T WORRY. I WON'T HIT ANY VITAL ORGANS.
SO JUST RELAX AND GET READY TO BE CUT UP.
HEY, FORGET WHAT I SAID ABOUT THIS GUY HAVING A PAIR...
HE'S A WUSS!
ZA
KIIYAAAY!!
WHOA!! HEY, THAT'S CUTTIN' IT TOO CLOSE!
FWIP
WELL, IF YOU WOULD JUST STAND STILL, I CAN FINISH IN A JIFF! ♡
LEAVE EVERYTHING TO ME. ♡
SWISH
ONE WRONG MOVE AND... TALK ABOUT REAL PAIN.
SLICE

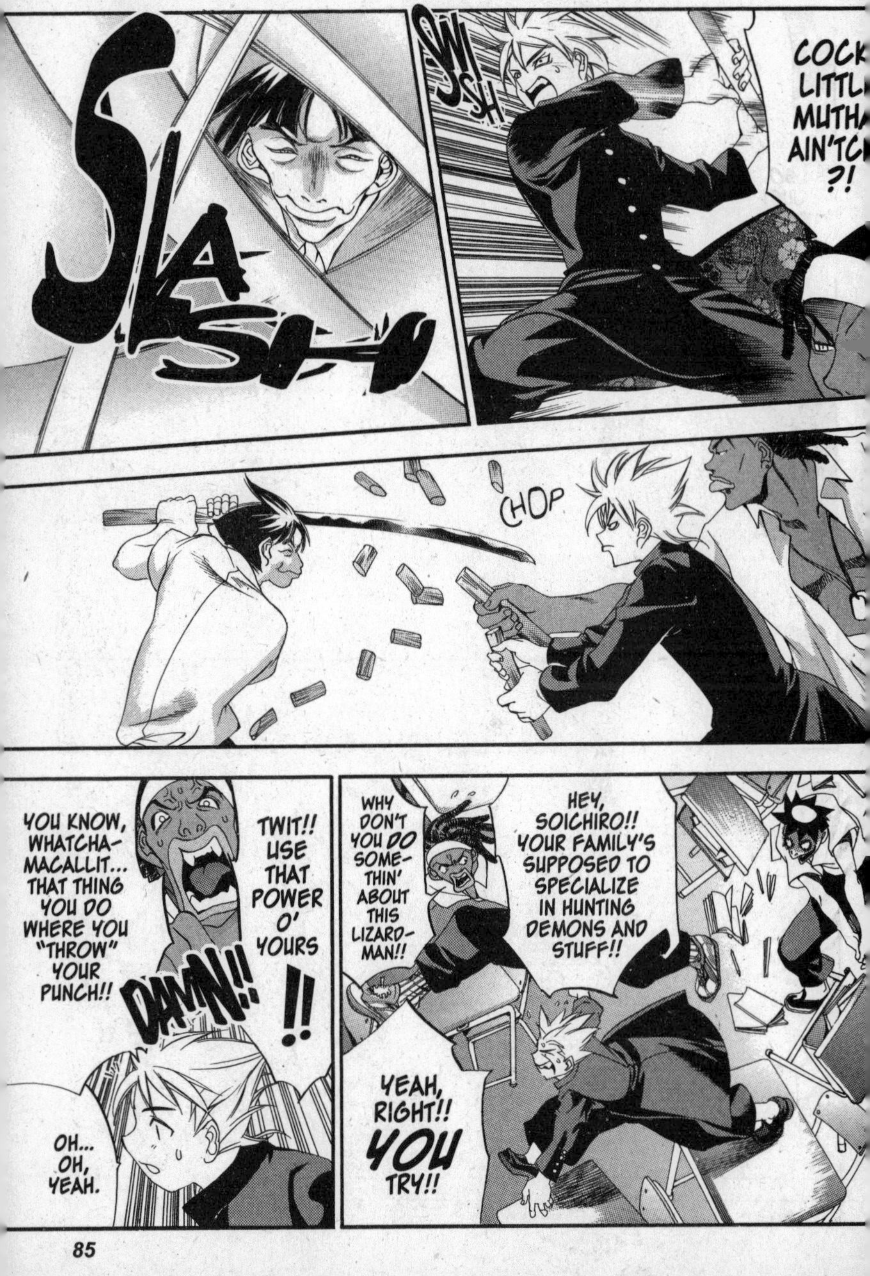
SWISH
COCK
LITTL
MUTHA
AIN'TCH
?!
SLASH
CHOP
HEY, SOICHIRO!! YOUR FAMILY'S SUPPOSED TO SPECIALIZE IN HUNTING DEMONS AND STUFF!!
WHY DON'T YOU DO SOMETHIN' ABOUT THIS LIZARD-MAN!!
YEAH, RIGHT!! YOU TRY!!
TWIT!! USE THAT POWER O' YOURS
!!
YOU KNOW, WHATCHA-MACALLIT... THAT THING YOU DO WHERE YOU "THROW" YOUR PUNCH!!
DAMN!!
OH... OH, YEAH.

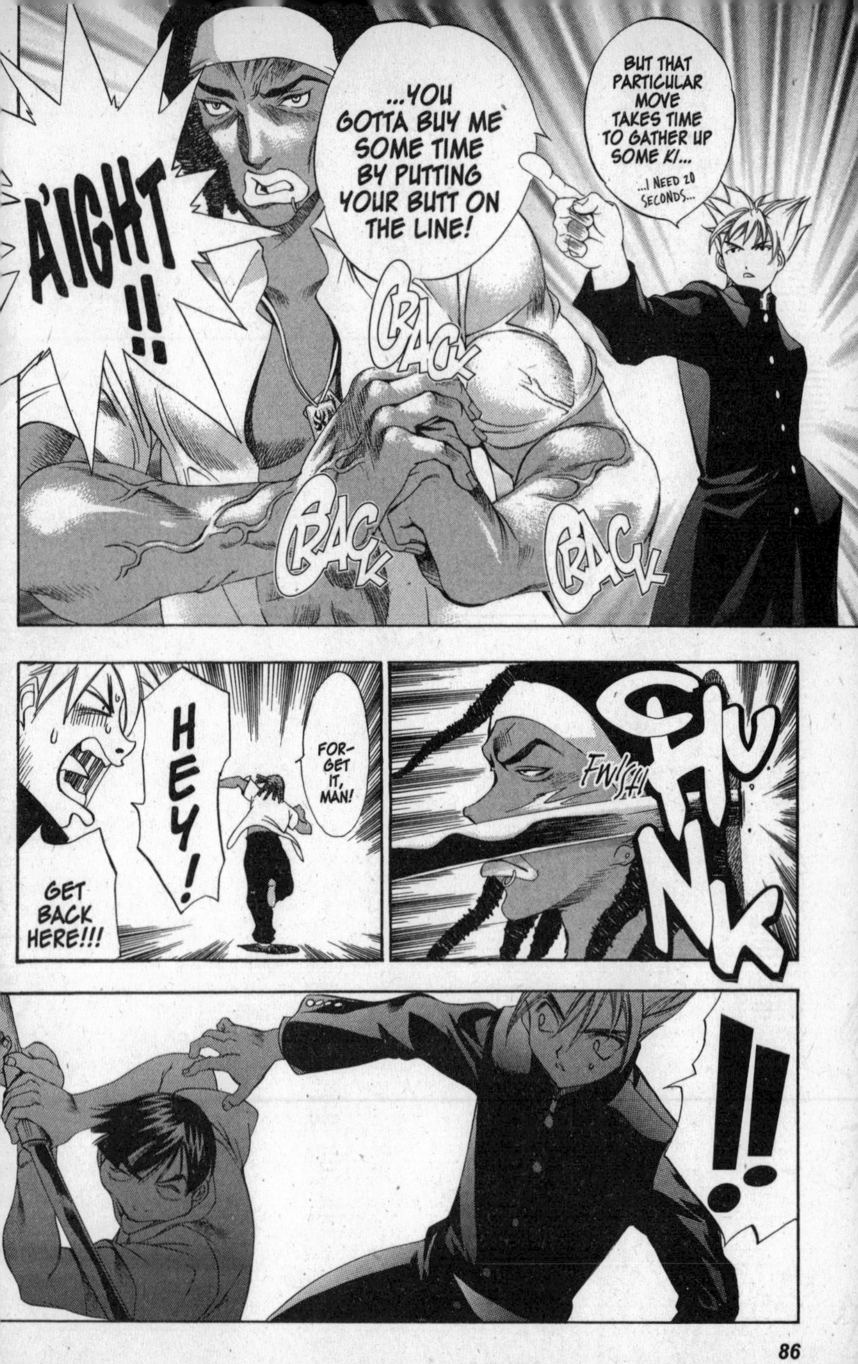
BUT THAT PARTICULAR MOVE TAKES TIME TO GATHER UP SOME KI...
...I NEED 20 SECONDS...
...YOU GOTTA BUY ME SOME TIME BY PUTTING YOUR BUTT ON THE LINE!
A'IGHT!!
CRACK
CRACK
CRACK
CHUNK
FWISH
FOR-GET IT, MAN!
HEY!
GET BACK HERE!!!
!!

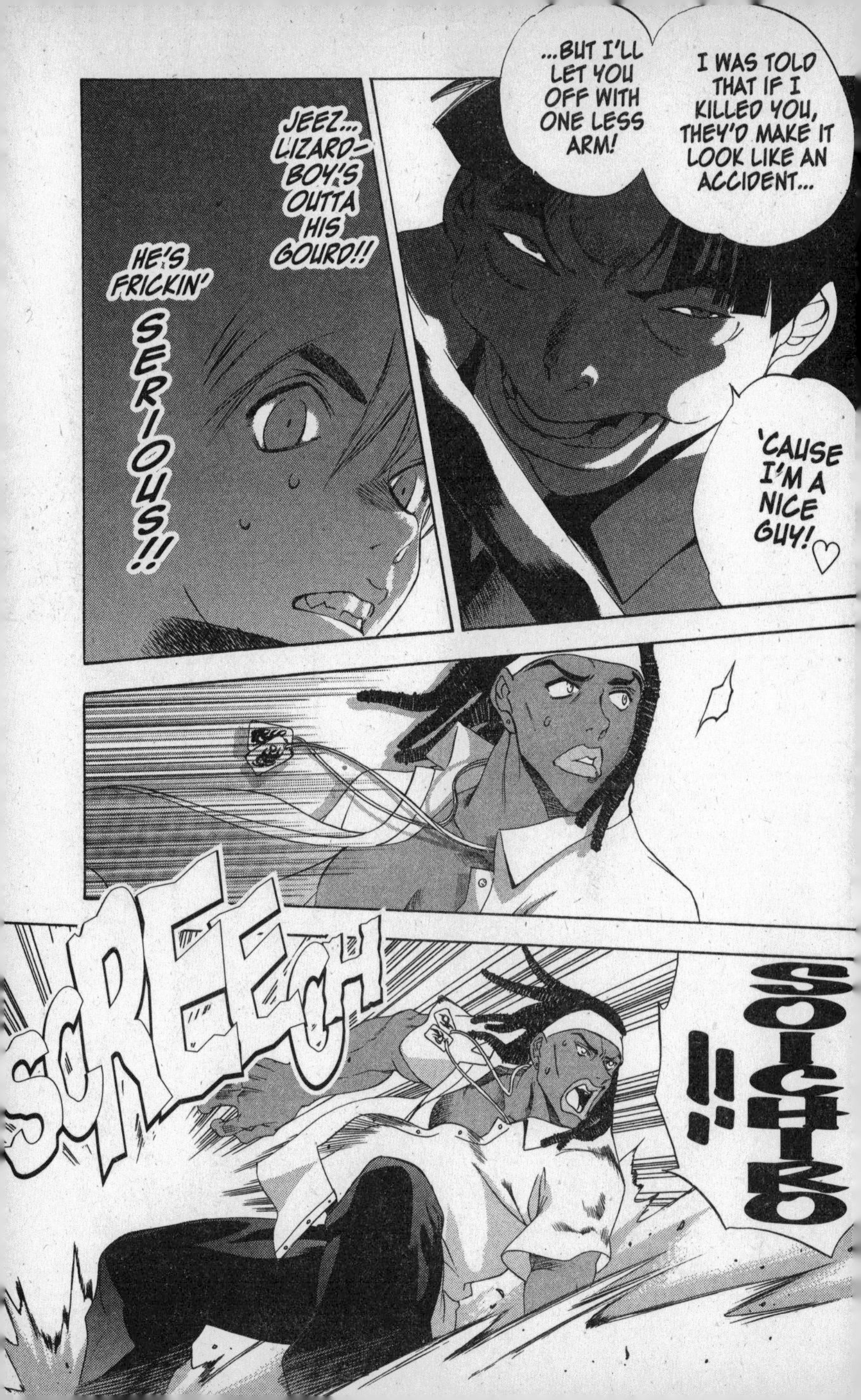
I WAS TOLD THAT IF I KILLED YOU, THEY'D MAKE IT LOOK LIKE AN ACCIDENT...
...BUT I'LL LET YOU OFF WITH ONE LESS ARM!
'CAUSE I'M A NICE GUY! ♥
JEEZ... LIZARD-BOY'S OUTTA HIS GOURD!!
HE'S FRICKIN' SERIOUS!!
SOICHIRO!!
SCREECH

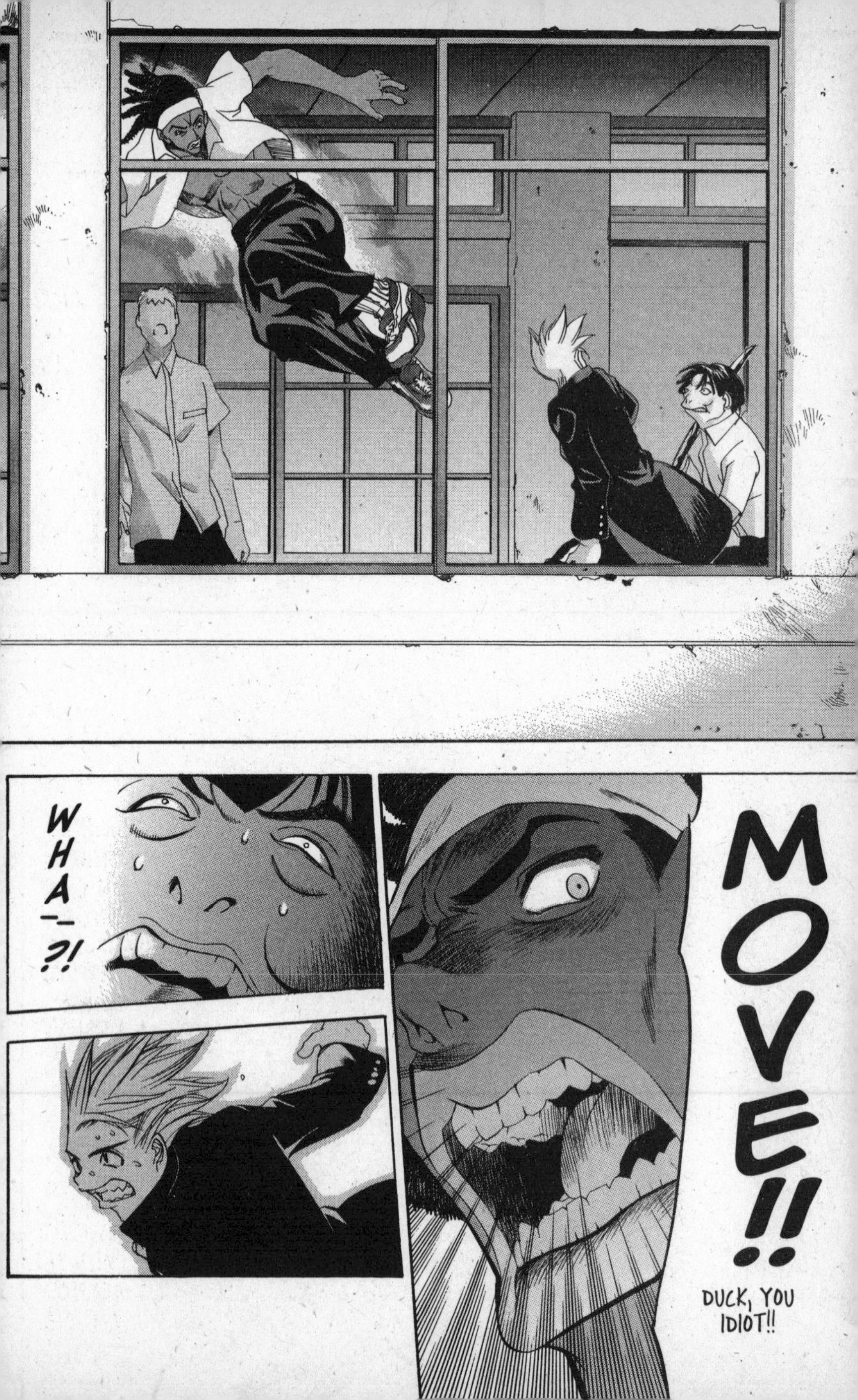
MOVE!!
DUCK, YOU IDIOT!!
WHA--?!

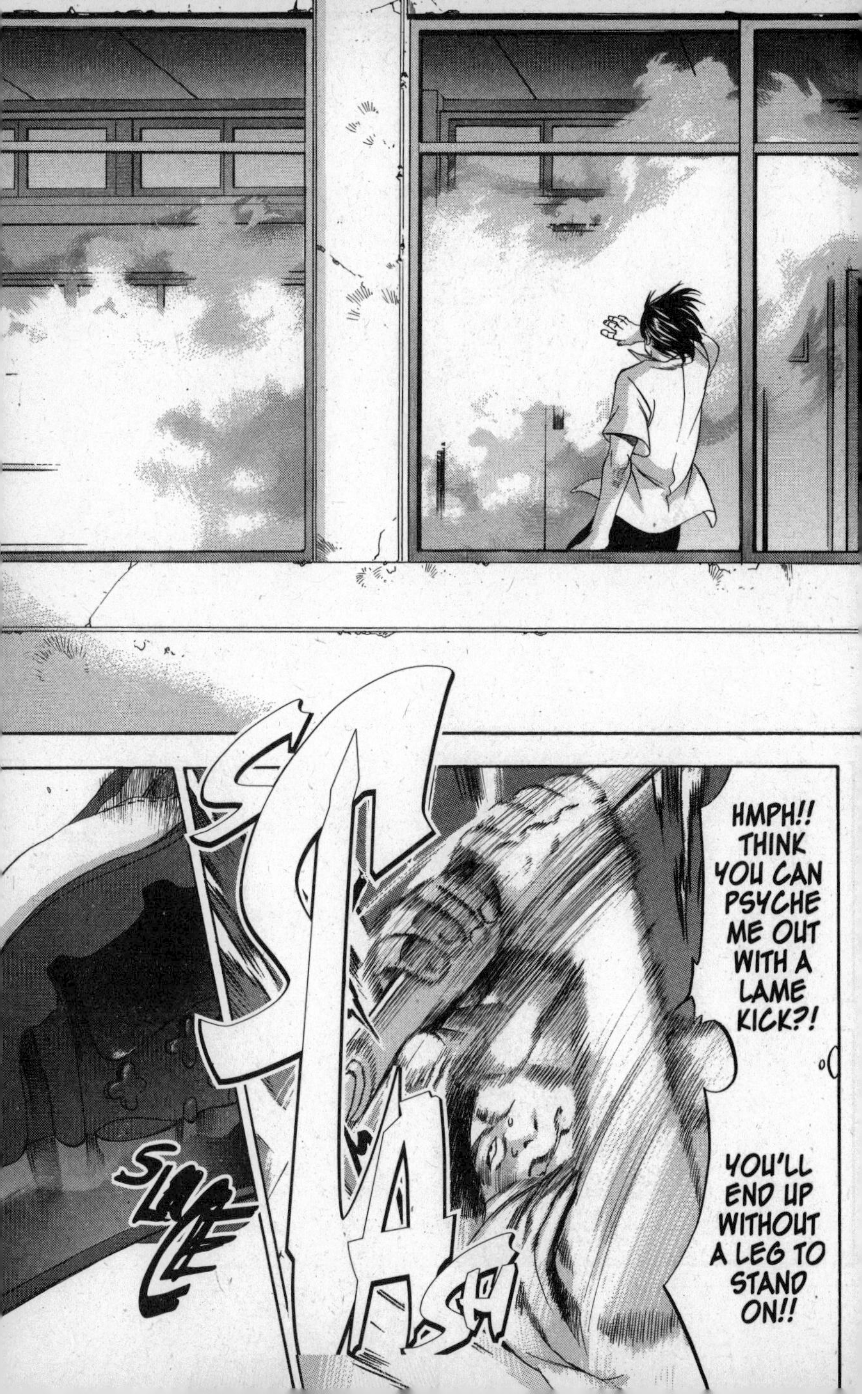
HMPH!! THINK YOU CAN PSYCHE ME OUT WITH A LAME KICK?!
YOU'LL END UP WITHOUT A LEG TO STAND ON!!

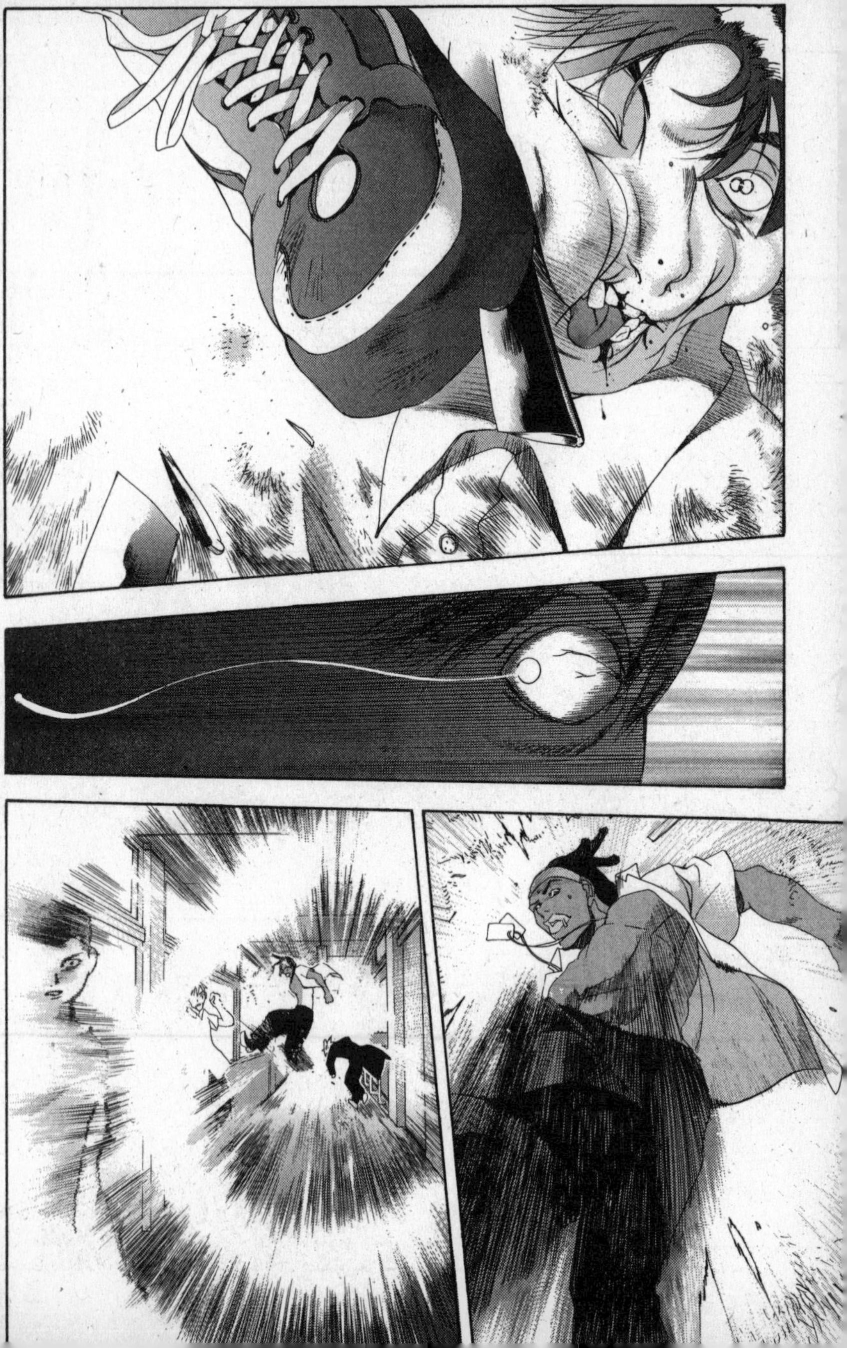

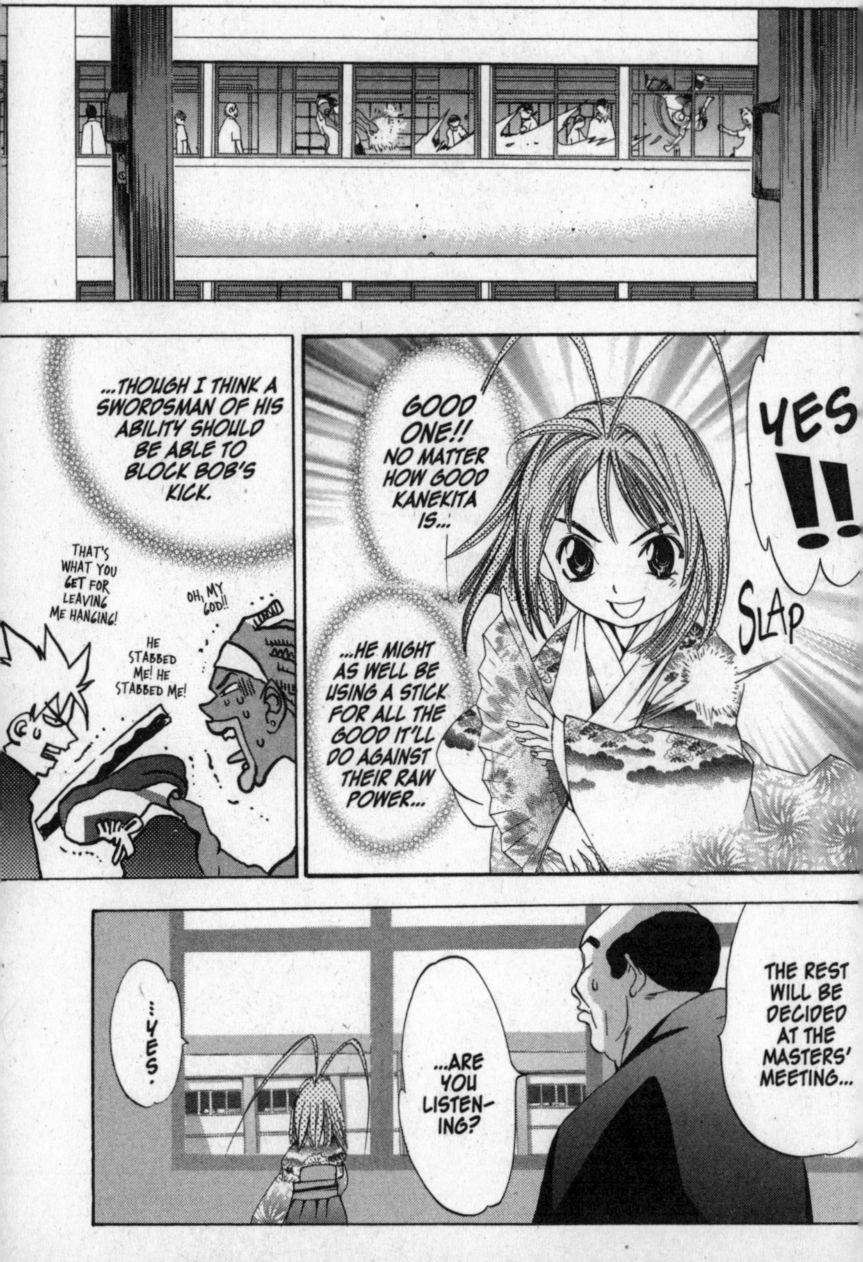
YES!!
SLAP
GOOD ONE!! NO MATTER HOW GOOD KANEKITA IS...
...HE MIGHT AS WELL BE USING A STICK FOR ALL THE GOOD IT'LL DO AGAINST THEIR RAW POWER...
...THOUGH I THINK A SWORDSMAN OF HIS ABILITY SHOULD BE ABLE TO BLOCK BOB'S KICK.
OH, MY GOD!!
HE STABBED ME! HE STABBED ME!
THAT'S WHAT YOU GET FOR LEAVING ME HANGING!
THE REST WILL BE DECIDED AT THE MASTERS' MEETING...
...ARE YOU LISTENING?
...YES.

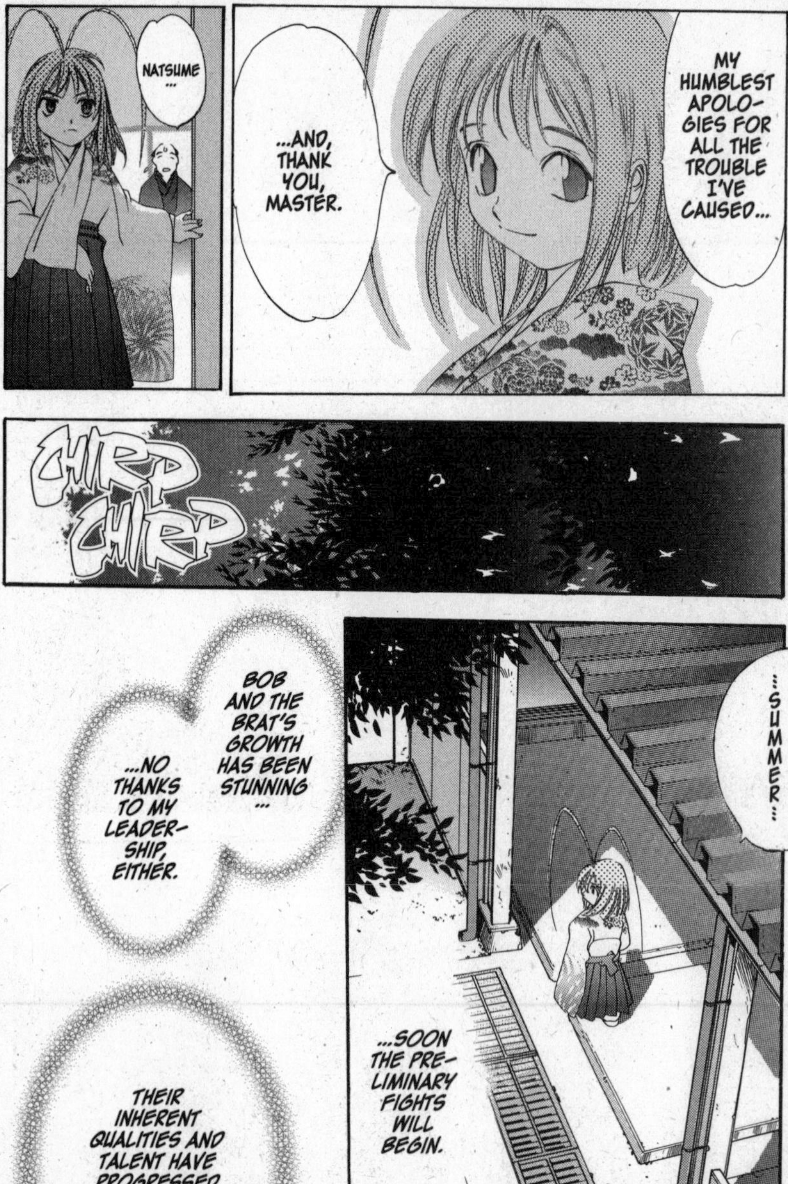
MY HUMBLEST APOLOGIES FOR ALL THE TROUBLE I'VE CAUSED...
...AND, THANK YOU, MASTER.
NATSUME...
CHIRP CHIRP
...SUMMER...
...SOON THE PRELIMINARY FIGHTS WILL BEGIN.
BOB AND THE BRAT'S GROWTH HAS BEEN STUNNING...
...NO THANKS TO MY LEADERSHIP, EITHER.
THEIR INHERENT QUALITIES AND TALENT HAVE PROGRESSED DUE TO INTENSE FIGHTING.

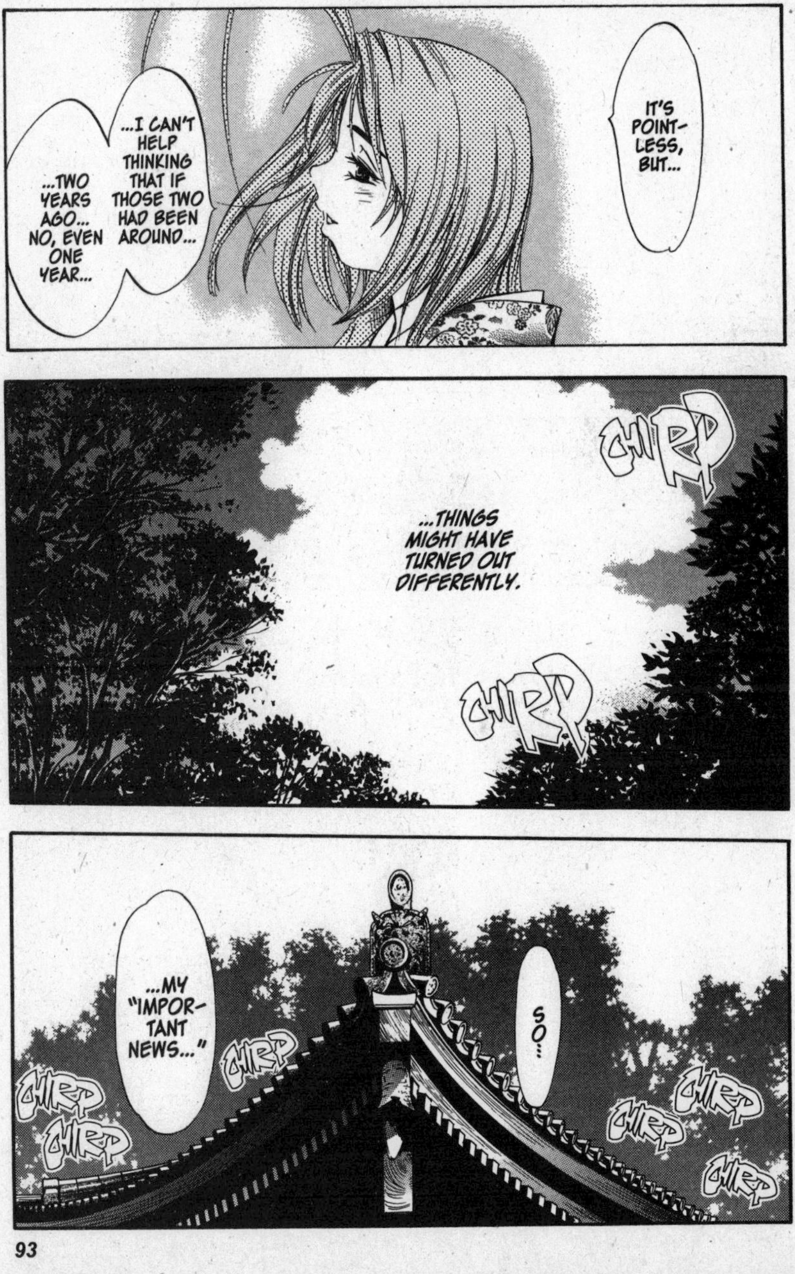
IT'S POINT-LESS, BUT...
...I CAN'T HELP THINKING THAT IF THOSE TWO HAD BEEN AROUND...
...TWO YEARS AGO... NO, EVEN ONE YEAR...
CHIRP
...THINGS MIGHT HAVE TURNED OUT DIFFERENTLY.
CHIRP
SO...
CHIRP
CHIRP
CHIRP
...MY "IMPORTANT NEWS..."
CHIRP
CHIRP
CHIRP

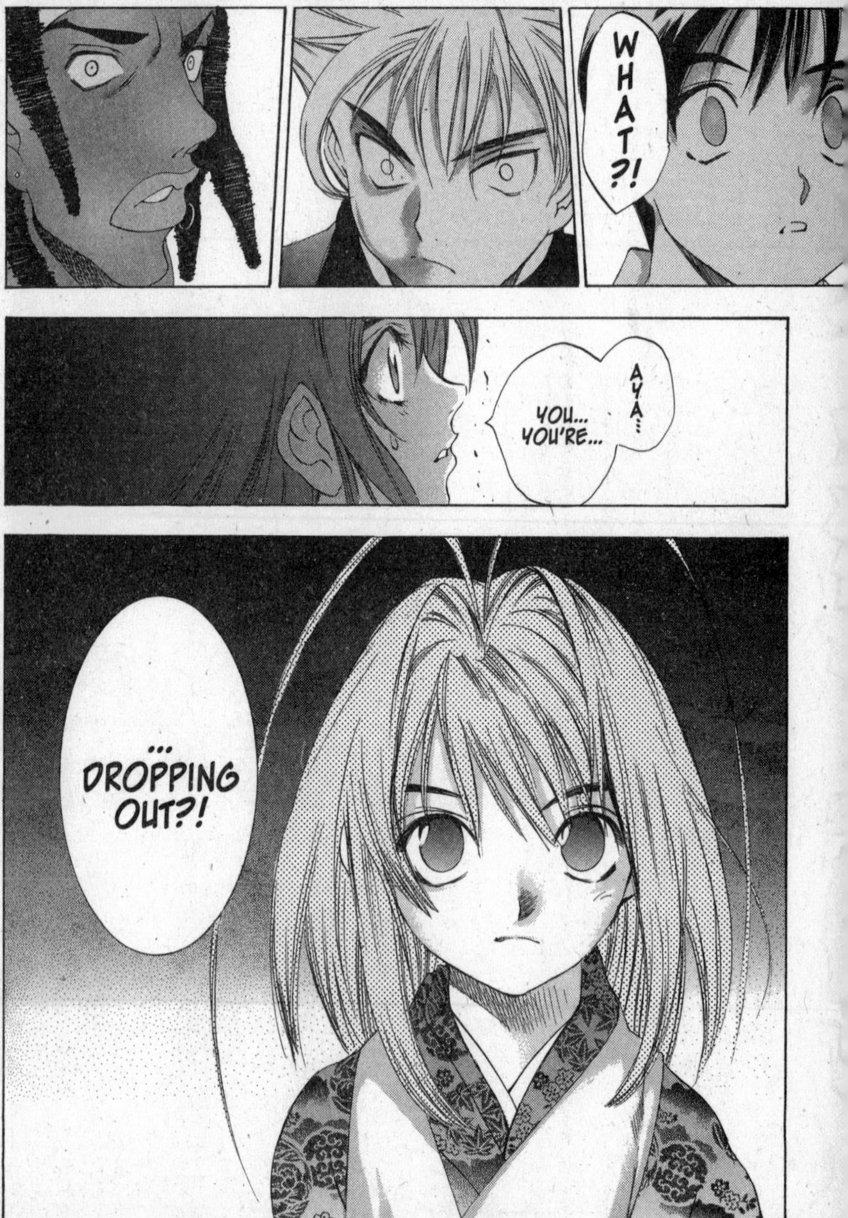
WHAT?!
AYA...
YOU... YOU'RE...
...DROPPING OUT?!

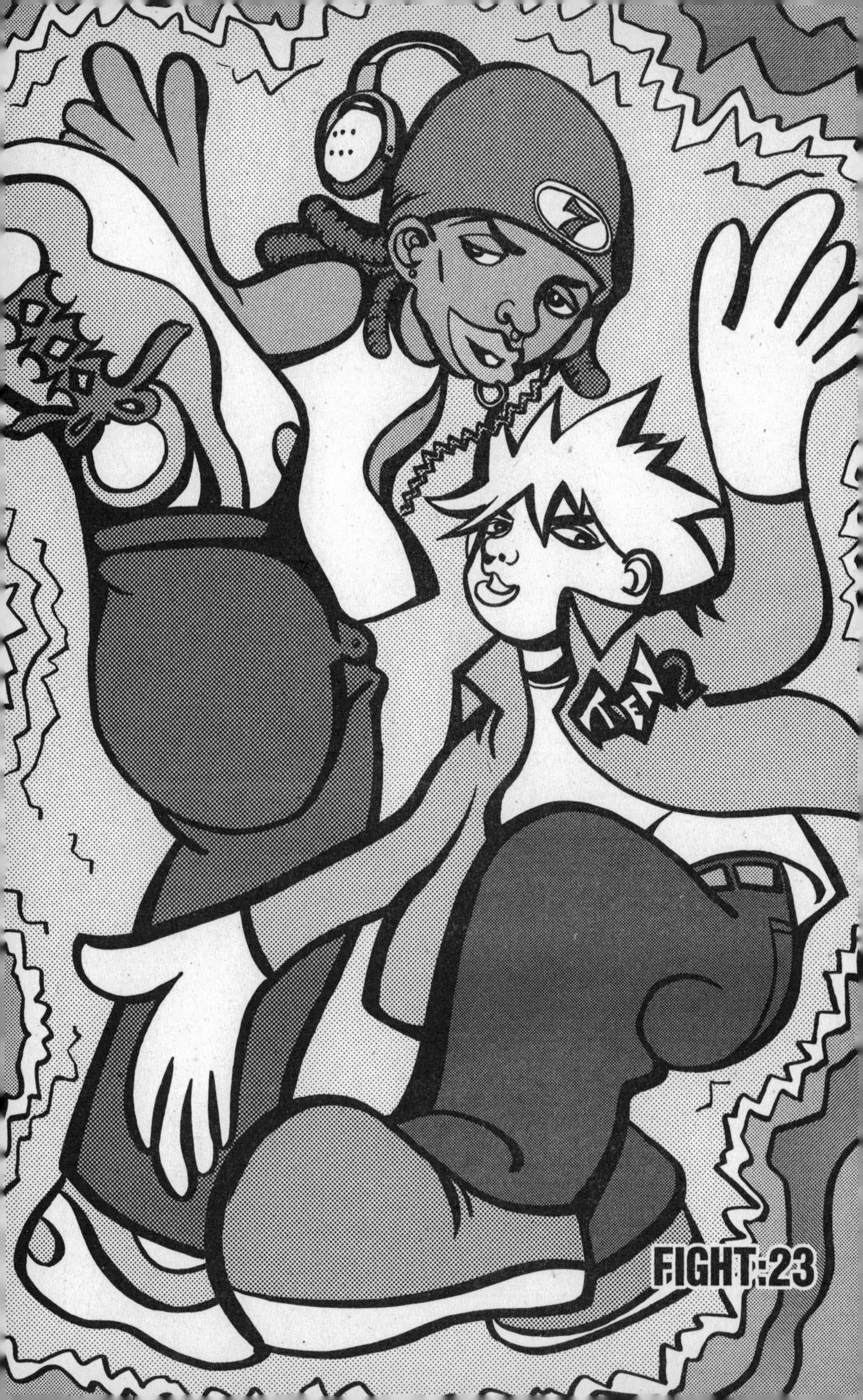
FIGHT:23

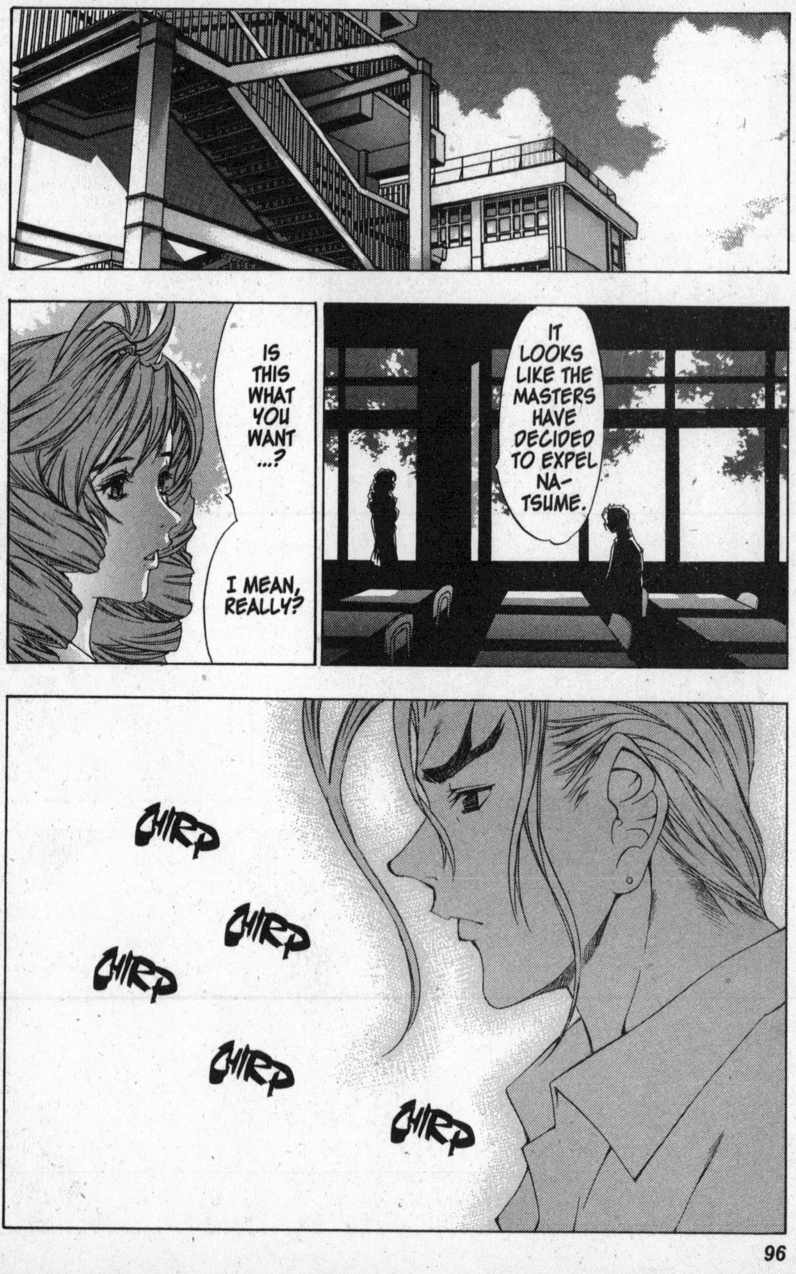
IT LOOKS LIKE THE MASTERS HAVE DECIDED TO EXPEL NATSUME.
IS THIS WHAT YOU WANT ...?
I MEAN, REALLY?
CHIRP
CHIRP
CHIRP
CHIRP
CHIRP

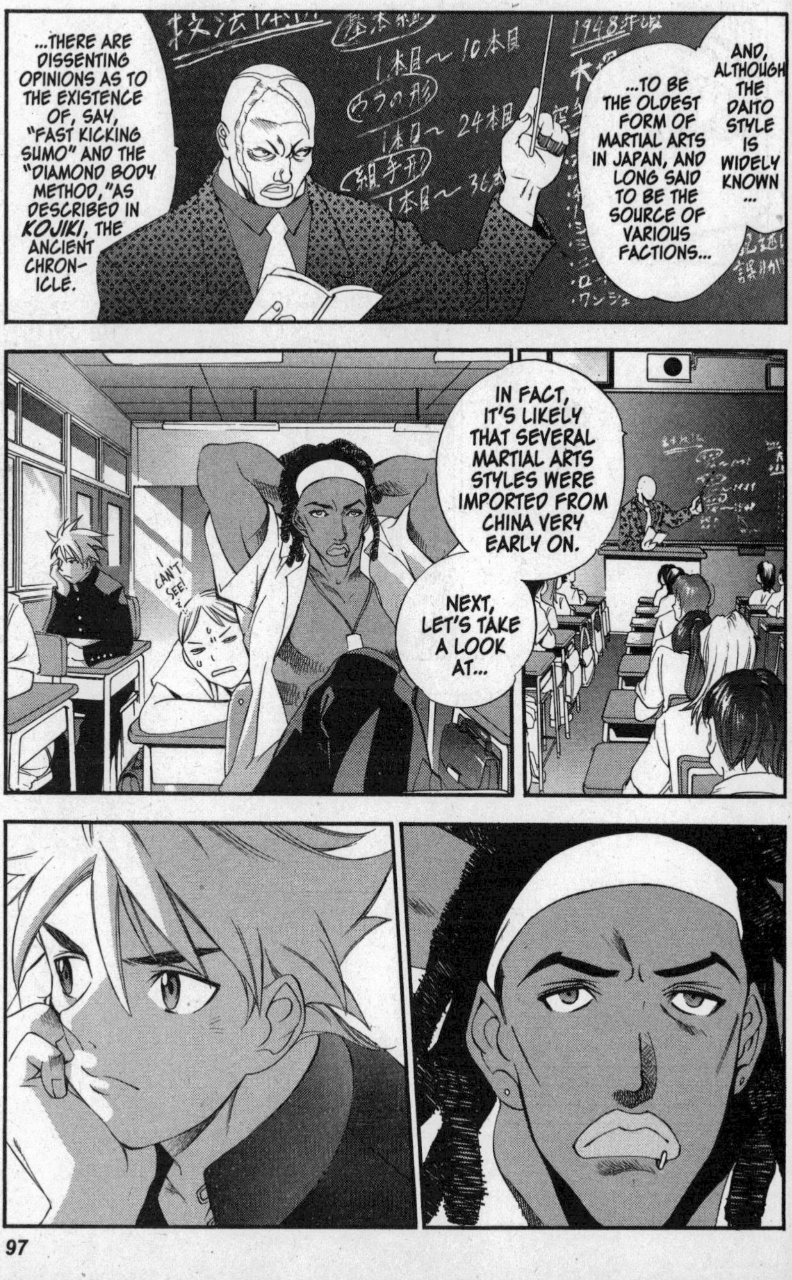
AND, ALTHOUGH THE DAITO STYLE IS WIDELY KNOWN ...
...TO BE THE OLDEST FORM OF MARTIAL ARTS IN JAPAN, AND LONG SAID TO BE THE SOURCE OF VARIOUS FACTIONS...
...THERE ARE DISSENTING OPINIONS AS TO THE EXISTENCE OF, SAY, "FAST KICKING SUMO" AND THE "DIAMOND BODY METHOD," AS DESCRIBED IN *KOJIKI*, THE ANCIENT CHRON-ICLE.
IN FACT, IT'S LIKELY THAT SEVERAL MARTIAL ARTS STYLES WERE IMPORTED FROM CHINA VERY EARLY ON.
NEXT, LET'S TAKE A LOOK AT...
I CAN'T SEE!

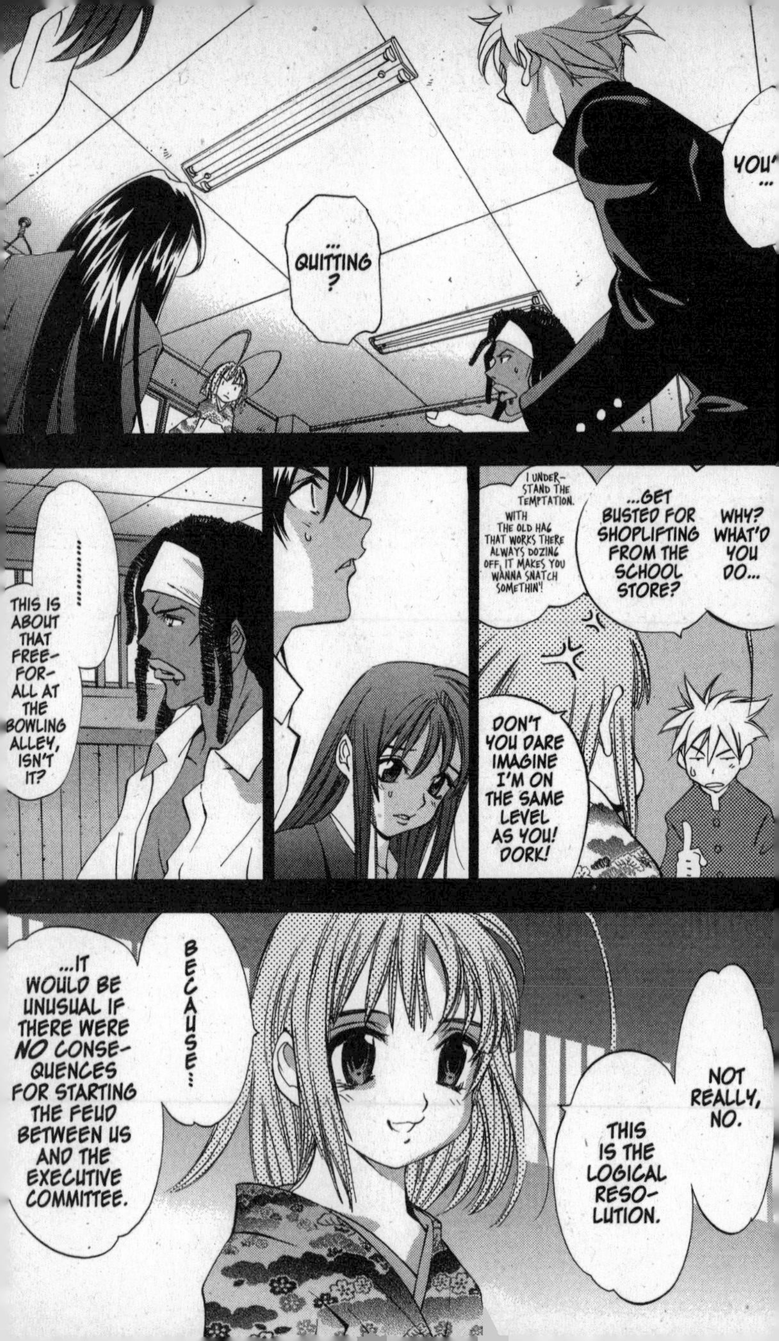
YOU' ...
... QUITTING?
WHY? WHAT'D YOU DO...
...GET BUSTED FOR SHOPLIFTING FROM THE SCHOOL STORE?
I UNDER-STAND THE TEMPTATION. WITH THE OLD HAG THAT WORKS THERE ALWAYS DOZING OFF, IT MAKES YOU WANNA SNATCH SOMETHIN'!
DON'T YOU DARE IMAGINE I'M ON THE SAME LEVEL AS YOU! DORK!
....
THIS IS ABOUT THAT FREE-FOR-ALL AT THE BOWLING ALLEY, ISN'T IT?
NOT REALLY, NO.
THIS IS THE LOGICAL RESO-LUTION.
BECAUSE...
...IT WOULD BE UNUSUAL IF THERE WERE NO CONSE-QUENCES FOR STARTING THE FEUD BETWEEN US AND THE EXECUTIVE COMMITTEE.

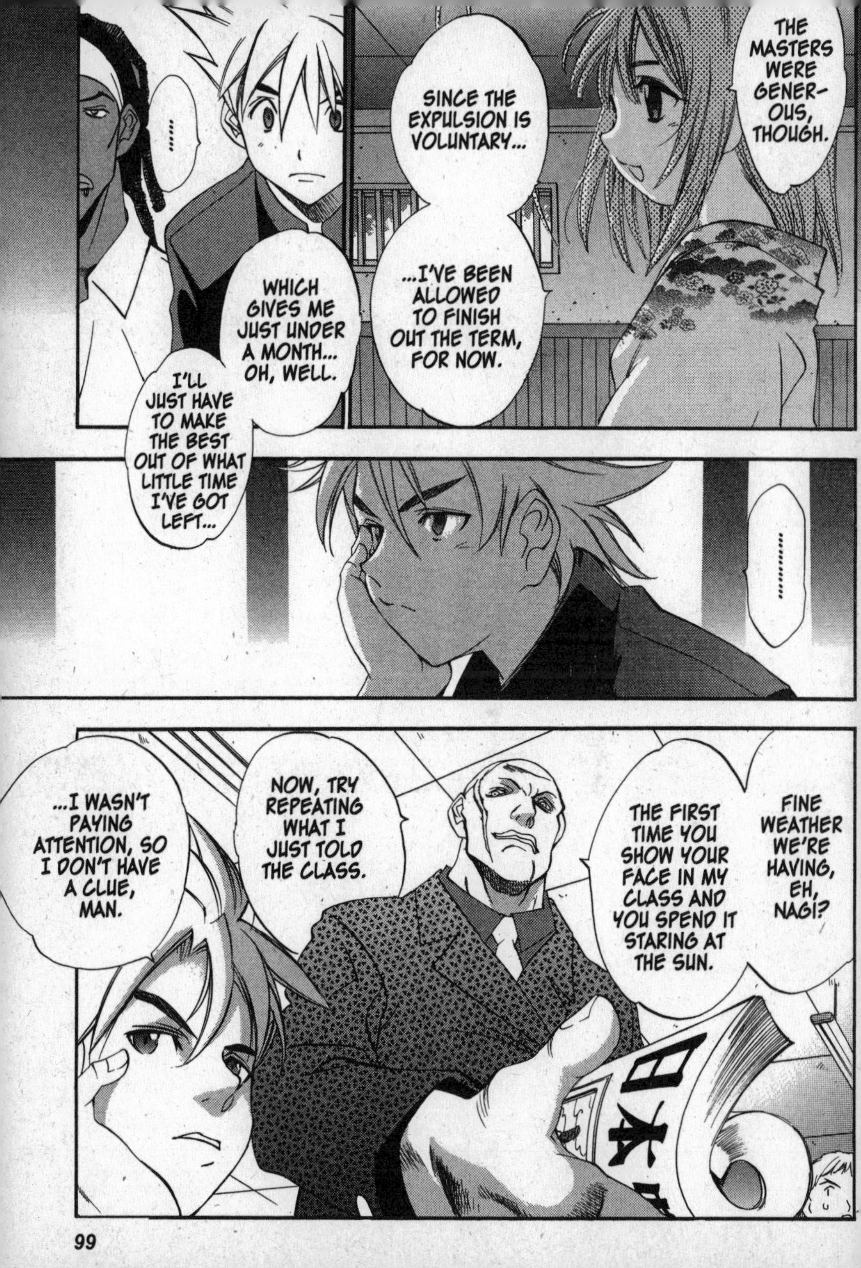
THE MASTERS WERE GENER-OUS, THOUGH.
SINCE THE EXPULSION IS VOLUNTARY...
...I'VE BEEN ALLOWED TO FINISH OUT THE TERM, FOR NOW.
......
WHICH GIVES ME JUST UNDER A MONTH... OH, WELL.
I'LL JUST HAVE TO MAKE THE BEST OUT OF WHAT LITTLE TIME I'VE GOT LEFT...
....
FINE WEATHER WE'RE HAVING, EH, NAGI?
THE FIRST TIME YOU SHOW YOUR FACE IN MY CLASS AND YOU SPEND IT STARING AT THE SUN.
NOW, TRY REPEATING WHAT I JUST TOLD THE CLASS.
...I WASN'T PAYING ATTENTION, SO I DON'T HAVE A CLUE, MAN.

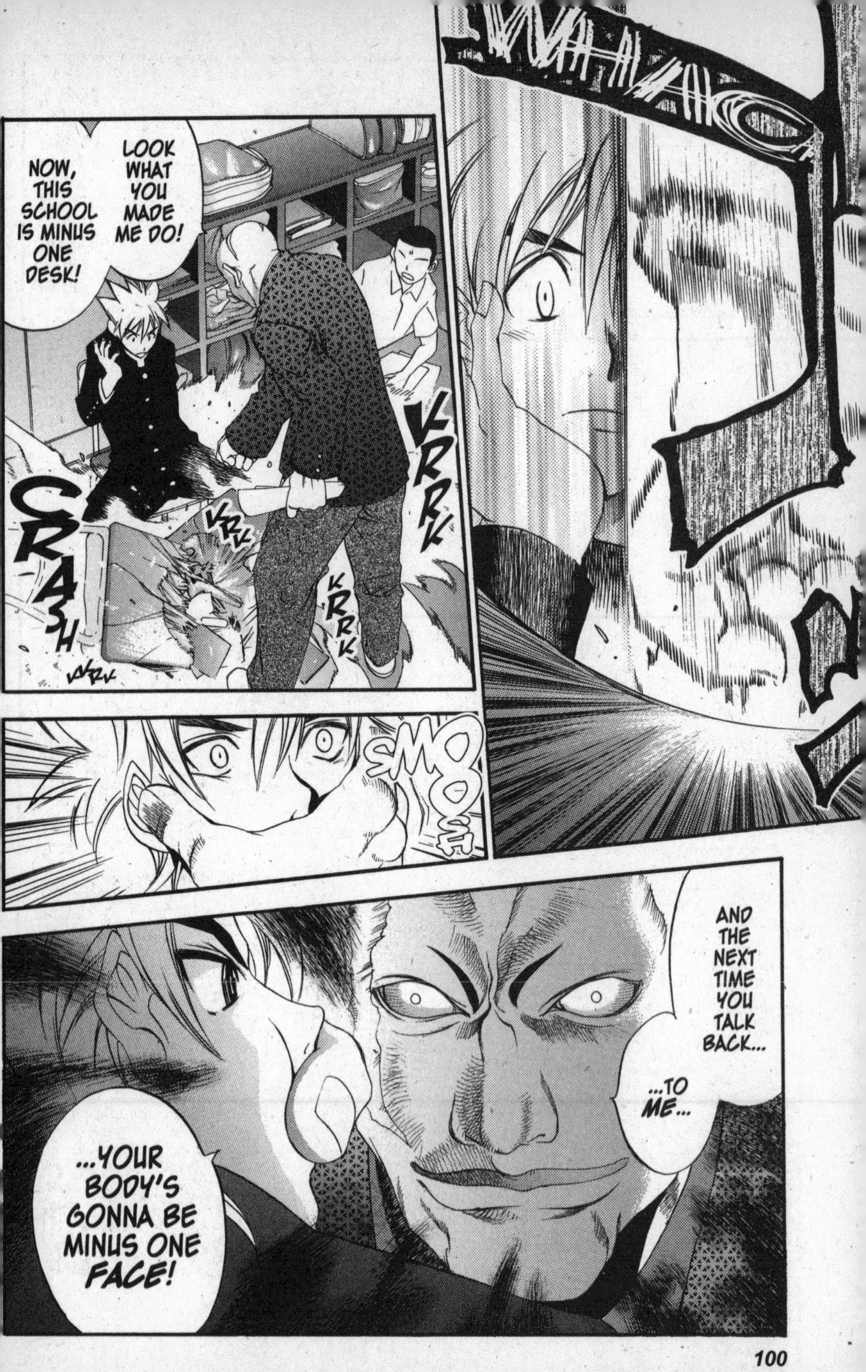
LOOK WHAT YOU MADE ME DO!
NOW, THIS SCHOOL IS MINUS ONE DESK!
KRRRK
KRK
CRASH
KRRRK
KRK
SMOOSH
AND THE NEXT TIME YOU TALK BACK...
...TO ME...
...YOUR BODY'S GONNA BE MINUS ONE FACE!

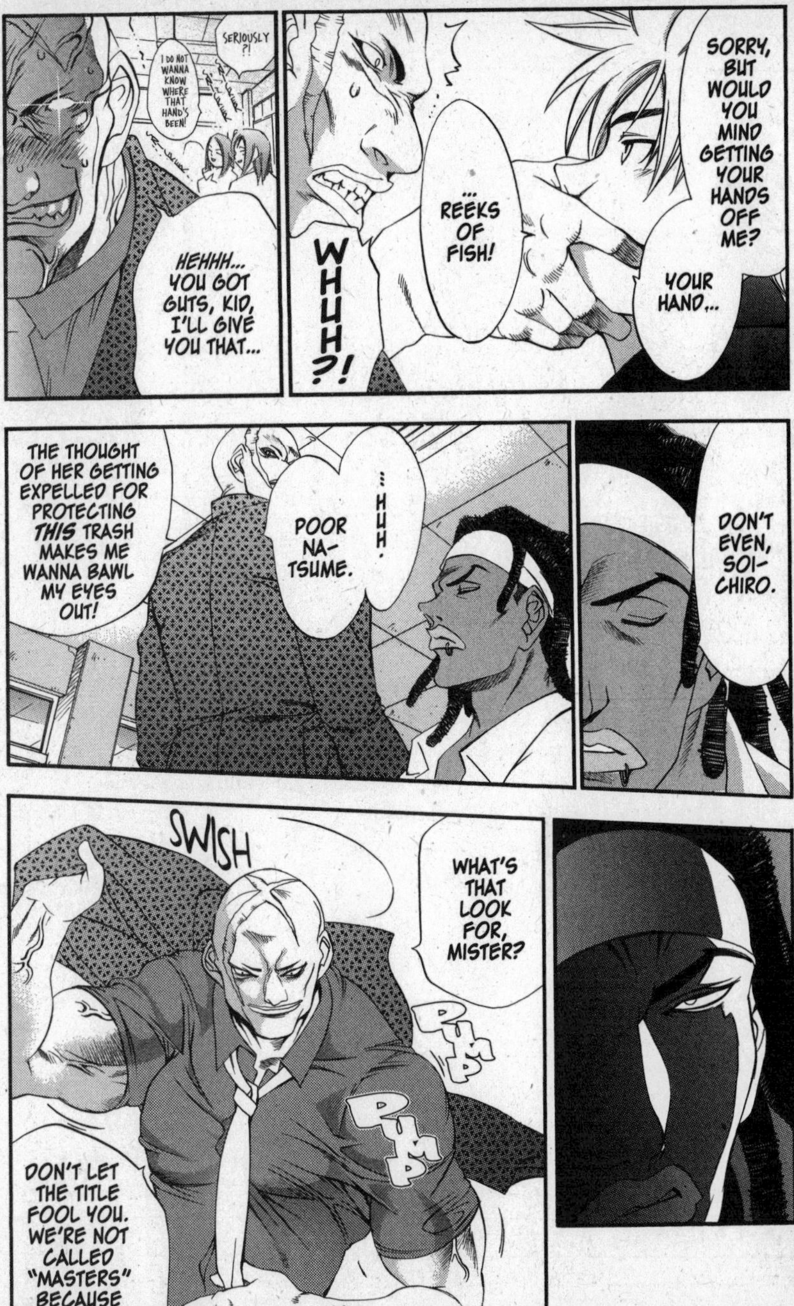
SORRY, BUT WOULD YOU MIND GETTING YOUR HANDS OFF ME?
YOUR HAND...
...REEKS OF FISH!
WHUHH?!
SERIOUSLY?!
I DO NOT WANNA KNOW WHERE THAT HAND'S BEEN!
HEHHH... YOU GOT GUTS, KID, I'LL GIVE YOU THAT...
DON'T EVEN, SOI-CHIRO.
...HUH.
POOR NA-TSUME.
THE THOUGHT OF HER GETTING EXPELLED FOR PROTECTING THIS TRASH MAKES ME WANNA BAWL MY EYES OUT!
WHAT'S THAT LOOK FOR, MISTER?
SWISH
PUMP
PUMP
DON'T LET THE TITLE FOOL YOU. WE'RE NOT CALLED "MASTERS" BECAUSE WE'RE GREAT TEACHERS.

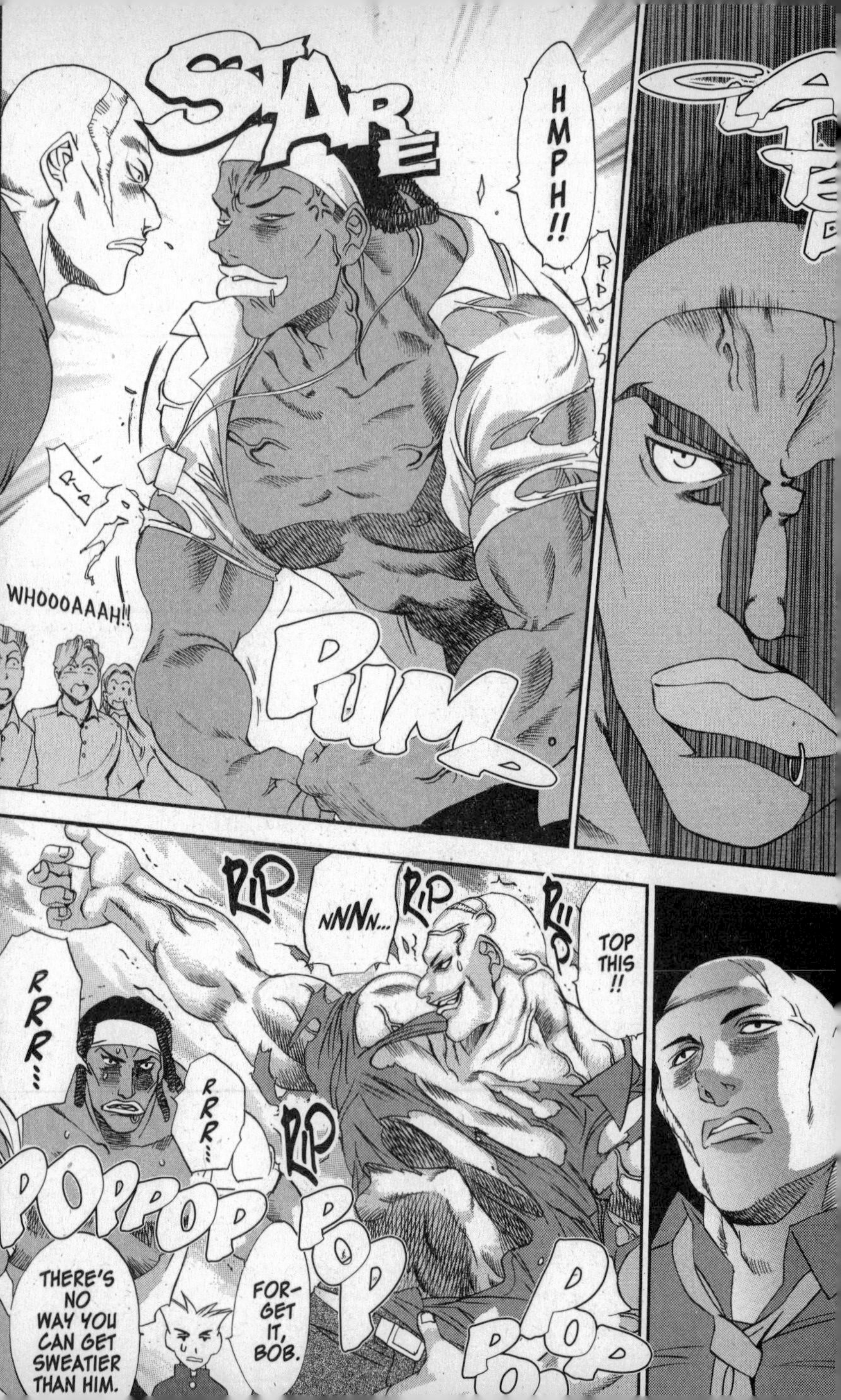
HMPH!!
STARE
RIP
RIP
WHOOOAAAH!!
PUMP
TOP THIS!!
RIIP
RIP
NNNN...
RIP
RRR...
RRR...
RIP
POPPOP
POP
POP
POP
FOR-GET IT, BOB.
THERE'S NO WAY YOU CAN GET SWEATIER THAN HIM.

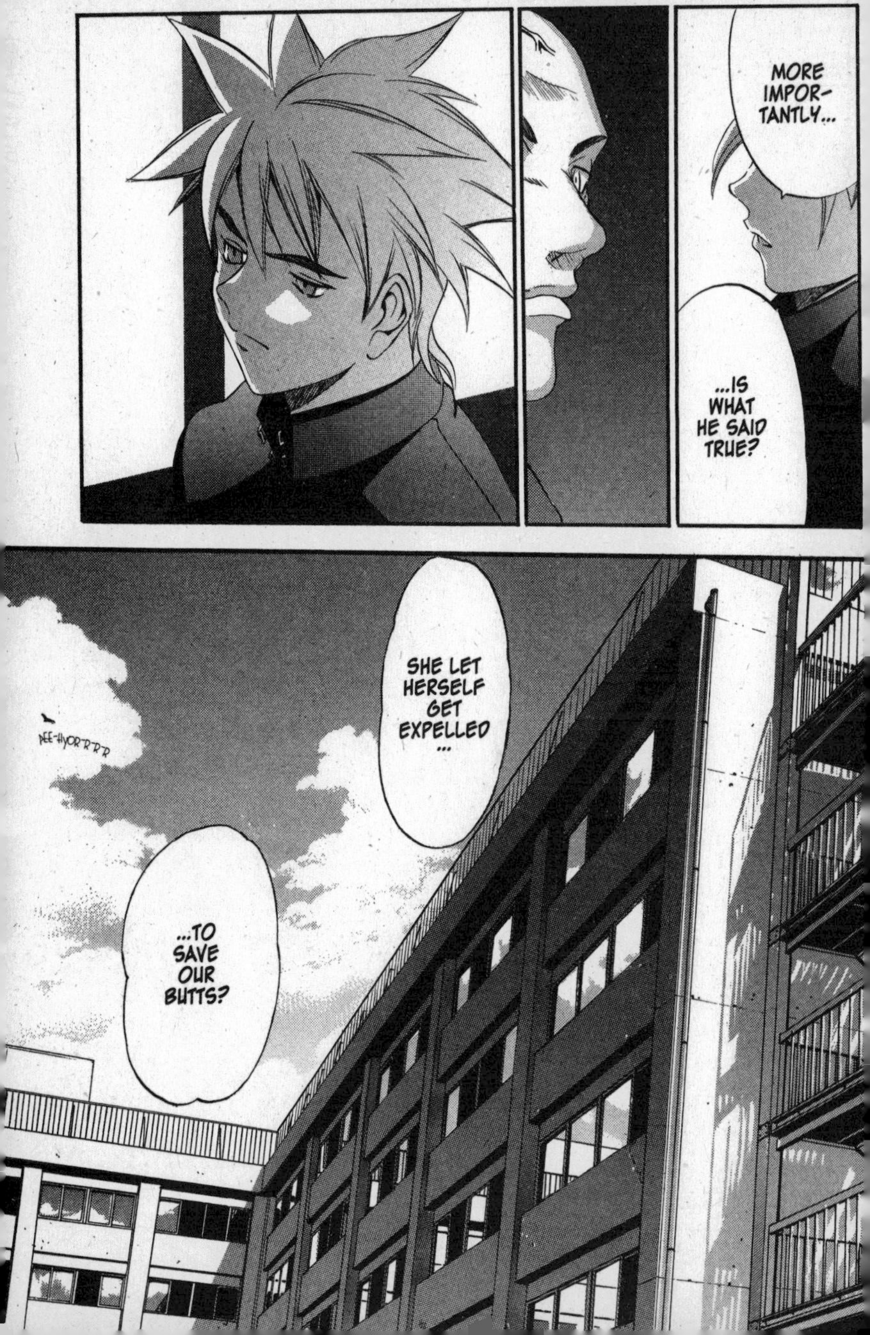
MORE IMPOR-TANTLY...
...IS WHAT HE SAID TRUE?
SHE LET HERSELF GET EXPELLED ...
...TO SAVE OUR BUTTS?
PEE-HYOR-R-R-R

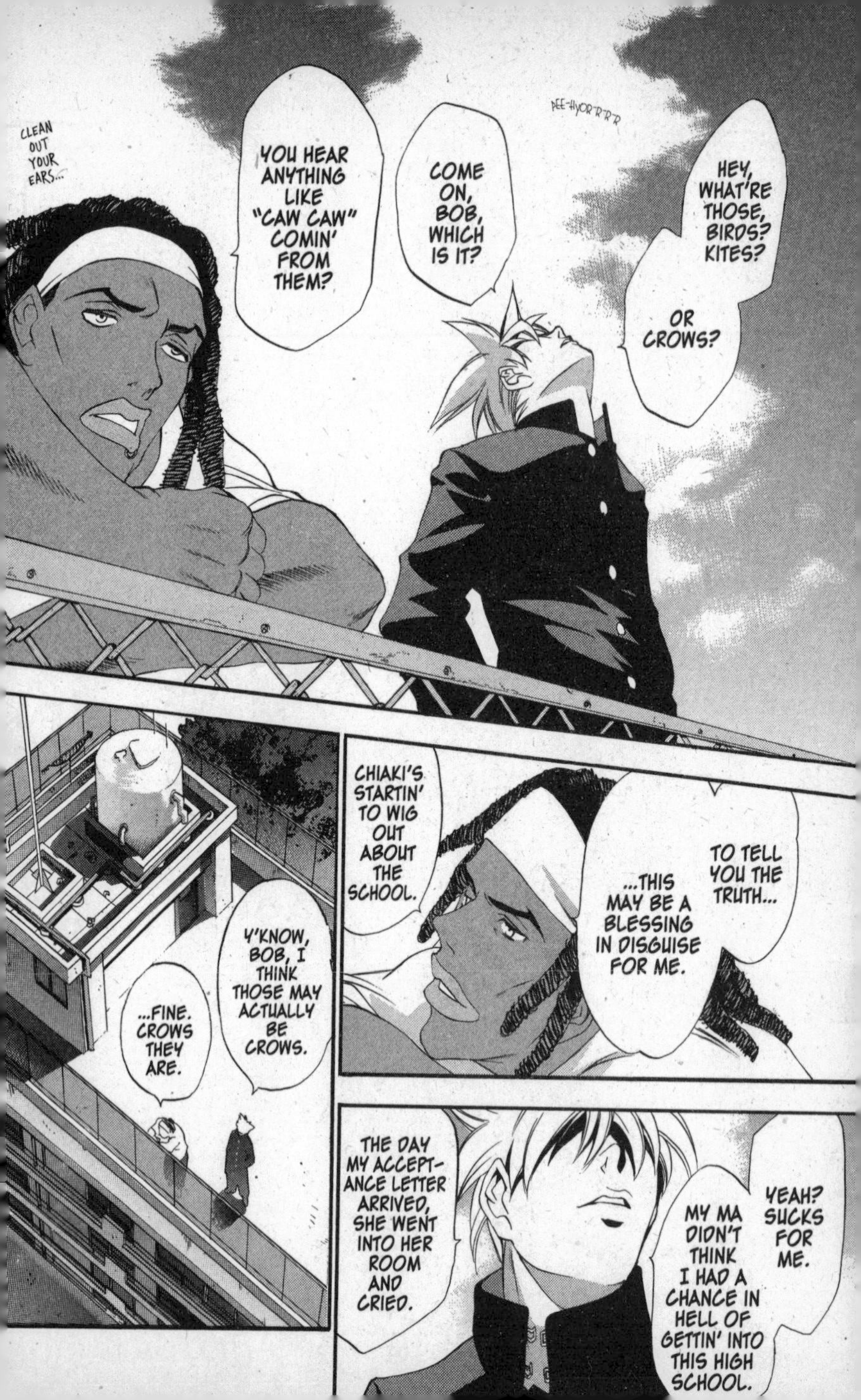
PEE-HYOR'R'R'R
HEY, WHAT'RE THOSE, BIRDS? KITES?
OR CROWS?
COME ON, BOB, WHICH IS IT?
YOU HEAR ANYTHING LIKE "CAW CAW" COMIN' FROM THEM?
CLEAN OUT YOUR EARS...
TO TELL YOU THE TRUTH...
...THIS MAY BE A BLESSING IN DISGUISE FOR ME.
CHIAKI'S STARTIN' TO WIG OUT ABOUT THE SCHOOL.
YEAH? SUCKS FOR ME.
MY MA DIDN'T THINK I HAD A CHANCE IN HELL OF GETTIN' INTO THIS HIGH SCHOOL.
THE DAY MY ACCEPTANCE LETTER ARRIVED, SHE WENT INTO HER ROOM AND CRIED.
Y'KNOW, BOB, I THINK THOSE MAY ACTUALLY BE CROWS.
...FINE. CROWS THEY ARE.

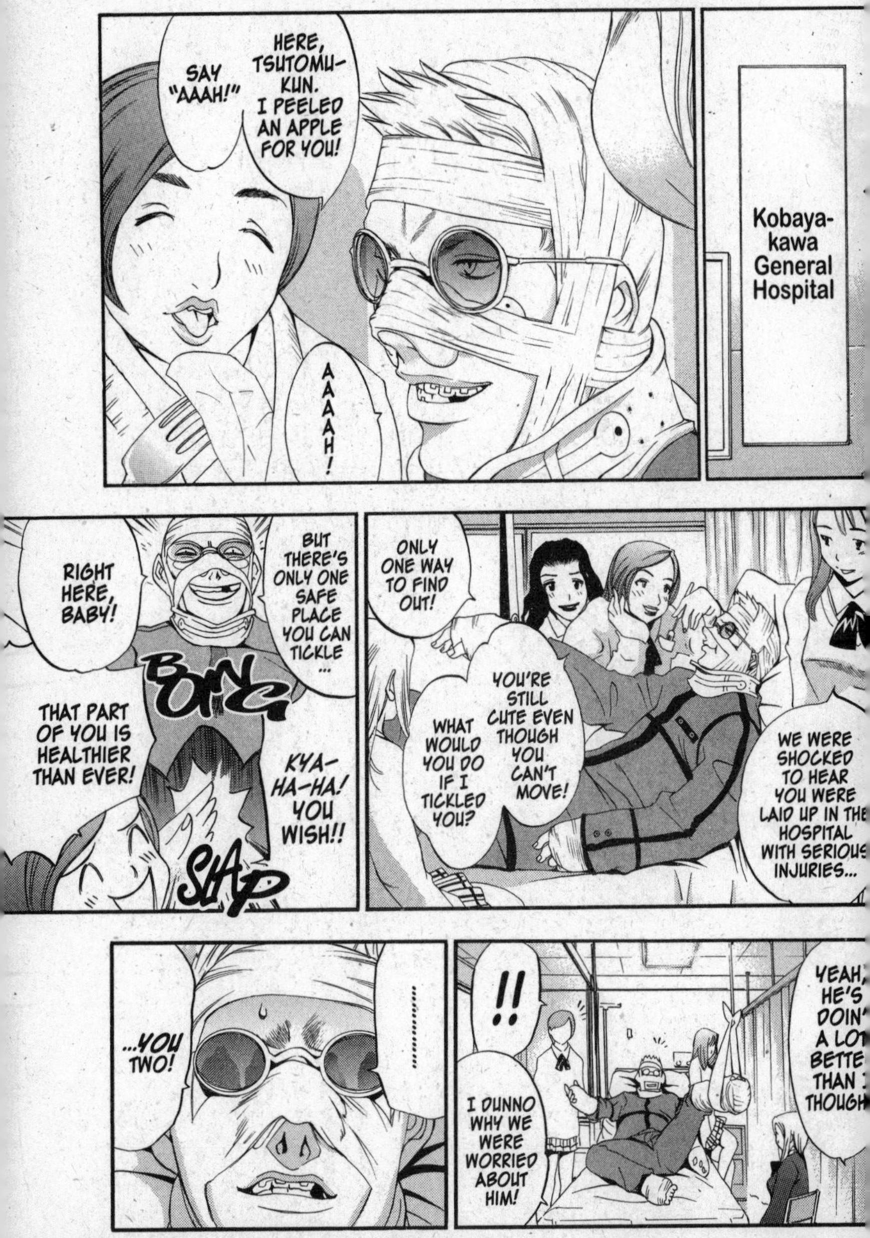
Kobayakawa General Hospital
HERE, TSUTOMU-KUN. I PEELED AN APPLE FOR YOU!
SAY "AAAH!"
AAAAH!
WE WERE SHOCKED TO HEAR YOU WERE LAID UP IN THE HOSPITAL WITH SERIOUS INJURIES...
YOU'RE STILL CUTE EVEN THOUGH YOU CAN'T MOVE!
WHAT WOULD YOU DO IF I TICKLED YOU?
ONLY ONE WAY TO FIND OUT!
BUT THERE'S ONLY ONE SAFE PLACE YOU CAN TICKLE ...
RIGHT HERE, BABY!
BOING
THAT PART OF YOU IS HEALTHIER THAN EVER!
KYA-HA-HA! YOU WISH!!
SLAP
YEAH, HE'S DOIN' A LOT BETTE THAN THOUGH
!!
I DUNNO WHY WE WERE WORRIED ABOUT HIM!
....
...YOU TWO!

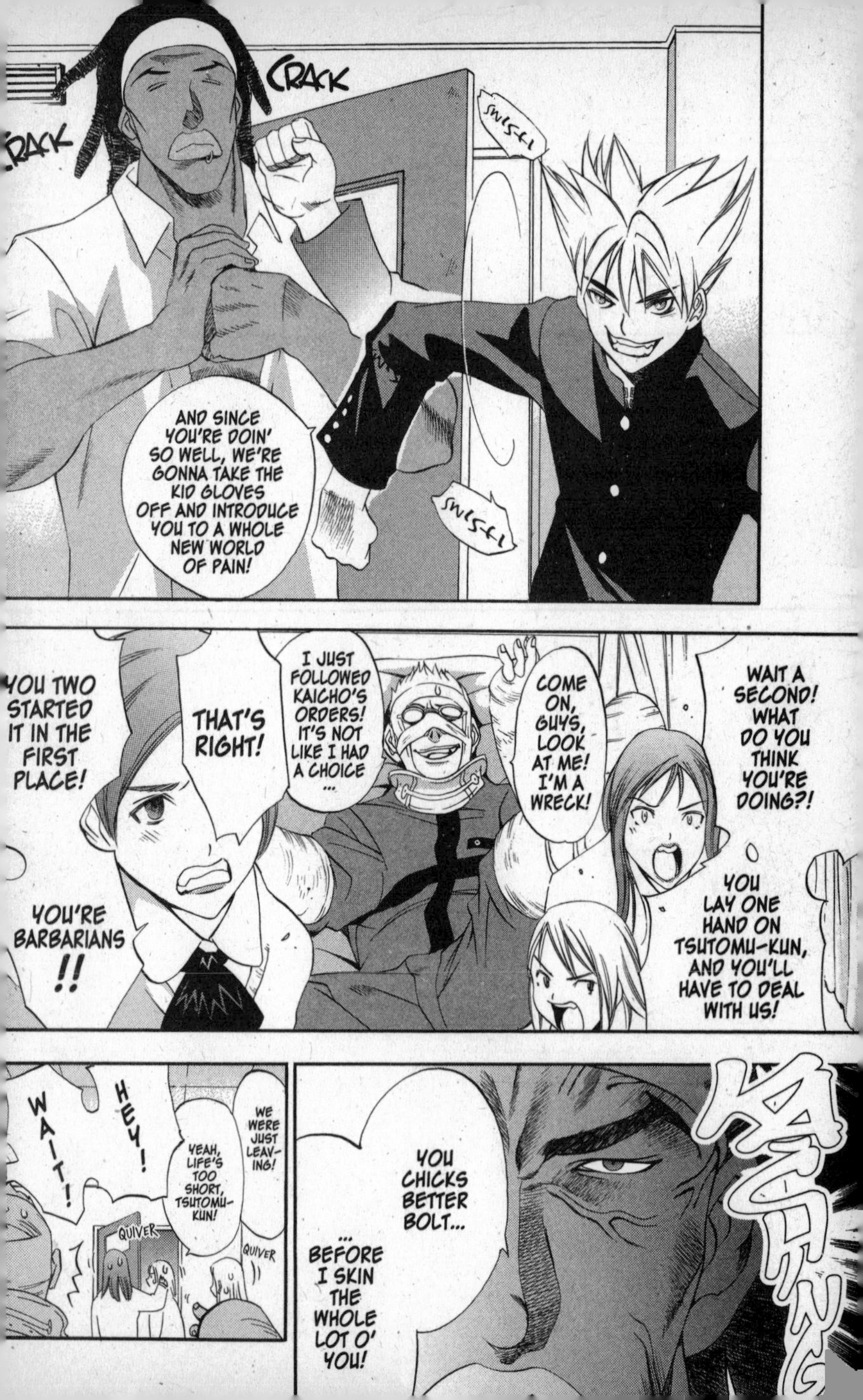
CRACK
CRACK
SWISH
AND SINCE YOU'RE DOIN' SO WELL, WE'RE GONNA TAKE THE KID GLOVES OFF AND INTRODUCE YOU TO A WHOLE NEW WORLD OF PAIN!
SWISH
WAIT A SECOND! WHAT DO YOU THINK YOU'RE DOING?!
YOU LAY ONE HAND ON TSUTOMU-KUN, AND YOU'LL HAVE TO DEAL WITH US!
COME ON, GUYS, LOOK AT ME! I'M A WRECK!
I JUST FOLLOWED KAICHO'S ORDERS! IT'S NOT LIKE I HAD A CHOICE ...
THAT'S RIGHT!
YOU TWO STARTED IT IN THE FIRST PLACE!
YOU'RE BARBARIANS !!
YOU CHICKS BETTER BOLT...
... BEFORE I SKIN THE WHOLE LOT O' YOU!
WE WERE JUST LEAVING!
HEY!
YEAH, LIFE'S TOO SHORT, TSUTOMU-KUN!
WAIT!
QUIVER
QUIVER

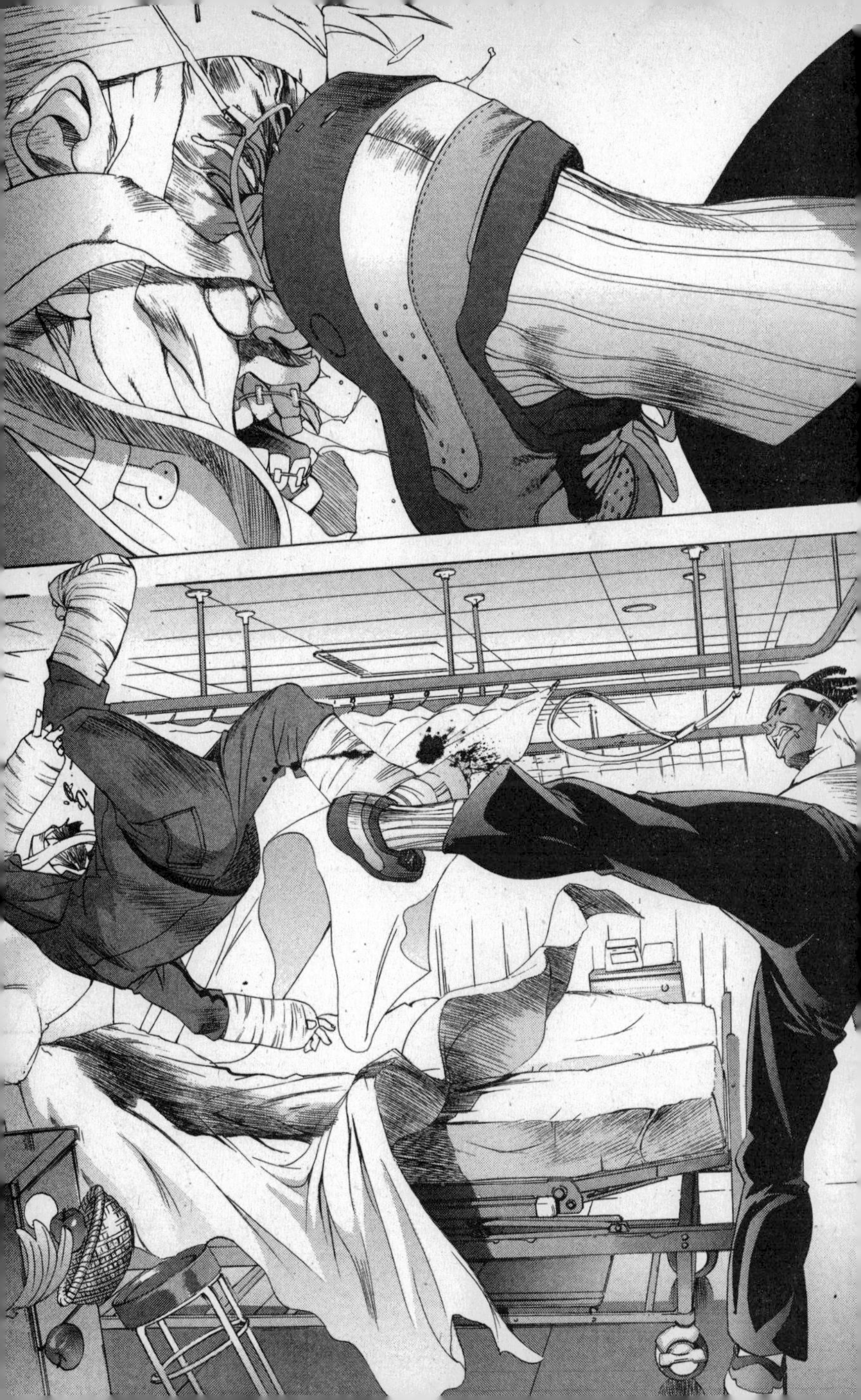

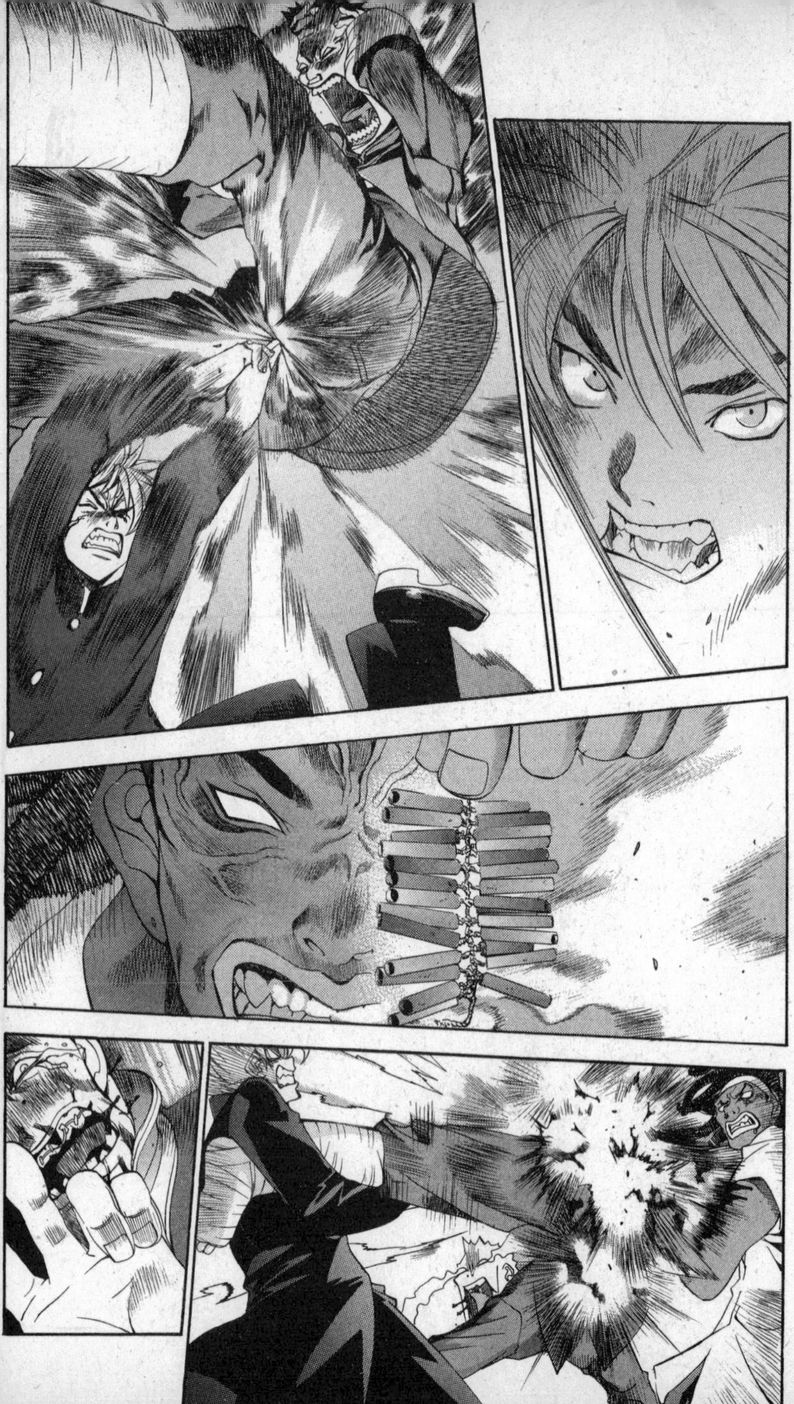

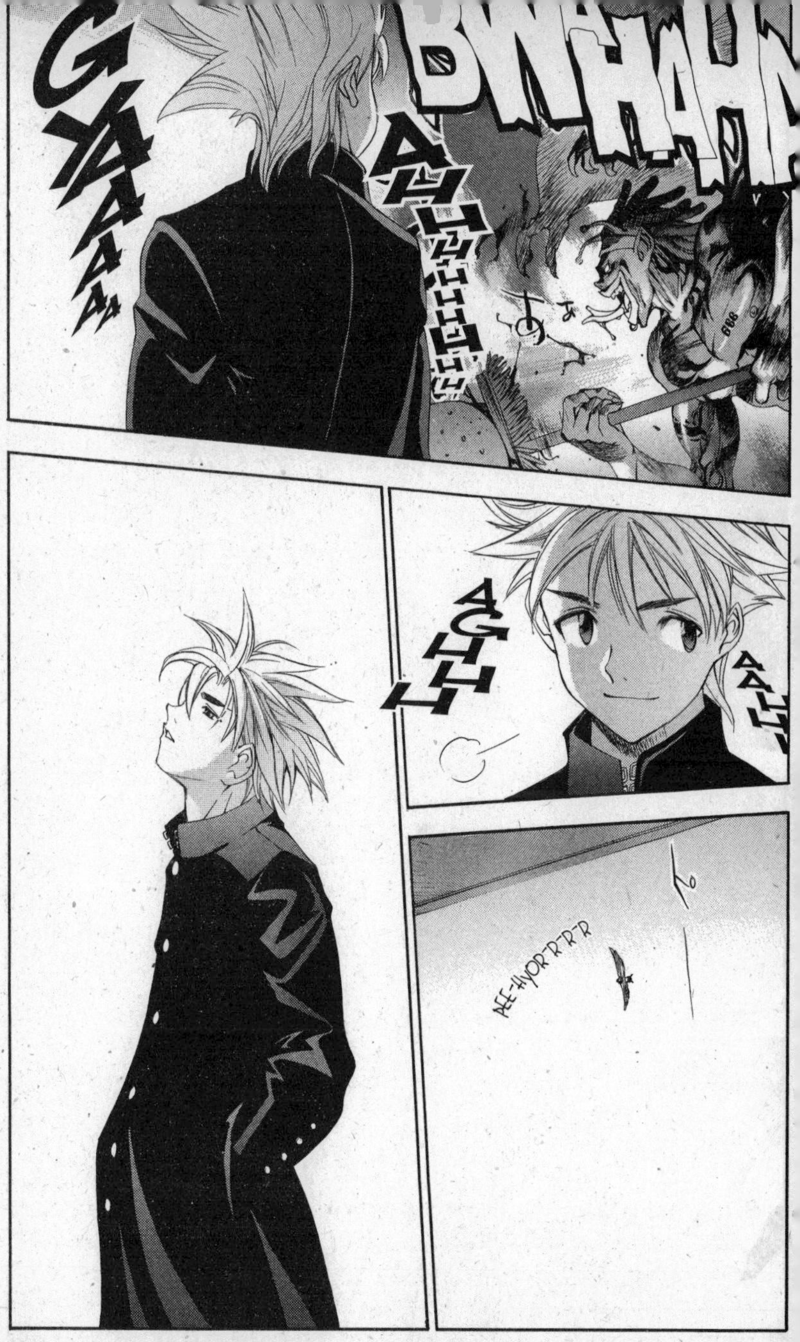
BWAHAH
AHHHHHHHHHHH
GYAAAAAA
AGHHH
AAHH
PEE-HYOR-R-R-R

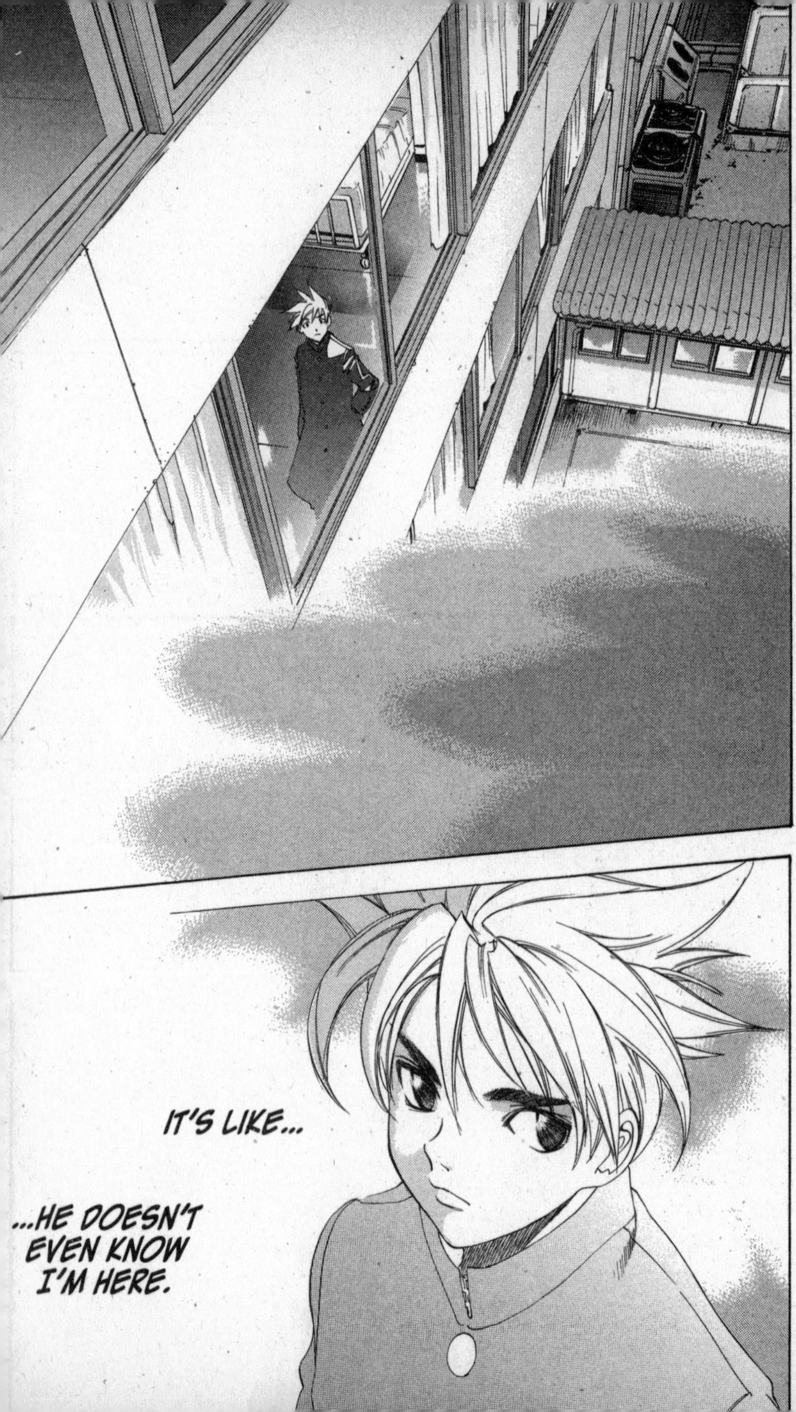
IT'S LIKE...
...HE DOESN'T EVEN KNOW I'M HERE.

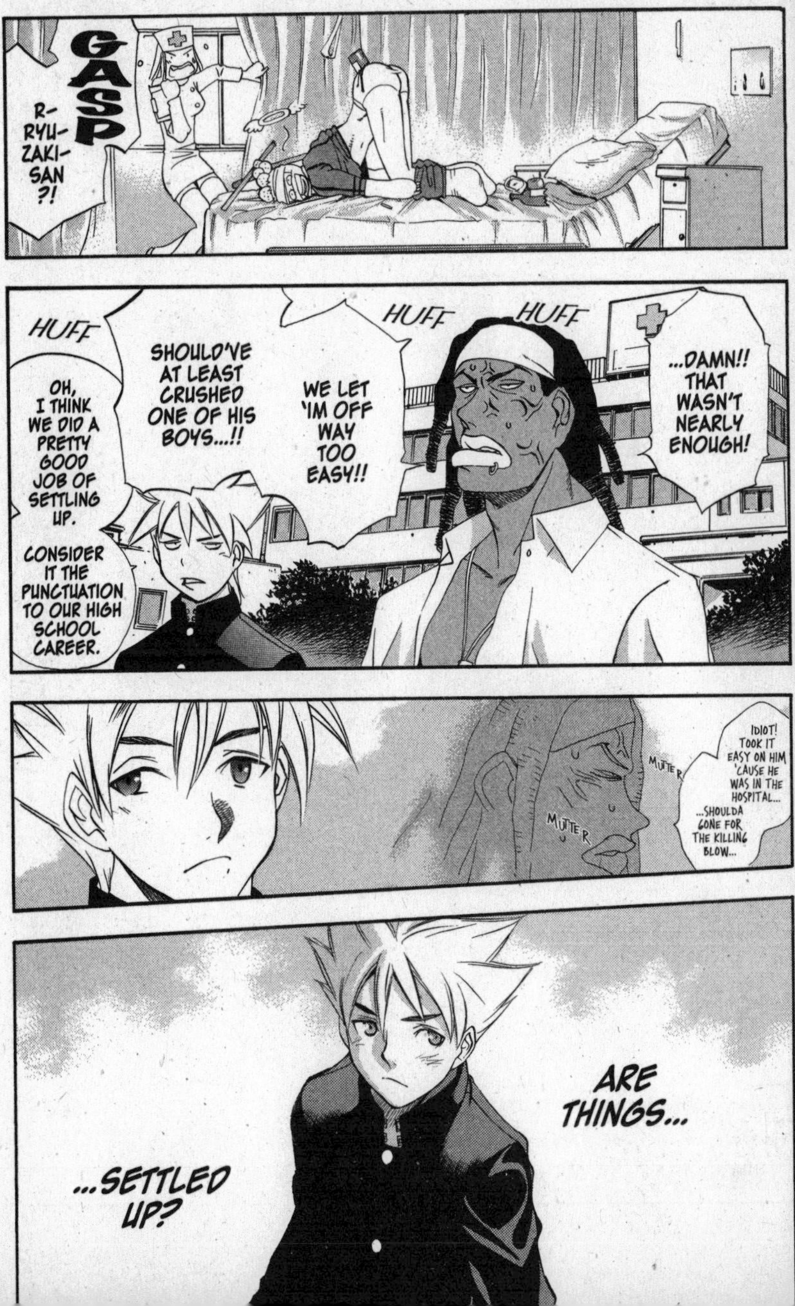
GASP
R-RYUZAKI-SAN?!
HUFF
...DAMN!! THAT WASN'T NEARLY ENOUGH!
HUFF
WE LET 'IM OFF WAY TOO EASY!!
SHOULD'VE AT LEAST CRUSHED ONE OF HIS BOYS...!!
HUFF
OH, I THINK WE DID A PRETTY GOOD JOB OF SETTLING UP.
CONSIDER IT THE PUNCTUATION TO OUR HIGH SCHOOL CAREER.
IDIOT! TOOK IT EASY ON HIM 'CAUSE HE WAS IN THE HOSPITAL... ...SHOULDA GONE FOR THE KILLING BLOW...
MUTTER
MUTTER
ARE THINGS...
...SETTLED UP?

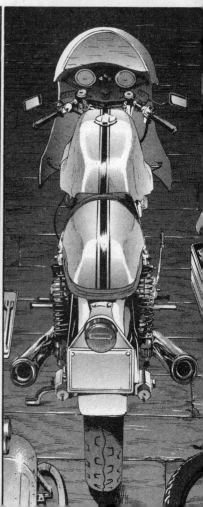

SHIN...
ARE
YOU...

...MAD
AT ME?

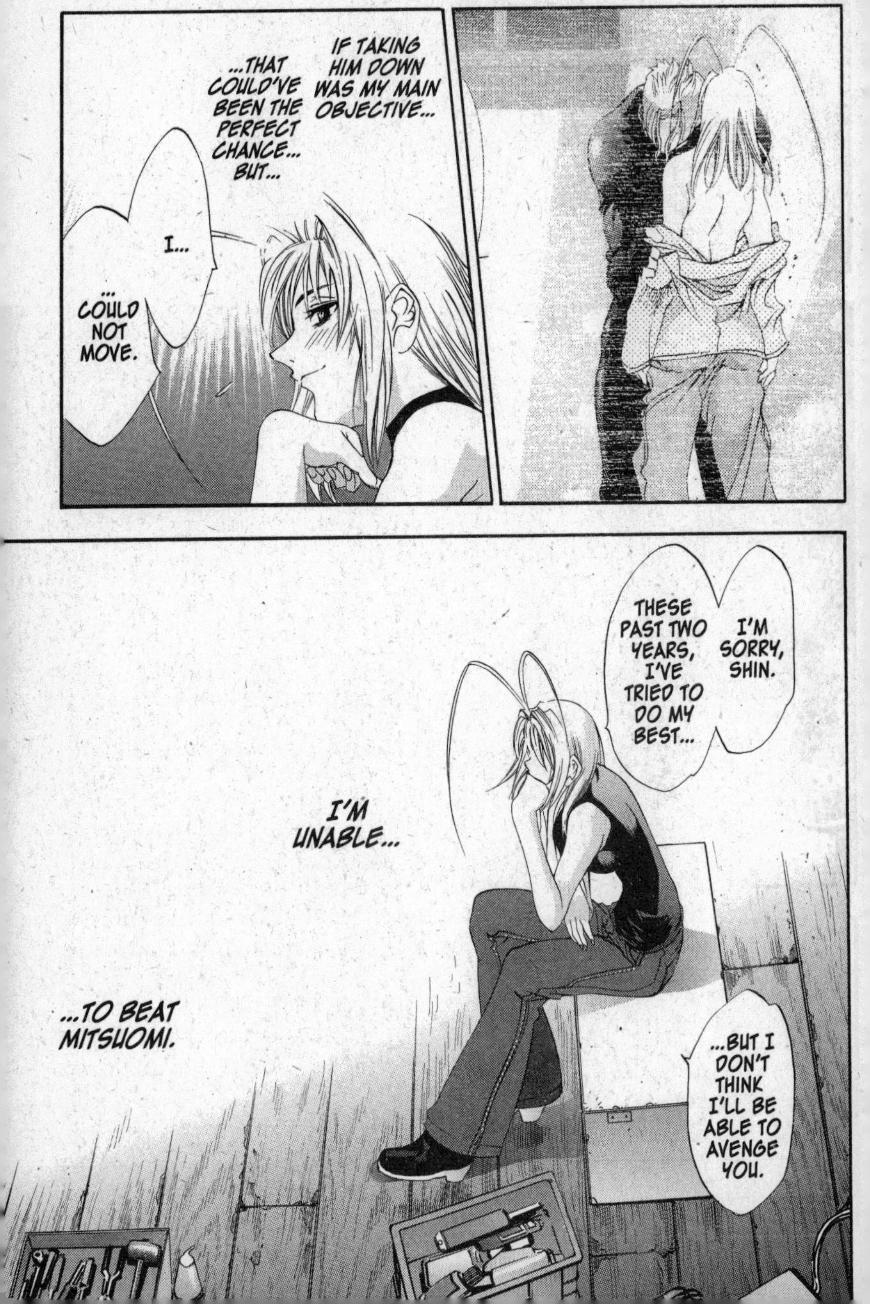
IF TAKING HIM DOWN WAS MY MAIN OBJECTIVE...
...THAT COULD'VE BEEN THE PERFECT CHANCE... BUT...
I...
...COULD NOT MOVE.
I'M SORRY, SHIN.
THESE PAST TWO YEARS, I'VE TRIED TO DO MY BEST...
...BUT I DON'T THINK I'LL BE ABLE TO AVENGE YOU.
I'M UNABLE...
...TO BEAT MITSUOMI.

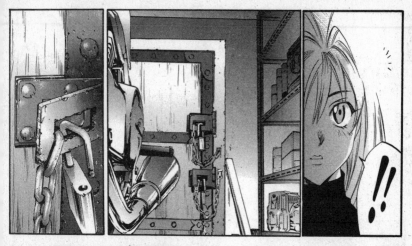

THE KEY...

...WHAT THE...? I'M THE ONLY ONE WHO HAS THE KEY TO THE STORAGE ROOM.

...IT'S GONE!!

CLATTER

NO...

...IT'S...

CLATTER CLATTER

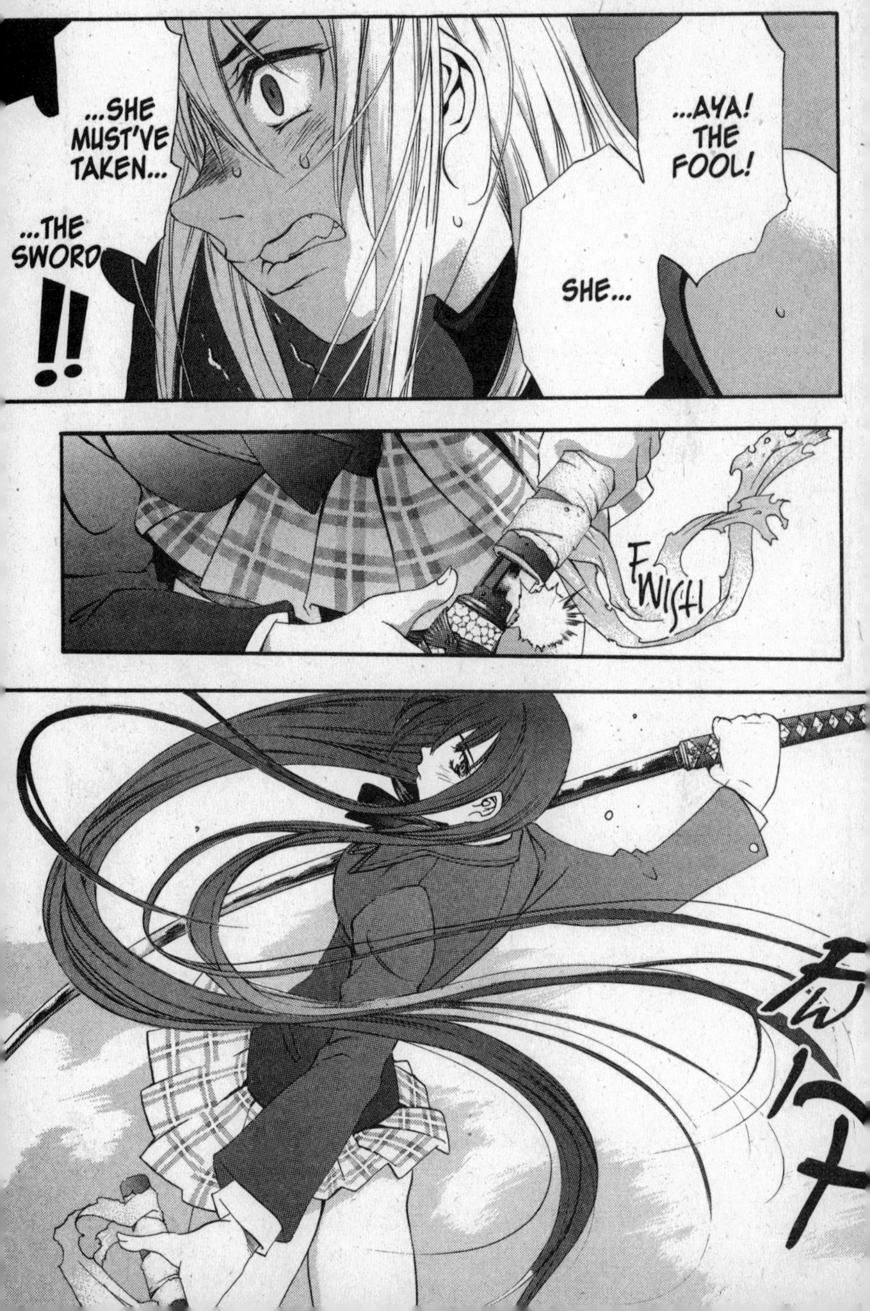
...AYA! THE FOOL!
SHE...
...SHE MUST'VE TAKEN...
...THE SWORD!!
FWISH!

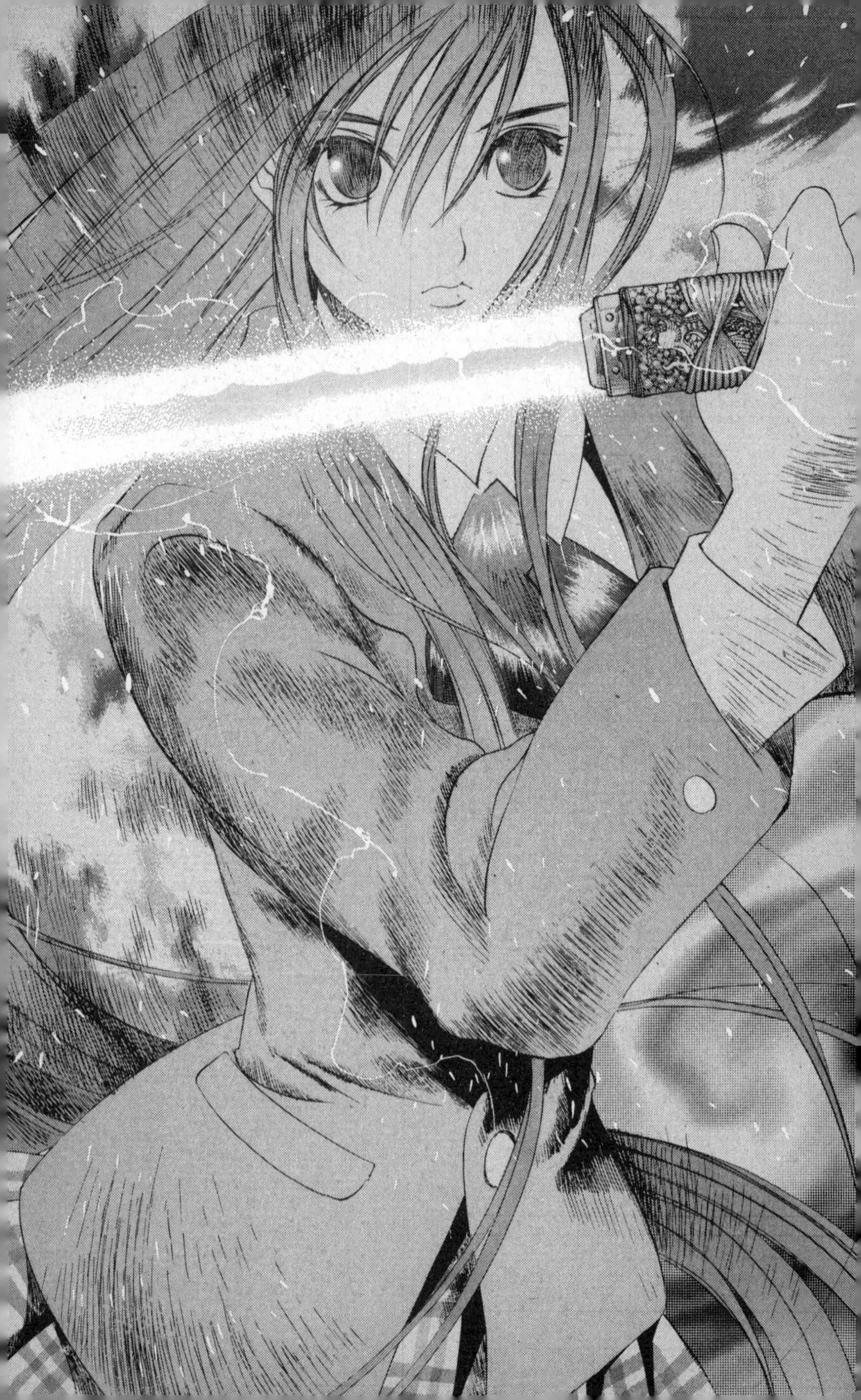

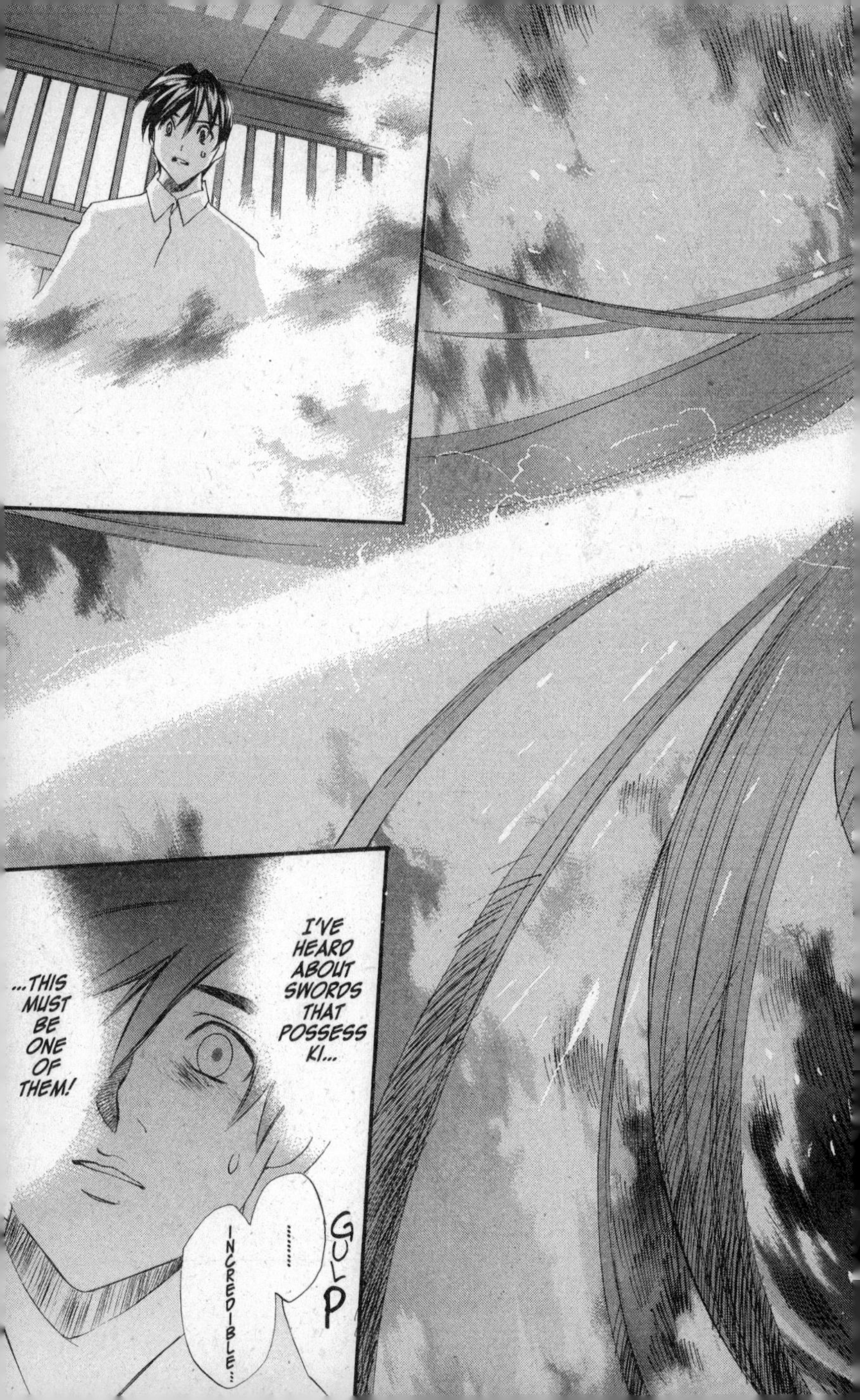
I'VE HEARD ABOUT SWORDS THAT POSSESS KI...
...THIS MUST BE ONE OF THEM!
GULP
......
INCREDIBLE...

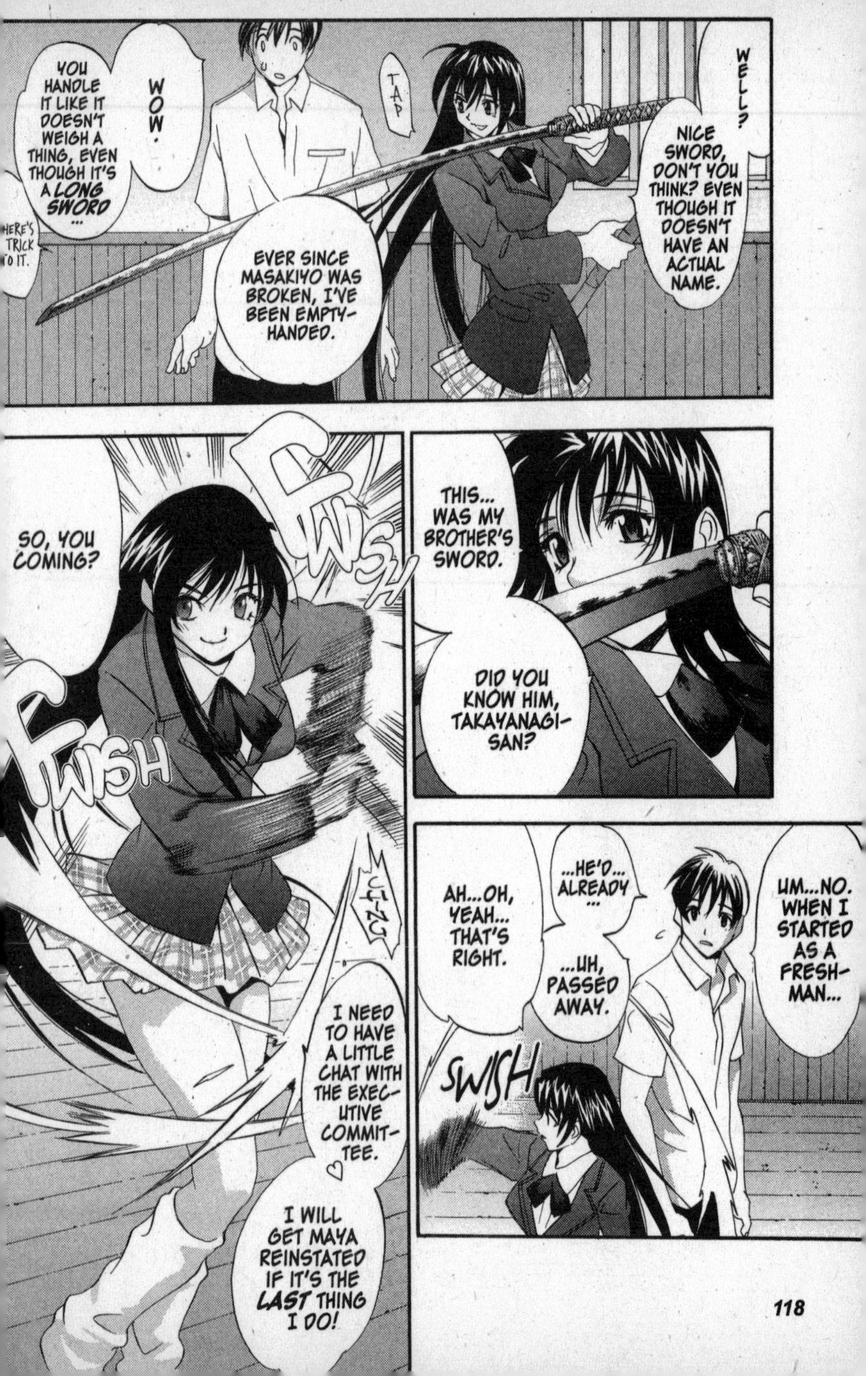
WELL?
NICE SWORD, DON'T YOU THINK? EVEN THOUGH IT DOESN'T HAVE AN ACTUAL NAME.
TAP
EVER SINCE MASAKIYO WAS BROKEN, I'VE BEEN EMPTY-HANDED.
WOW.
YOU HANDLE IT LIKE IT DOESN'T WEIGH A THING, EVEN THOUGH IT'S A *LONG SWORD*...
HERE'S TRICK TO IT.
THIS... WAS MY BROTHER'S SWORD.
DID YOU KNOW HIM, TAKAYANAGI-SAN?
UM...NO. WHEN I STARTED AS A FRESHMAN...
...HE'D... ALREADY...
...UH, PASSED AWAY.
AH...OH, YEAH... THAT'S RIGHT.
SWISH
SWISH
SO, YOU COMING?
FWISH
I NEED TO HAVE A LITTLE CHAT WITH THE EXEC-UTIVE COMMIT-TEE. ♡
I WILL GET MAYA REINSTATED IF IT'S THE *LAST* THING I DO!

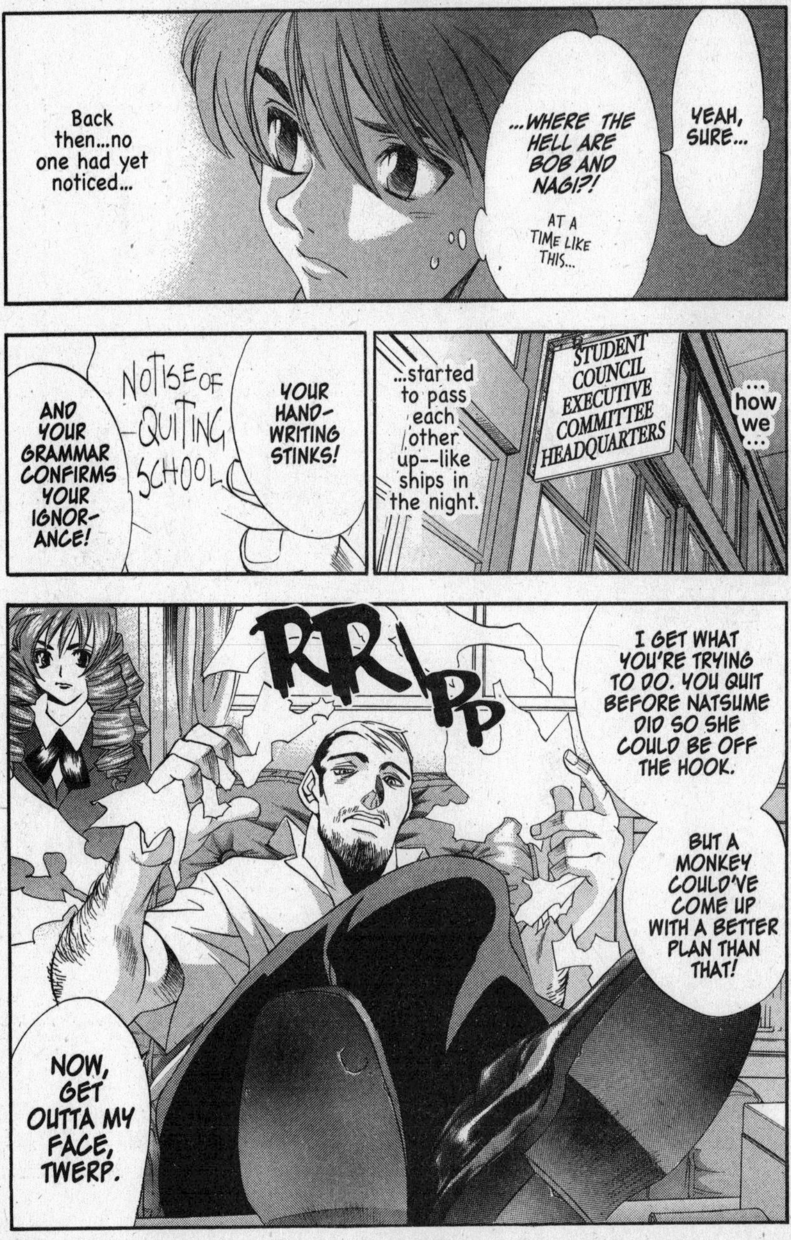
YEAH, SURE...
...WHERE THE HELL ARE BOB AND NAGI?!
AT A TIME LIKE THIS...
Back then...no one had yet noticed...
...how we...
STUDENT COUNCIL EXECUTIVE COMMITTEE HEADQUARTERS
...started to pass each other up--like ships in the night.
YOUR HAND-WRITING STINKS!
NOTISE OF QUITING SCHOOL
AND YOUR GRAMMAR CONFIRMS YOUR IGNOR-ANCE!
I GET WHAT YOU'RE TRYING TO DO. YOU QUIT BEFORE NATSUME DID SO SHE COULD BE OFF THE HOOK.
RRIPP
BUT A MONKEY COULD'VE COME UP WITH A BETTER PLAN THAN THAT!
NOW, GET OUTTA MY FACE, TWERP.

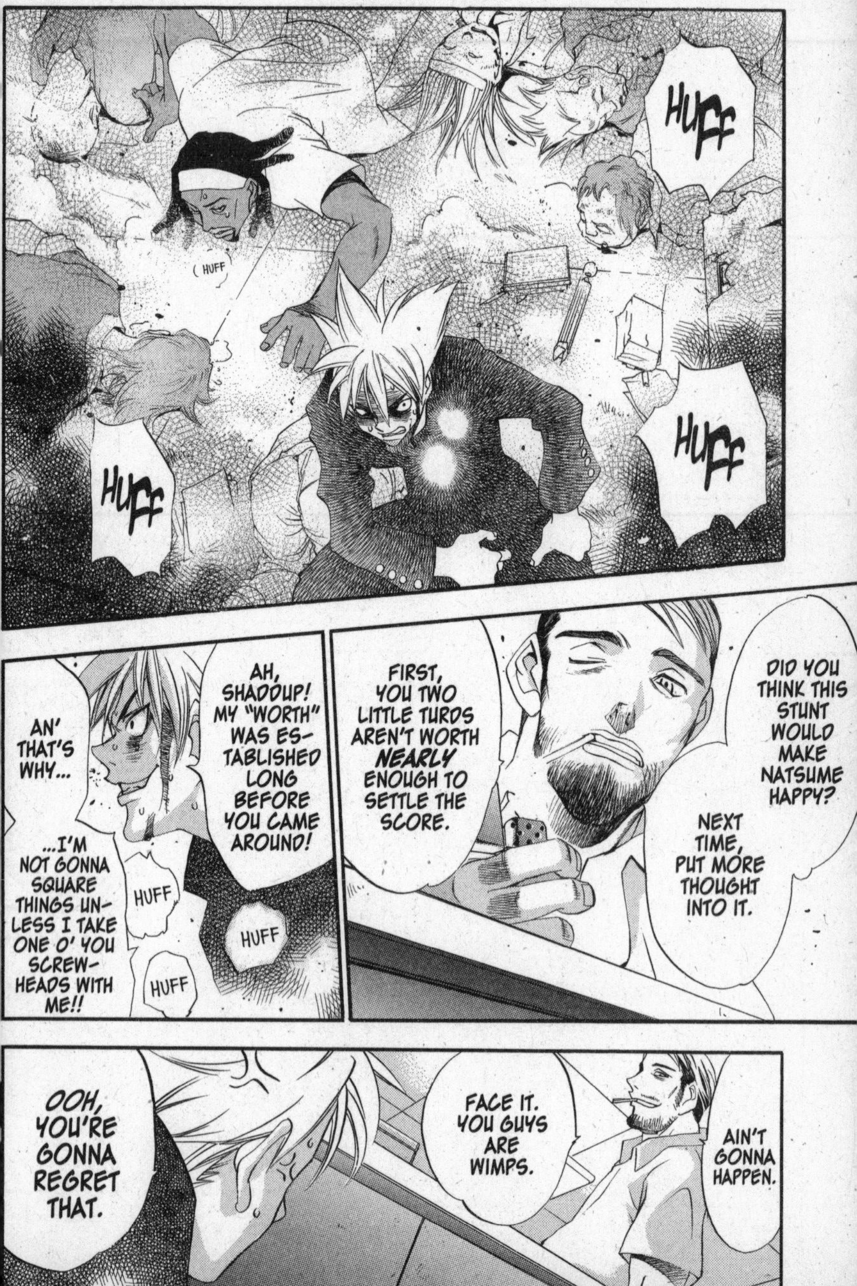
HUFF
HUFF
(HUFF
HUFF
DID YOU THINK THIS STUNT WOULD MAKE NATSUME HAPPY?
NEXT TIME, PUT MORE THOUGHT INTO IT.
FIRST, YOU TWO LITTLE TURDS AREN'T WORTH *NEARLY* ENOUGH TO SETTLE THE SCORE.
AH, SHADDUP! MY "WORTH" WAS ES-TABLISHED LONG BEFORE YOU CAME AROUND!
AN' THAT'S WHY...
...I'M NOT GONNA SQUARE THINGS UN-LESS I TAKE ONE O' YOU SCREW-HEADS WITH ME!!
HUFF
HUFF
HUFF
AIN'T GONNA HAPPEN.
FACE IT. YOU GUYS ARE WIMPS.
OOH, YOU'RE GONNA REGRET THAT.

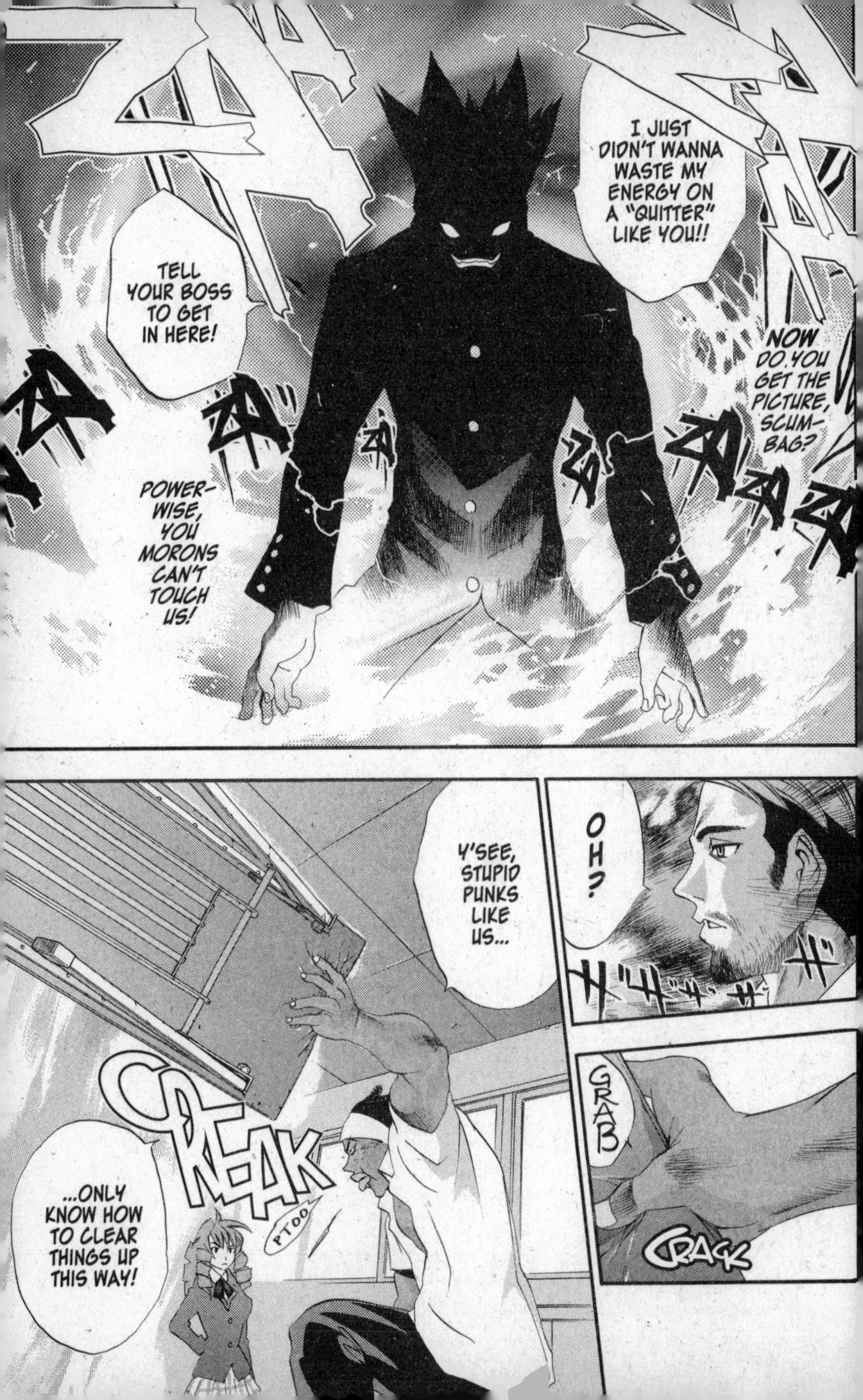
I JUST DIDN'T WANNA WASTE MY ENERGY ON A "QUITTER" LIKE YOU!!
TELL YOUR BOSS TO GET IN HERE!
NOW DO YOU GET THE PICTURE, SCUM-BAG?
POWER-WISE, YOU MORONS CAN'T TOUCH US!
OH?
GRAB
CRACK
Y'SEE, STUPID PUNKS LIKE US...
CREAK
PTOO
...ONLY KNOW HOW TO CLEAR THINGS UP THIS WAY!

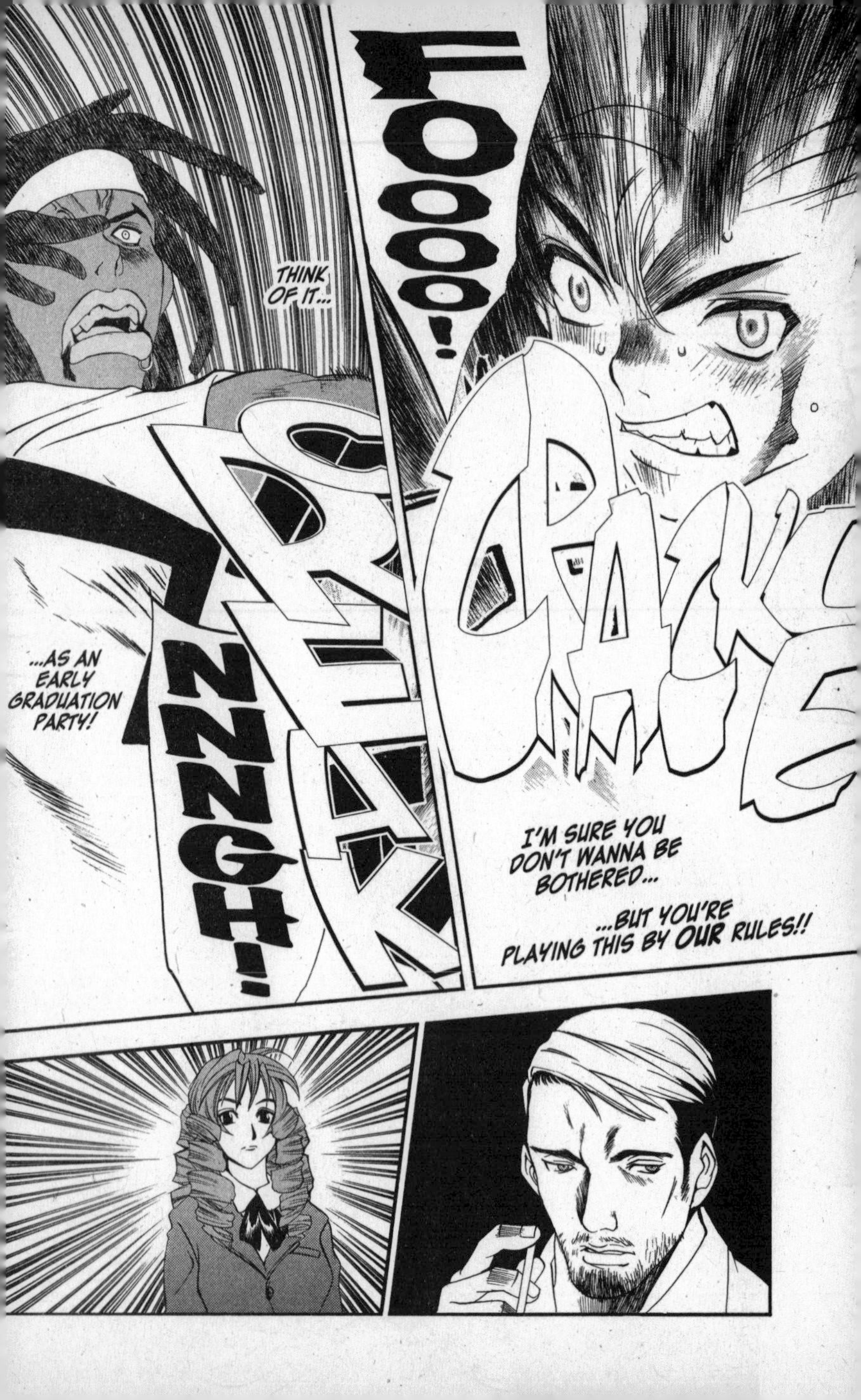
CRACK
I'M SURE YOU DON'T WANNA BE BOTHERED...
...BUT YOU'RE PLAYING THIS BY OUR RULES!!
FOOOO!
THINK OF IT...
...AS AN EARLY GRADUATION PARTY!

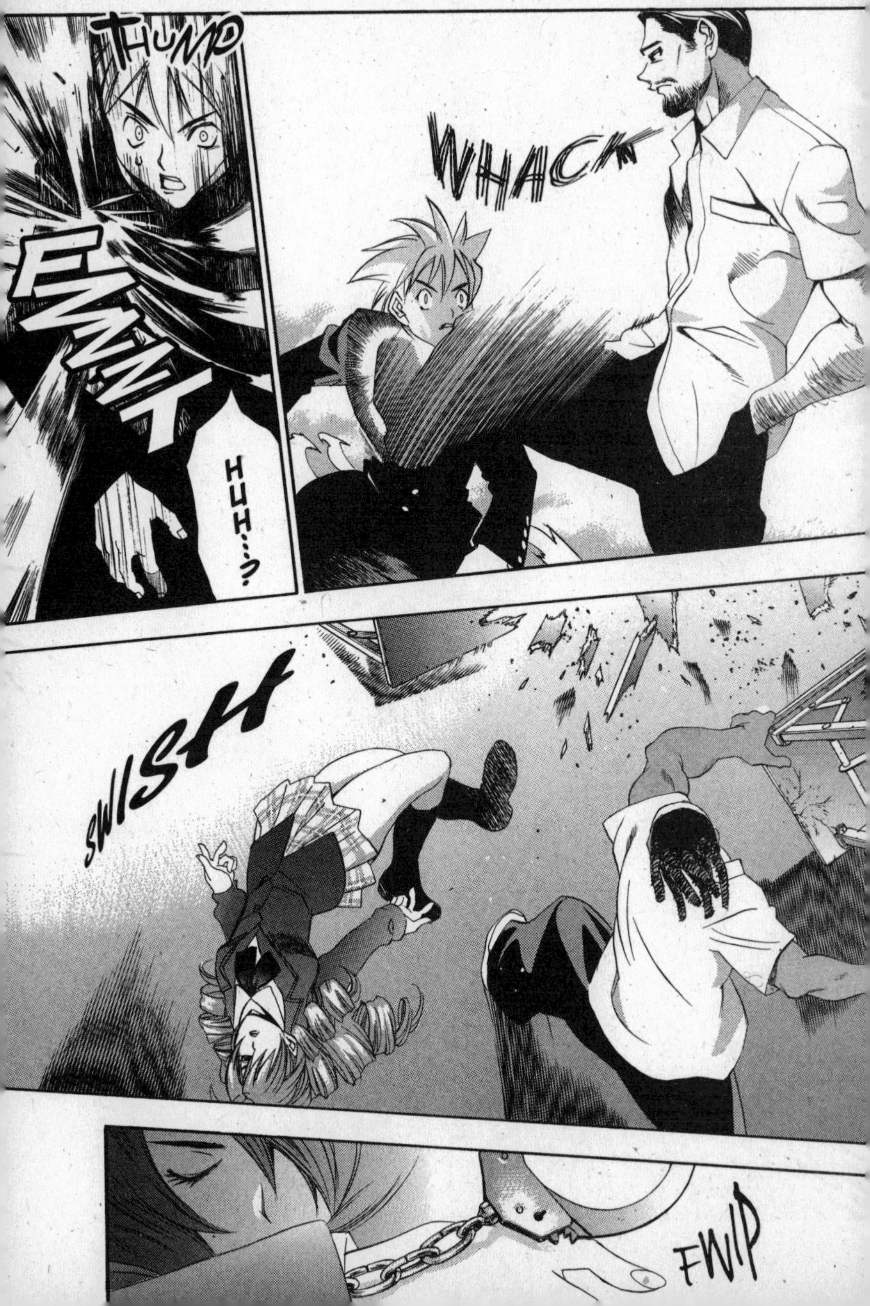
WHACK
THUMP
FWNNK
HUH...?
SWISH
FWIP

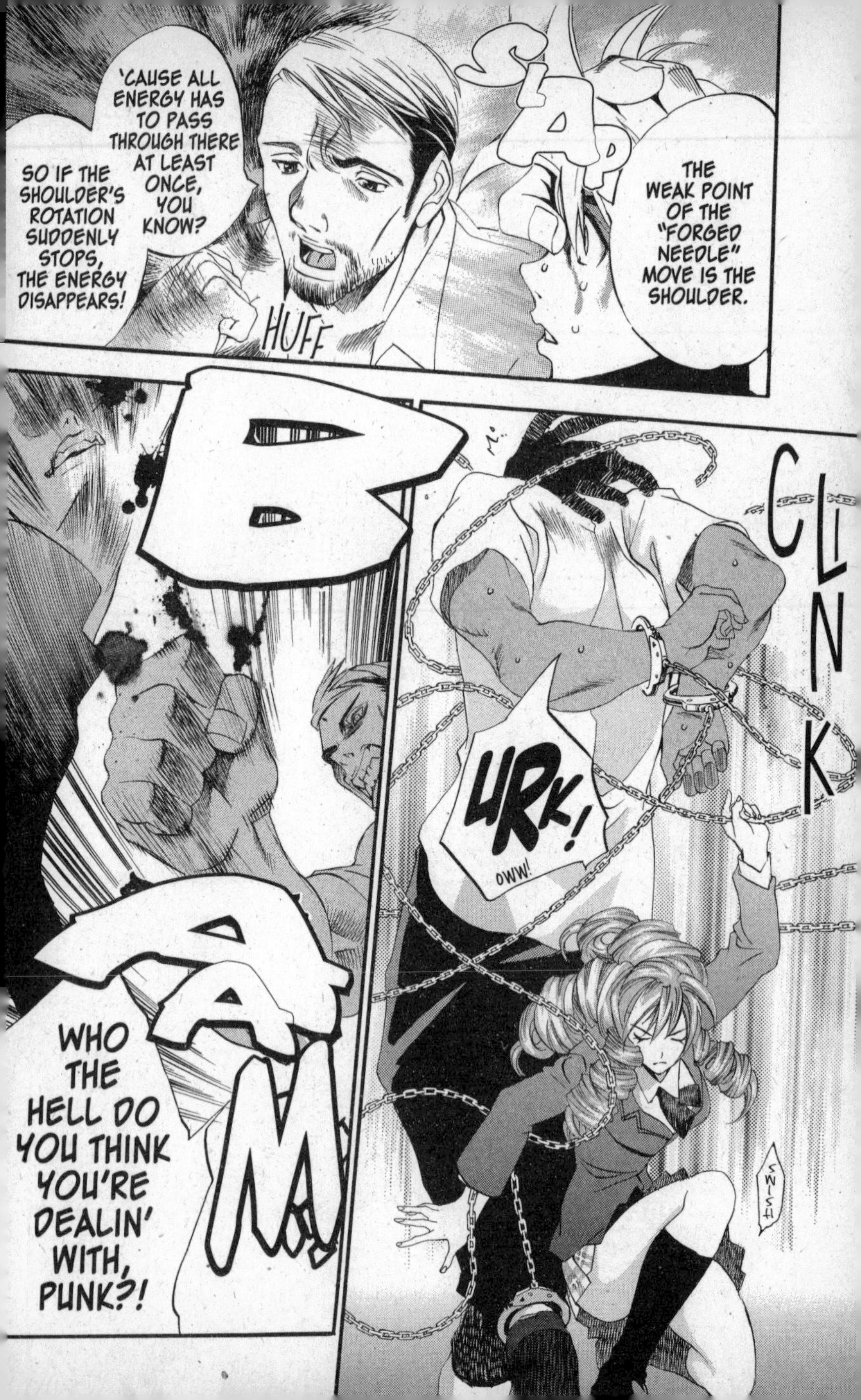
SLAP
THE WEAK POINT OF THE "FORGED NEEDLE" MOVE IS THE SHOULDER.
'CAUSE ALL ENERGY HAS TO PASS THROUGH THERE AT LEAST ONCE, YOU KNOW?
SO IF THE SHOULDER'S ROTATION SUDDENLY STOPS, THE ENERGY DISAPPEARS!
HUFF
CLINK
URK!
OWW!
SWISH
BAM
WHO THE HELL DO YOU THINK YOU'RE DEALIN' WITH, PUNK?!

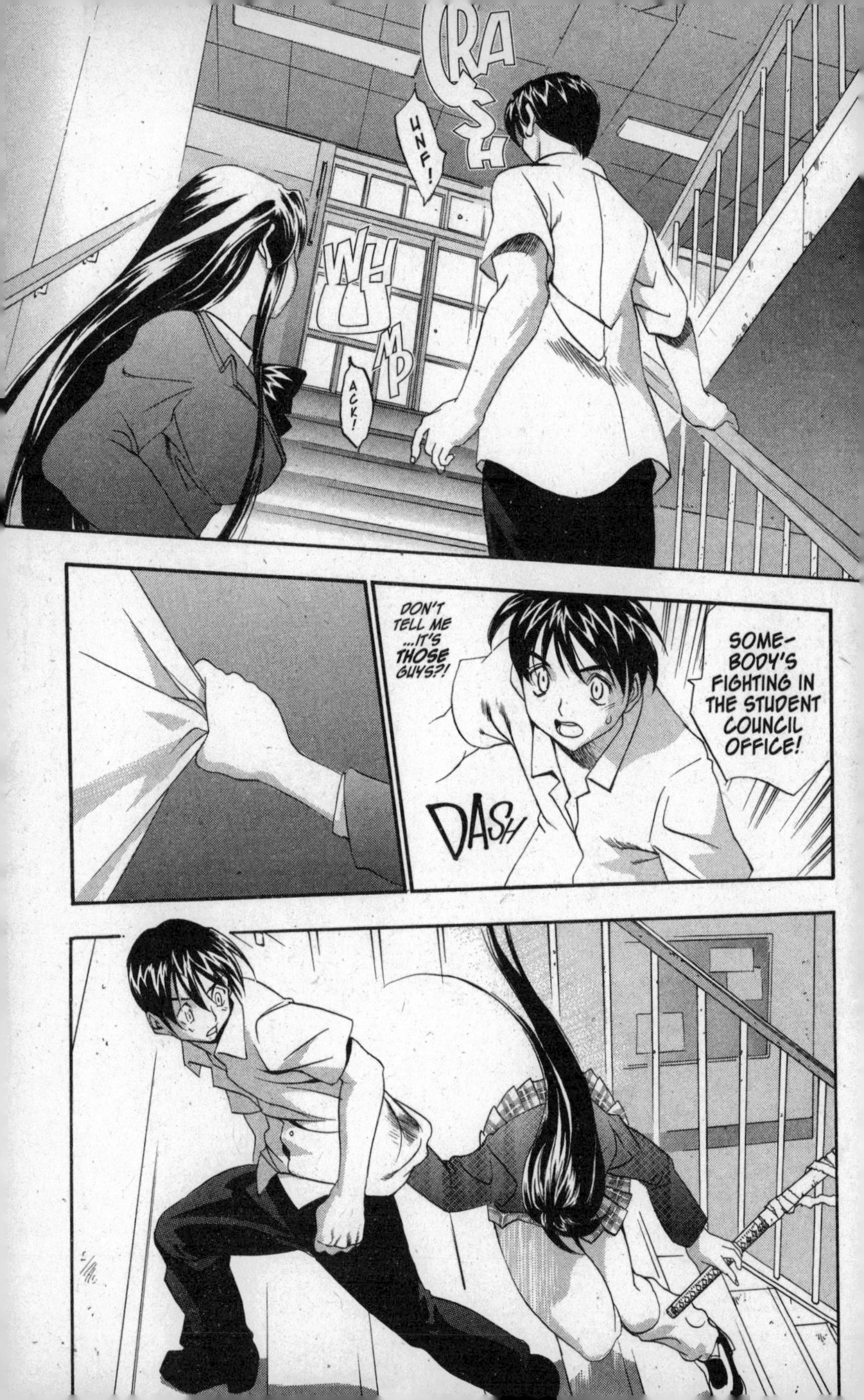
CRASH
UNF!
WHUMP
ACK!
SOME-BODY'S FIGHTING IN THE STUDENT COUNCIL OFFICE!
DON'T TELL ME ...IT'S THOSE GUYS?!
DASH

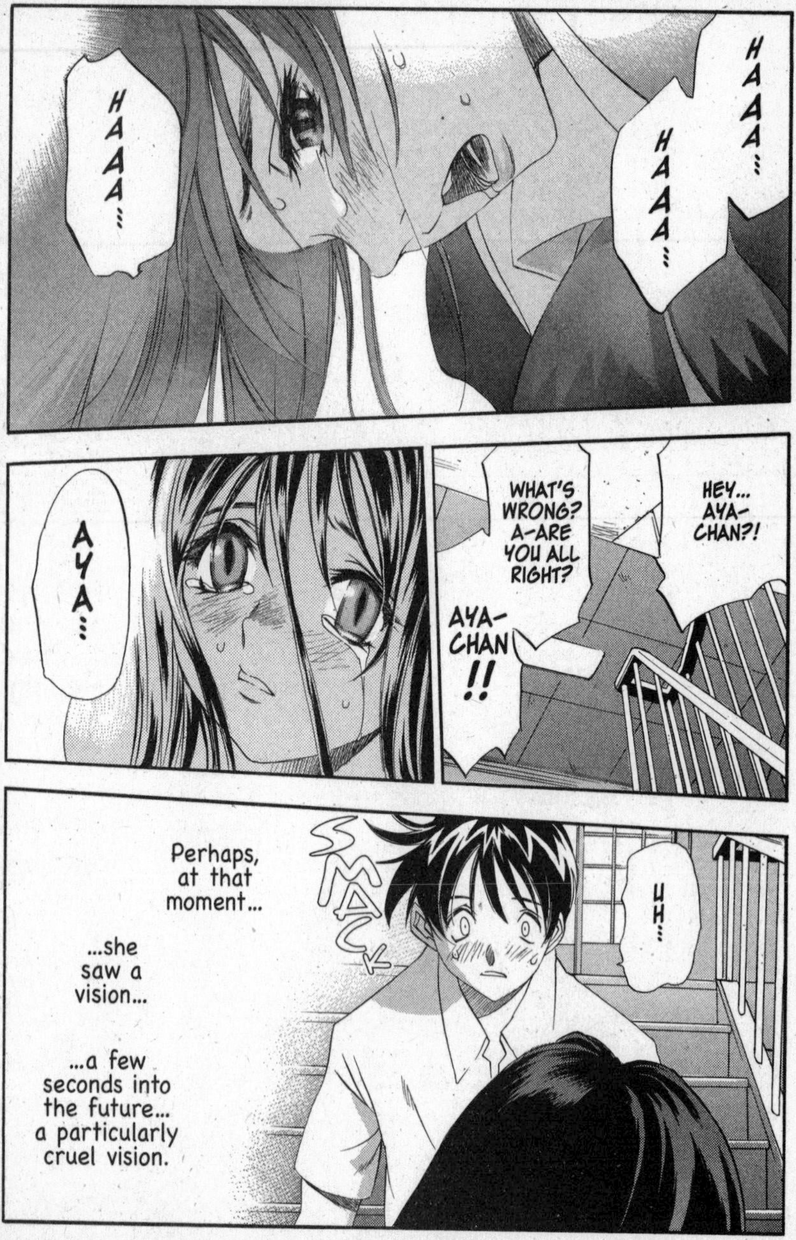
HAAAA...
HAAAA...
HAAAA...
HEY... AYA-CHAN?!
WHAT'S WRONG? A-ARE YOU ALL RIGHT?
AYA-CHAN!!
AYA...
UH...
SMACK
Perhaps, at that moment...
...she saw a vision...
...a few seconds into the future... a particularly cruel vision.

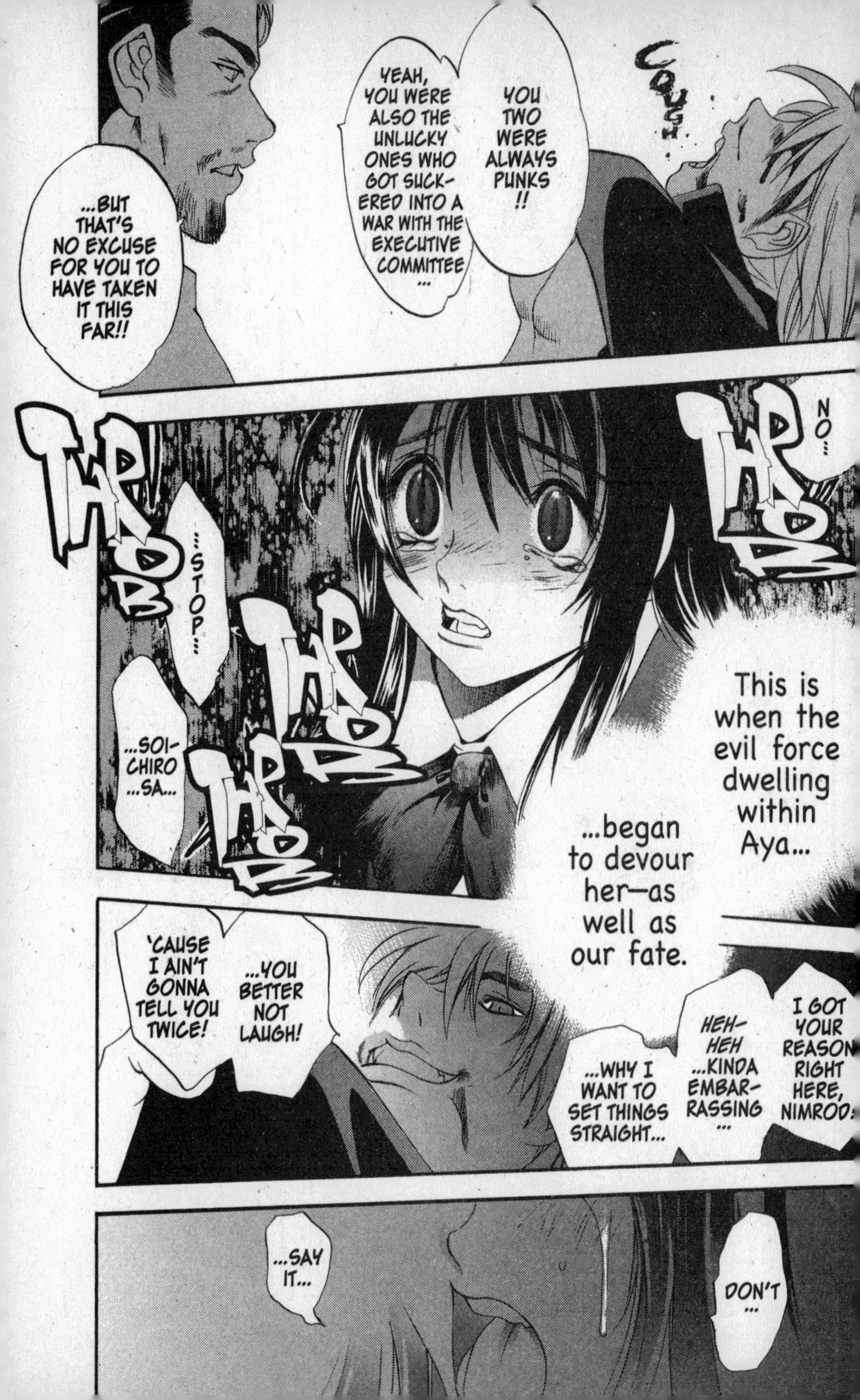
COUGH
YOU TWO WERE ALWAYS PUNKS!!
YEAH, YOU WERE ALSO THE UNLUCKY ONES WHO GOT SUCKERED INTO A WAR WITH THE EXECUTIVE COMMITTEE...
...BUT THAT'S NO EXCUSE FOR YOU TO HAVE TAKEN IT THIS FAR!!
NO...
THROB
This is when the evil force dwelling within Aya...
...began to devour her—as well as our fate.
THROB
THROB
...STOP...
THROB
...SOI-CHIRO ...SA...
I GOT YOUR REASON RIGHT HERE, NIMROD:
HEH-HEH ...KINDA EMBARRASSING...
...WHY I WANT TO SET THINGS STRAIGHT...
...YOU BETTER NOT LAUGH!
'CAUSE I AIN'T GONNA TELL YOU TWICE!
DON'T...
...SAY IT...

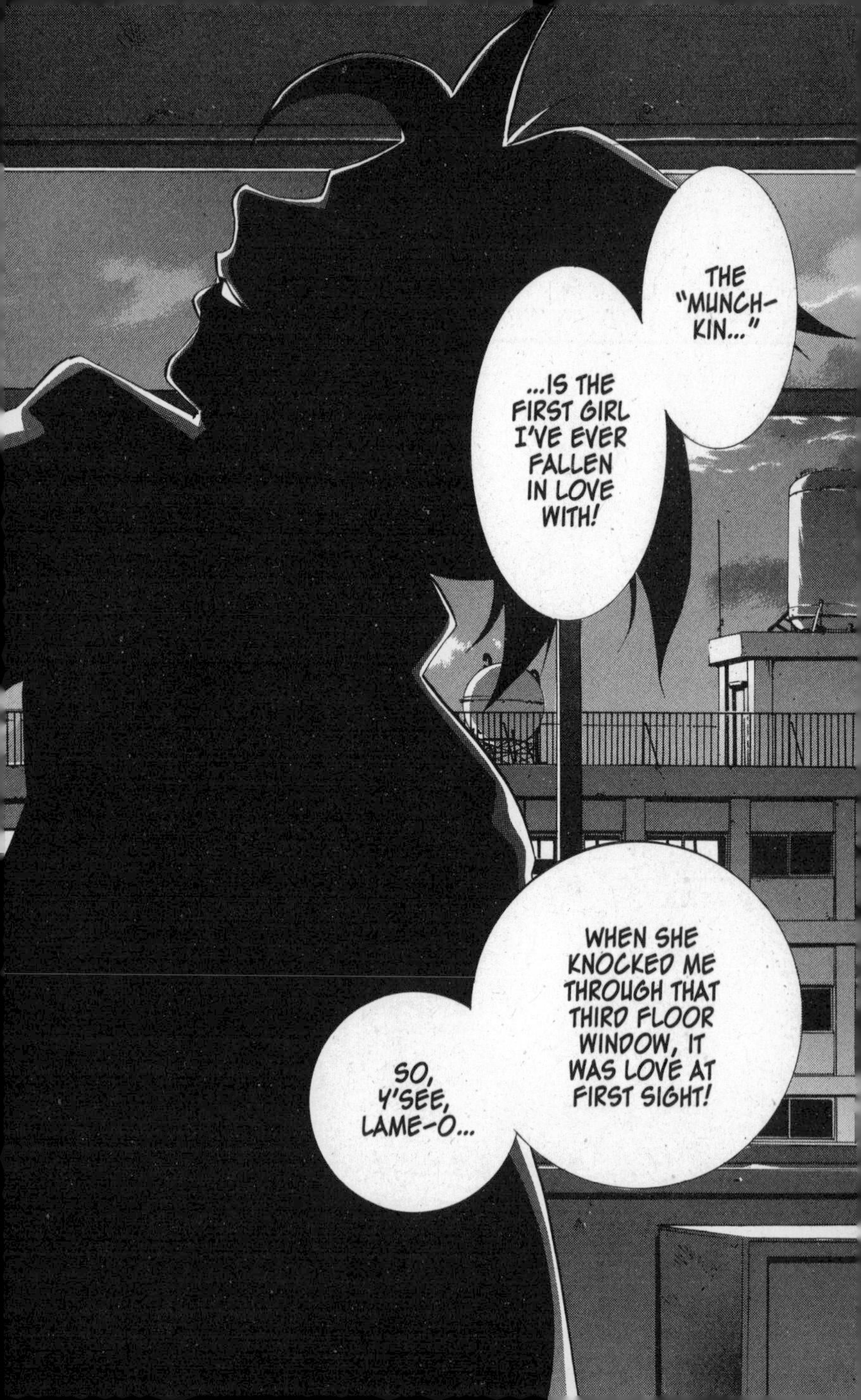
THE "MUNCH-KIN..."
...IS THE FIRST GIRL I'VE EVER FALLEN IN LOVE WITH!
WHEN SHE KNOCKED ME THROUGH THAT THIRD FLOOR WINDOW, IT WAS LOVE AT FIRST SIGHT!
SO, Y'SEE, LAME-O...

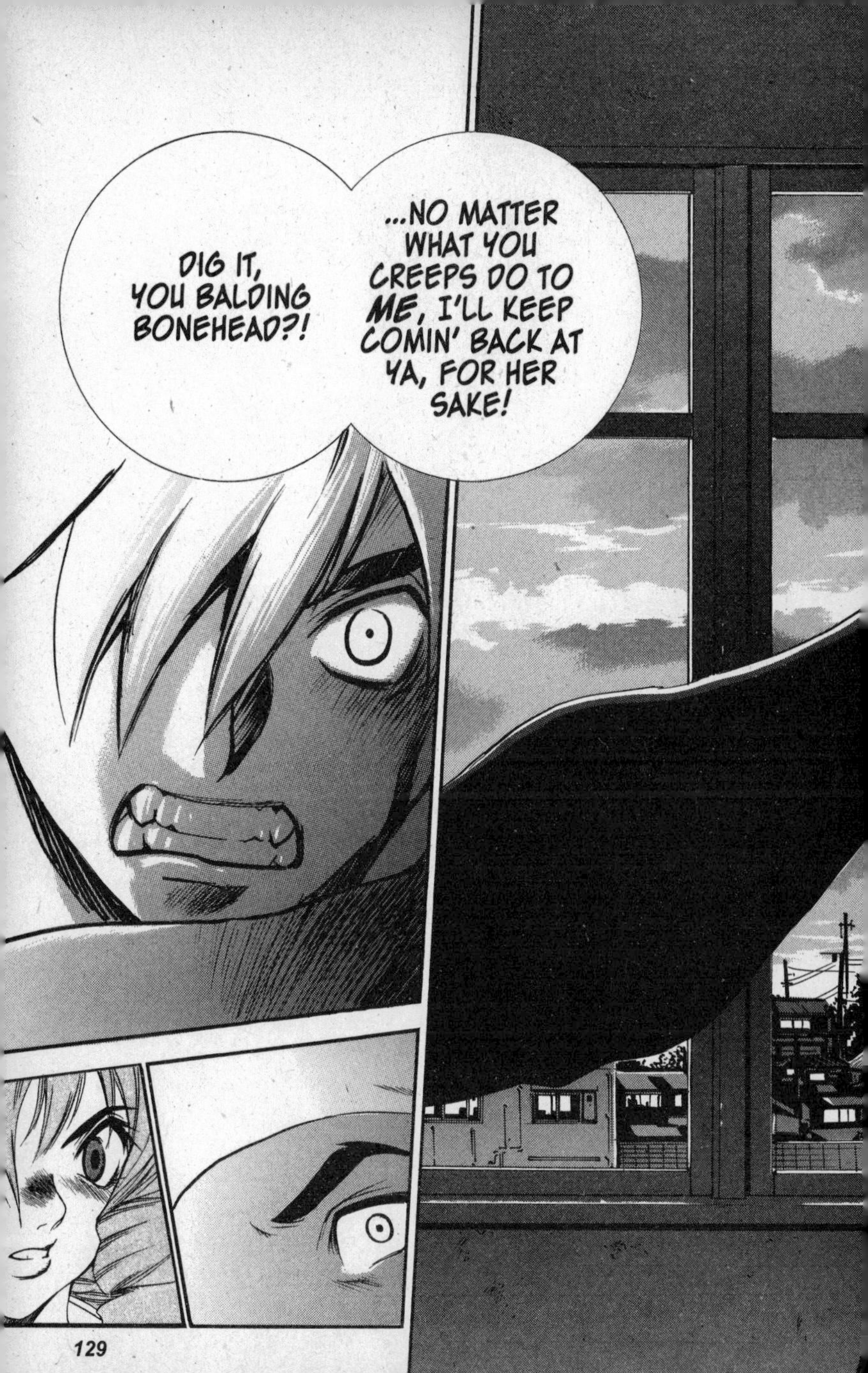
...NO MATTER WHAT YOU CREEPS DO TO *ME*, I'LL KEEP COMIN' BACK AT YA, FOR HER SAKE!
DIG IT, YOU BALDING BONEHEAD?!

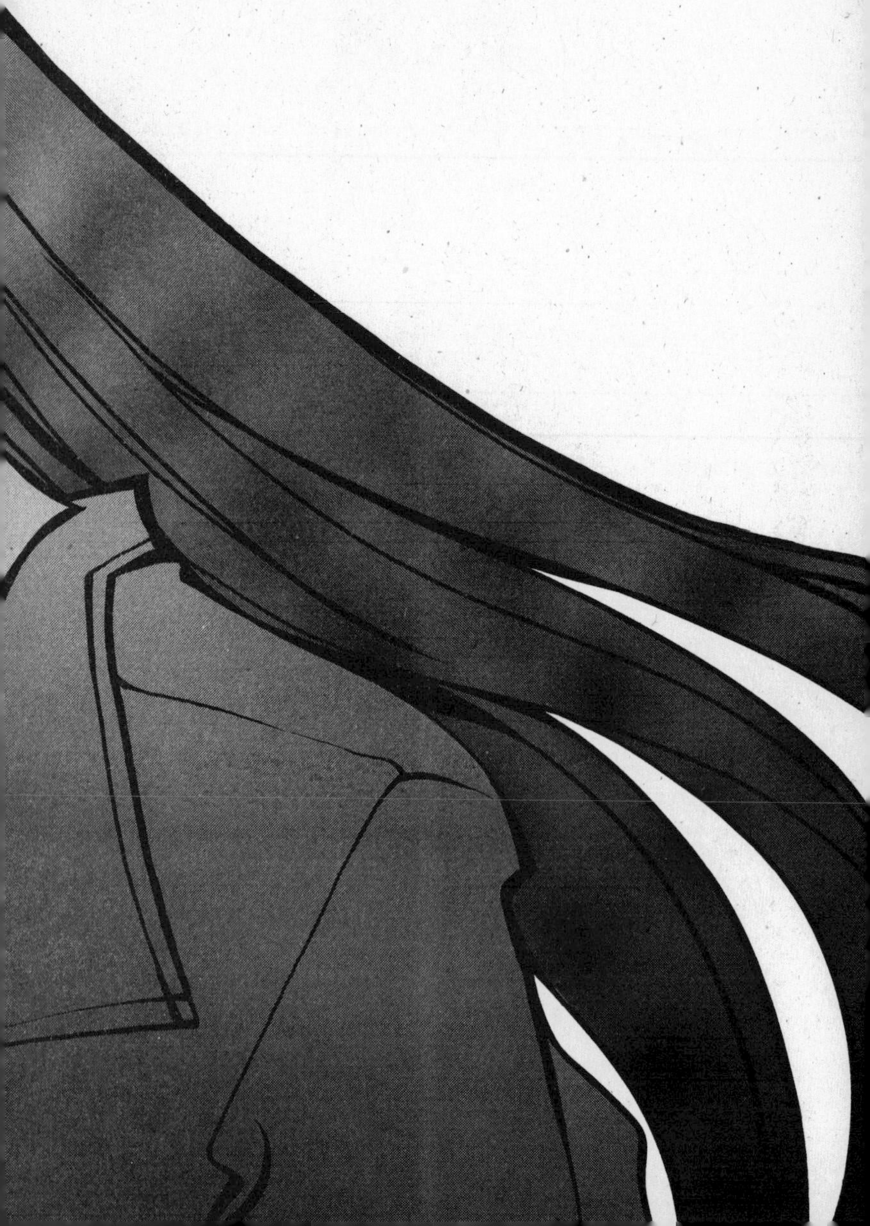

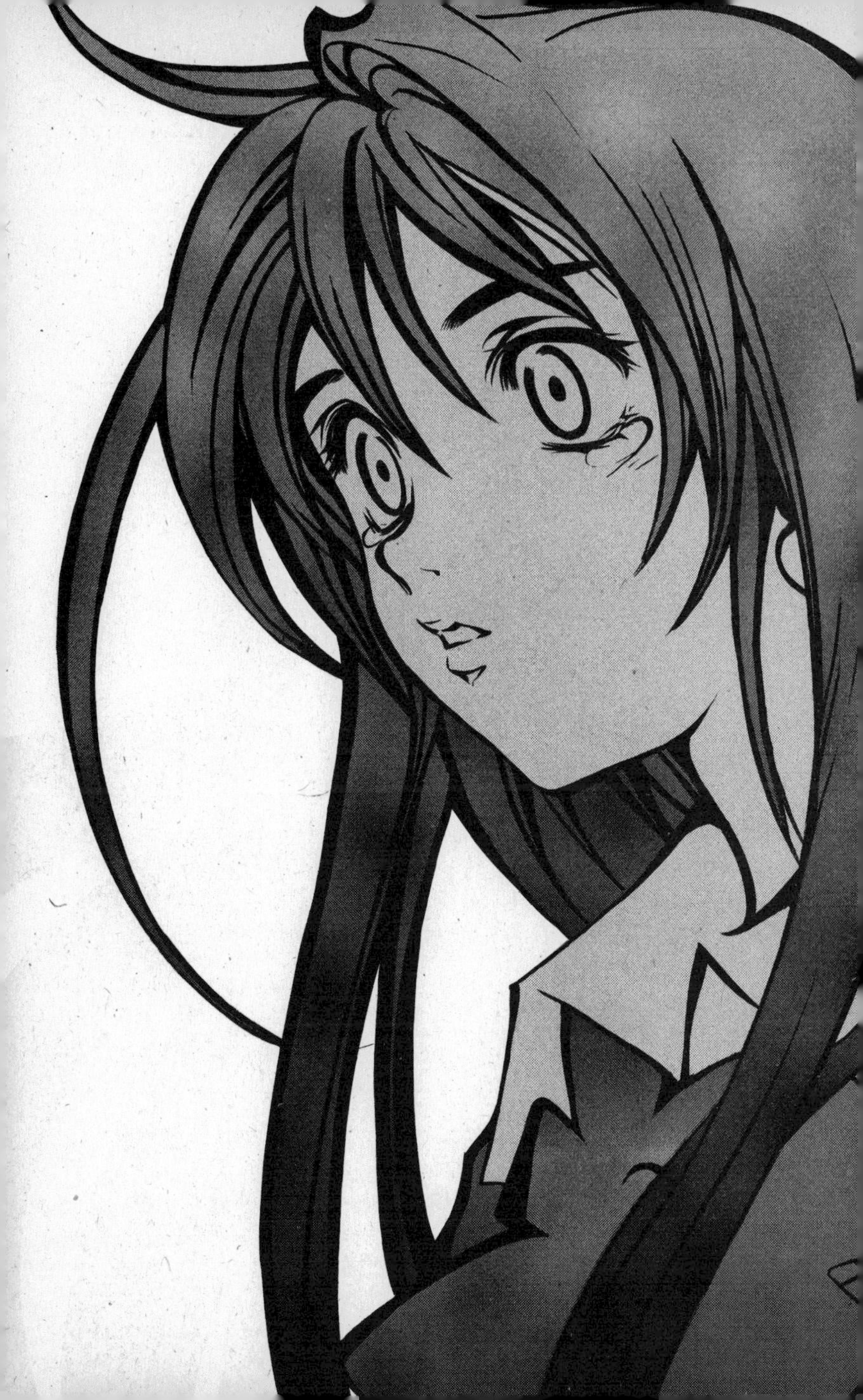

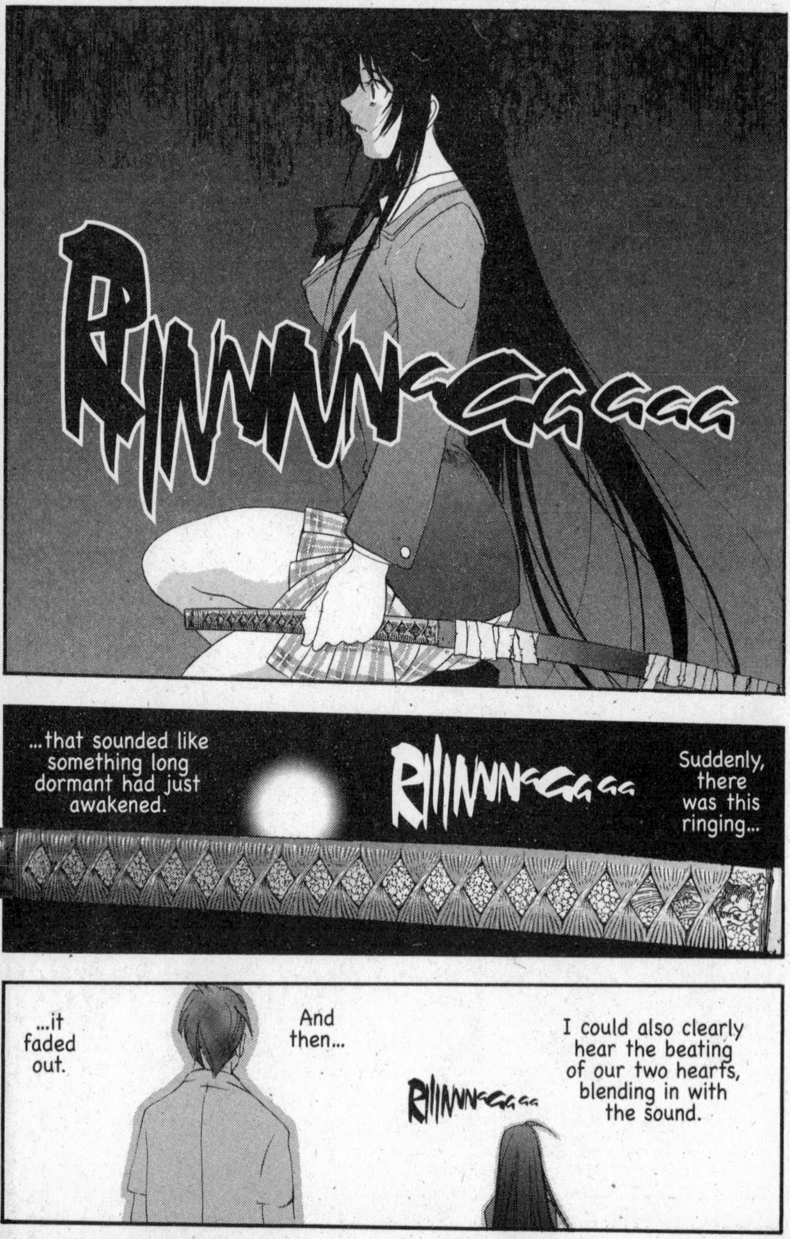
RIINNNNgggggg
Suddenly, there was this ringing...
RIIINNNggggg
...that sounded like something long dormant had just awakened.
I could also clearly hear the beating of our two hearts, blending in with the sound.
RIIINNNggggg
And then...
...it faded out.

FIGHT:24

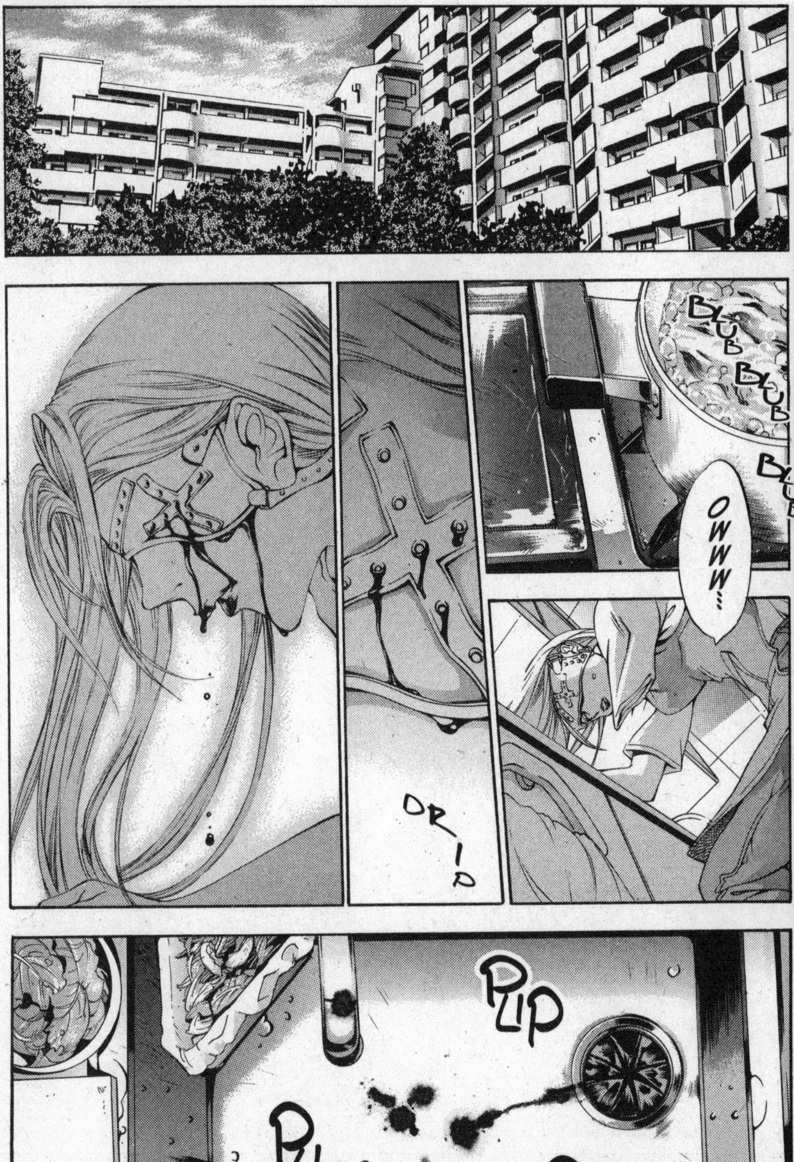
BLUB
BLUB
BLUB
OWWW...
DRIP
PLIP
PLIP
PLIPP

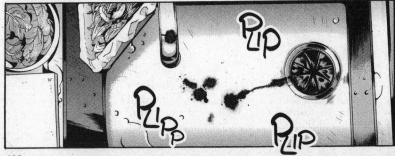

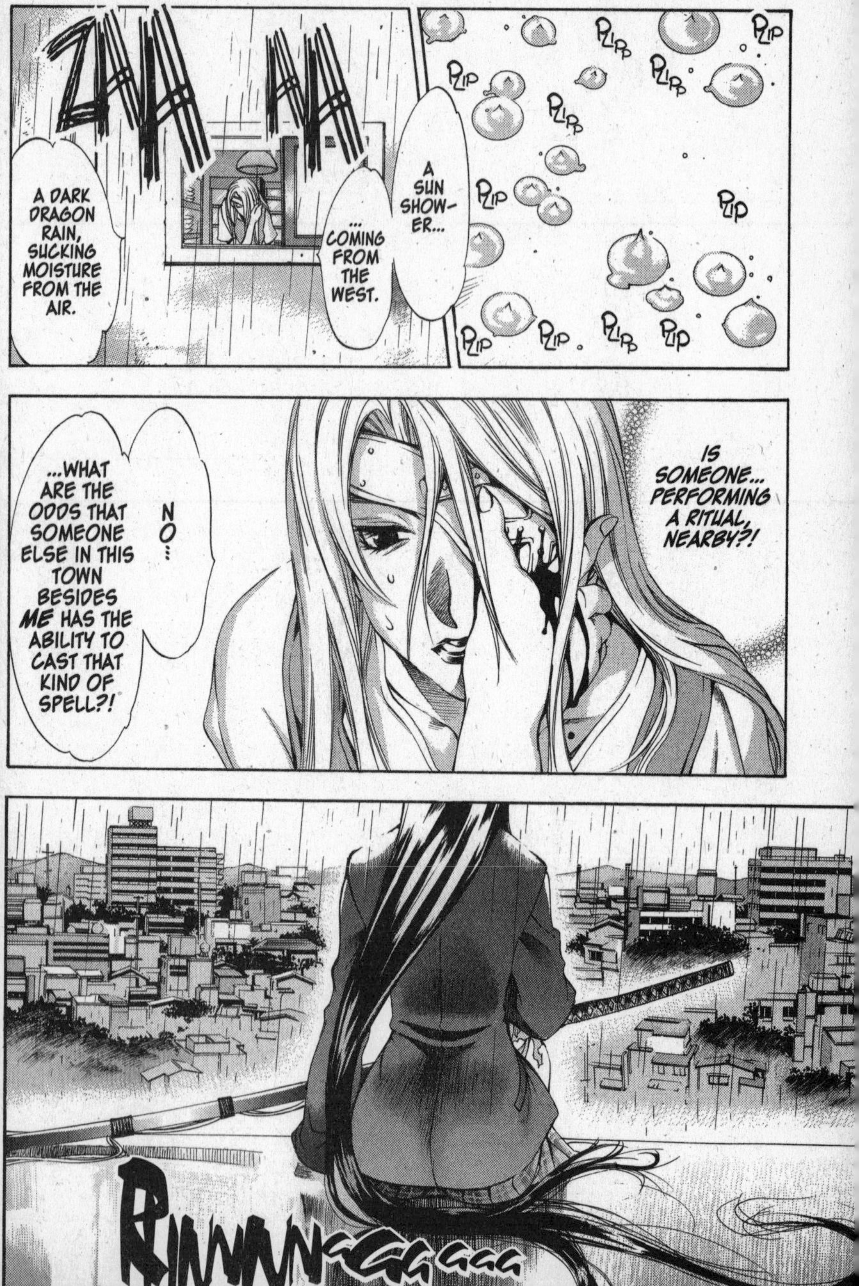

PZIP
PZIPP
PZIP
PZIPP
PZIP
PZIP
PZIP
PZIPP
PZIP
A SUN SHOWER...
...COMING FROM THE WEST.
ZAA AA
A DARK DRAGON RAIN, SUCKING MOISTURE FROM THE AIR.
IS SOMEONE... PERFORMING A RITUAL, NEARBY?!
NO...
...WHAT ARE THE ODDS THAT SOMEONE ELSE IN THIS TOWN BESIDES *ME* HAS THE ABILITY TO CAST THAT KIND OF SPELL?!
RINNNNGGGGGGG

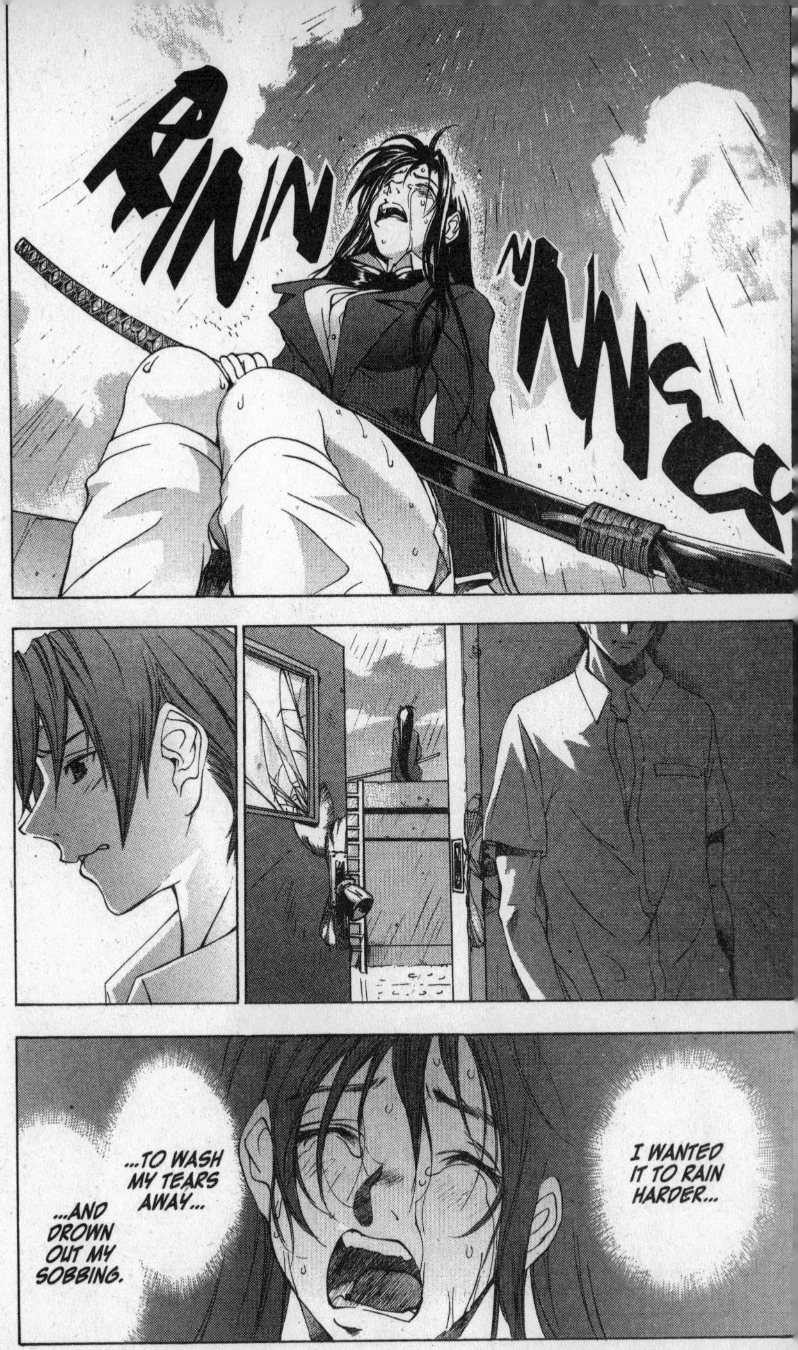
I WANTED IT TO RAIN HARDER...
...TO WASH MY TEARS AWAY...
...AND DROWN OUT MY SOBBING.

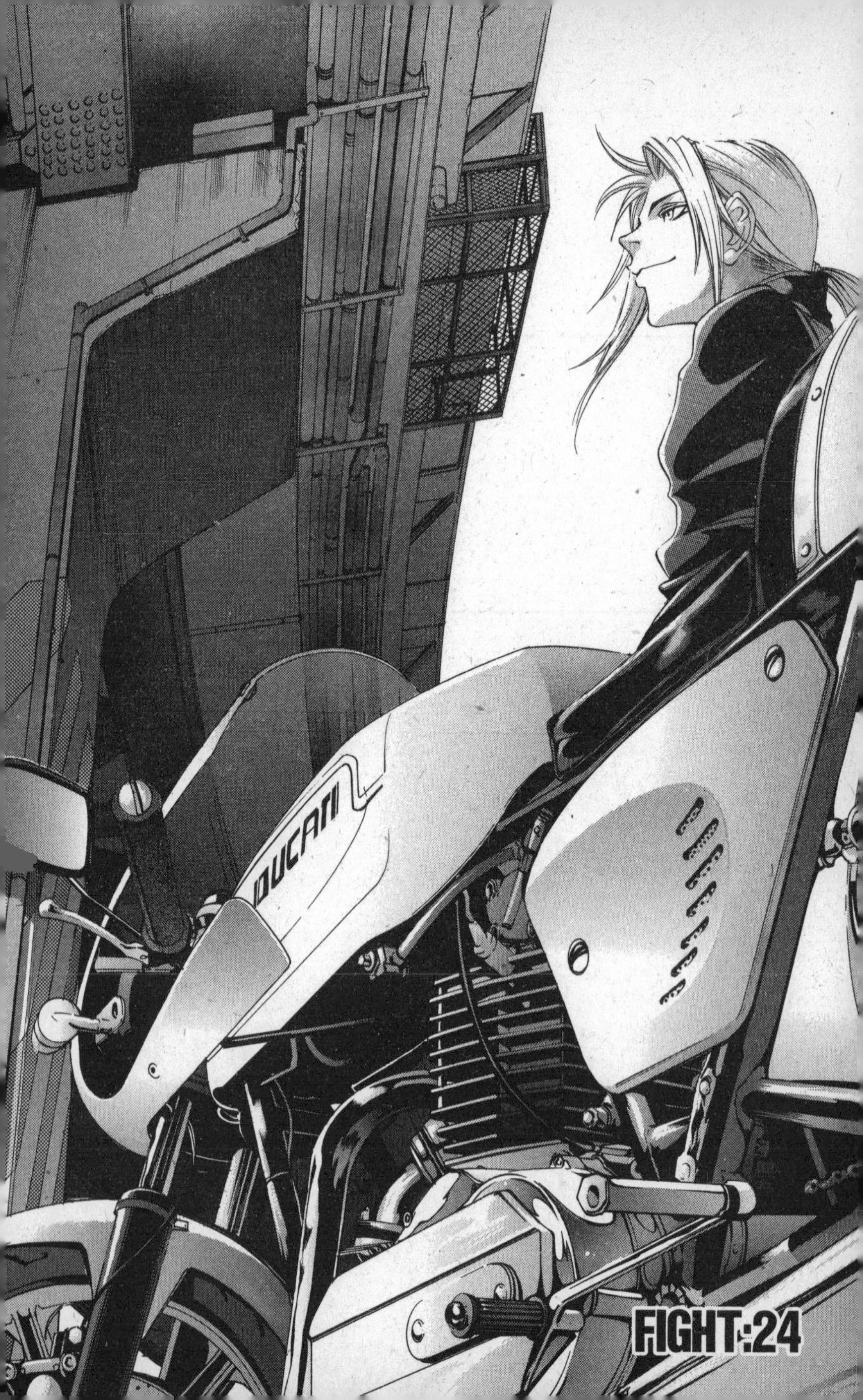
DUCATI
FIGHT:24

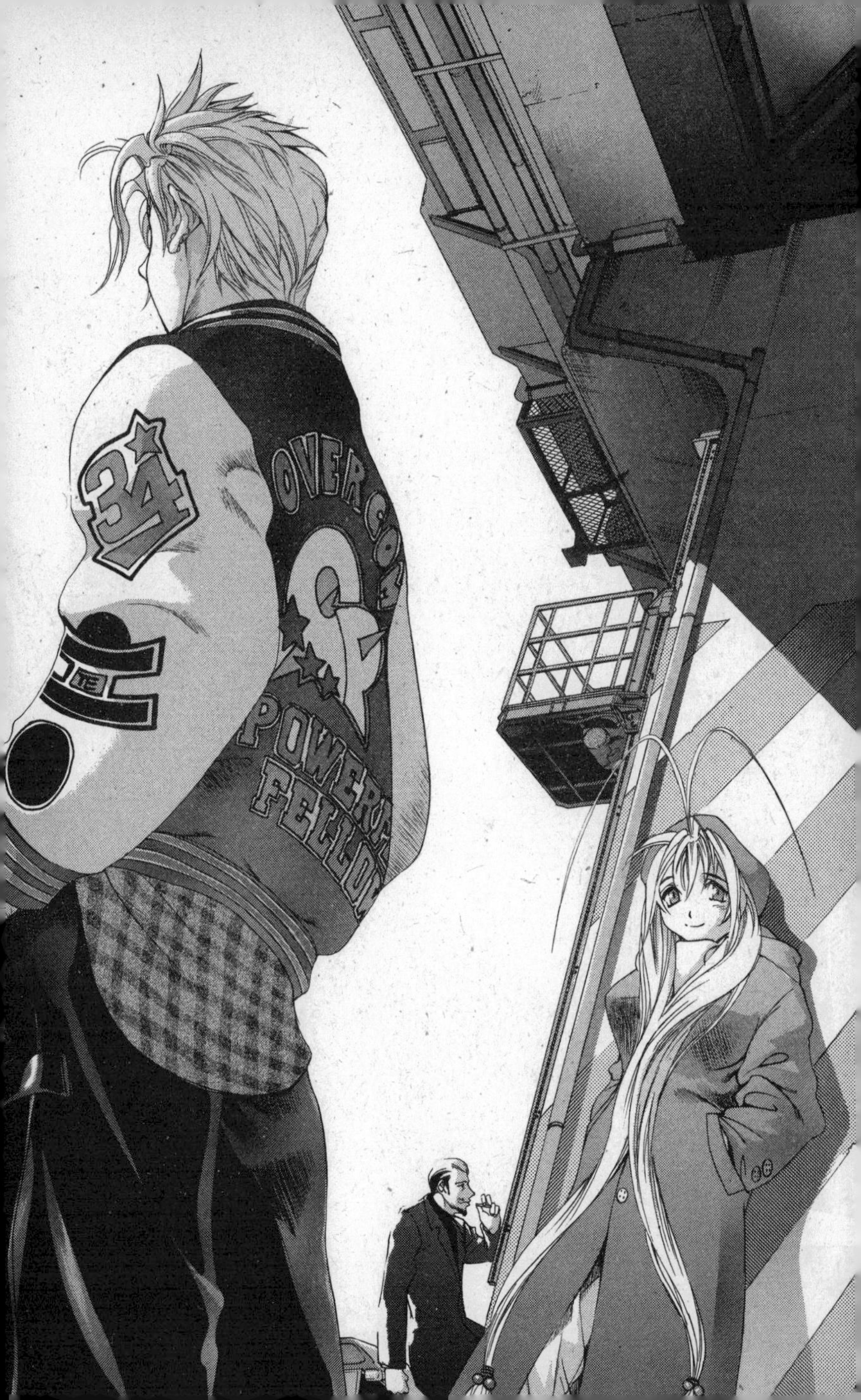
34

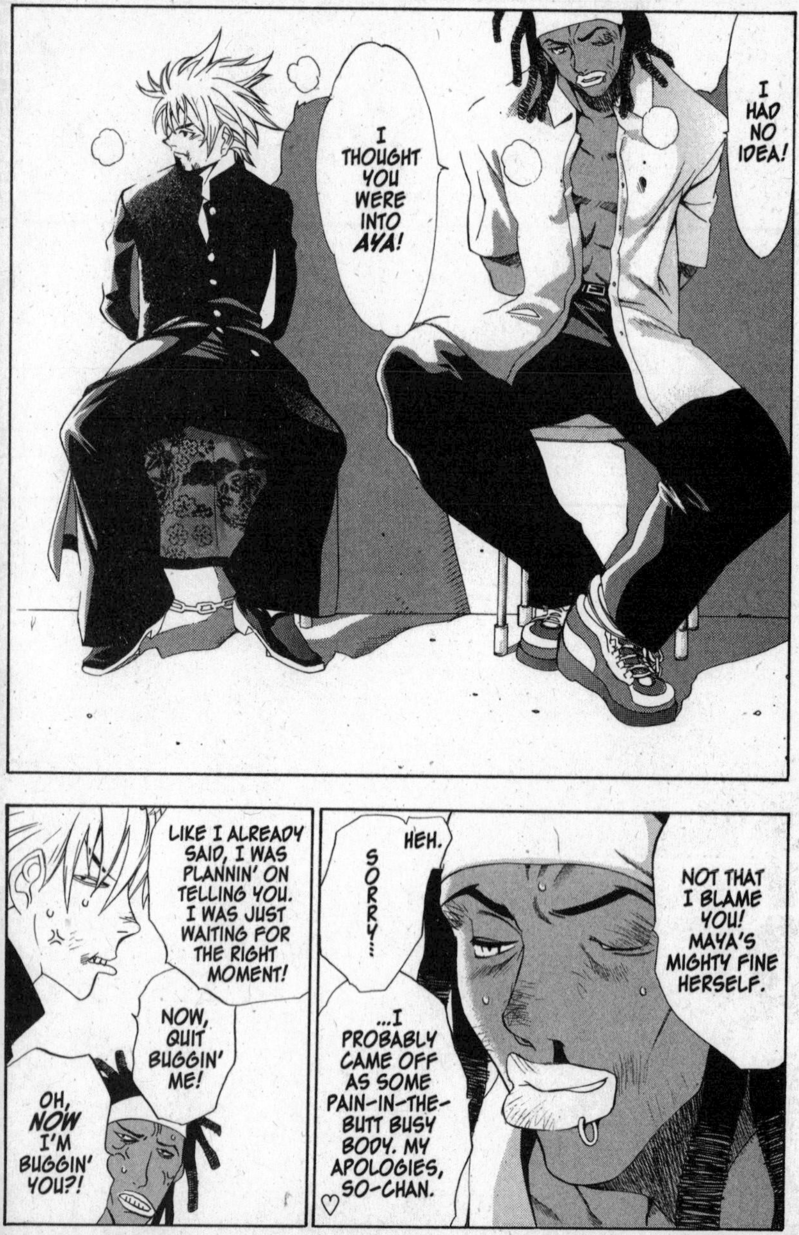
I HAD NO IDEA!
I THOUGHT YOU WERE INTO AYA!
NOT THAT I BLAME YOU! MAYA'S MIGHTY FINE HERSELF.
HEH.
SORRY...
...I PROBABLY CAME OFF AS SOME PAIN-IN-THE-BUTT BUSY BODY. MY APOLOGIES, SO-CHAN. ♡
LIKE I ALREADY SAID, I WAS PLANNIN' ON TELLING YOU. I WAS JUST WAITING FOR THE RIGHT MOMENT!
NOW, QUIT BUGGIN' ME!
OH, NOW I'M BUGGIN' YOU?!

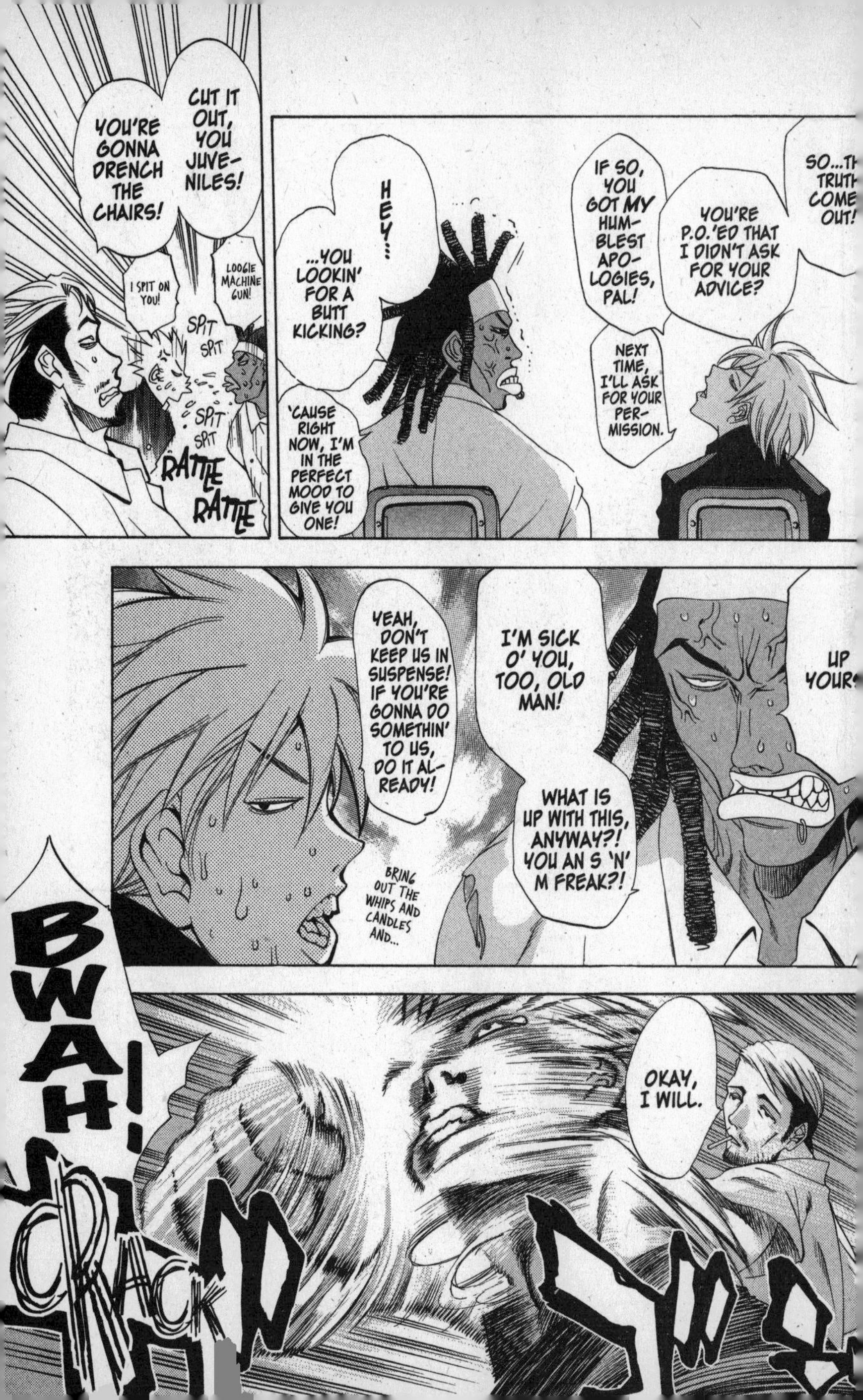
SO...TH TRUTH COME OUT!
YOU'RE P.O.'ED THAT I DIDN'T ASK FOR YOUR ADVICE?
IF SO, YOU GOT MY HUMBLEST APOLOGIES, PAL!
NEXT TIME, I'LL ASK FOR YOUR PERMISSION.
HEY...
...YOU LOOKIN' FOR A BUTT KICKING?
'CAUSE RIGHT NOW, I'M IN THE PERFECT MOOD TO GIVE YOU ONE!
CUT IT OUT, YOU JUVENILES!
YOU'RE GONNA DRENCH THE CHAIRS!
LOOGIE MACHINE GUN!
I SPIT ON YOU!
SPIT SPIT
SPIT SPIT
RATTLE RATTLE
UP YOUR
I'M SICK O' YOU, TOO, OLD MAN!
WHAT IS UP WITH THIS, ANYWAY?! YOU AN S 'N' M FREAK?!
YEAH, DON'T KEEP US IN SUSPENSE! IF YOU'RE GONNA DO SOMETHIN' TO US, DO IT ALREADY!
BRING OUT THE WHIPS AND CANDLES AND...
OKAY, I WILL.
BWAH!
CRACK

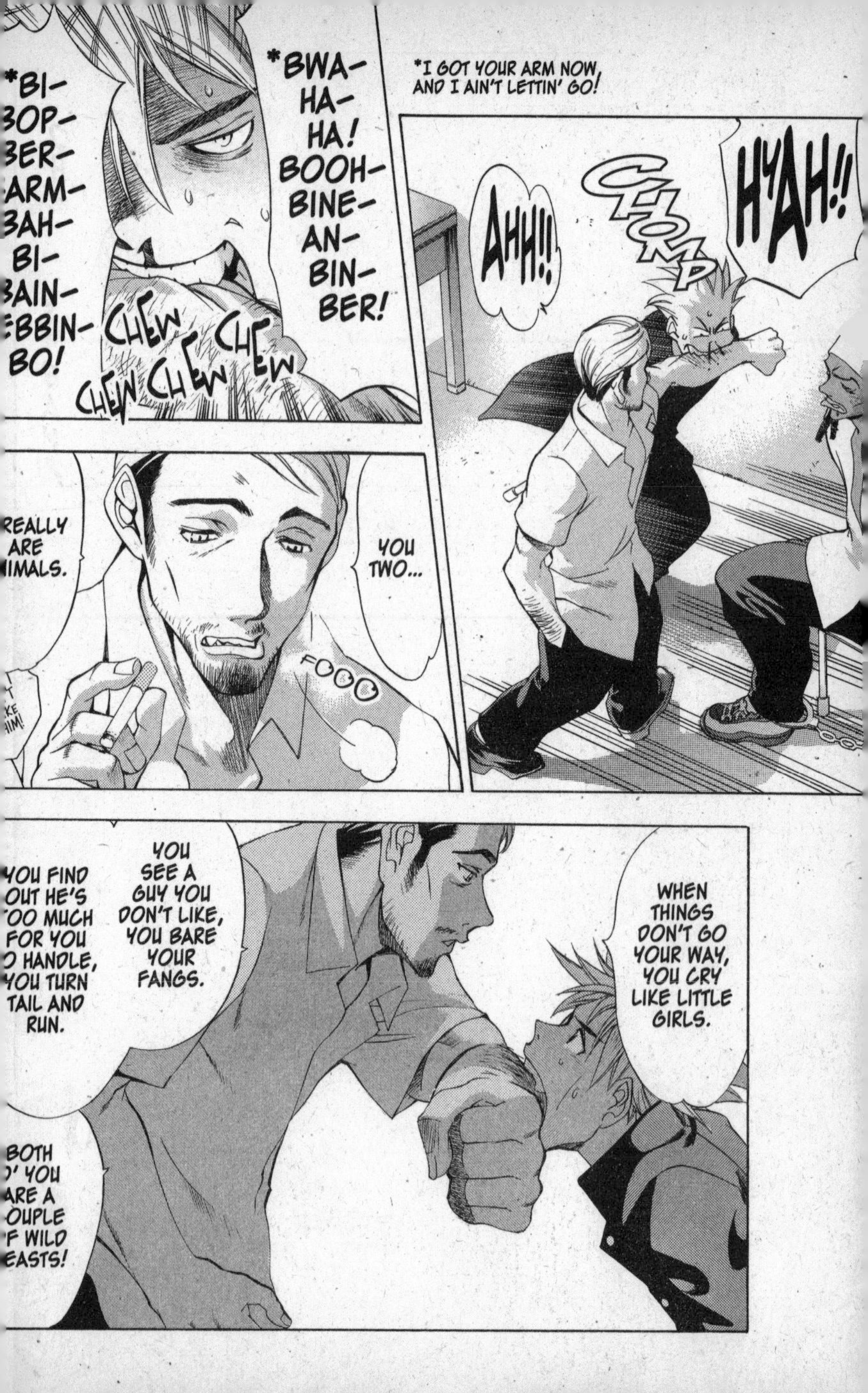
HYAH!!
CHOMP
AHH!!!
*BWA-HA-HA! BOOH-BINE-AN-BIN-BER!
*BI-BOP-BER-ARM-BAH-BI-BAIN-EBBIN-BO!
CHEW CHEW CHEW CHEW CHEW
*I GOT YOUR ARM NOW, AND I AIN'T LETTIN' GO!
YOU TWO...
REALLY ARE IMALS.
FOOO
WHEN THINGS DON'T GO YOUR WAY, YOU CRY LIKE LITTLE GIRLS.
YOU SEE A GUY YOU DON'T LIKE, YOU BARE YOUR FANGS.
YOU FIND OUT HE'S OO MUCH FOR YOU O HANDLE, YOU TURN TAIL AND RUN.
BOTH ' YOU ARE A OUPLE F WILD EASTS!

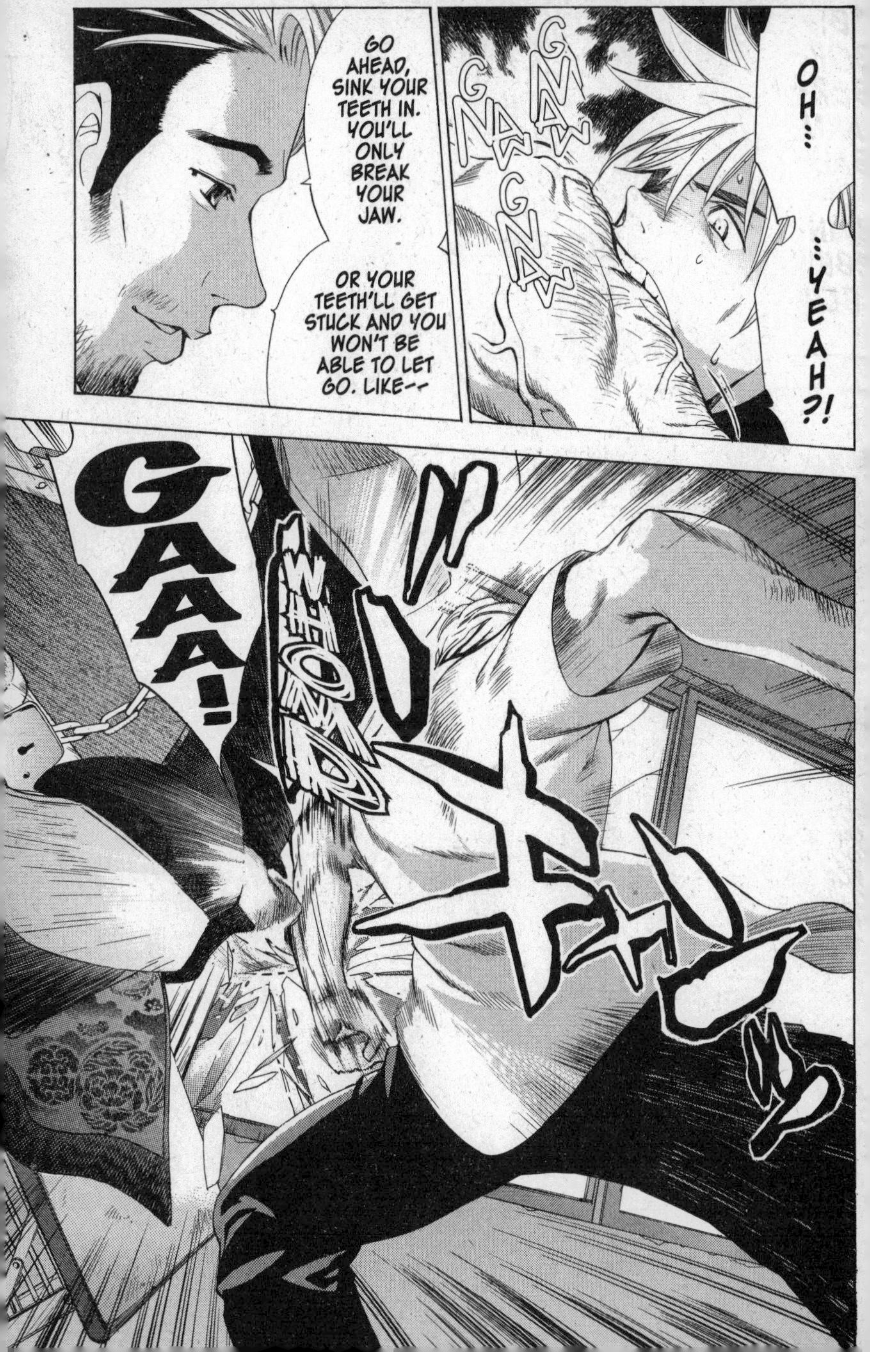
OH... ...YEAH?!
GNAW GNAW GNAW
GO AHEAD, SINK YOUR TEETH IN. YOU'LL ONLY BREAK YOUR JAW.
OR YOUR TEETH'LL GET STUCK AND YOU WON'T BE ABLE TO LET GO. LIKE--
WHOMP
GAAA!

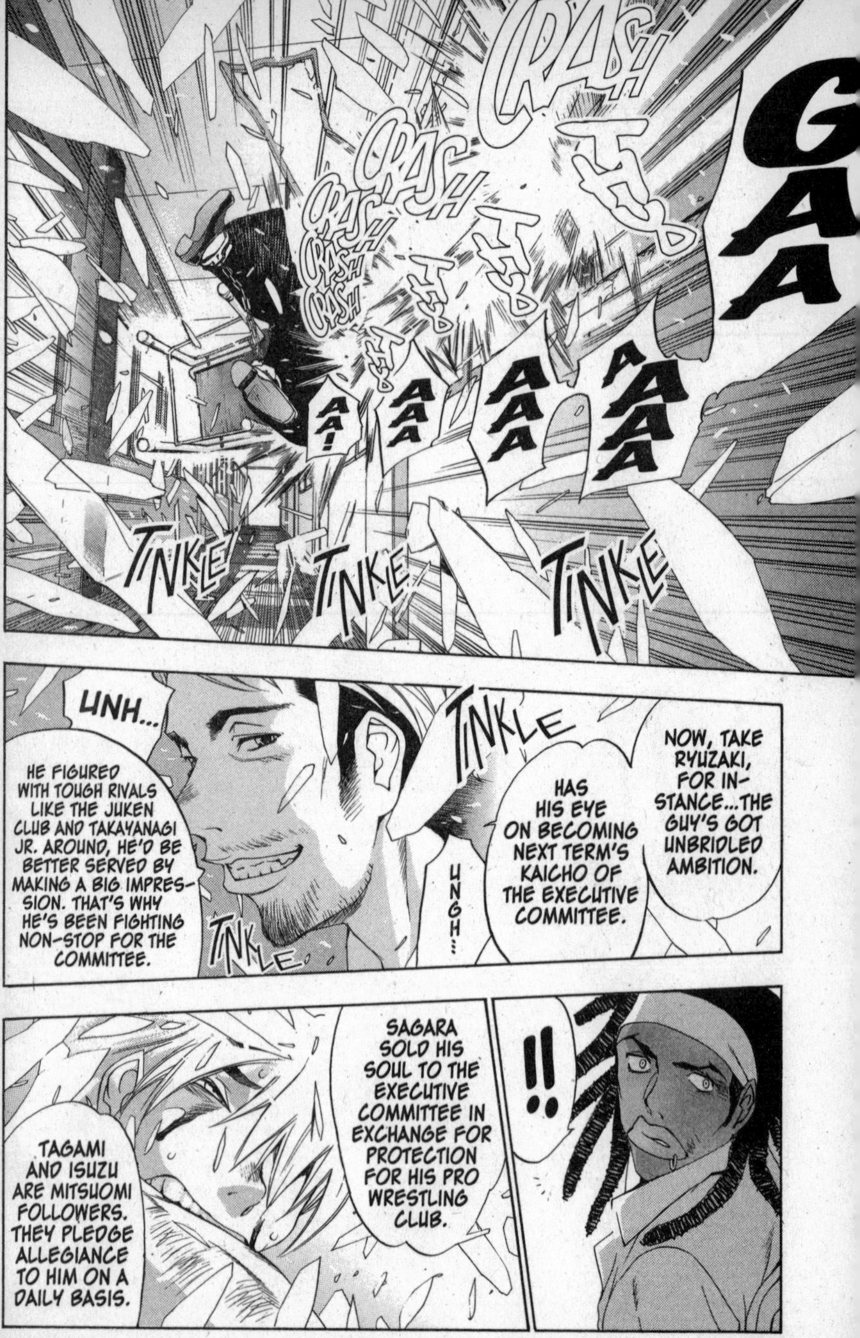
GAA
AAAA
AAAA
AAA
AAA
AA!
CRASH
CRASH
CRASH
CRASH
CRASH
CRASH
TINKLE
TINKLE
TINKLE
NOW, TAKE RYUZAKI, FOR IN-STANCE...THE GUY'S GOT UNBRIDLED AMBITION.
HAS HIS EYE ON BECOMING NEXT TERM'S KAICHO OF THE EXECUTIVE COMMITTEE.
TINKLE
UNGH...
UNH...
HE FIGURED WITH TOUGH RIVALS LIKE THE JUKEN CLUB AND TAKAYANAGI JR. AROUND, HE'D BE BETTER SERVED BY MAKING A BIG IMPRES-SION. THAT'S WHY HE'S BEEN FIGHTING NON-STOP FOR THE COMMITTEE.
TINKLE
!!
SAGARA SOLD HIS SOUL TO THE EXECUTIVE COMMITTEE IN EXCHANGE FOR PROTECTION FOR HIS PRO WRESTLING CLUB.
TAGAMI AND ISUZU ARE MITSUOMI FOLLOWERS. THEY PLEDGE ALLEGIANCE TO HIM ON A DAILY BASIS.

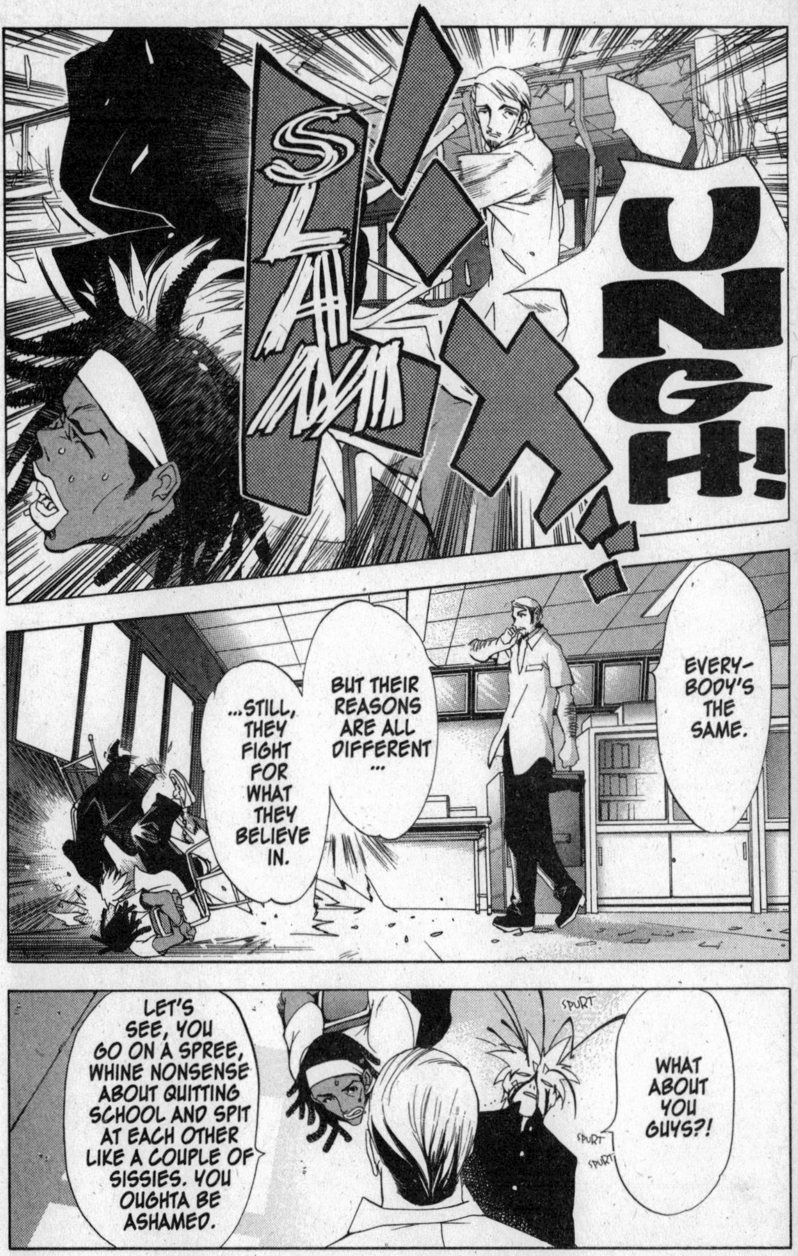
SLAM
UNGH!
EVERYBODY'S THE SAME.
BUT THEIR REASONS ARE ALL DIFFERENT...
...STILL, THEY FIGHT FOR WHAT THEY BELIEVE IN.
SPURT
WHAT ABOUT YOU GUYS?!
SPURT
SPURT
LET'S SEE, YOU GO ON A SPREE, WHINE NONSENSE ABOUT QUITTING SCHOOL AND SPIT AT EACH OTHER LIKE A COUPLE OF SISSIES. YOU OUGHTA BE ASHAMED.

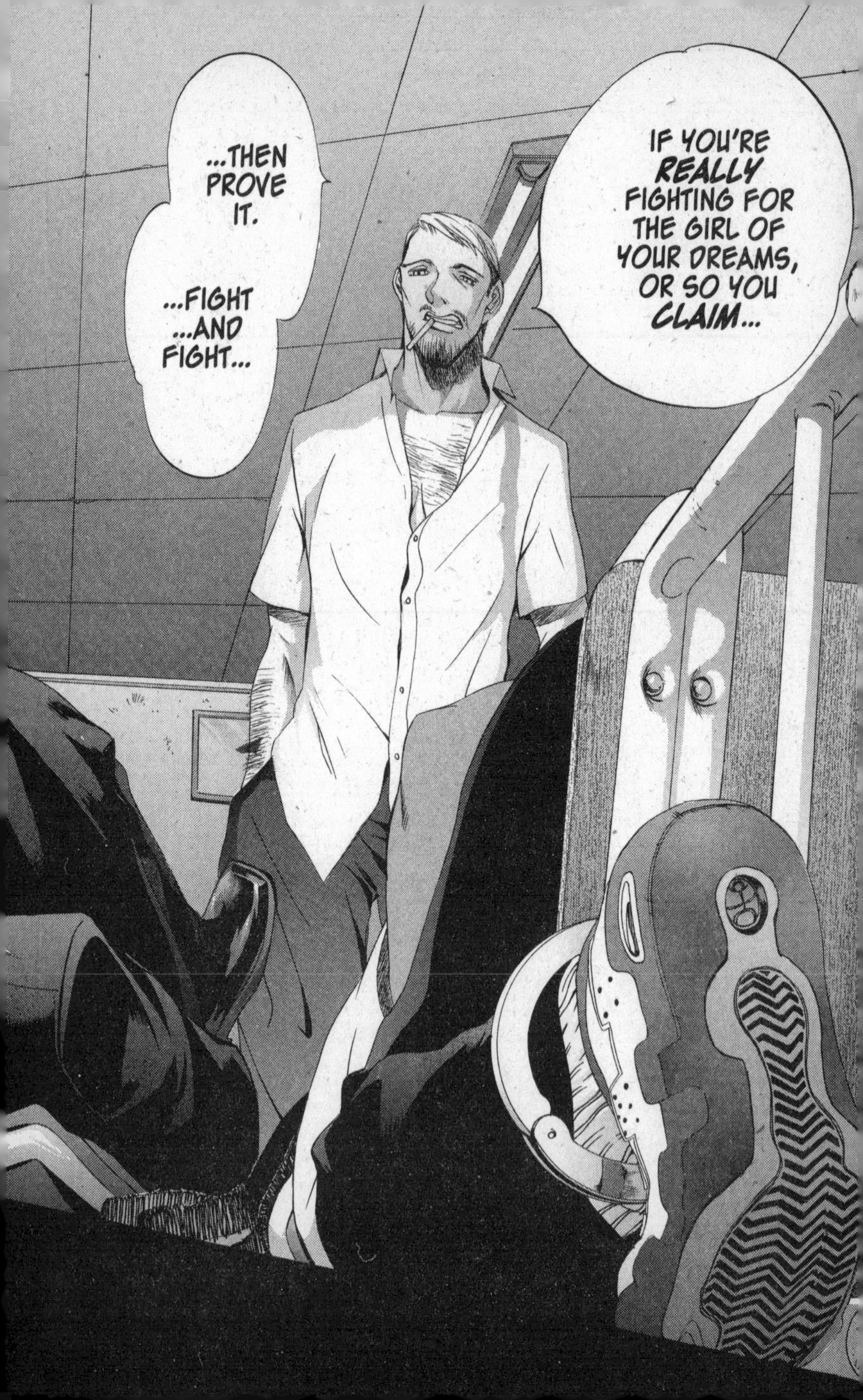
IF YOU'RE *REALLY* FIGHTING FOR THE GIRL OF YOUR DREAMS, OR SO YOU **CLAIM**...
...THEN PROVE IT.
...FIGHT ...AND FIGHT...

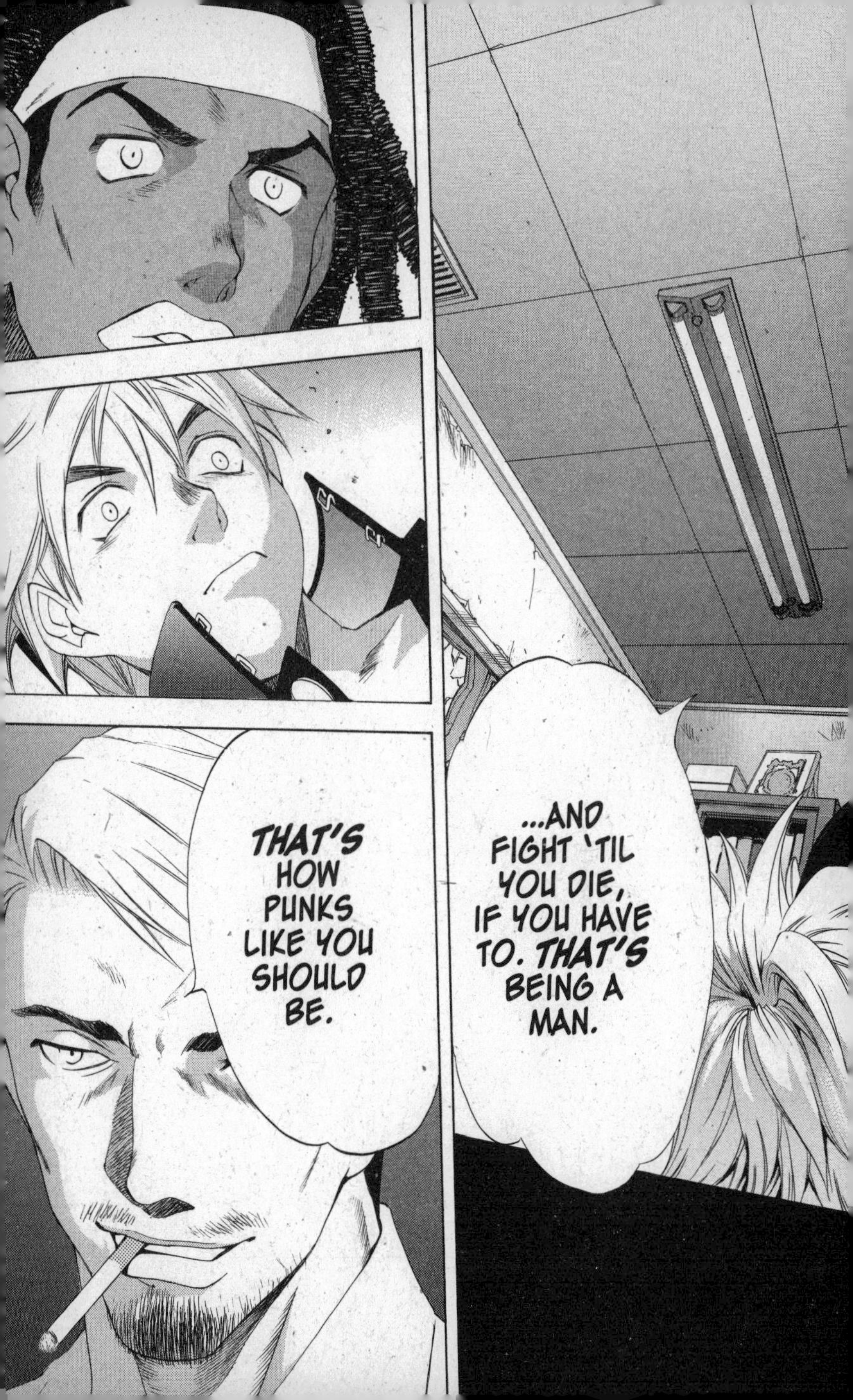
...AND FIGHT 'TIL YOU DIE, IF YOU HAVE TO. THAT'S BEING A MAN.
THAT'S HOW PUNKS LIKE YOU SHOULD BE.

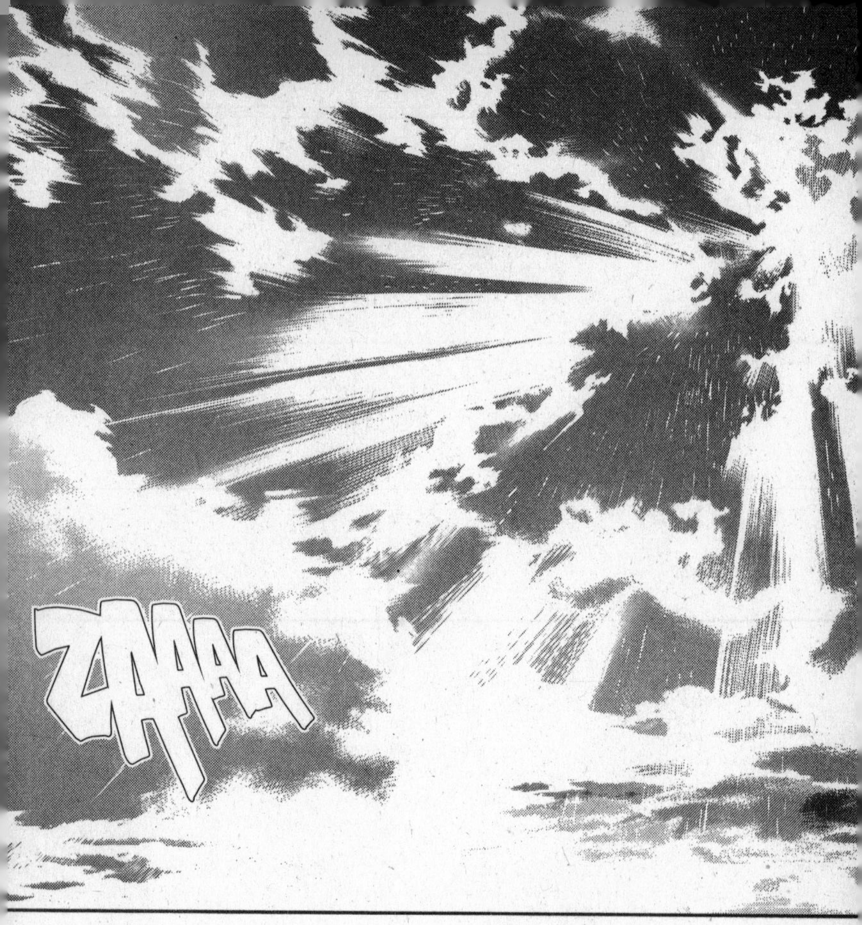
ZAAAA

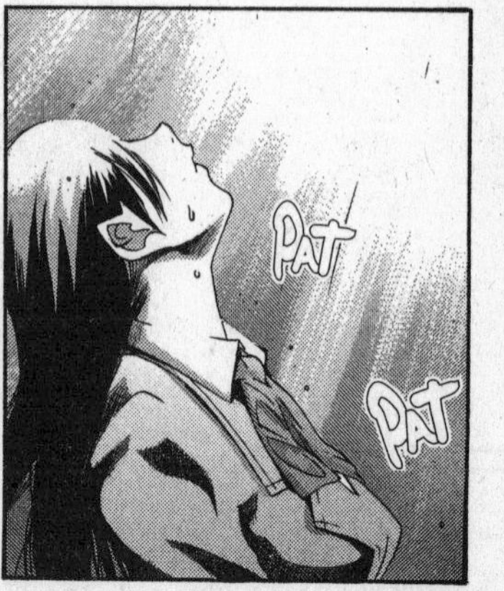
PAT
PAT

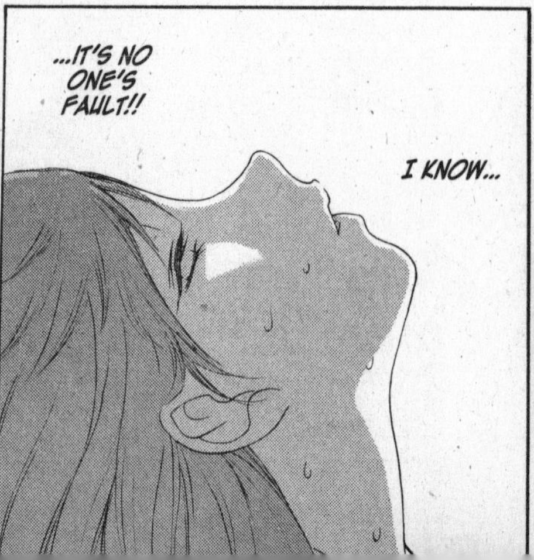
...IT'S NO ONE'S FAULT!!
I KNOW...

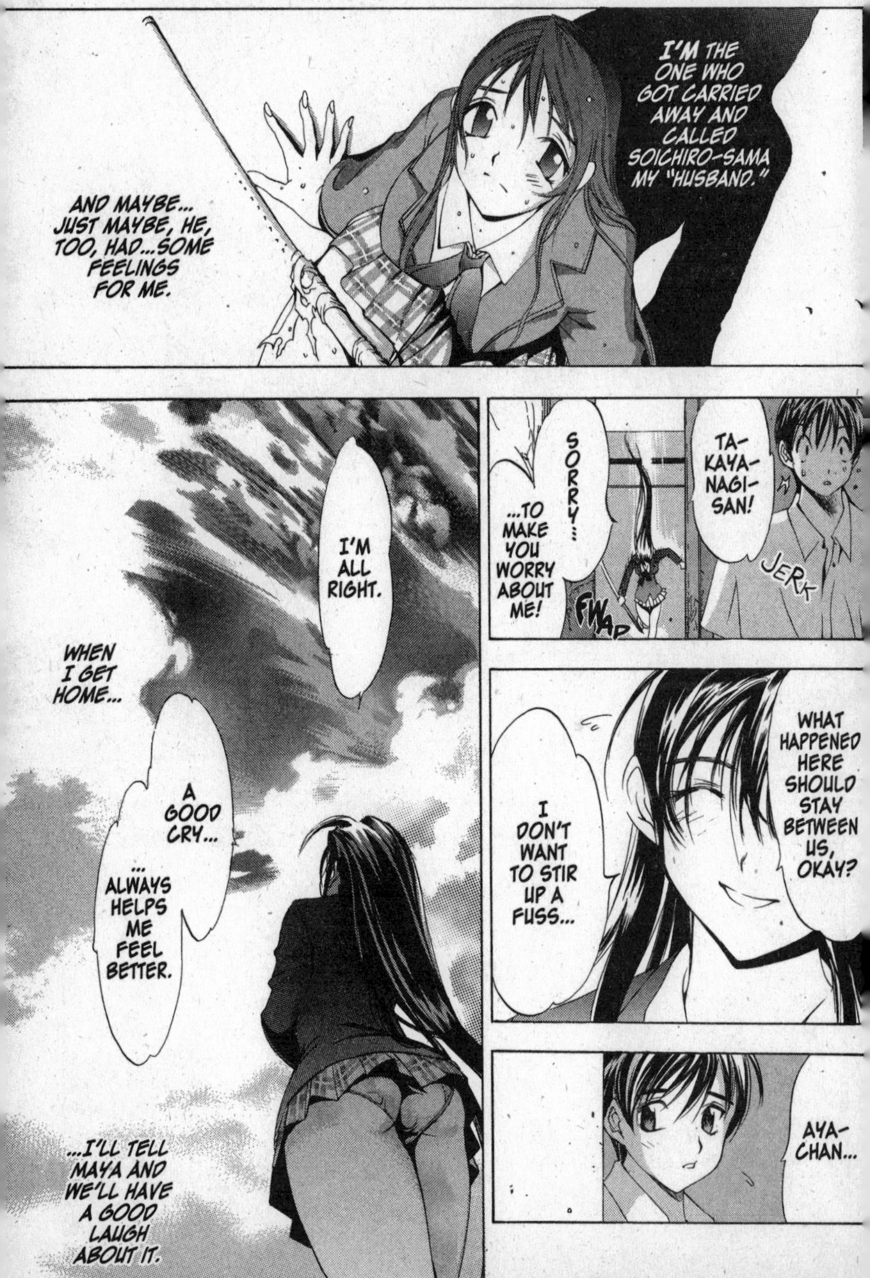
I'M THE ONE WHO GOT CARRIED AWAY AND CALLED SOICHIRO-SAMA MY "HUSBAND."
AND MAYBE... JUST MAYBE, HE, TOO, HAD...SOME FEELINGS FOR ME.
TA-KAYA-NAGI-SAN!
JERK
SORRY... ...TO MAKE YOU WORRY ABOUT ME!
FWAP
WHAT HAPPENED HERE SHOULD STAY BETWEEN US, OKAY?
I DON'T WANT TO STIR UP A FUSS...
AYA-CHAN...
I'M ALL RIGHT.
WHEN I GET HOME...
A GOOD CRY... ...ALWAYS HELPS ME FEEL BETTER.
...I'LL TELL MAYA AND WE'LL HAVE A GOOD LAUGH ABOUT IT.

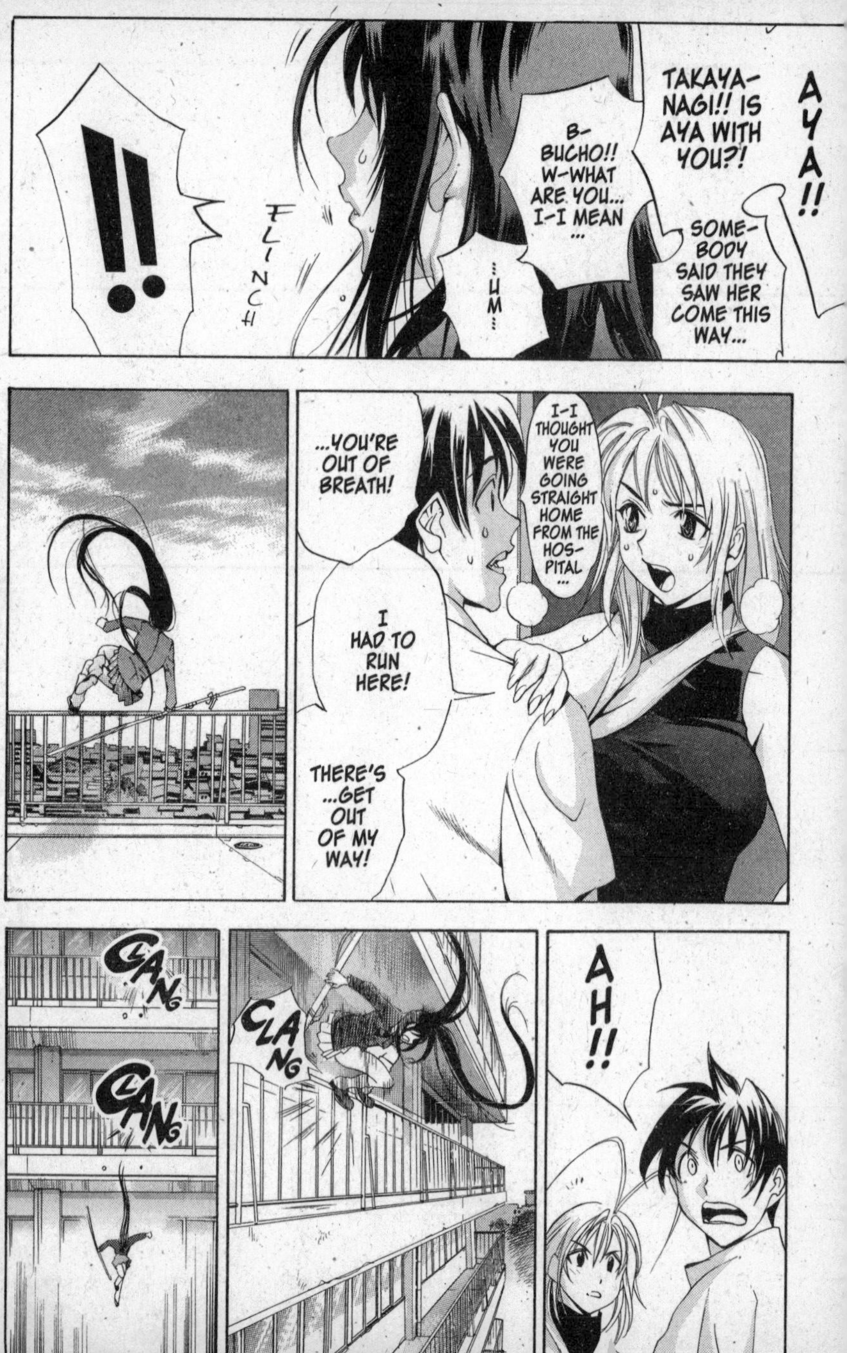
AYA!!
TAKAYA-NAGI!! IS AYA WITH YOU?!
SOME-BODY SAID THEY SAW HER COME THIS WAY...
B-BUCHO!! W-WHAT ARE YOU... I-I MEAN ...
...UM...
FLINCH
!!
I-I THOUGHT YOU WERE GOING STRAIGHT HOME FROM THE HOS-PITAL ...
...YOU'RE OUT OF BREATH!
I HAD TO RUN HERE!
THERE'S ...GET OUT OF MY WAY!
AH!!
CLANG
CLANG
CLANG

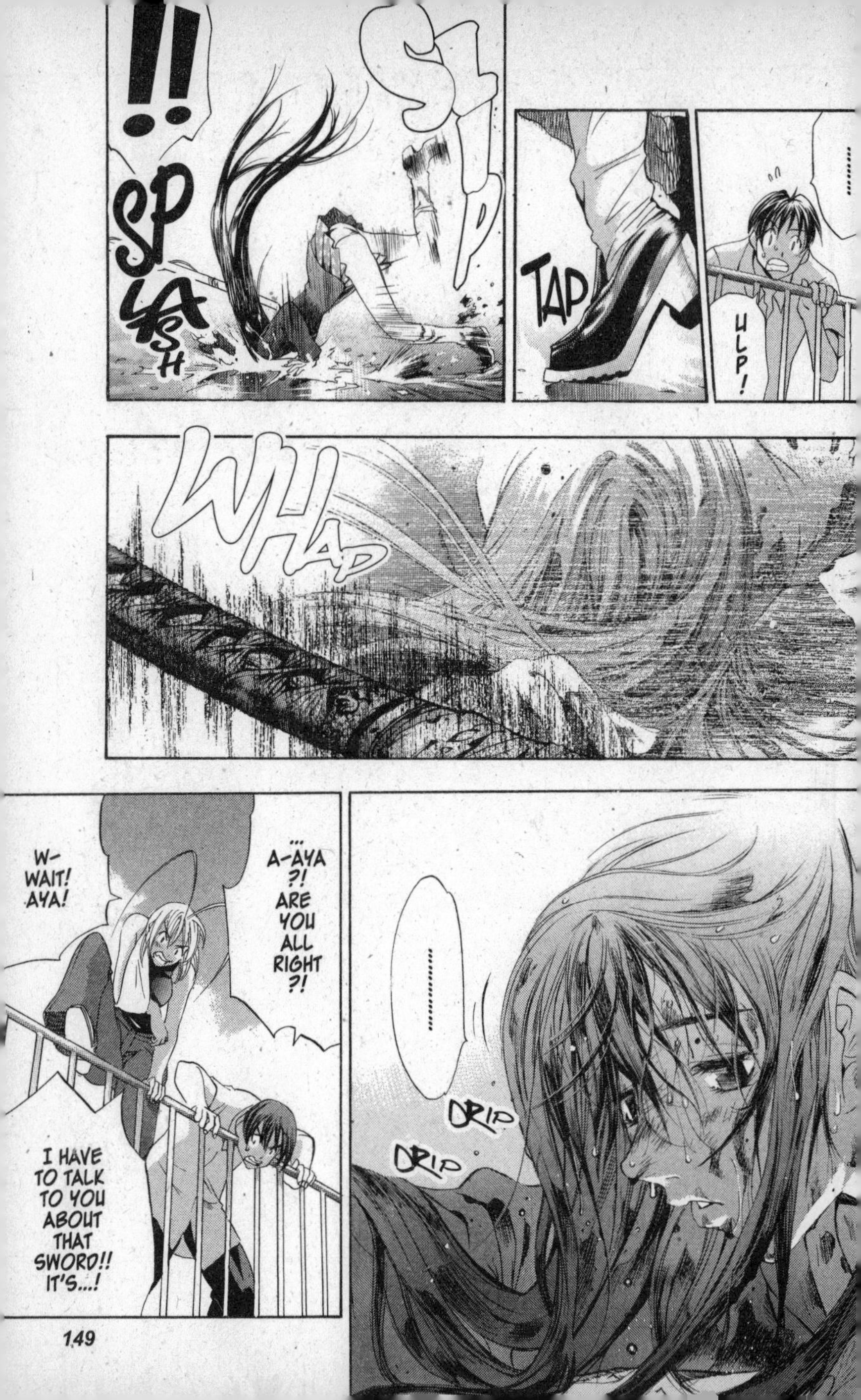

......
HLP!
TAP
SLIP
!!
SPLASH
WHAP
......
DRIP
DRIP
...A-AYA?! ARE YOU ALL RIGHT?!
W-WAIT! AYA!
I HAVE TO TALK TO YOU ABOUT THAT SWORD!! IT'S...!

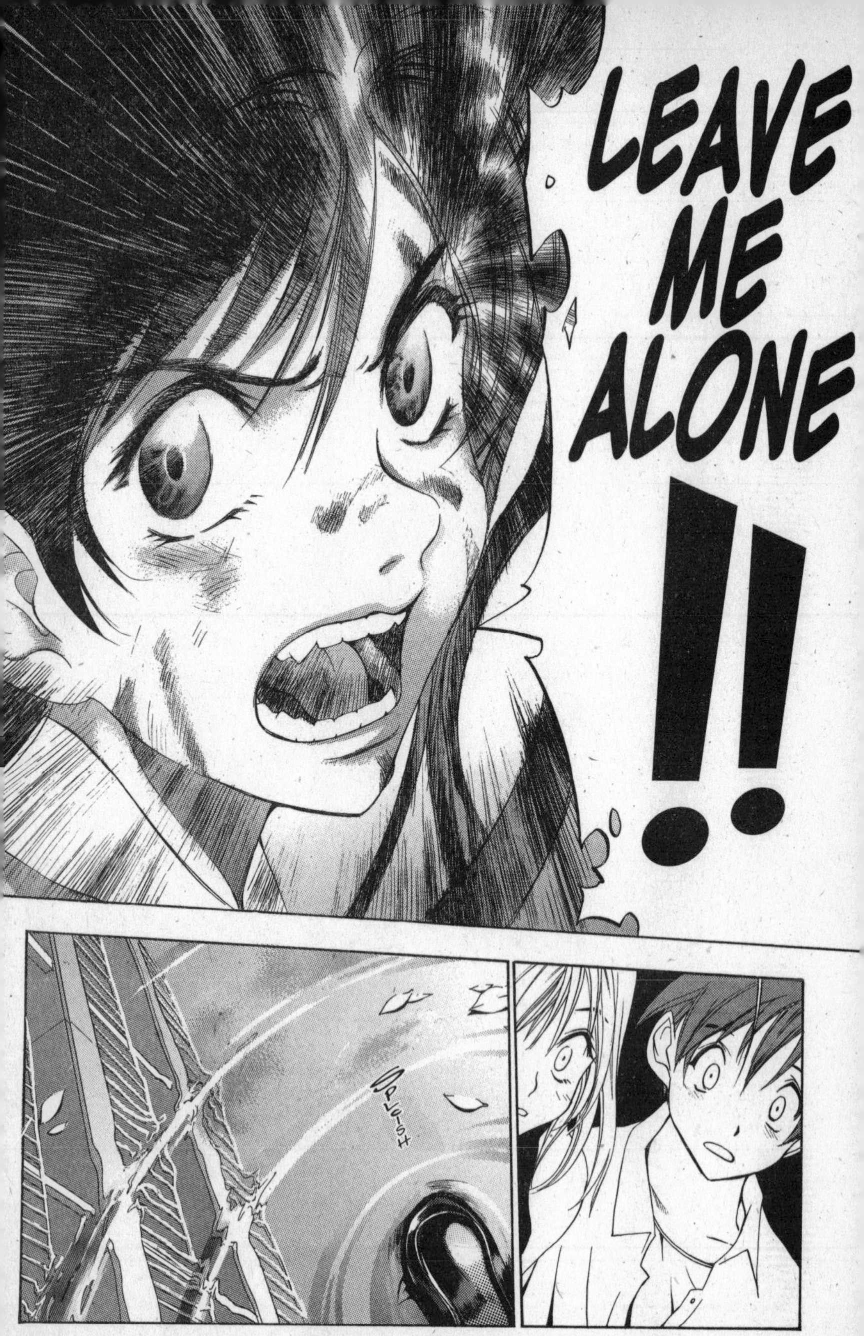
LEAVE ME ALONE!!
SPLISH

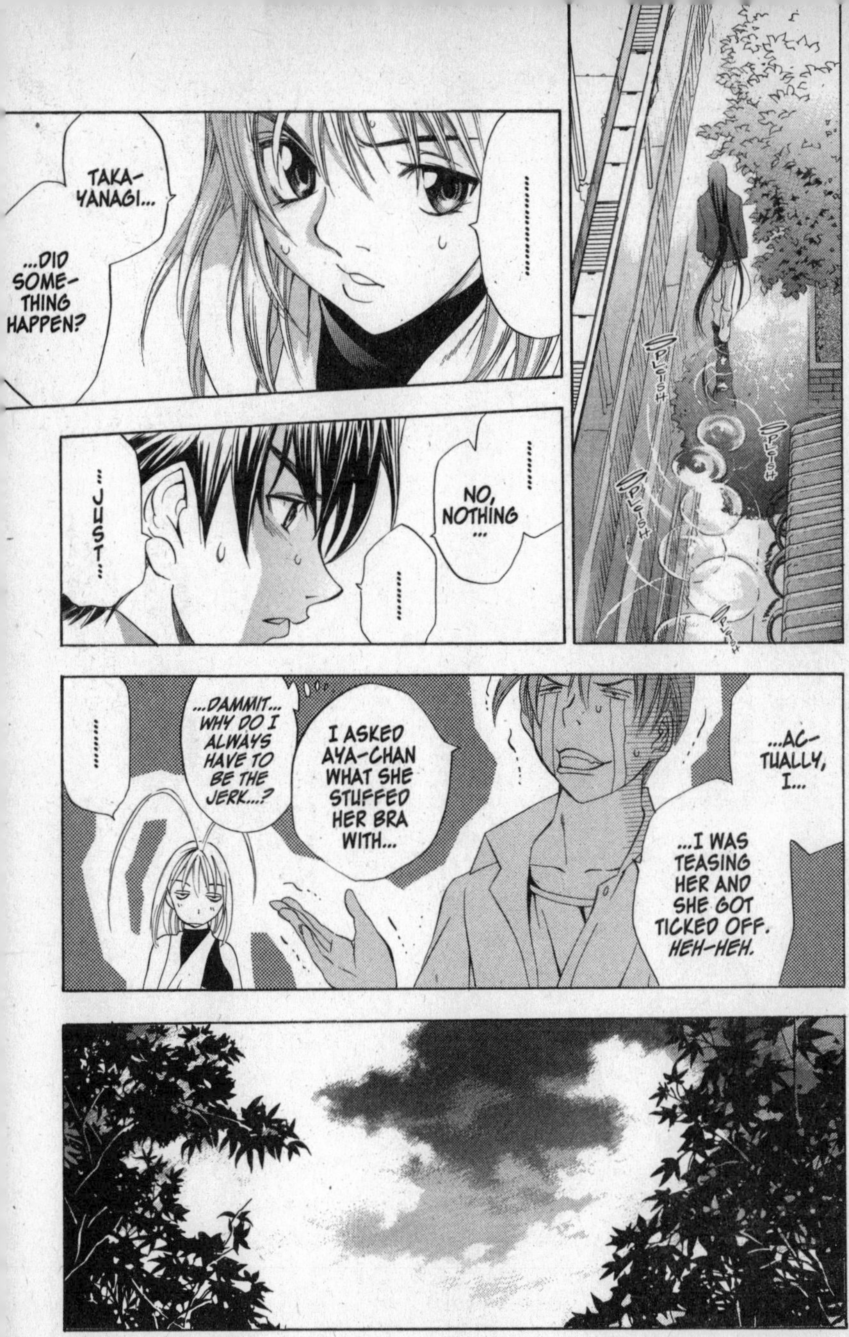
SPLISH
SPLISH
SPLISH
....
TAKA-YANAGI...
...DID SOME-THING HAPPEN?
......
NO, NOTHING ...
......
...JUST...
...AC-TUALLY, I...
...I WAS TEASING HER AND SHE GOT TICKED OFF. HEH-HEH.
I ASKED AYA-CHAN WHAT SHE STUFFED HER BRA WITH...
...DAMMIT... WHY DO I ALWAYS HAVE TO BE THE JERK...?
......

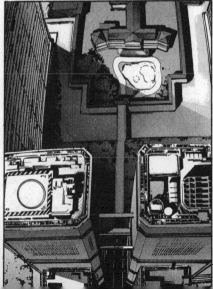

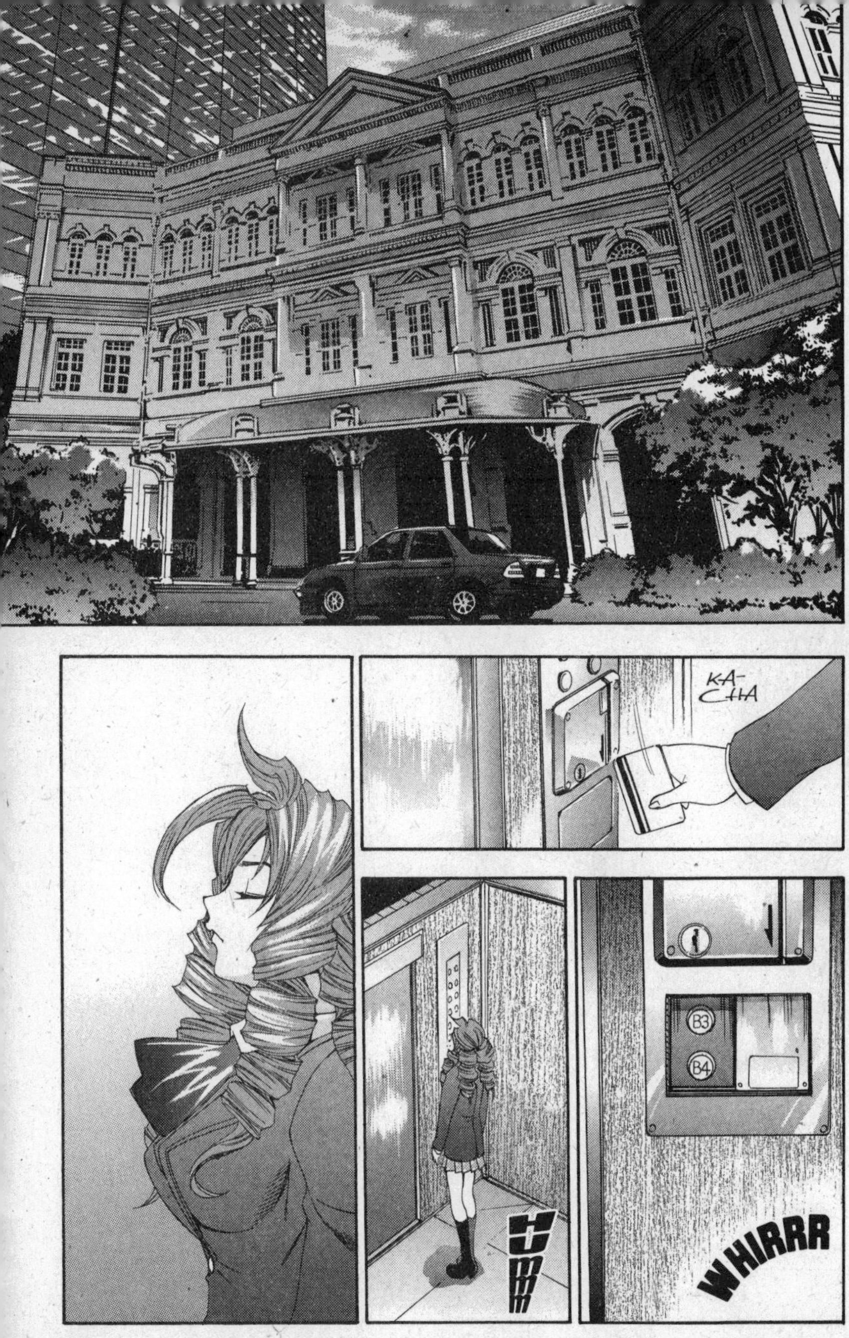
KA-CHA
WHIRRR
HUMMM

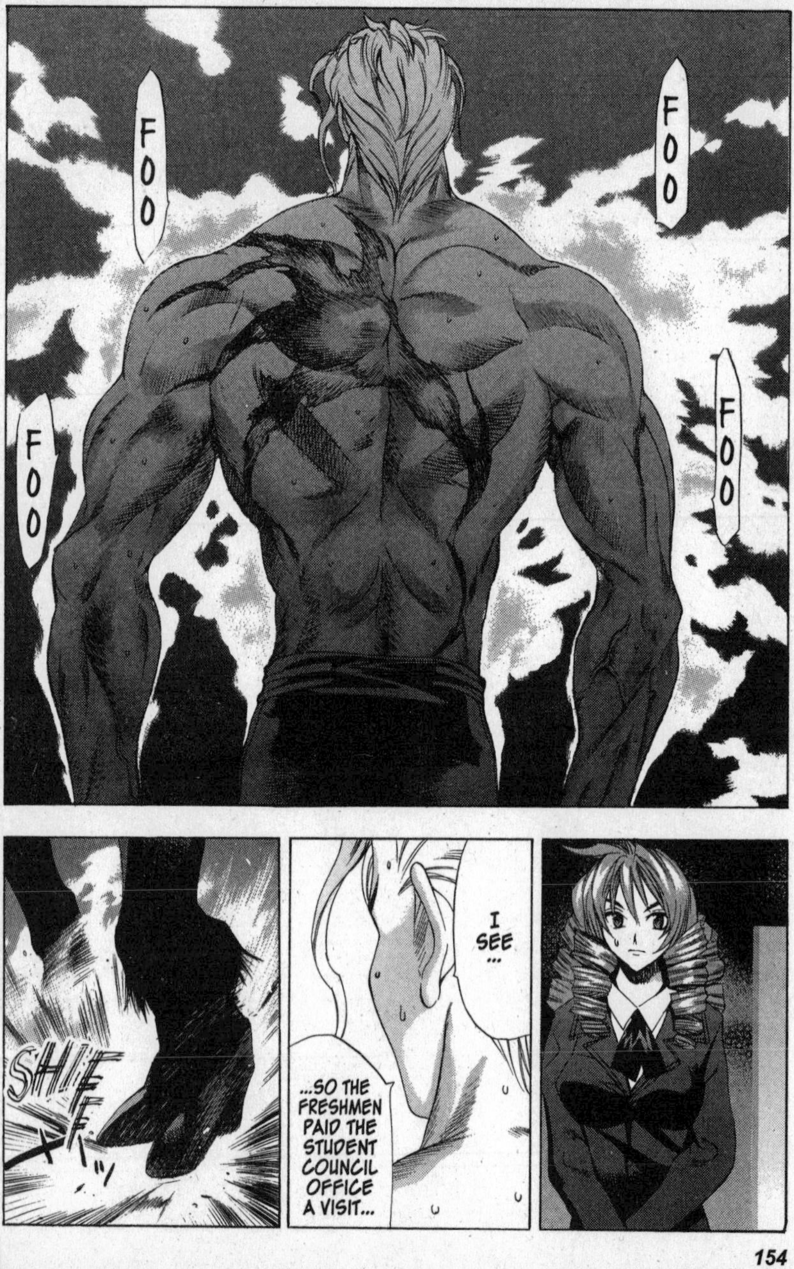
FOO
FOO
FOO
FOO
I SEE...
...SO THE FRESHMEN PAID THE STUDENT COUNCIL OFFICE A VISIT...
SHIFF

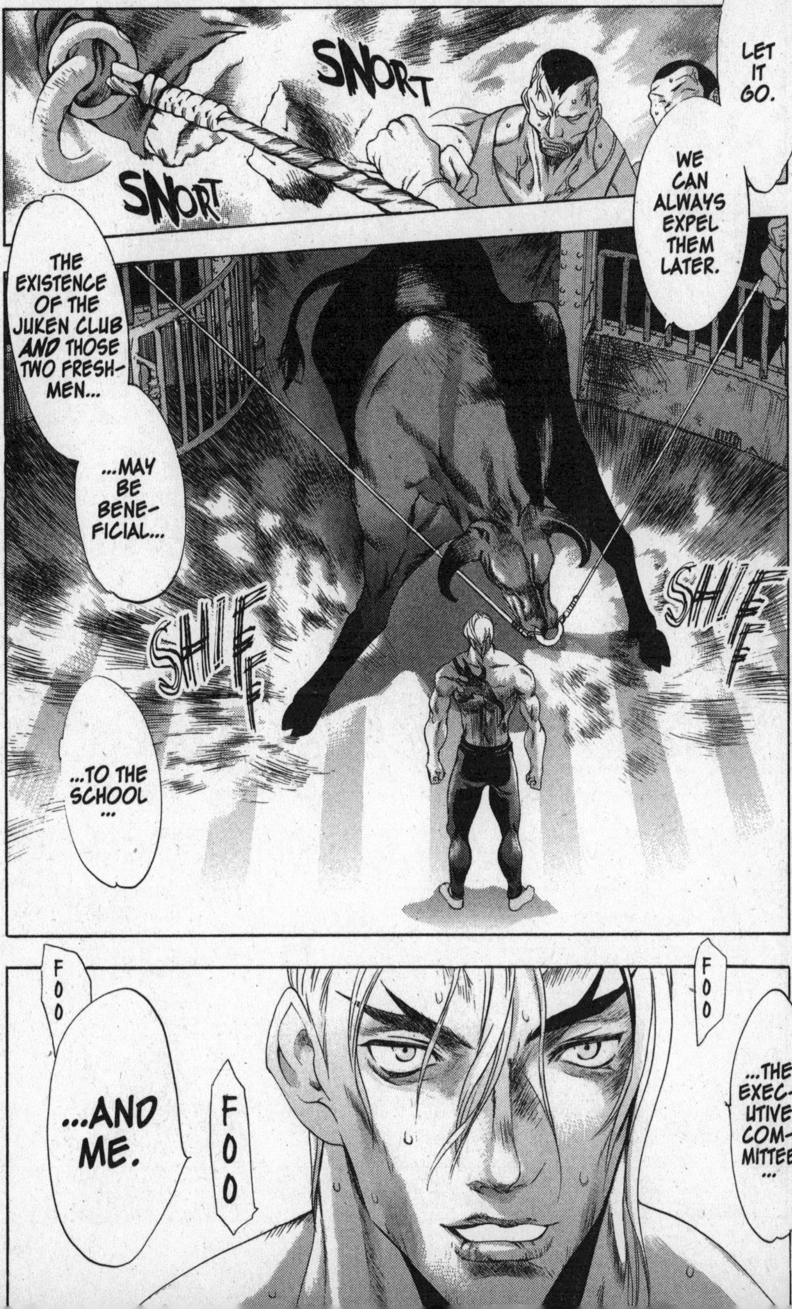

LET IT GO.
WE CAN ALWAYS EXPEL THEM LATER.
SNORT
SNORT
THE EXISTENCE OF THE JUKEN CLUB AND THOSE TWO FRESH-MEN...
...MAY BE BENE-FICIAL...
SHIFF
SHIFF
...TO THE SCHOOL...
FOO
...THE EXEC-UTIVE COM-MITTEE...
FOO
FOO
...AND ME.

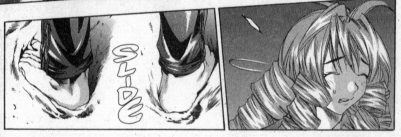

SLIDE

...I'VE GRANTED HER A ONE-MONTH POST-PONEMENT OF HER EXPULSION. CALL IT A SECOND CHANCE.

AS FOR MAYA...

WHOA!

WHOA!

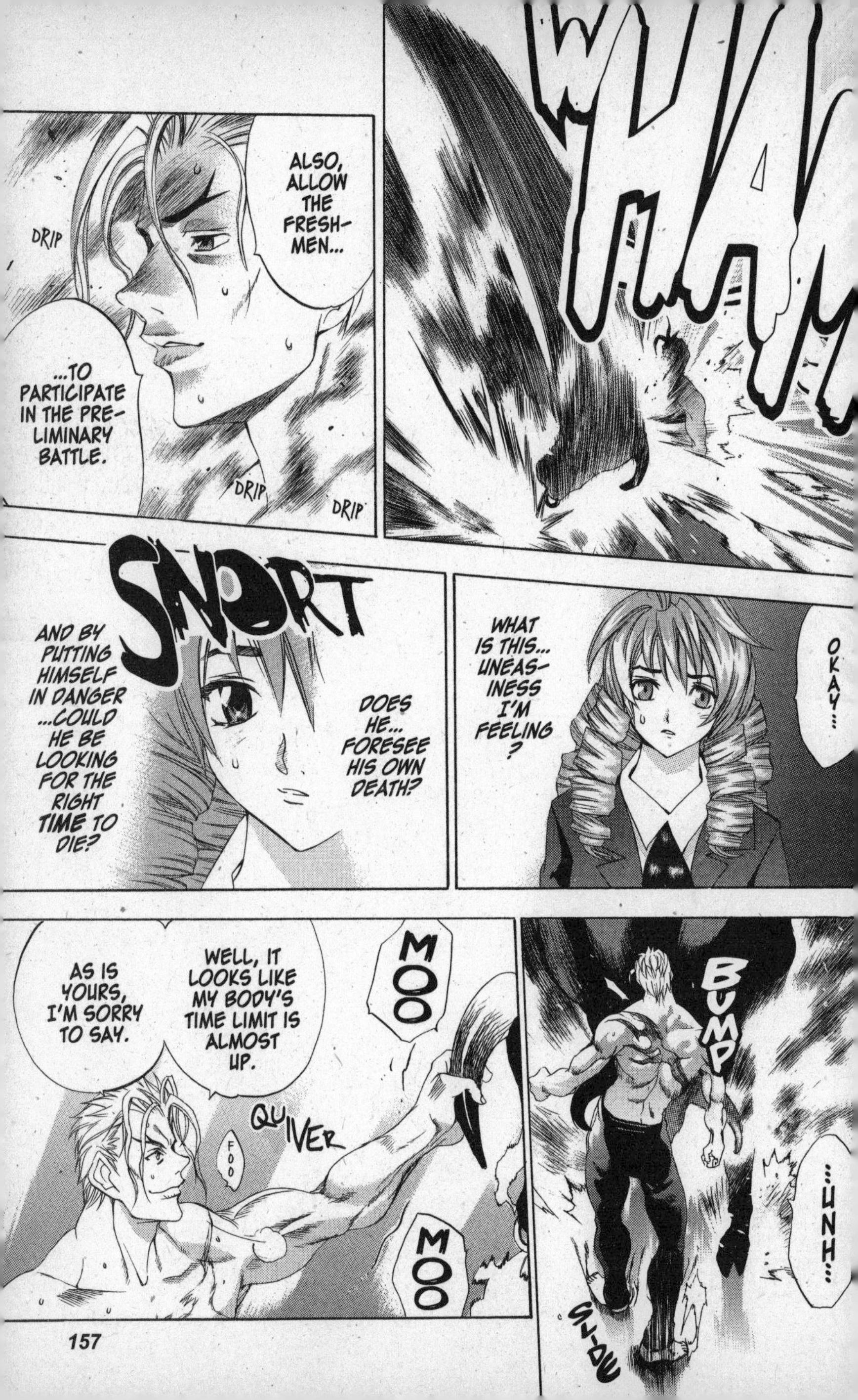
WHAM
ALSO, ALLOW THE FRESHMEN...
DRIP
...TO PARTICIPATE IN THE PRELIMINARY BATTLE.
DRIP
DRIP
OKAY...
WHAT IS THIS... UNEASINESS I'M FEELING?
SNORT
DOES HE... FORESEE HIS OWN DEATH?
AND BY PUTTING HIMSELF IN DANGER ...COULD HE BE LOOKING FOR THE RIGHT TIME TO DIE?
BUMP
...UNH...
SLIDE
MOO
WELL, IT LOOKS LIKE MY BODY'S TIME LIMIT IS ALMOST UP.
AS IS YOURS, I'M SORRY TO SAY.
QUIVER
FOO
MOO

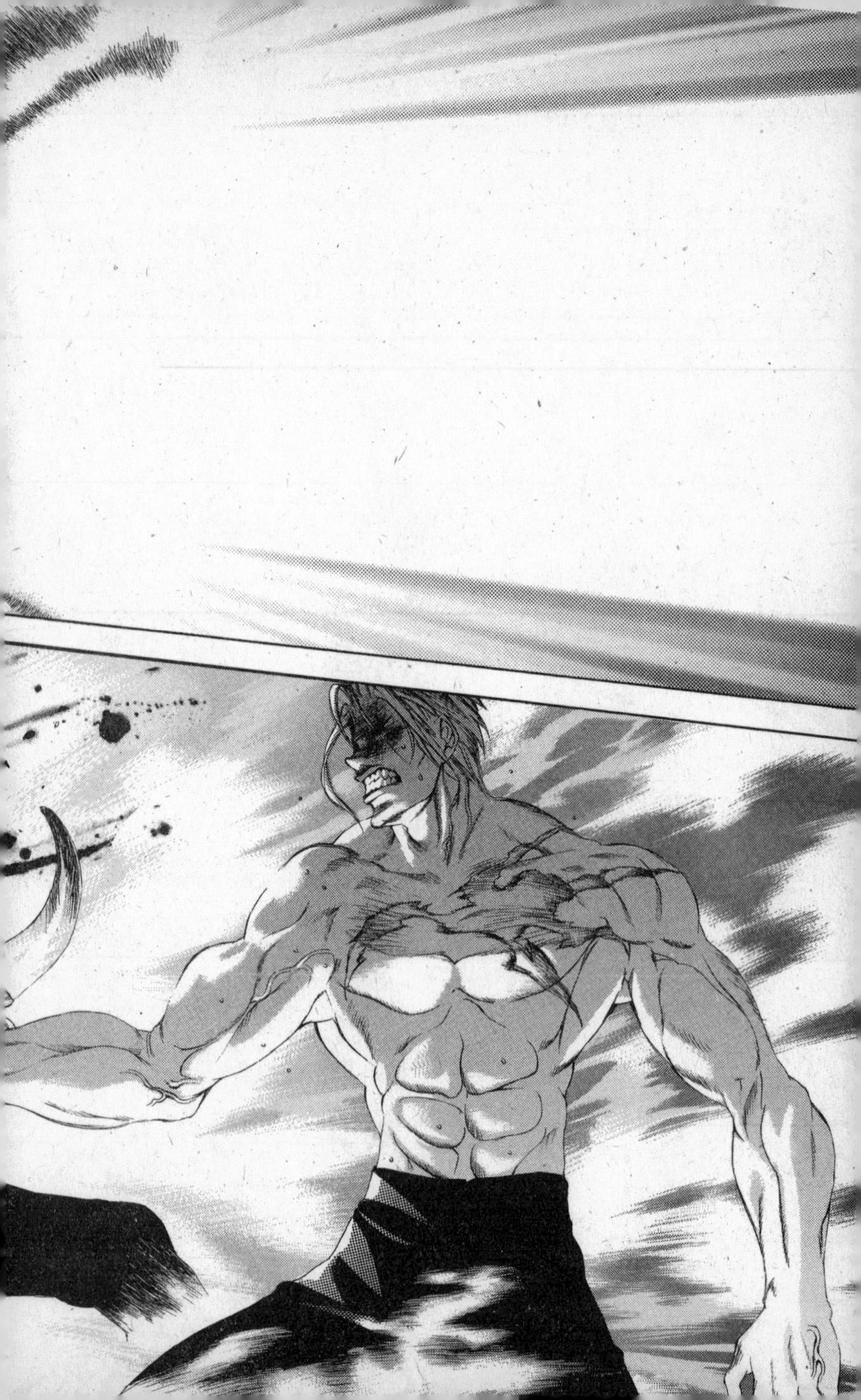

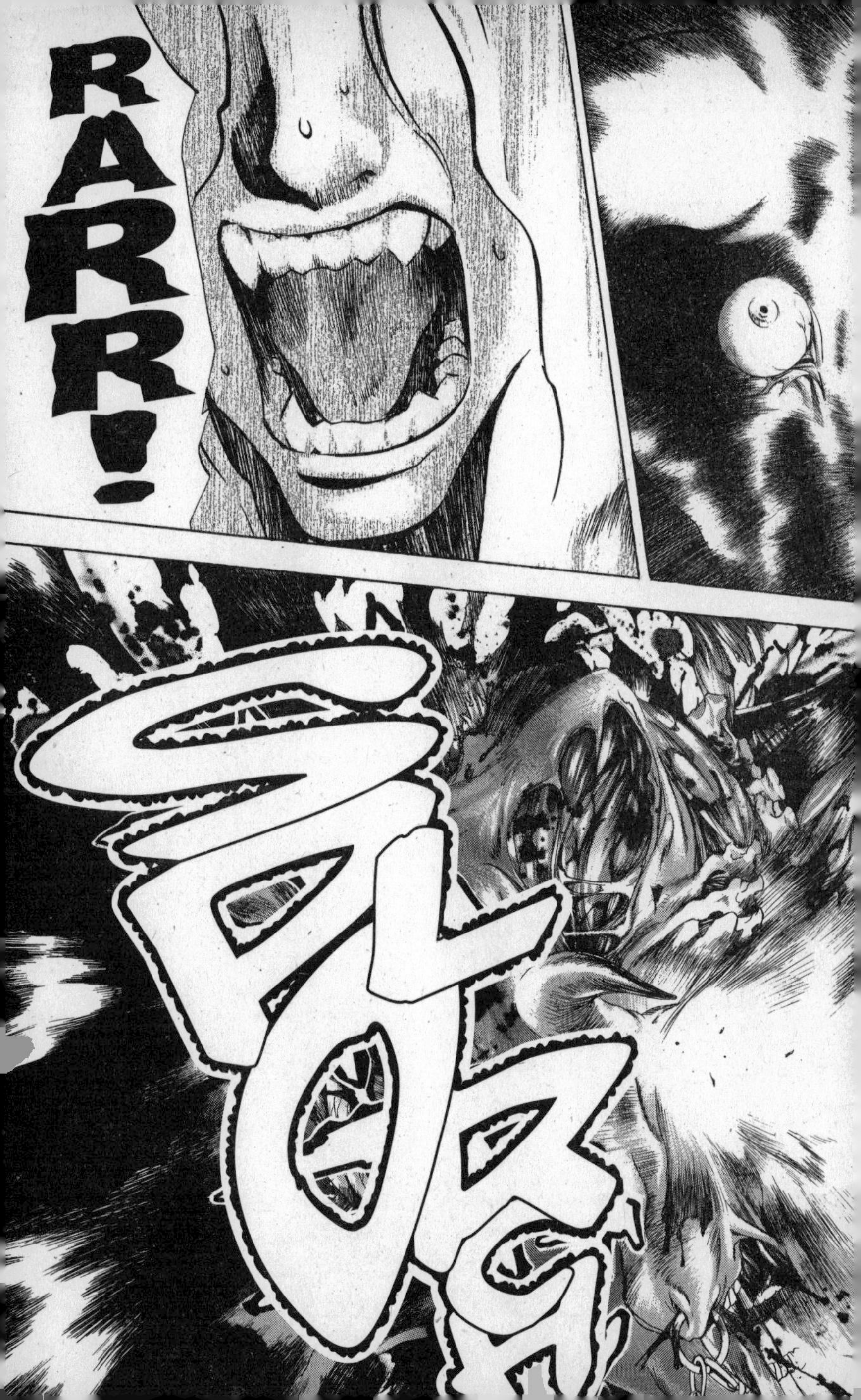
RARR!

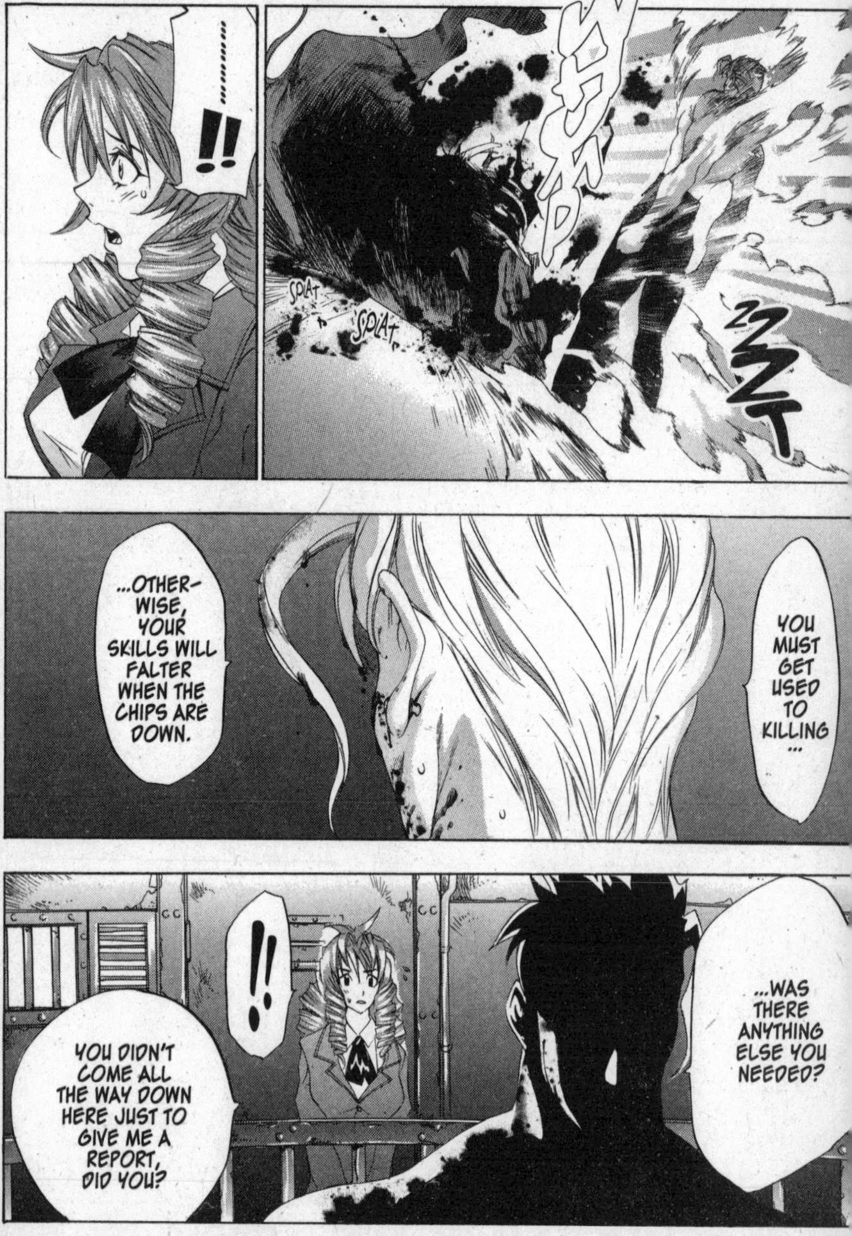
SPLAT
SPLAT
ZZZZT
......!!
YOU MUST GET USED TO KILLING...
...OTHERWISE, YOUR SKILLS WILL FALTER WHEN THE CHIPS ARE DOWN.
...WAS THERE ANYTHING ELSE YOU NEEDED?
!!
YOU DIDN'T COME ALL THE WAY DOWN HERE JUST TO GIVE ME A REPORT, DID YOU?

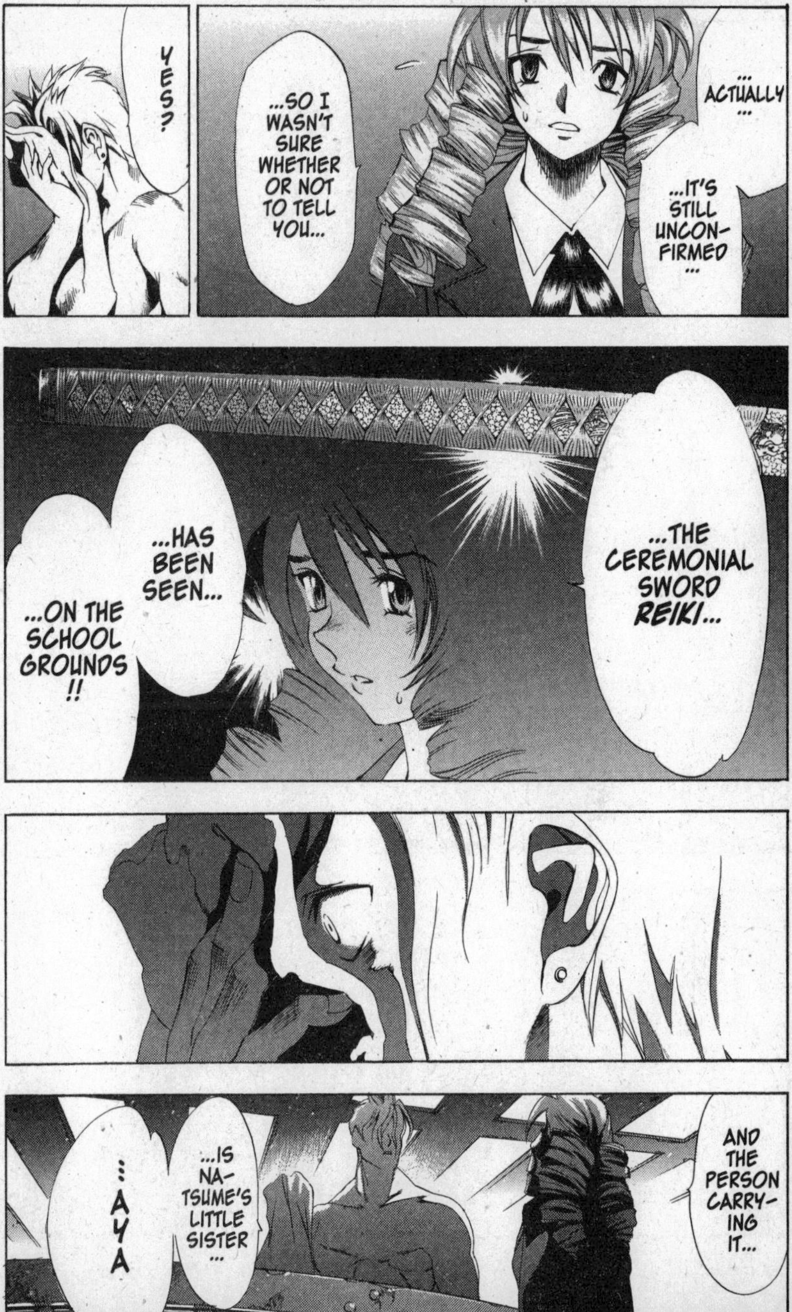
...ACTUALLY...
...IT'S STILL UNCONFIRMED...
...SO I WASN'T SURE WHETHER OR NOT TO TELL YOU...
YES?
...THE CEREMONIAL SWORD *REIKI*...
...HAS BEEN SEEN...
...ON THE SCHOOL GROUNDS!!
AND THE PERSON CARRYING IT...
...IS NATSUME'S LITTLE SISTER...
...AYA

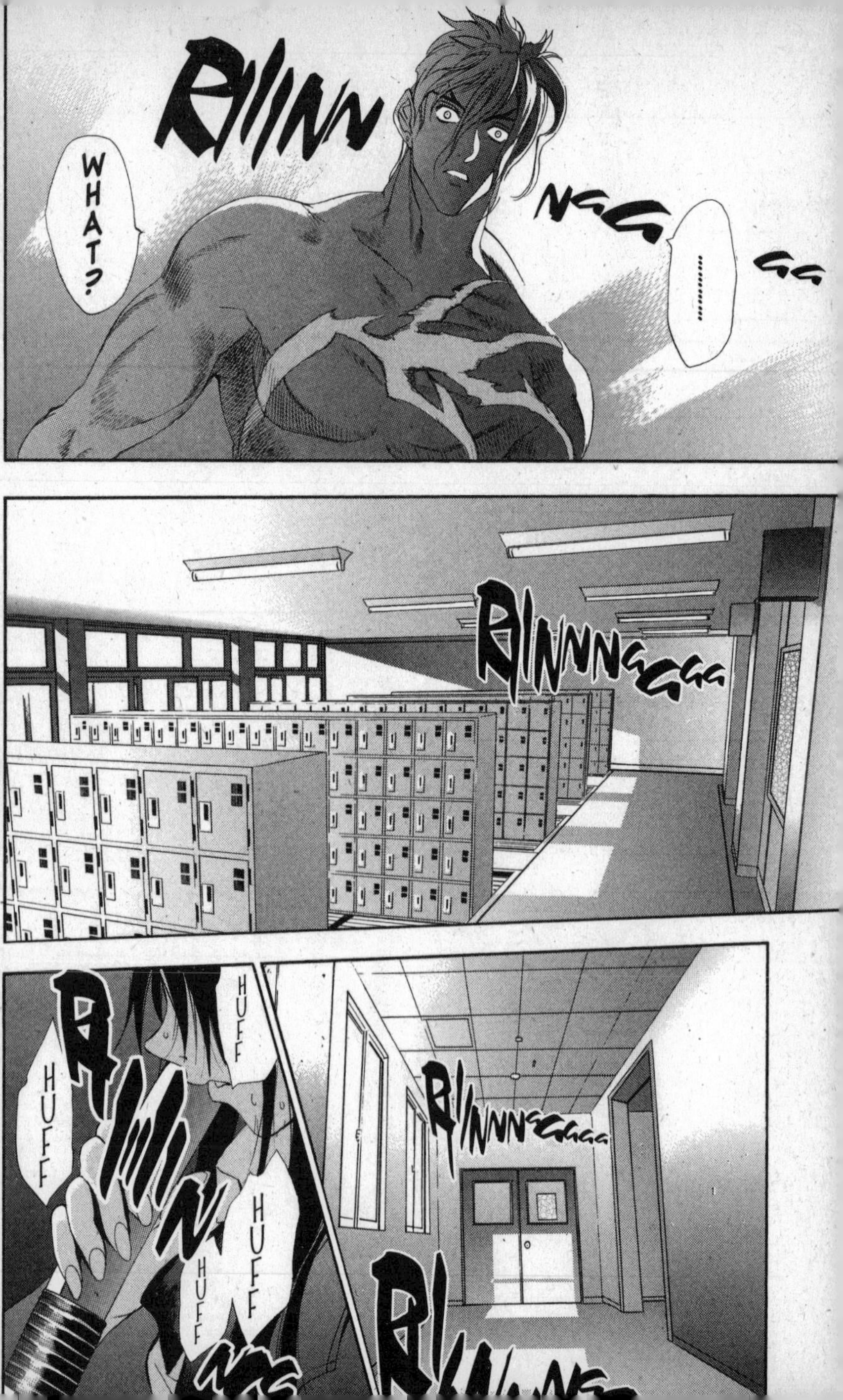
RIINN NGG GG
......
WHAT?
RINNNGGGG
RIINNNGGGGG
HUFF
HUFF
HUFF
HUFF
HUFF

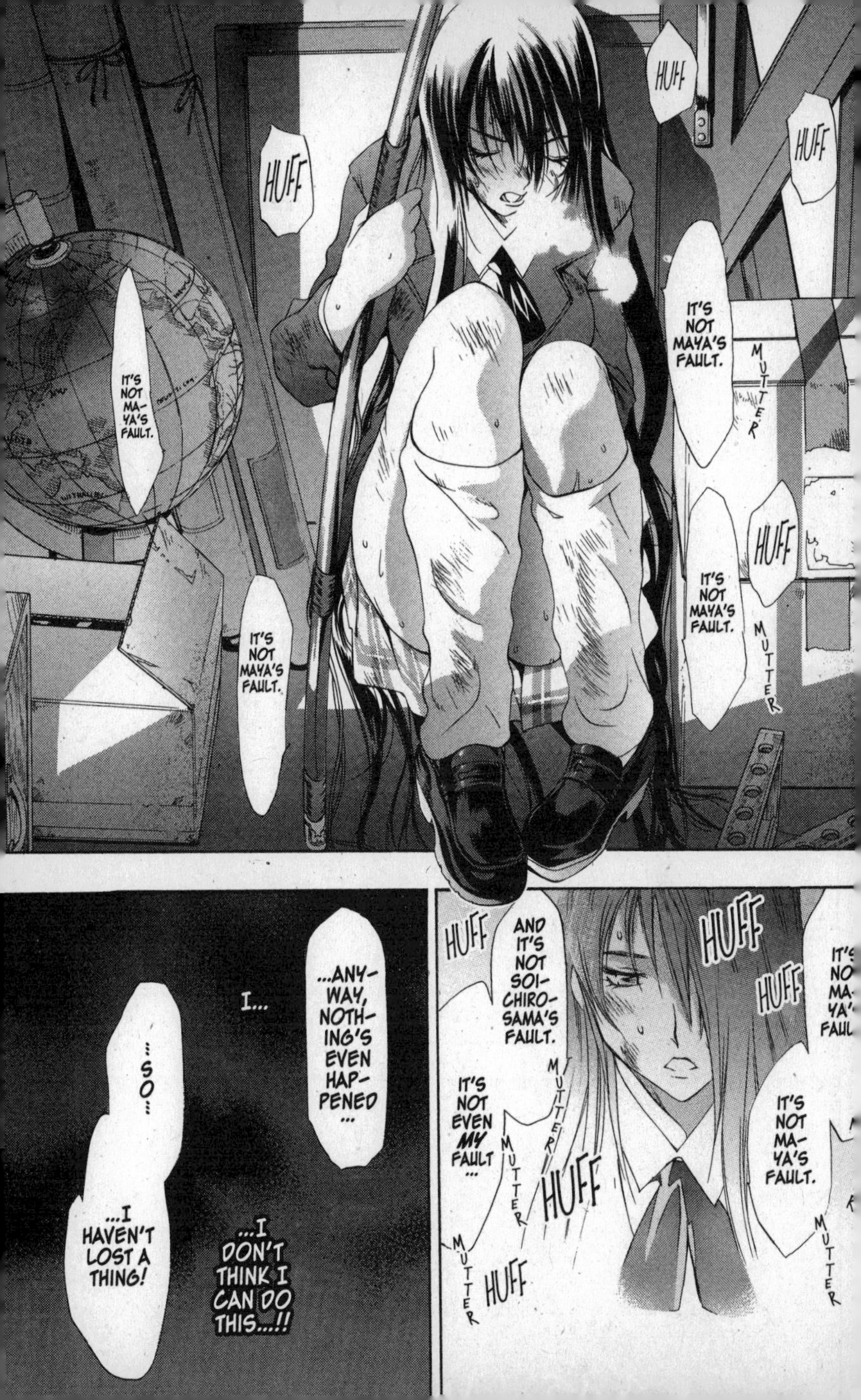
HUFF
HUFF
IT'S NOT MAYA'S FAULT.
MUTTER
HUFF
IT'S NOT MAYA'S FAULT.
MUTTER
HUFF
IT'S NOT MAYA'S FAULT.
IT'S NOT MAYA'S FAULT.
IT'S NOT MA-YA'S FAUL
HUFF
HUFF
AND IT'S NOT SOI-CHIRO-SAMA'S FAULT.
HUFF
MUTTER
IT'S NOT MA-YA'S FAULT.
MUTTER
IT'S NOT EVEN *MY* FAULT...
MUTTER
HUFF
MUTTER
HUFF
...ANY-WAY, NOTH-ING'S EVEN HAP-PENED...
I...
...SO...
...I HAVEN'T LOST A THING!
...I DON'T THINK I CAN DO THIS...!!

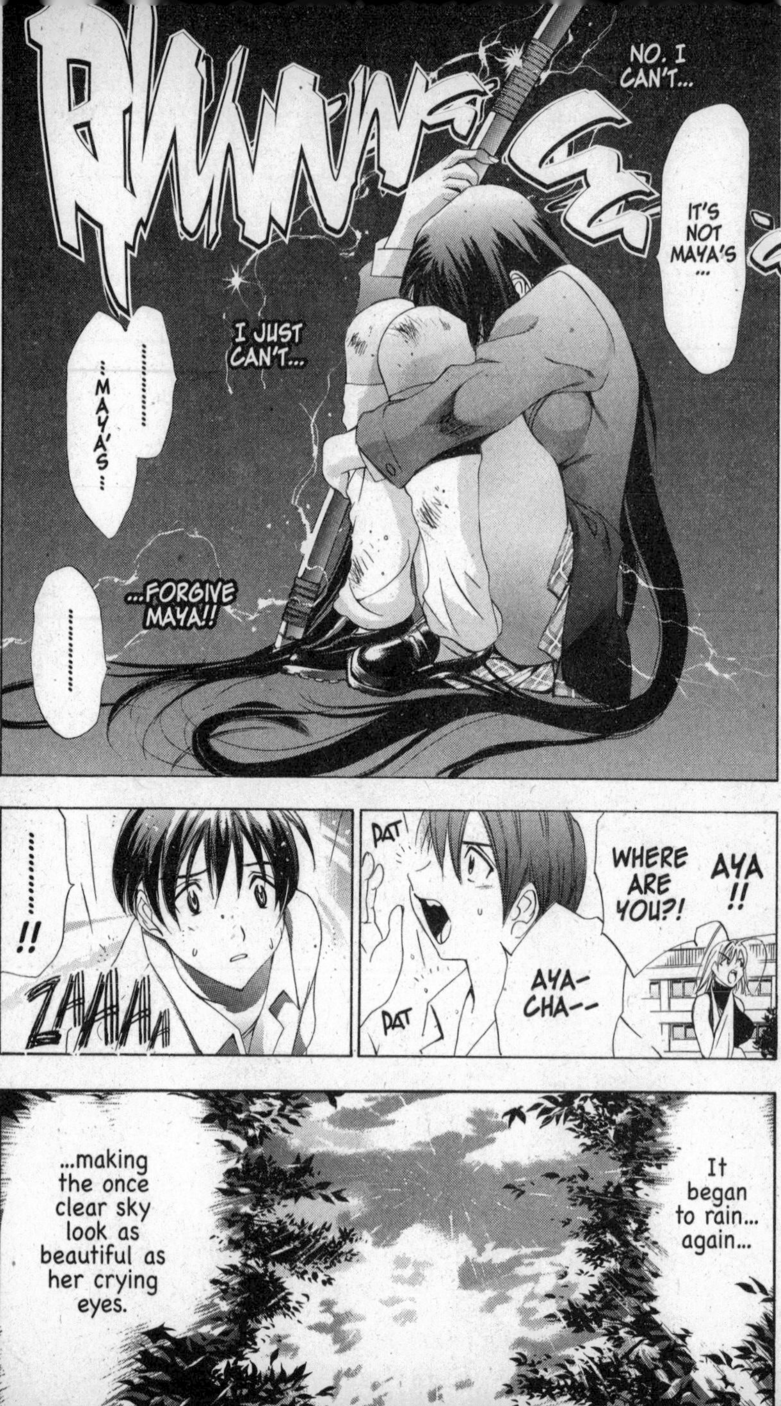
NO. I CAN'T...
IT'S NOT MAYA'S...
I JUST CAN'T...
......MAYA'S...
...FORGIVE MAYA!!
......
AYA!!
WHERE ARE YOU?!
PAT
AYA-CHA--
PAT
......!!
It began to rain... again...
...making the once clear sky look as beautiful as her crying eyes.

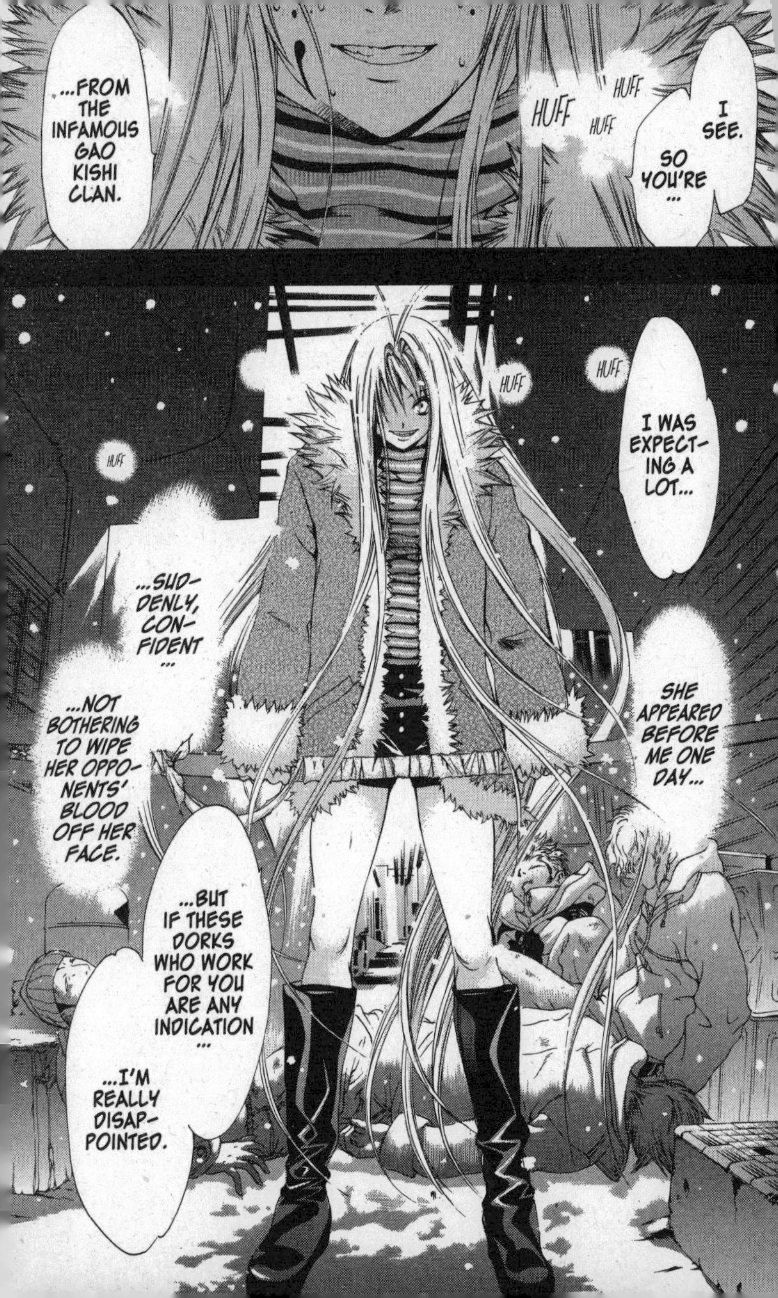
HUFF HUFF HUFF
I SEE. SO YOU'RE...
...FROM THE INFAMOUS GAO KISHI CLAN.
HUFF
HUFF
I WAS EXPECTING A LOT...
SHE APPEARED BEFORE ME ONE DAY...
HUFF
...SUDDENLY, CONFIDENT...
...NOT BOTHERING TO WIPE HER OPPONENTS' BLOOD OFF HER FACE.
...BUT IF THESE DORKS WHO WORK FOR YOU ARE ANY INDICATION...
...I'M REALLY DISAPPOINTED.

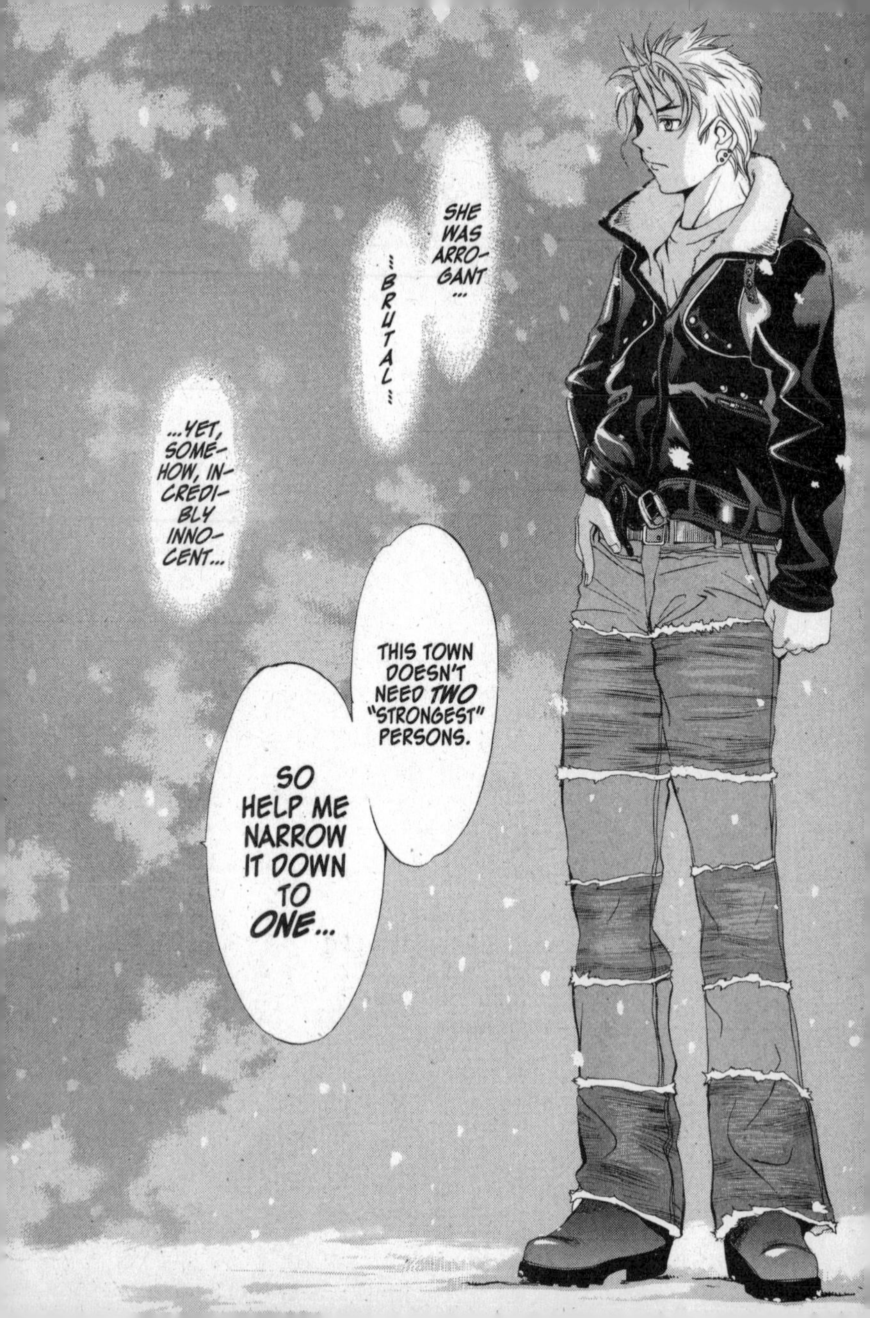
SHE WAS ARROGANT...
...BRUTAL...
...YET, SOMEHOW, INCREDIBLY INNOCENT...
THIS TOWN DOESN'T NEED TWO "STRONGEST" PERSONS.
SO HELP ME NARROW IT DOWN TO ONE...

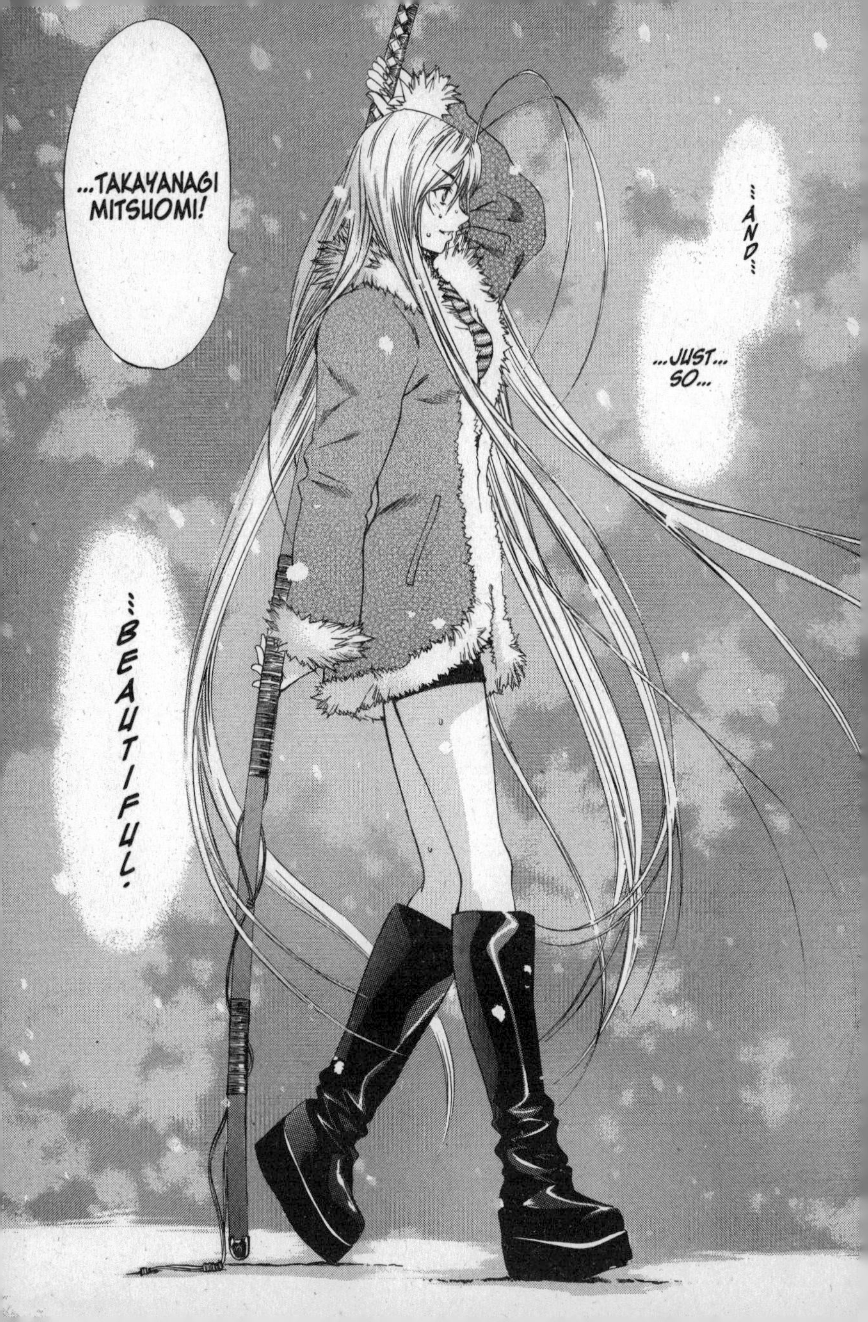
...AND...
...JUST... SO...
...TAKAYANAGI MITSUOMI!
...BEAUTIFUL.

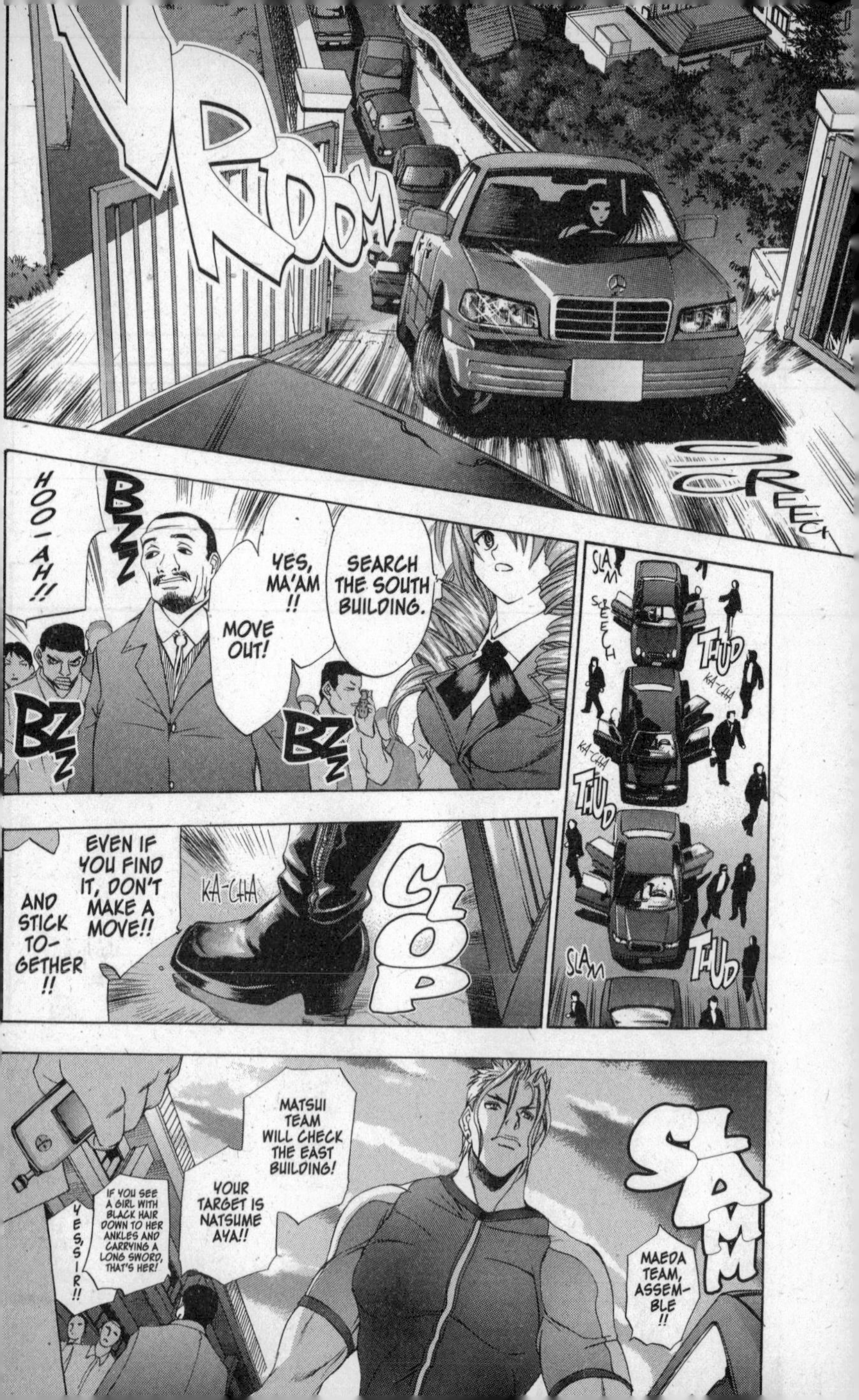
VROOM
SCREECH
SLAM
SCREECH
THUD
KA-CHA
KA-CHA
THUD
SLAM
THUD
SEARCH THE SOUTH BUILDING.
YES, MA'AM!!
MOVE OUT!
BZZ
HOO-AH!!
BZZ
BZZ
CLOP
KA-CHA
EVEN IF YOU FIND IT, DON'T MAKE A MOVE!!
AND STICK TO-GETHER!!
SLAMM
MAEDA TEAM, ASSEM-BLE!!
MATSUI TEAM WILL CHECK THE EAST BUILDING!
YOUR TARGET IS NATSUME AYA!!
IF YOU SEE A GIRL WITH BLACK HAIR DOWN TO HER ANKLES AND CARRYING A LONG SWORD, THAT'S HER!
YESSIR!!

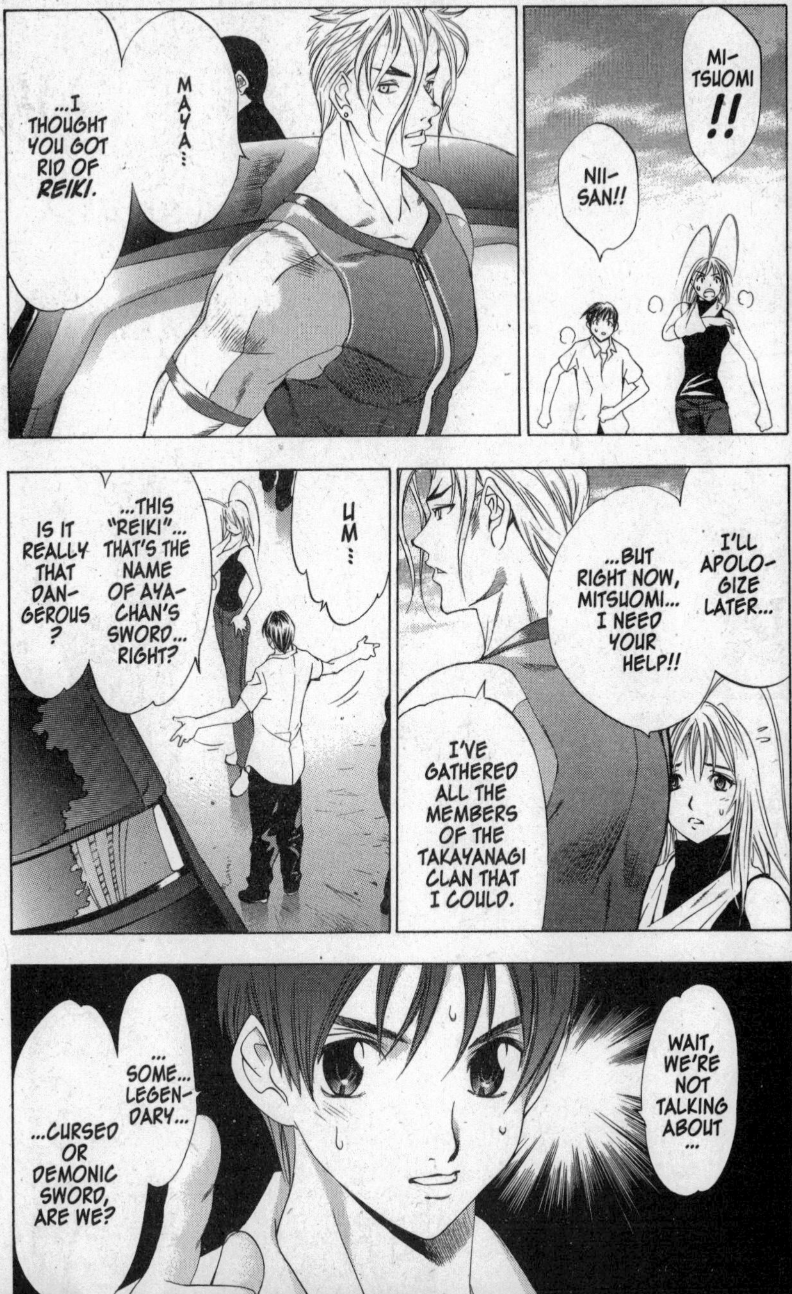
MI-TSUOMI!!
NII-SAN!!
MAYA...
...I THOUGHT YOU GOT RID OF *REIKI*.
I'LL APOLO-GIZE LATER...
...BUT RIGHT NOW, MITSUOMI... I NEED YOUR HELP!!
I'VE GATHERED ALL THE MEMBERS OF THE TAKAYANAGI CLAN THAT I COULD.
UM...
...THIS "REIKI"... THAT'S THE NAME OF AYA-CHAN'S SWORD... RIGHT?
IS IT REALLY THAT DAN-GEROUS?
WAIT, WE'RE NOT TALKING ABOUT...
...SOME... LEGEN-DARY...
...CURSED OR DEMONIC SWORD, ARE WE?

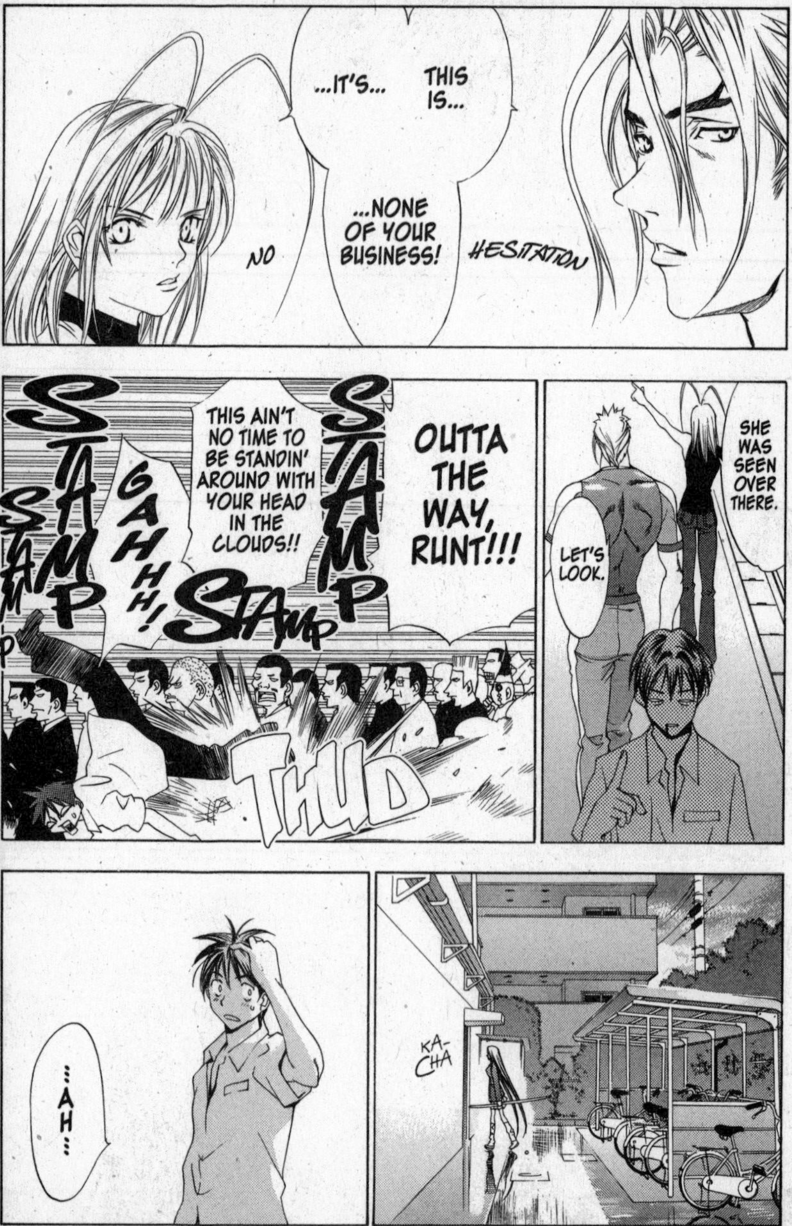
THIS IS...
...IT'S...
...NONE OF YOUR BUSINESS!
HESITATION
NO
SHE WAS SEEN OVER THERE.
LET'S LOOK.
OUTTA THE WAY, RUNT!!!
STAMP
THIS AIN'T NO TIME TO BE STANDIN' AROUND WITH YOUR HEAD IN THE CLOUDS!!
GAHHH!
STAMP
STAMP
STAMP
STAMP
THUD
KA-CHA
...AH...

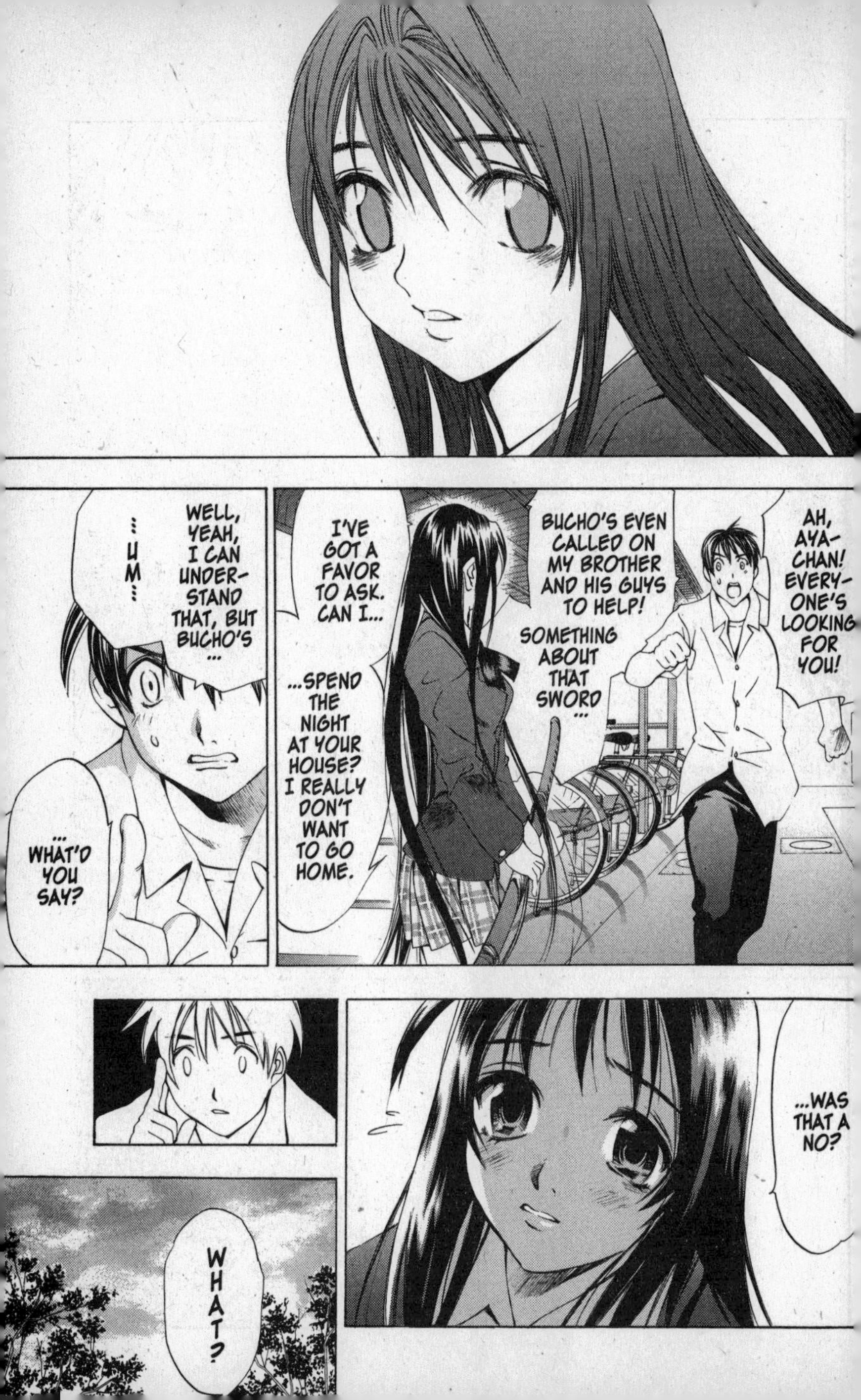
AH, AYA-CHAN! EVERY-ONE'S LOOKING FOR YOU!
BUCHO'S EVEN CALLED ON MY BROTHER AND HIS GUYS TO HELP!
SOMETHING ABOUT THAT SWORD ...
I'VE GOT A FAVOR TO ASK. CAN I...
...SPEND THE NIGHT AT YOUR HOUSE? I REALLY DON'T WANT TO GO HOME.
WELL, YEAH, I CAN UNDERSTAND THAT, BUT BUCHO'S ...
...UM...
...WHAT'D YOU SAY?
...WAS THAT A NO?
WHAT?

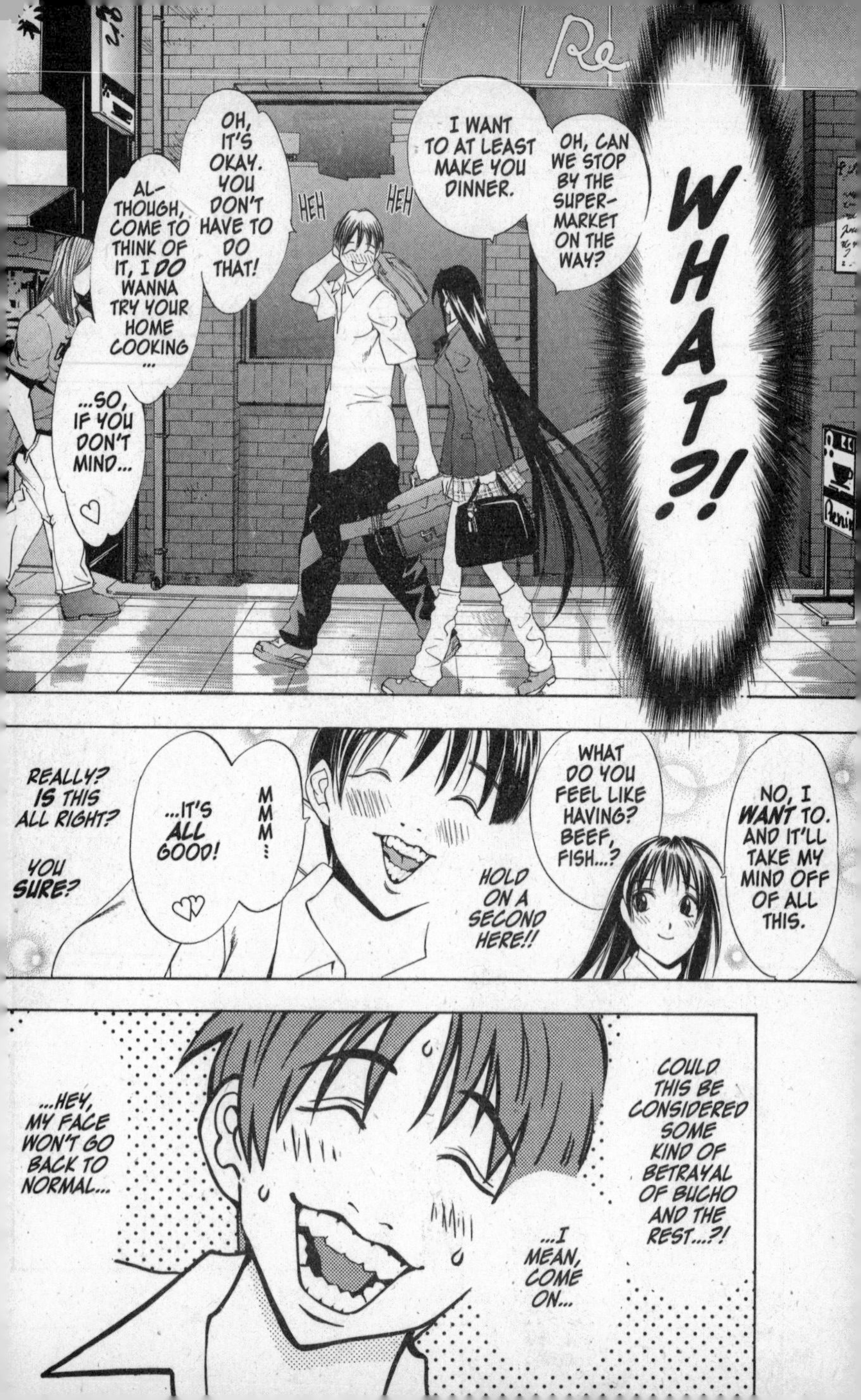
OH, CAN WE STOP BY THE SUPER-MARKET ON THE WAY?
I WANT TO AT LEAST MAKE YOU DINNER.
HEH HEH
OH, IT'S OKAY. YOU DON'T HAVE TO DO THAT!
AL-THOUGH, COME TO THINK OF IT, I DO WANNA TRY YOUR HOME COOKING...
...SO, IF YOU DON'T MIND...
WHAT?!
NO, I WANT TO. AND IT'LL TAKE MY MIND OFF OF ALL THIS.
WHAT DO YOU FEEL LIKE HAVING? BEEF, FISH...?
HOLD ON A SECOND HERE!!
MMM...
...IT'S ALL GOOD!
REALLY? IS THIS ALL RIGHT?
YOU SURE?
COULD THIS BE CONSIDERED SOME KIND OF BETRAYAL OF BUCHO AND THE REST...?!
...I MEAN, COME ON...
...HEY, MY FACE WON'T GO BACK TO NORMAL...

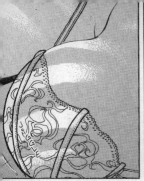

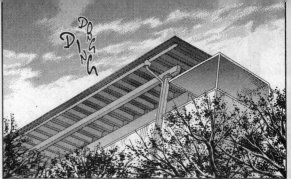

DING DONG
JIGGLE
MMM...
MAKIHARA-SAN! SPECIAL DELIVERY!
AH...
...OKAY!
DAMMIT! I MISSED SCHOOL AGAIN! OH, WELL.
WHAT AM I GONNA DO? I ALWAYS PASS OUT AFTER SEX...
...UM, I NEED A PEN? WHERE ...?
DRAG
DRAG

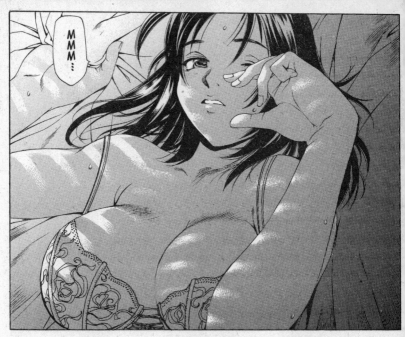

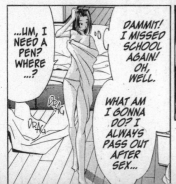

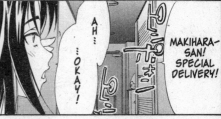

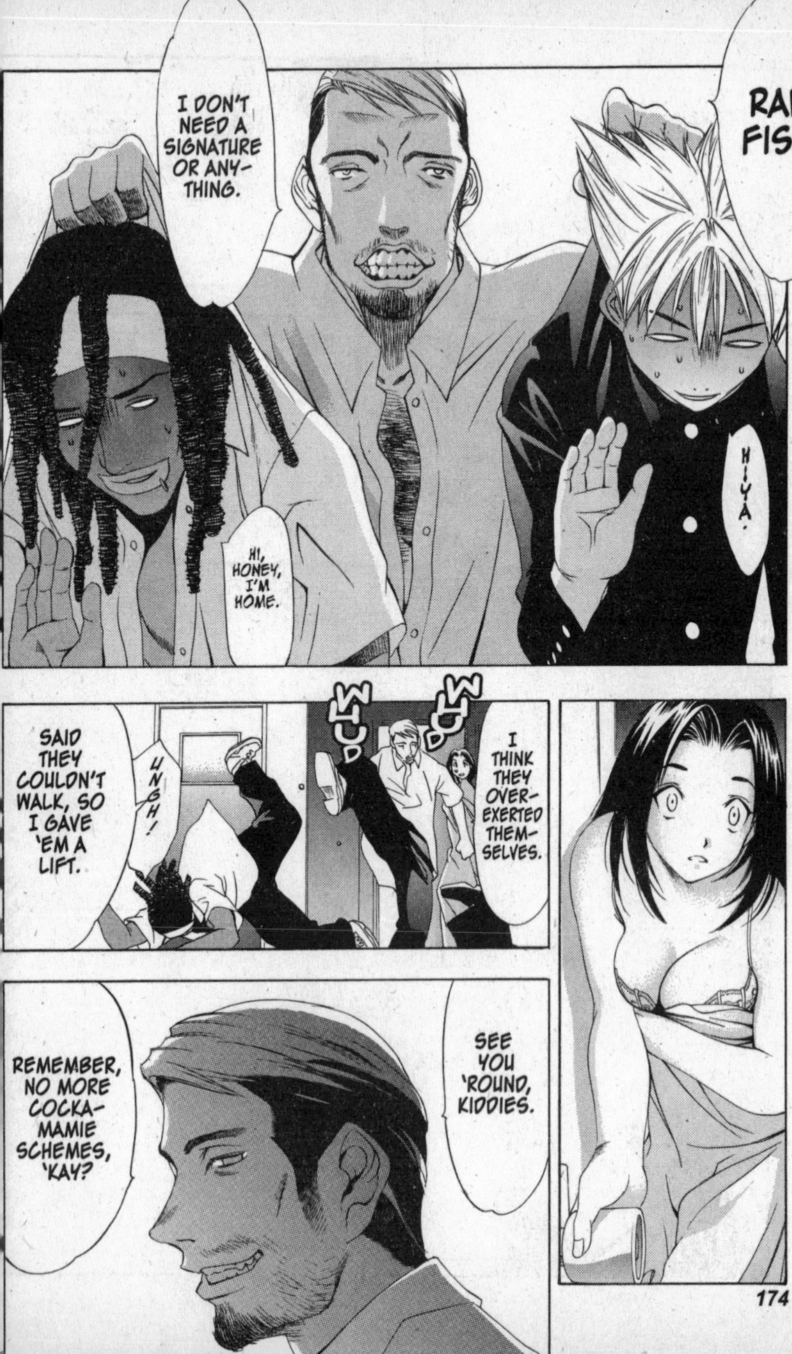
RAW FISH.
I DON'T NEED A SIGNATURE OR ANY-THING.
HIYA.
HI, HONEY, I'M HOME.
I THINK THEY OVER-EXERTED THEM-SELVES.
WHUD
WHUD
UNGH!
SAID THEY COULDN'T WALK, SO I GAVE 'EM A LIFT.
SEE YOU 'ROUND, KIDDIES.
REMEMBER, NO MORE COCKA-MAMIE SCHEMES, 'KAY?

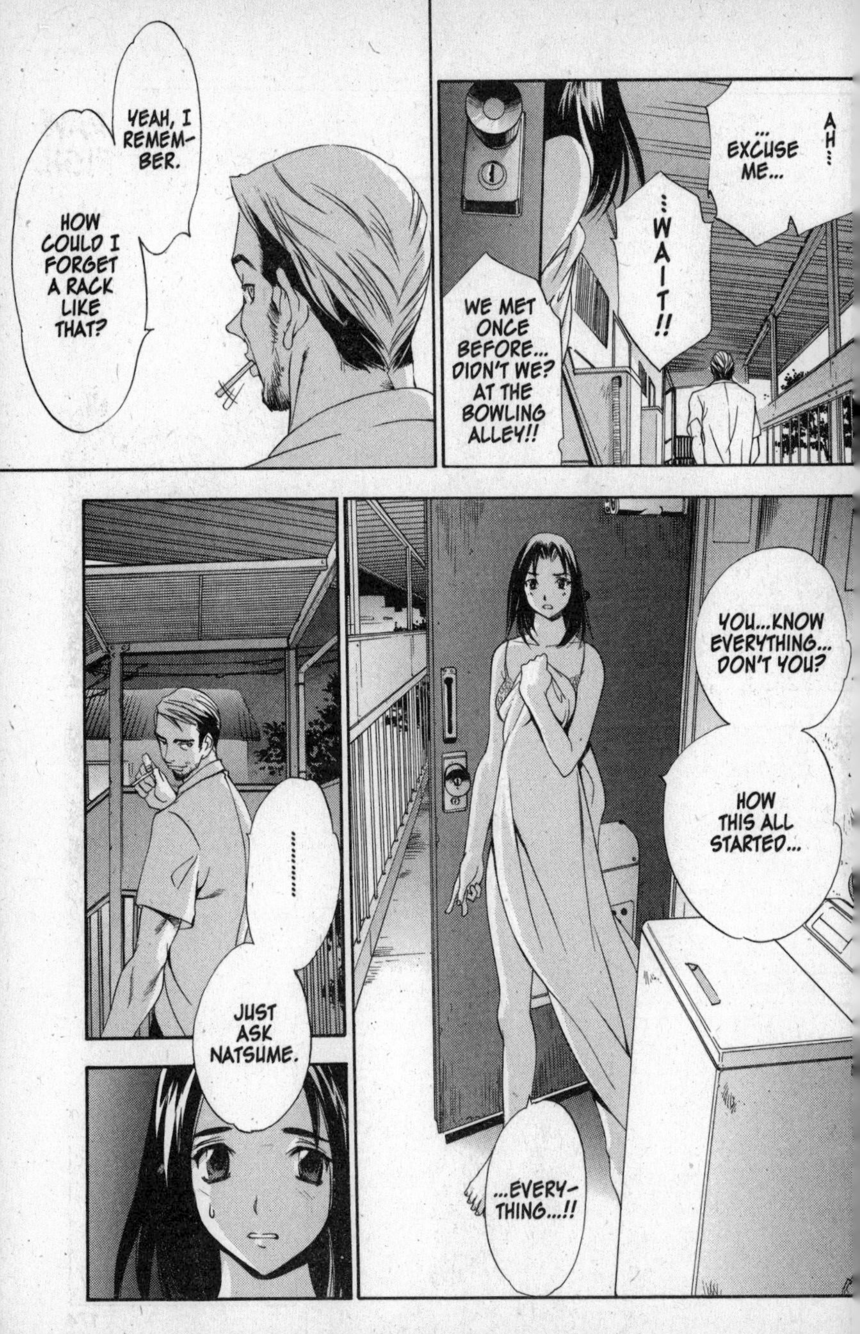
AH...
...EXCUSE ME...
...WAIT!!
WE MET ONCE BEFORE... DIDN'T WE? AT THE BOWLING ALLEY!!
YEAH, I REMEMBER.
HOW COULD I FORGET A RACK LIKE THAT?
YOU...KNOW EVERYTHING... DON'T YOU?
HOW THIS ALL STARTED...
...EVERYTHING...!!
......
JUST ASK NATSUME.

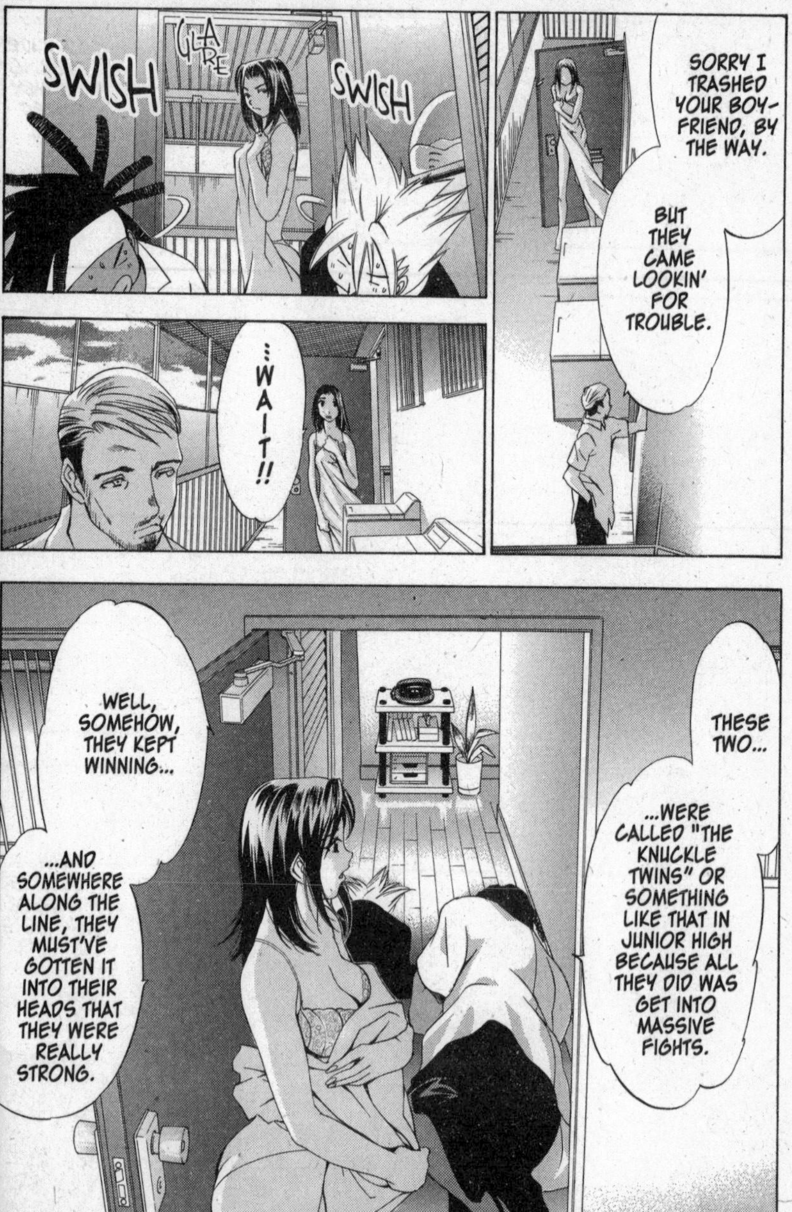
SORRY I TRASHED YOUR BOY-FRIEND, BY THE WAY.
BUT THEY CAME LOOKIN' FOR TROUBLE.
SWISH
GLARE
SWISH
...WAIT!!
THESE TWO...
...WERE CALLED "THE KNUCKLE TWINS" OR SOMETHING LIKE THAT IN JUNIOR HIGH BECAUSE ALL THEY DID WAS GET INTO MASSIVE FIGHTS.
WELL, SOMEHOW, THEY KEPT WINNING...
...AND SOMEWHERE ALONG THE LINE, THEY MUST'VE GOTTEN IT INTO THEIR HEADS THAT THEY WERE REALLY STRONG.

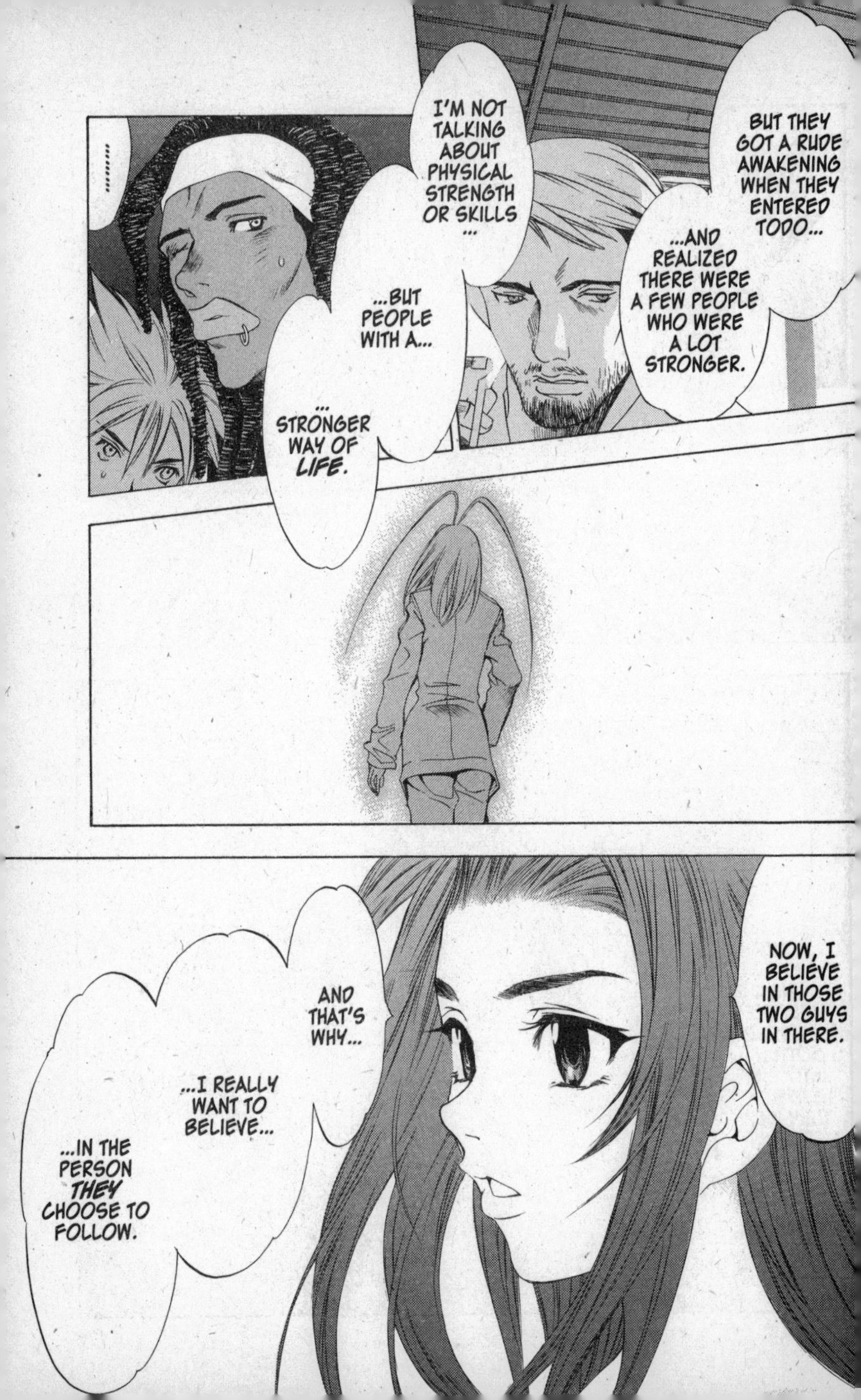
BUT THEY GOT A RUDE AWAKENING WHEN THEY ENTERED TODO...
...AND REALIZED THERE WERE A FEW PEOPLE WHO WERE A LOT STRONGER.
I'M NOT TALKING ABOUT PHYSICAL STRENGTH OR SKILLS...
...BUT PEOPLE WITH A...
...STRONGER WAY OF *LIFE*.
......
NOW, I BELIEVE IN THOSE TWO GUYS IN THERE.
AND THAT'S WHY...
...I REALLY WANT TO BELIEVE...
...IN THE PERSON *THEY* CHOOSE TO FOLLOW.

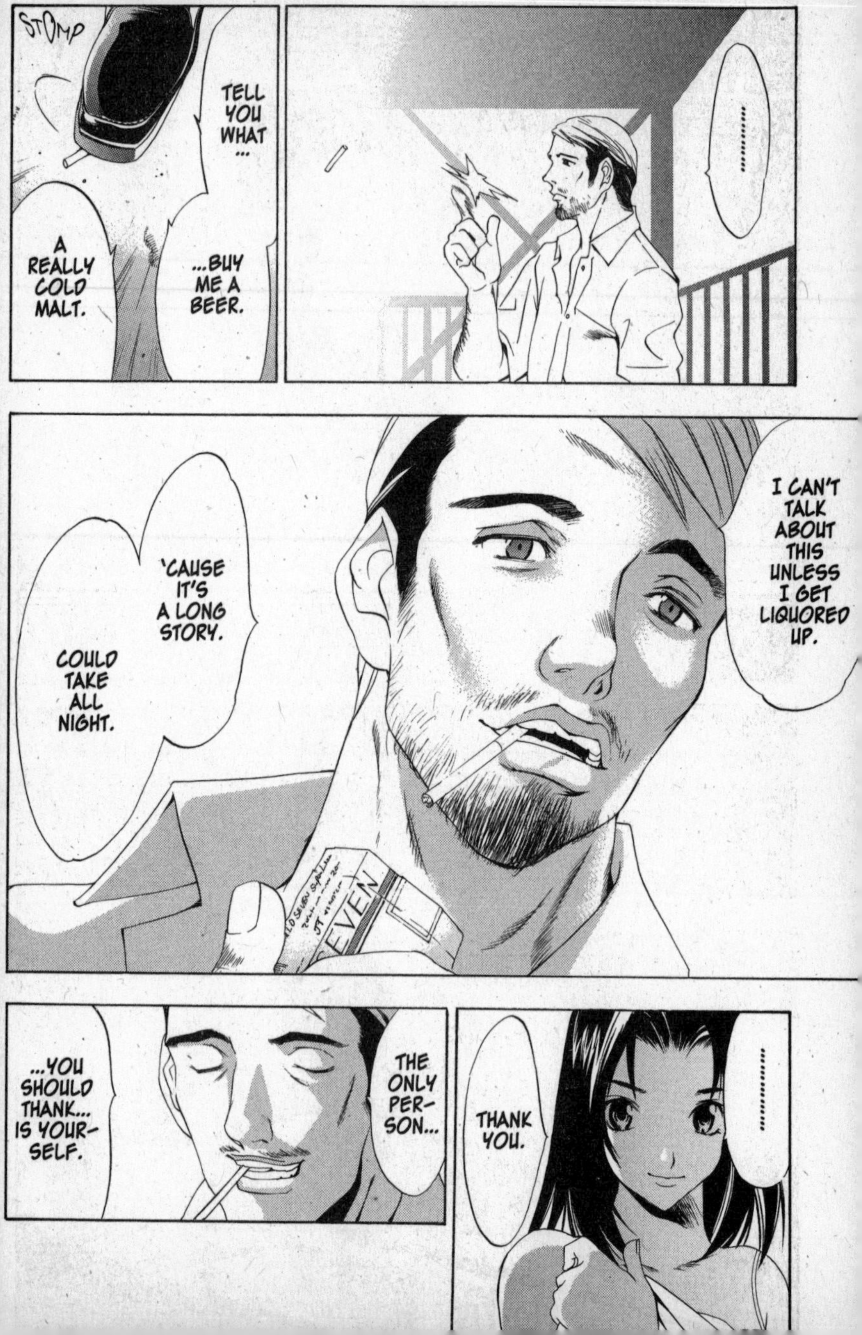
......
TELL YOU WHAT ...
STOMP
...BUY ME A BEER.
A REALLY COLD MALT.
I CAN'T TALK ABOUT THIS UNLESS I GET LIQUORED UP.
'CAUSE IT'S A LONG STORY.
COULD TAKE ALL NIGHT.
......
THANK YOU.
THE ONLY PER-SON...
...YOU SHOULD THANK... IS YOUR-SELF.

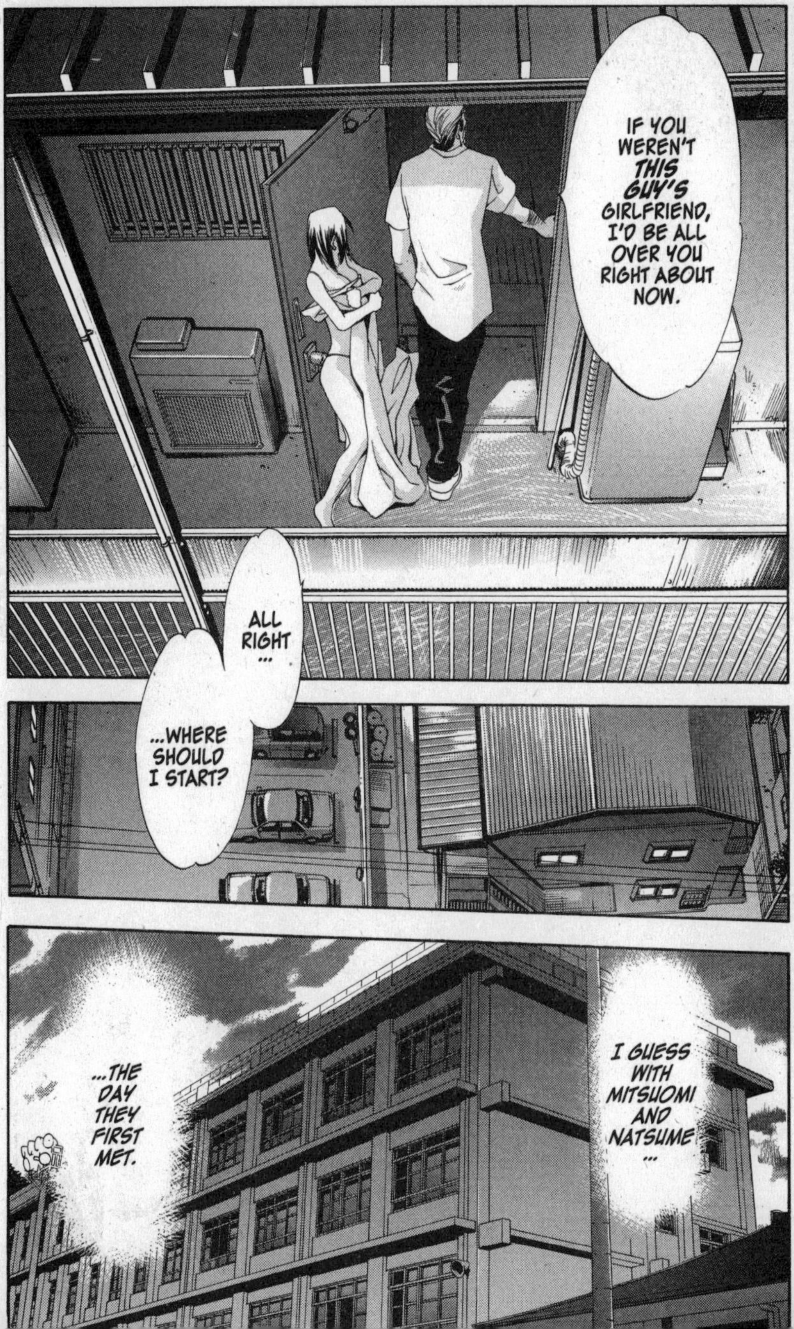
IF YOU WEREN'T ***THIS GUY'S*** GIRLFRIEND, I'D BE ALL OVER YOU RIGHT ABOUT NOW.
ALL RIGHT...
...WHERE SHOULD I START?
I GUESS WITH MITSUOMI AND NATSUME...
...THE DAY THEY FIRST MET.

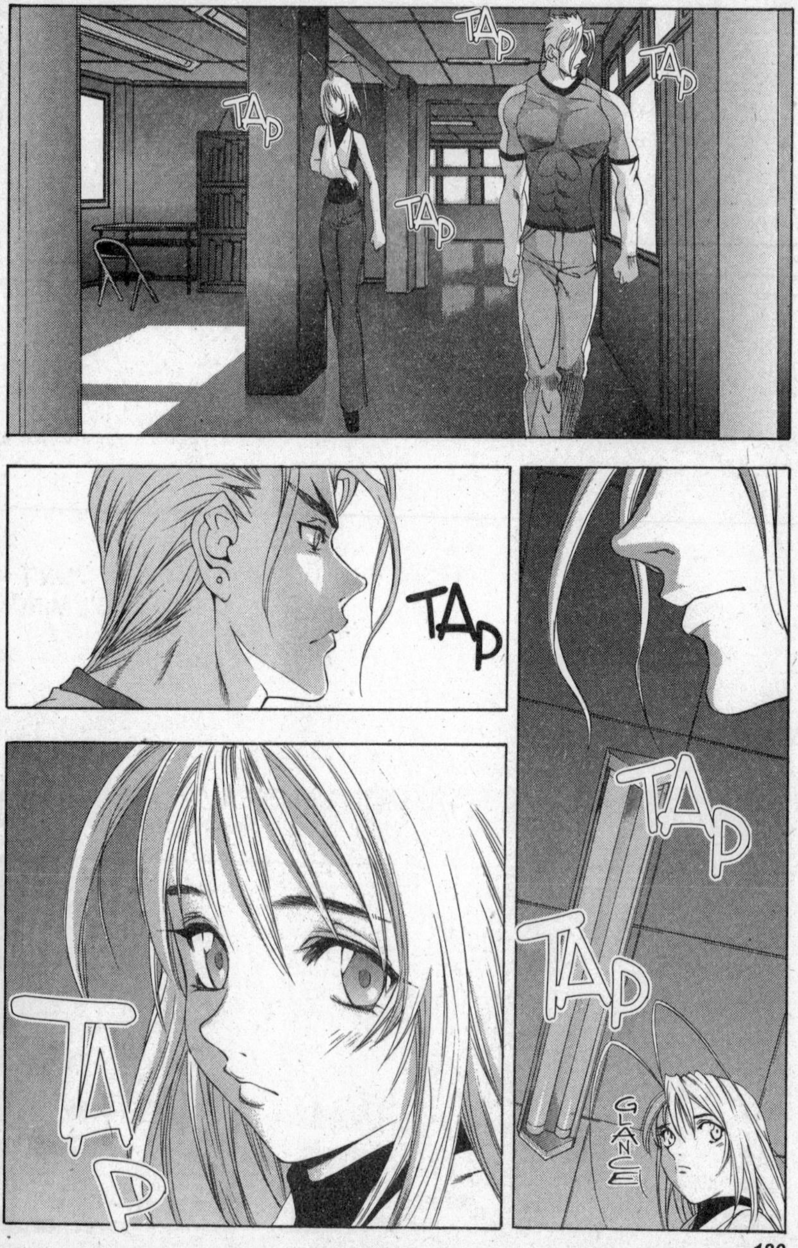
TAP
TAP
TAP
TAP
TAP
TAP
GLANCE
TAP
TAP

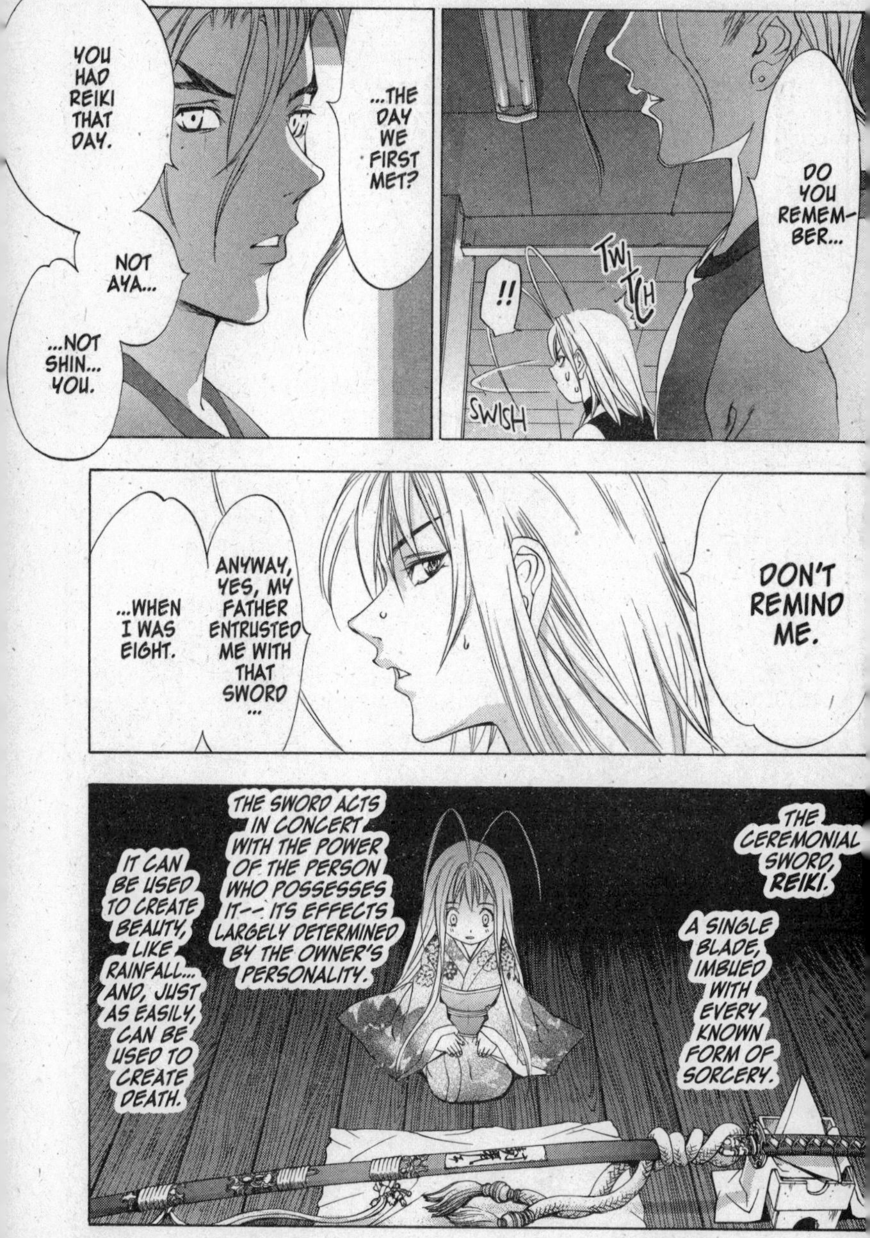
DO YOU REMEMBER...
!!
TWITCH
SWISH
...THE DAY WE FIRST MET?
YOU HAD REIKI THAT DAY.
NOT AYA...
...NOT SHIN... YOU.
DON'T REMIND ME.
ANYWAY, YES, MY FATHER ENTRUSTED ME WITH THAT SWORD ...
...WHEN I WAS EIGHT.
THE CEREMONIAL SWORD, REIKI.
A SINGLE BLADE, IMBUED WITH EVERY KNOWN FORM OF SORCERY.
THE SWORD ACTS IN CONCERT WITH THE POWER OF THE PERSON WHO POSSESSES IT-- ITS EFFECTS LARGELY DETERMINED BY THE OWNER'S PERSONALITY.
IT CAN BE USED TO CREATE BEAUTY, LIKE RAINFALL... AND, JUST AS EASILY, CAN BE USED TO CREATE DEATH.

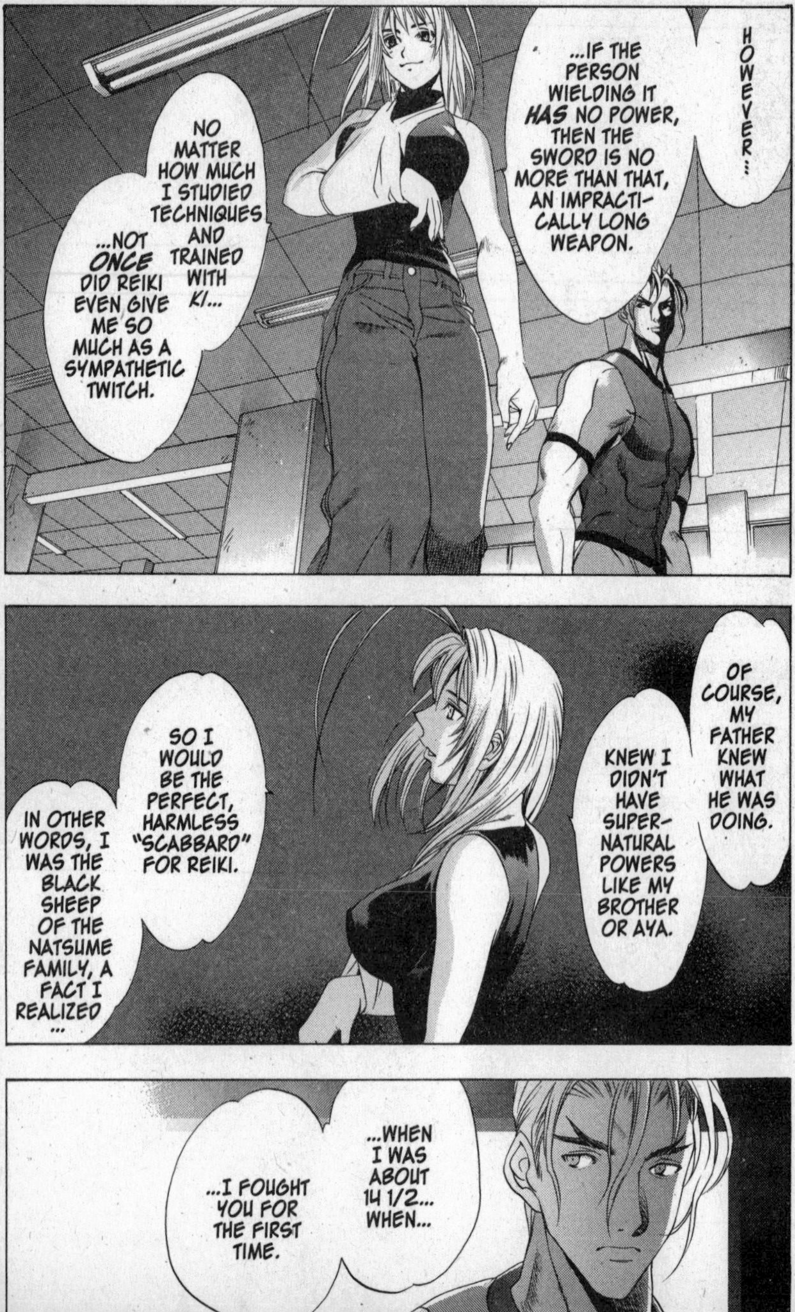
HOWEVER...
...IF THE PERSON WIELDING IT HAS NO POWER, THEN THE SWORD IS NO MORE THAN THAT, AN IMPRACTICALLY LONG WEAPON.
NO MATTER HOW MUCH I STUDIED TECHNIQUES AND TRAINED WITH KI...
...NOT ONCE DID REIKI EVEN GIVE ME SO MUCH AS A SYMPATHETIC TWITCH.
OF COURSE, MY FATHER KNEW WHAT HE WAS DOING.
KNEW I DIDN'T HAVE SUPERNATURAL POWERS LIKE MY BROTHER OR AYA.
SO I WOULD BE THE PERFECT, HARMLESS "SCABBARD" FOR REIKI.
IN OTHER WORDS, I WAS THE BLACK SHEEP OF THE NATSUME FAMILY, A FACT I REALIZED ...
...WHEN I WAS ABOUT 14 1/2... WHEN...
...I FOUGHT YOU FOR THE FIRST TIME.

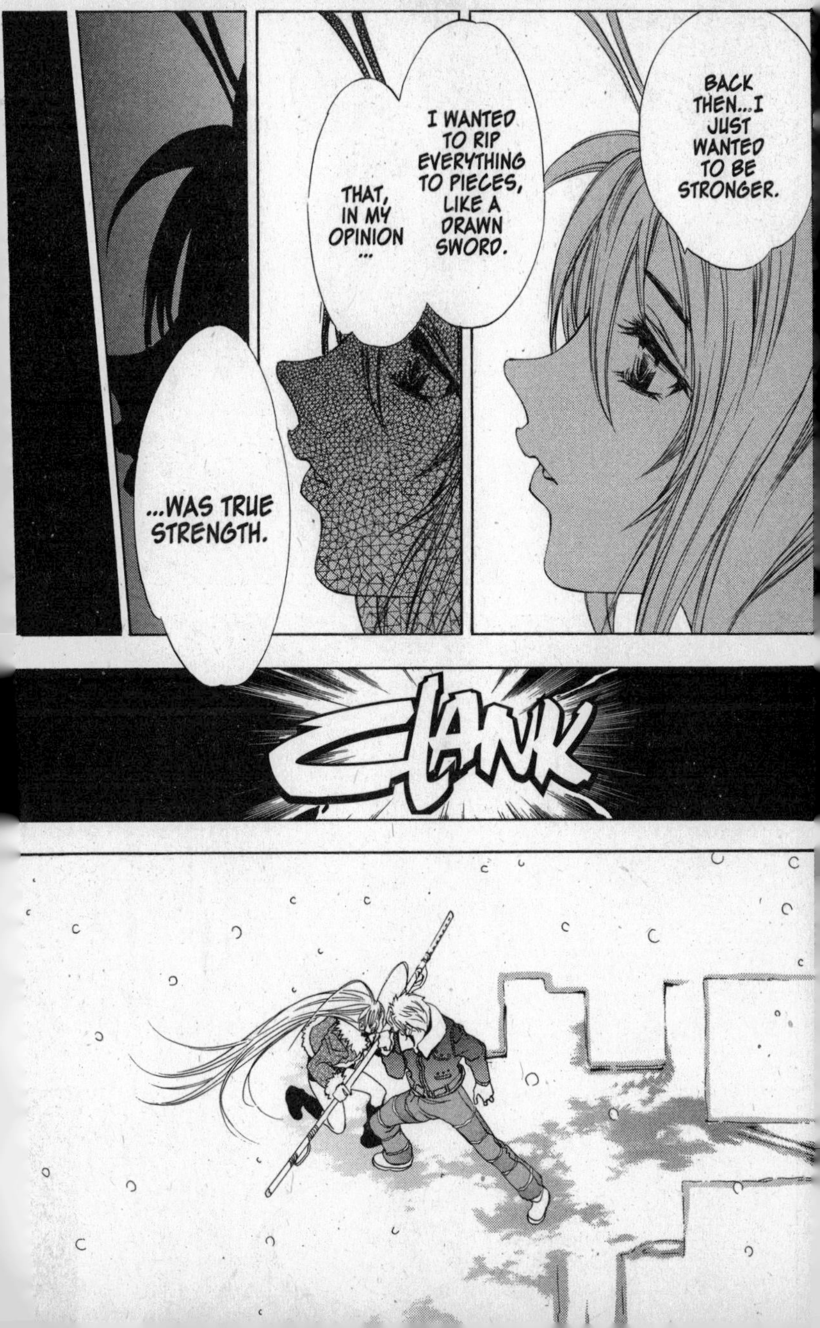
BACK THEN...I JUST WANTED TO BE STRONGER.
I WANTED TO RIP EVERYTHING TO PIECES, LIKE A DRAWN SWORD.
THAT, IN MY OPINION ...
...WAS TRUE STRENGTH.
CLANK

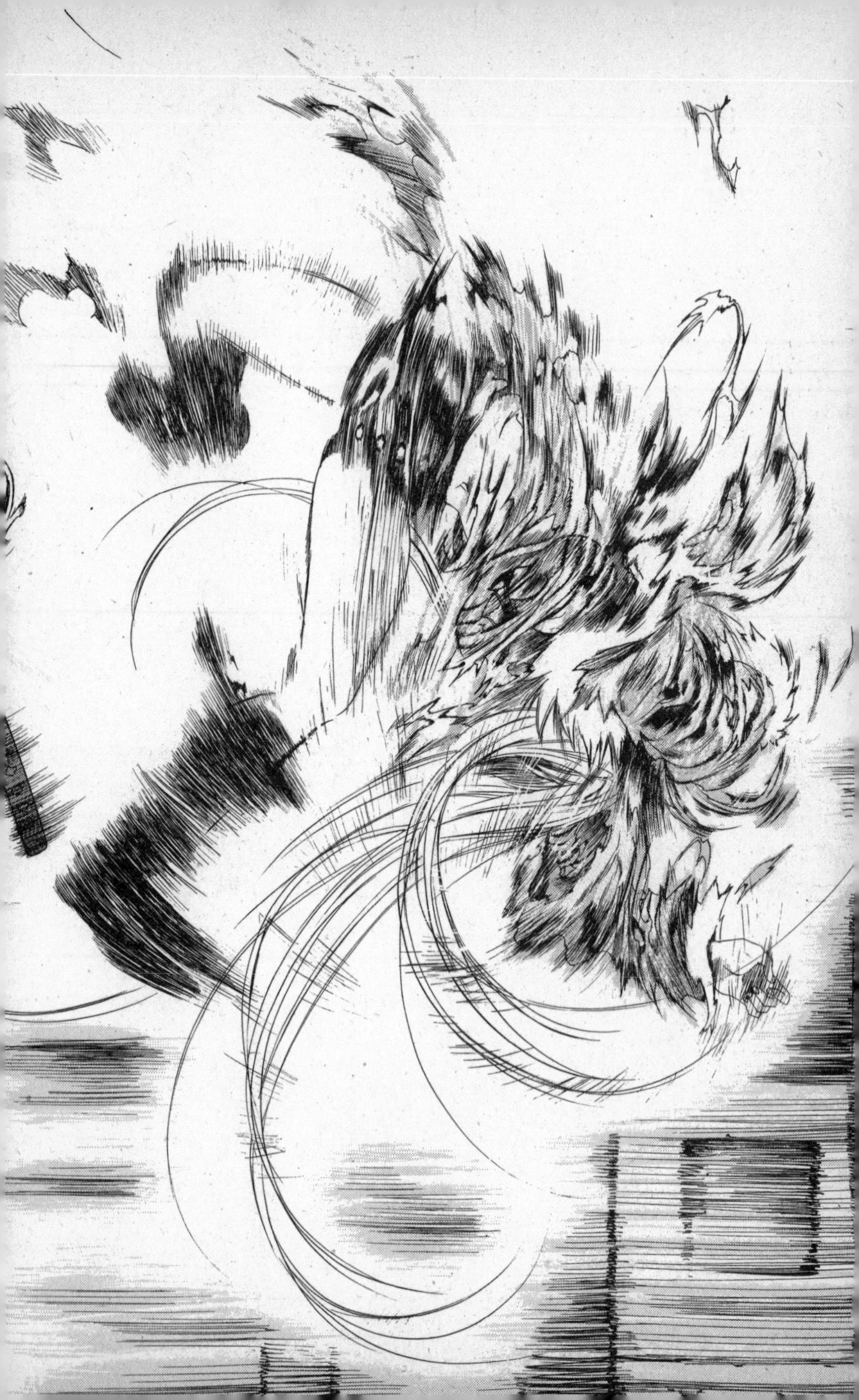

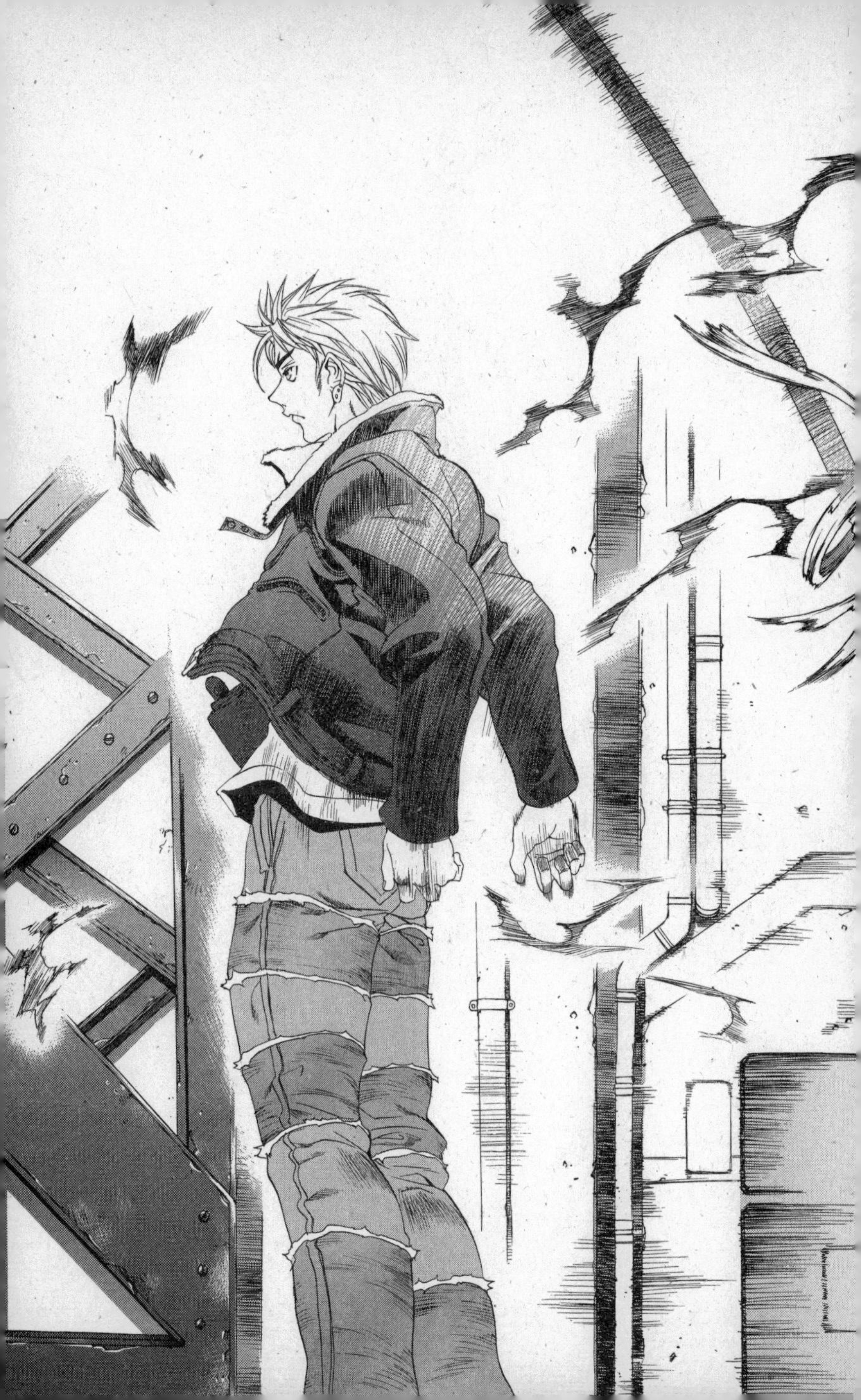

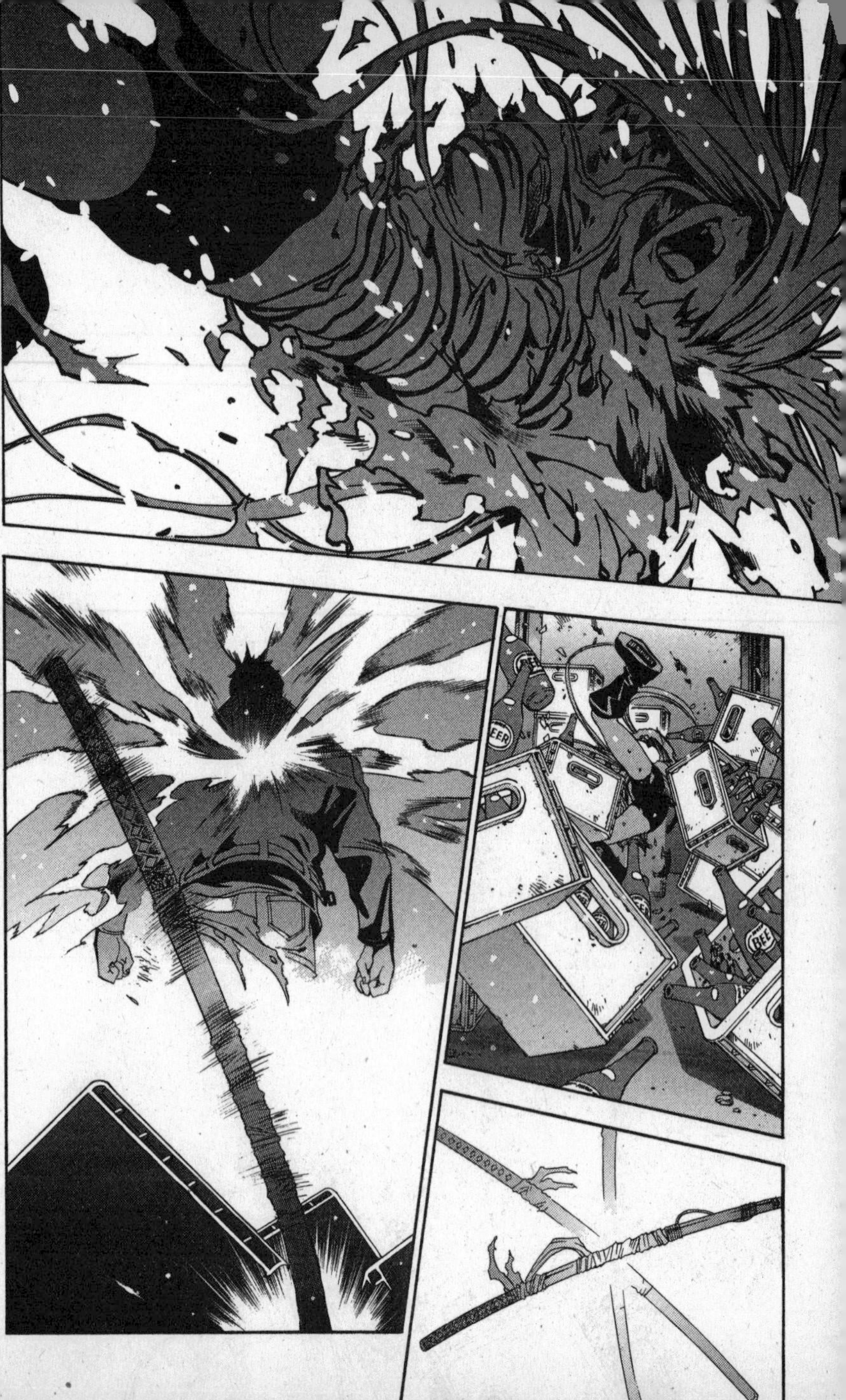
BEER

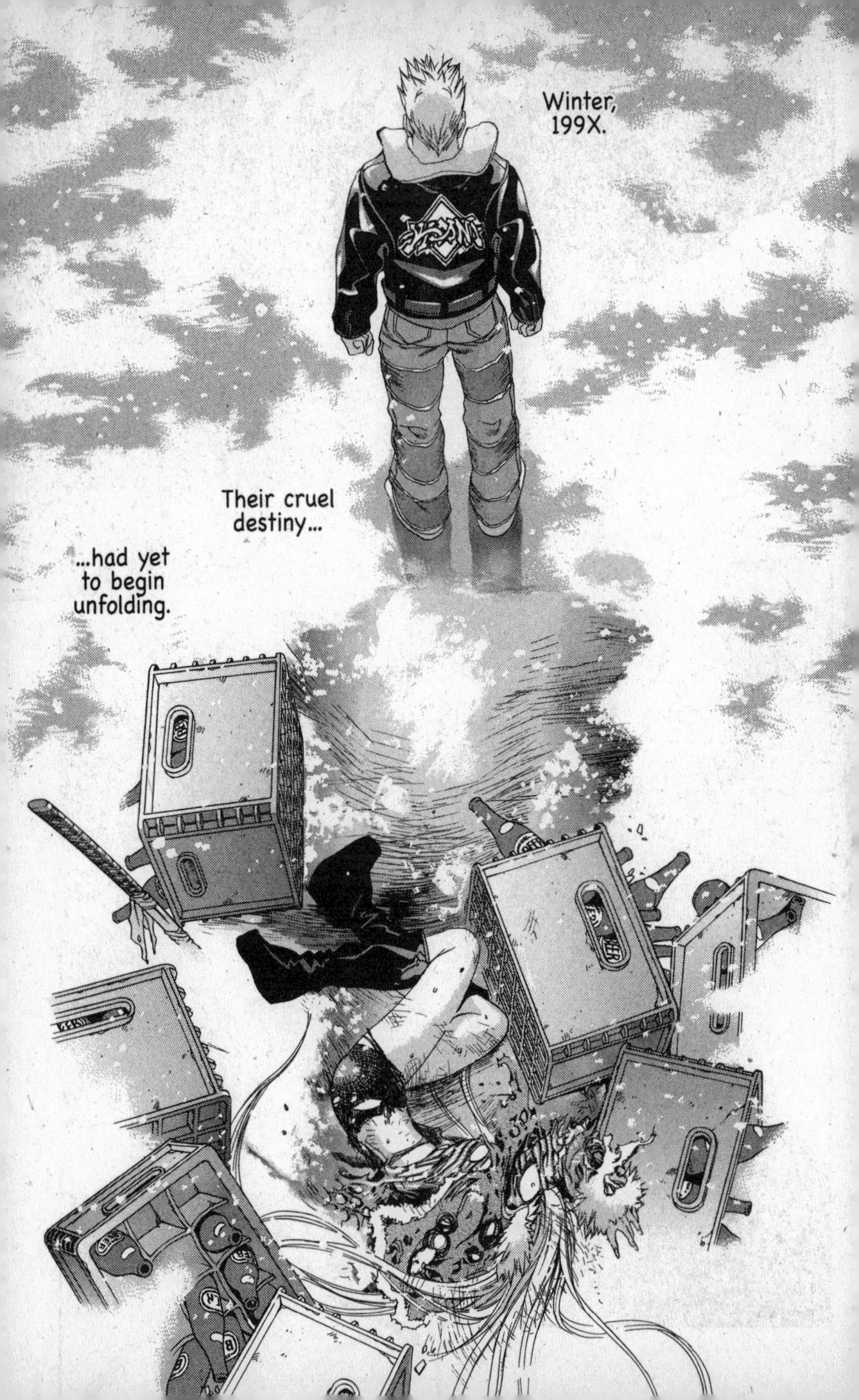
Winter, 199X.
Their cruel destiny...
...had yet to begin unfolding.

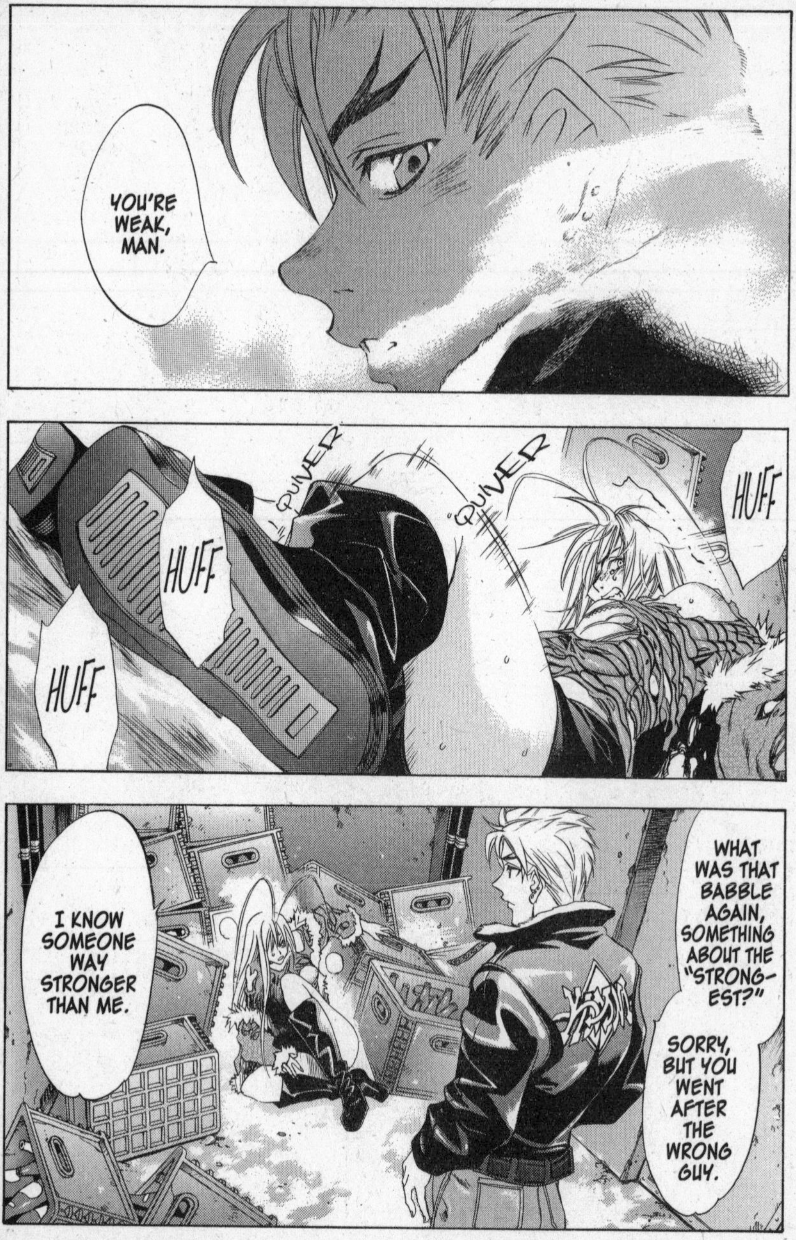
YOU'RE WEAK, MAN.
HUFF
QUIVER
QUIVER
HUFF
HUFF
WHAT WAS THAT BABBLE AGAIN, SOMETHING ABOUT THE "STRONG-EST?"
SORRY, BUT YOU WENT AFTER THE WRONG GUY.
I KNOW SOMEONE WAY STRONGER THAN ME.

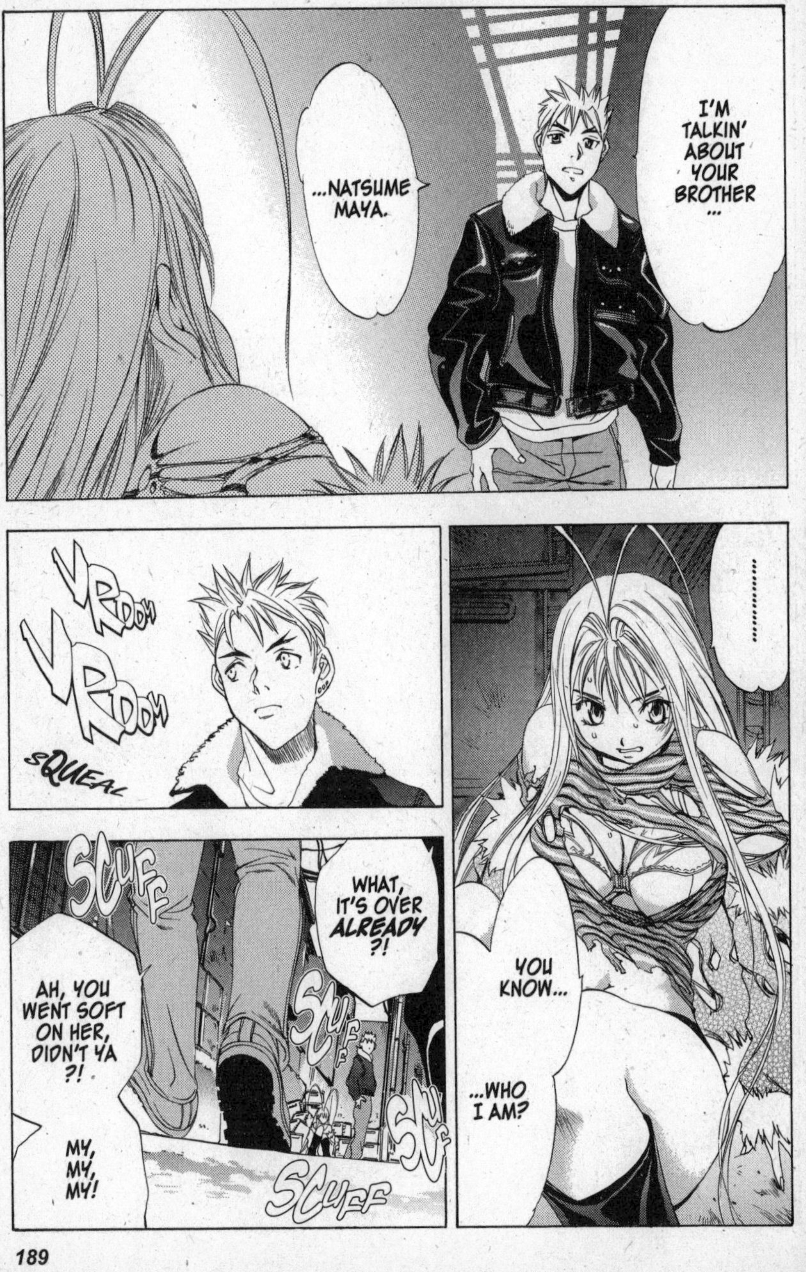
I'M TALKIN' ABOUT YOUR BROTHER ...
...NATSUME MAYA.
....
YOU KNOW...
...WHO I AM?
VROOM
VROOM
SQUEAL
SCUFF
WHAT, IT'S OVER ALREADY ?!
SCUFF
AH, YOU WENT SOFT ON HER, DIDN'T YA ?!
SCUFF
SCUFF
MY, MY, MY!

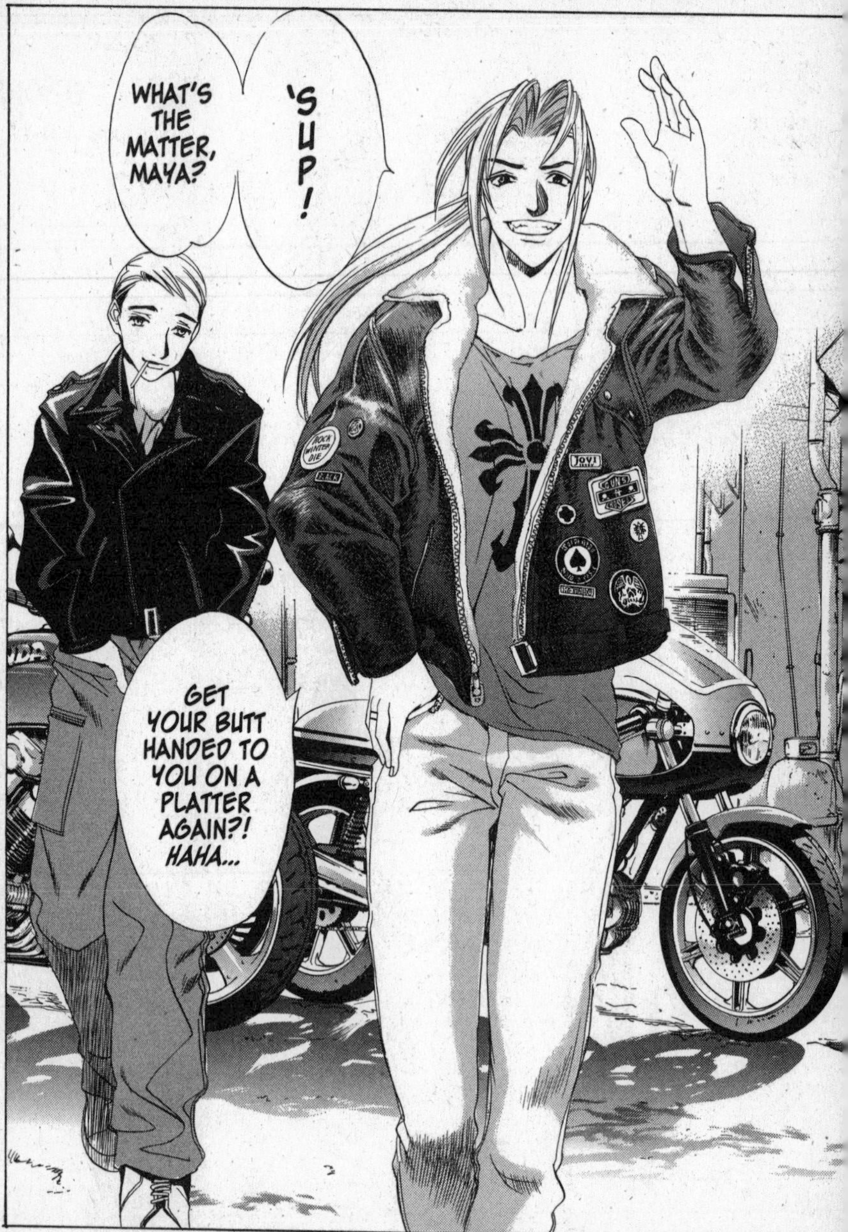
'SUP!
WHAT'S THE MATTER, MAYA?
GET YOUR BUTT HANDED TO YOU ON A PLATTER AGAIN?! HAHA...

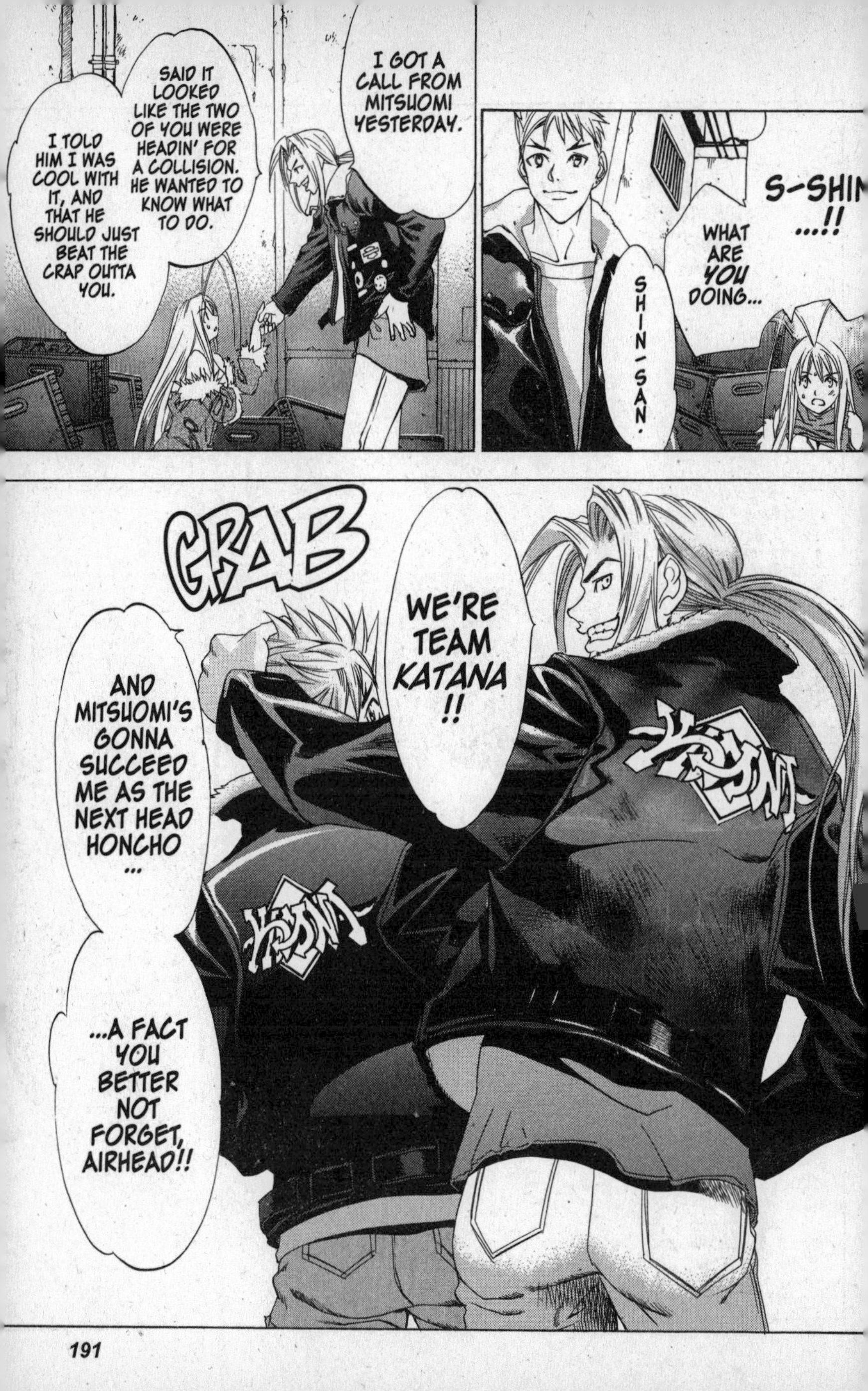
S-SHIN ...!!
WHAT ARE YOU DOING...
SHIN-SAN.
I GOT A CALL FROM MITSUOMI YESTERDAY.
SAID IT LOOKED LIKE THE TWO OF YOU WERE HEADIN' FOR A COLLISION. HE WANTED TO KNOW WHAT TO DO.
I TOLD HIM I WAS COOL WITH IT, AND THAT HE SHOULD JUST BEAT THE CRAP OUTTA YOU.
GRAB
WE'RE TEAM KATANA!!
AND MITSUOMI'S GONNA SUCCEED ME AS THE NEXT HEAD HONCHO ...
...A FACT YOU BETTER NOT FORGET, AIRHEAD!!

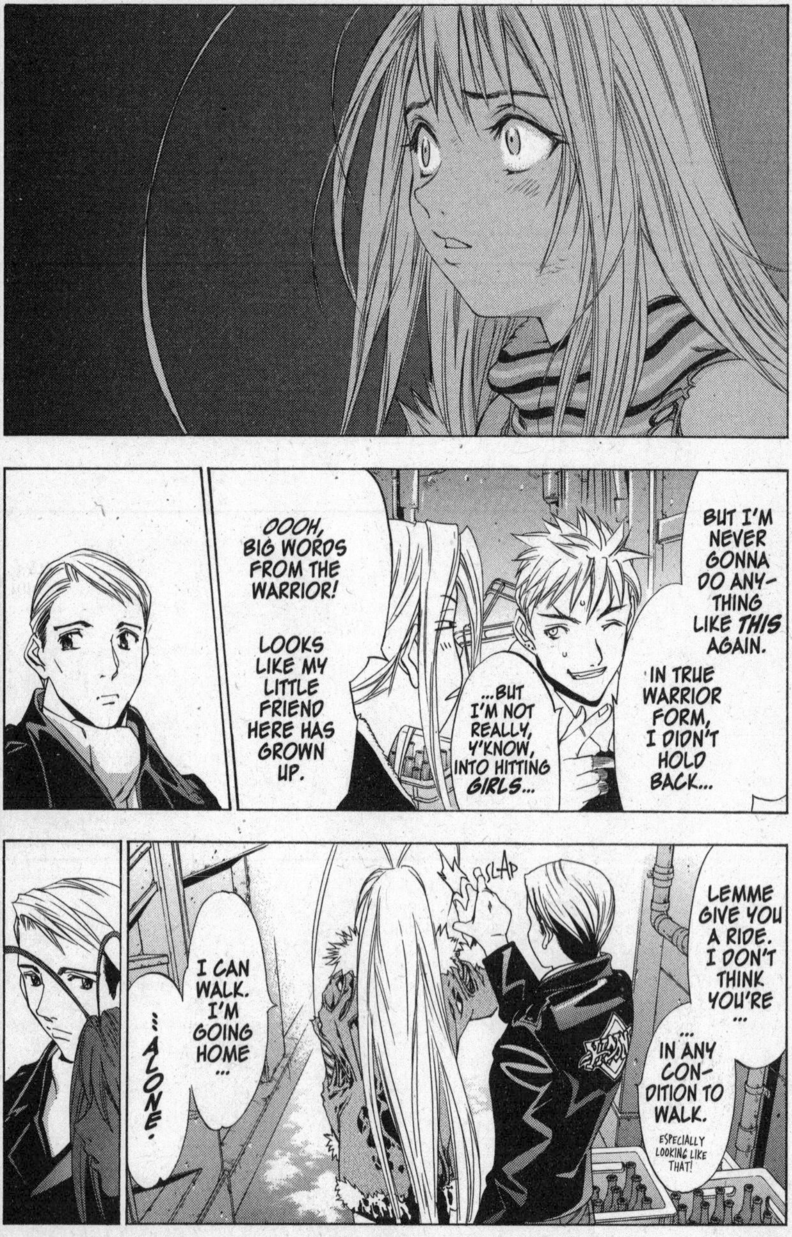
BUT I'M NEVER GONNA DO ANY-THING LIKE THIS AGAIN.
IN TRUE WARRIOR FORM, I DIDN'T HOLD BACK...
...BUT I'M NOT REALLY, Y'KNOW, INTO HITTING GIRLS...
OOOH, BIG WORDS FROM THE WARRIOR!
LOOKS LIKE MY LITTLE FRIEND HERE HAS GROWN UP.
LEMME GIVE YOU A RIDE. I DON'T THINK YOU'RE...
...IN ANY CON-DITION TO WALK.
ESPECIALLY LOOKING LIKE THAT!
SLAP
I CAN WALK. I'M GOING HOME...
...ALONE.

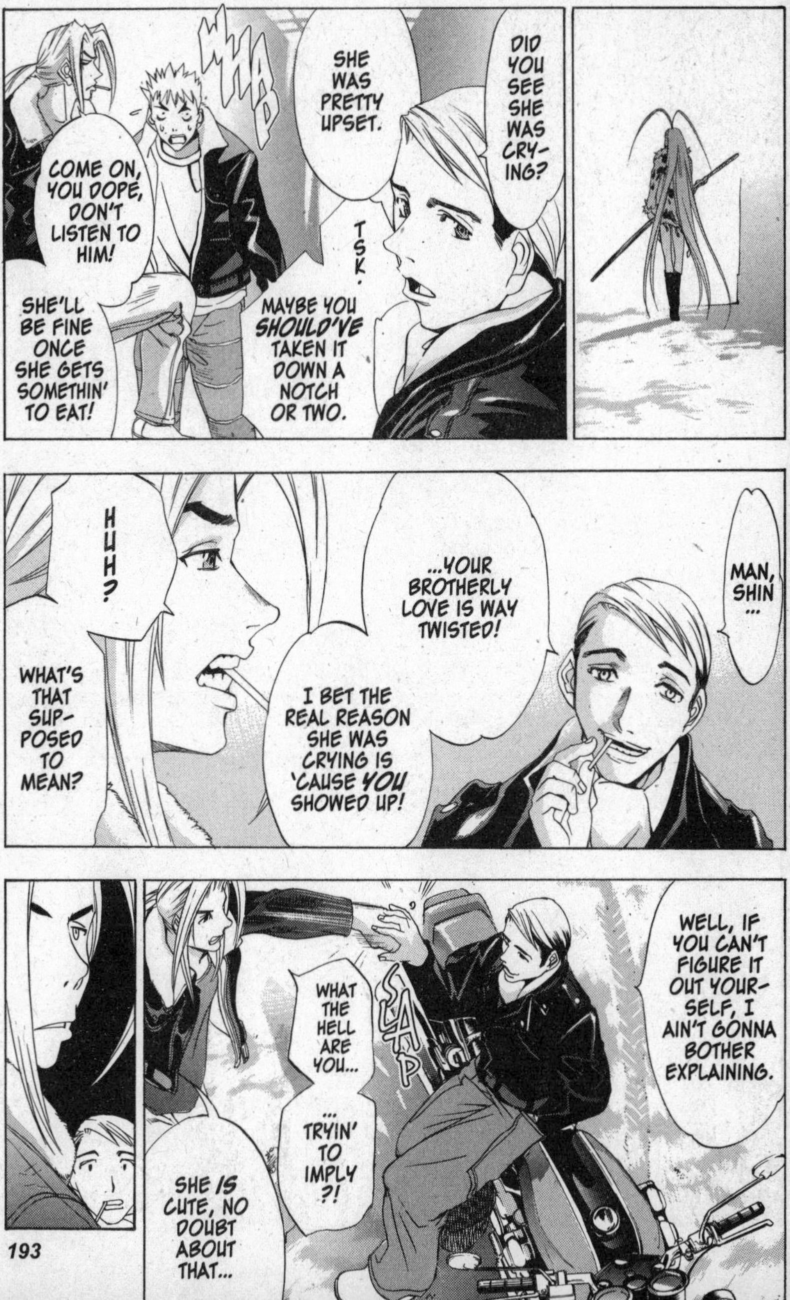
DID YOU SEE SHE WAS CRY-ING?
SHE WAS PRETTY UPSET.
WHAP
TSK.
MAYBE YOU SHOULD'VE TAKEN IT DOWN A NOTCH OR TWO.
COME ON, YOU DOPE, DON'T LISTEN TO HIM!
SHE'LL BE FINE ONCE SHE GETS SOMETHIN' TO EAT!
MAN, SHIN...
...YOUR BROTHERLY LOVE IS WAY TWISTED!
I BET THE REAL REASON SHE WAS CRYING IS 'CAUSE YOU SHOWED UP!
HUH?
WHAT'S THAT SUP-POSED TO MEAN?
WELL, IF YOU CAN'T FIGURE IT OUT YOUR-SELF, I AIN'T GONNA BOTHER EXPLAINING.
SLAP
WHAT THE HELL ARE YOU...
...TRYIN' TO IMPLY?!
SHE IS CUTE, NO DOUBT ABOUT THAT...

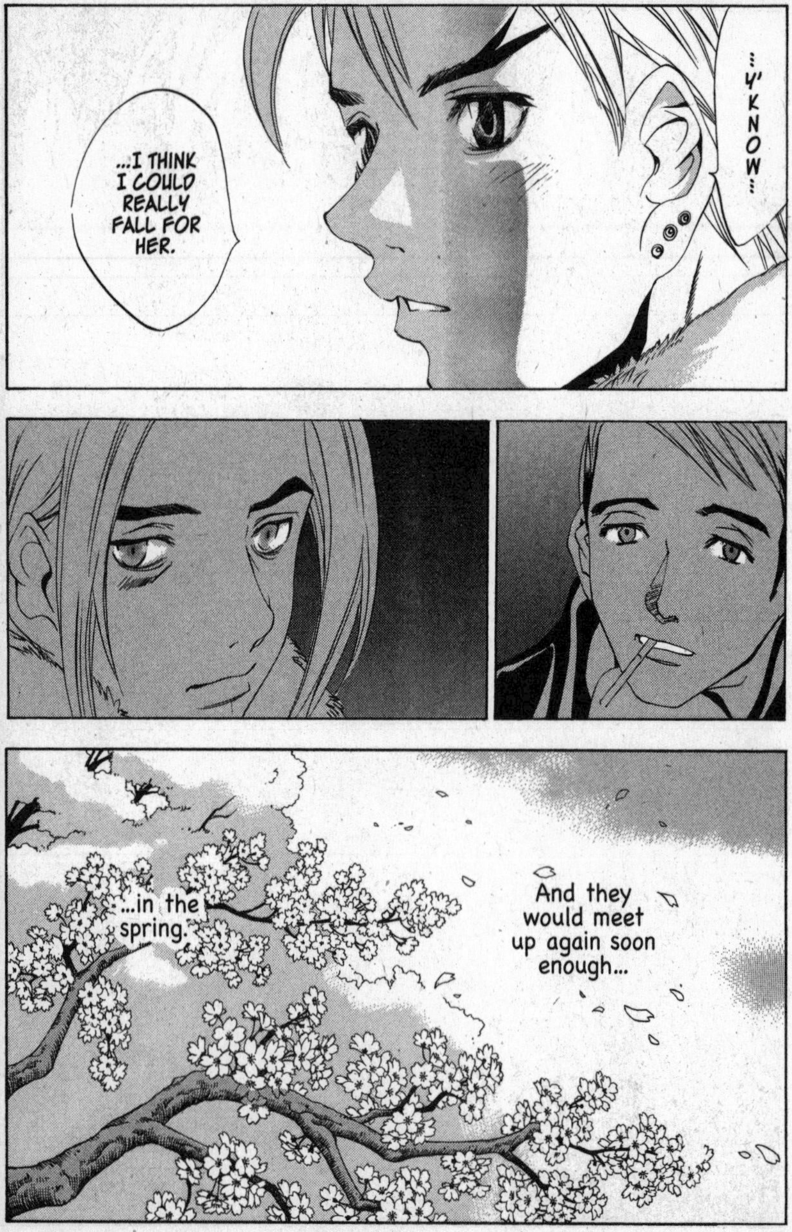
...Y'KNOW...
...I THINK I COULD REALLY FALL FOR HER.
And they would meet up again soon enough...
...in the spring.

FIGHT:26

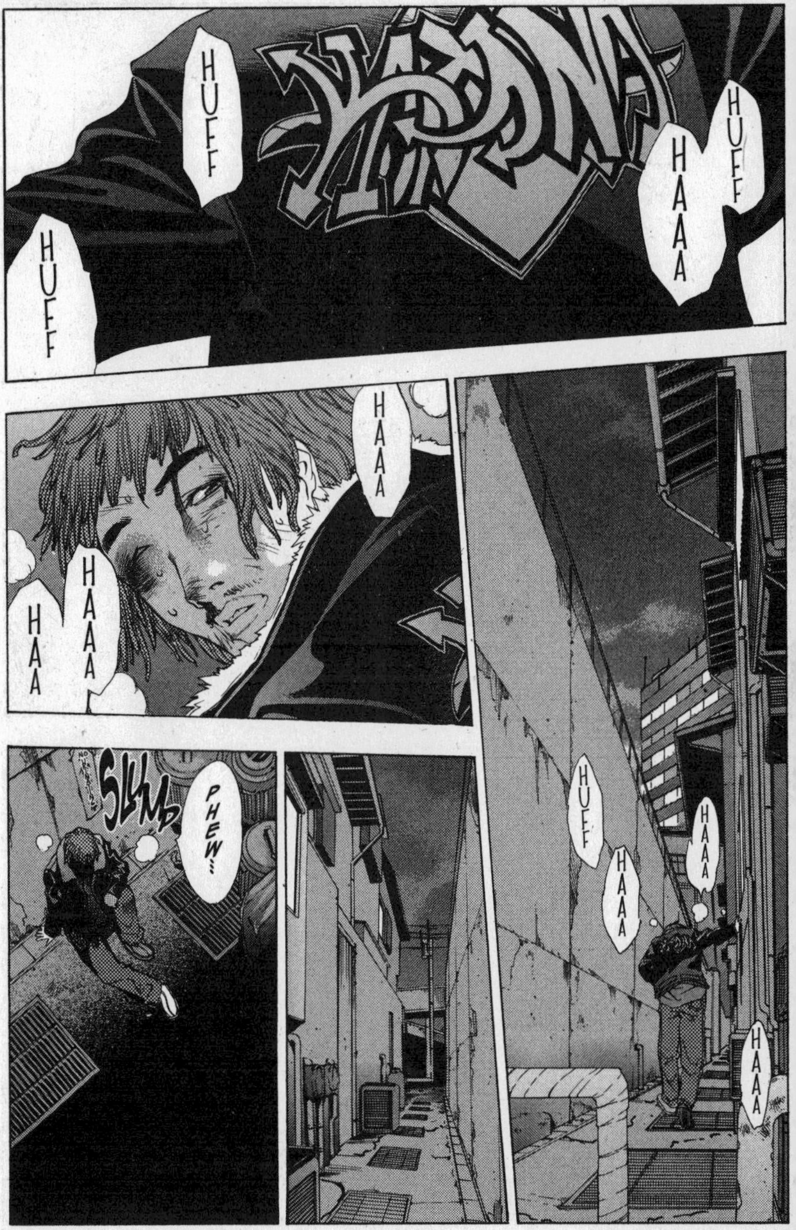
HUFF
HAAA
HUFF
HUFF
HAAA
HUFF
HAAA
HAAA
HAAA
HAAA
HAA
SLUMP
PHEW...

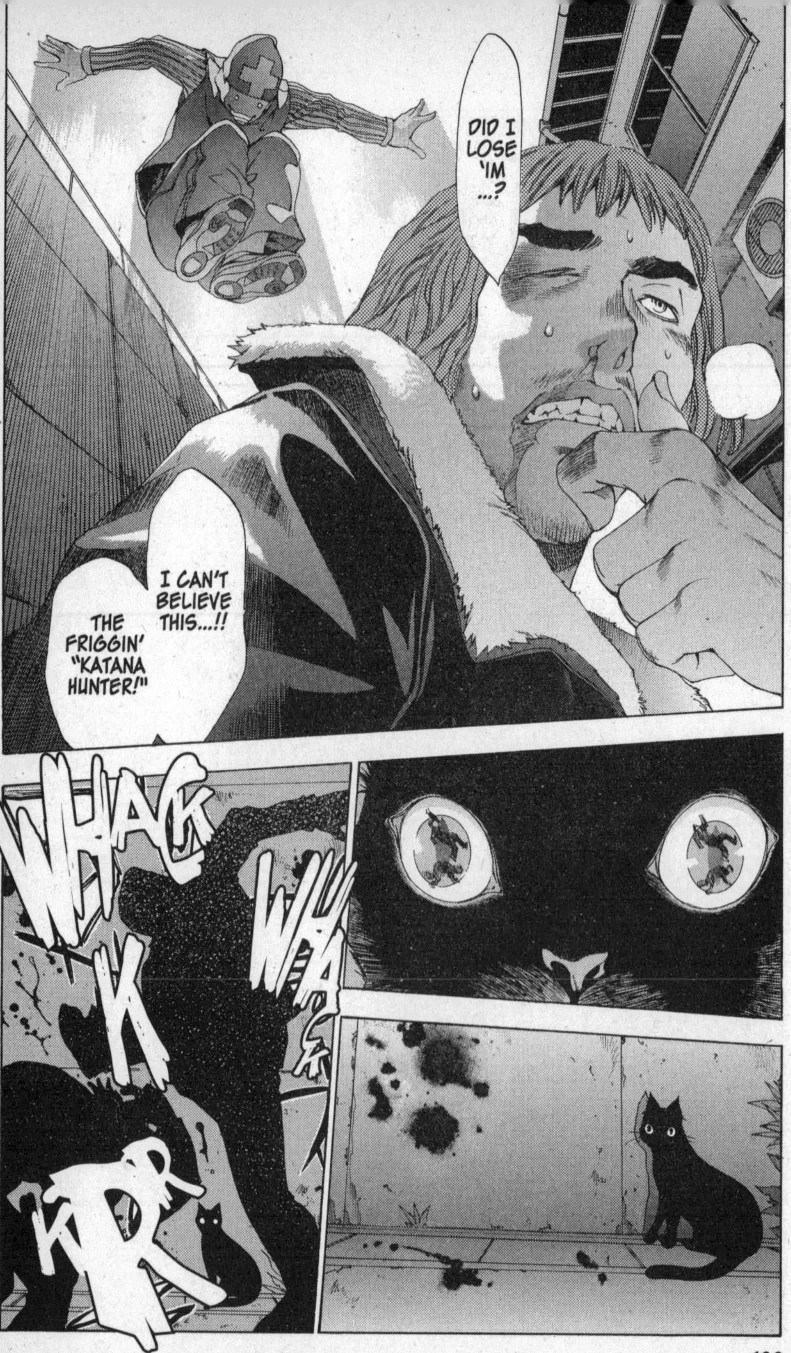
DID I LOSE 'IM ...?
I CAN'T BELIEVE THIS...!!
THE FRIGGIN' "KATANA HUNTER!"
WHACK
WHACK

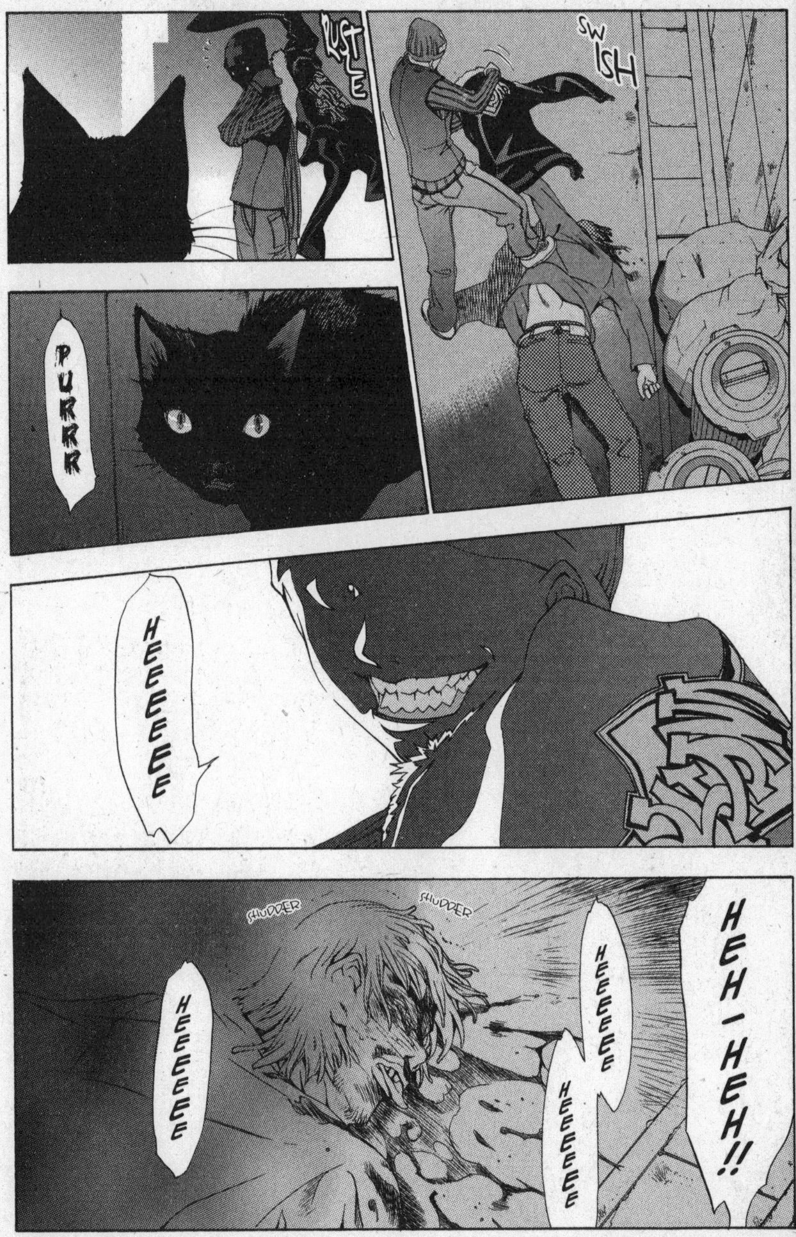
SWISH
RUSTLE
PURRR
HEEEEEEE
HEH-HEH!!
HEEEEEE
HEEEEEE
SHUDDER
SHUDDER
HEEEEEE

FIGHT:26

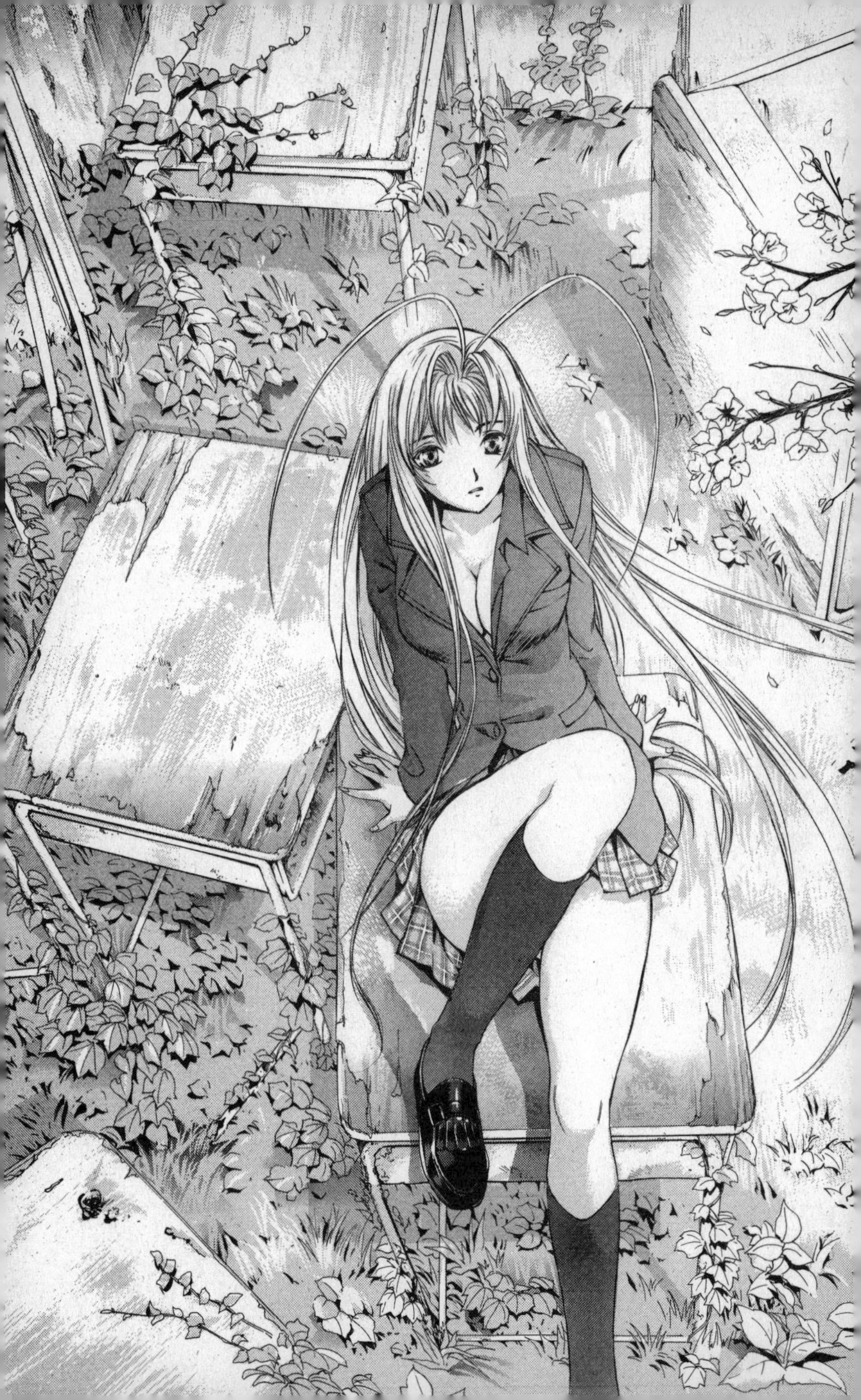

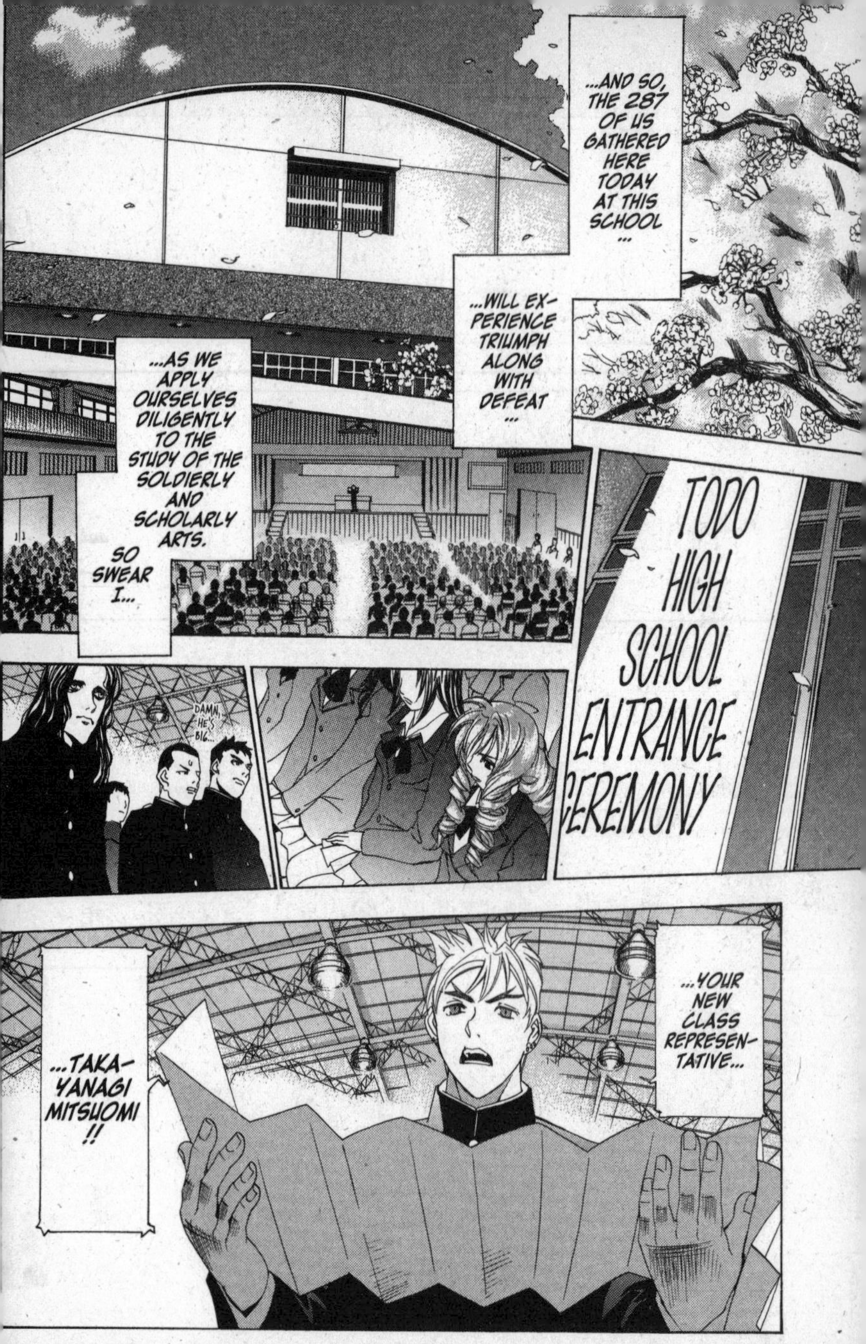
...AND SO, THE 287 OF US GATHERED HERE TODAY AT THIS SCHOOL...
...WILL EXPERIENCE TRIUMPH ALONG WITH DEFEAT...
...AS WE APPLY OURSELVES DILIGENTLY TO THE STUDY OF THE SOLDIERLY AND SCHOLARLY ARTS.
TODO HIGH SCHOOL ENTRANCE CEREMONY
SO SWEAR I...
DAMN, HE'S BIG...
...YOUR NEW CLASS REPRESENTATIVE...
...TAKAYANAGI MITSUOMI!!

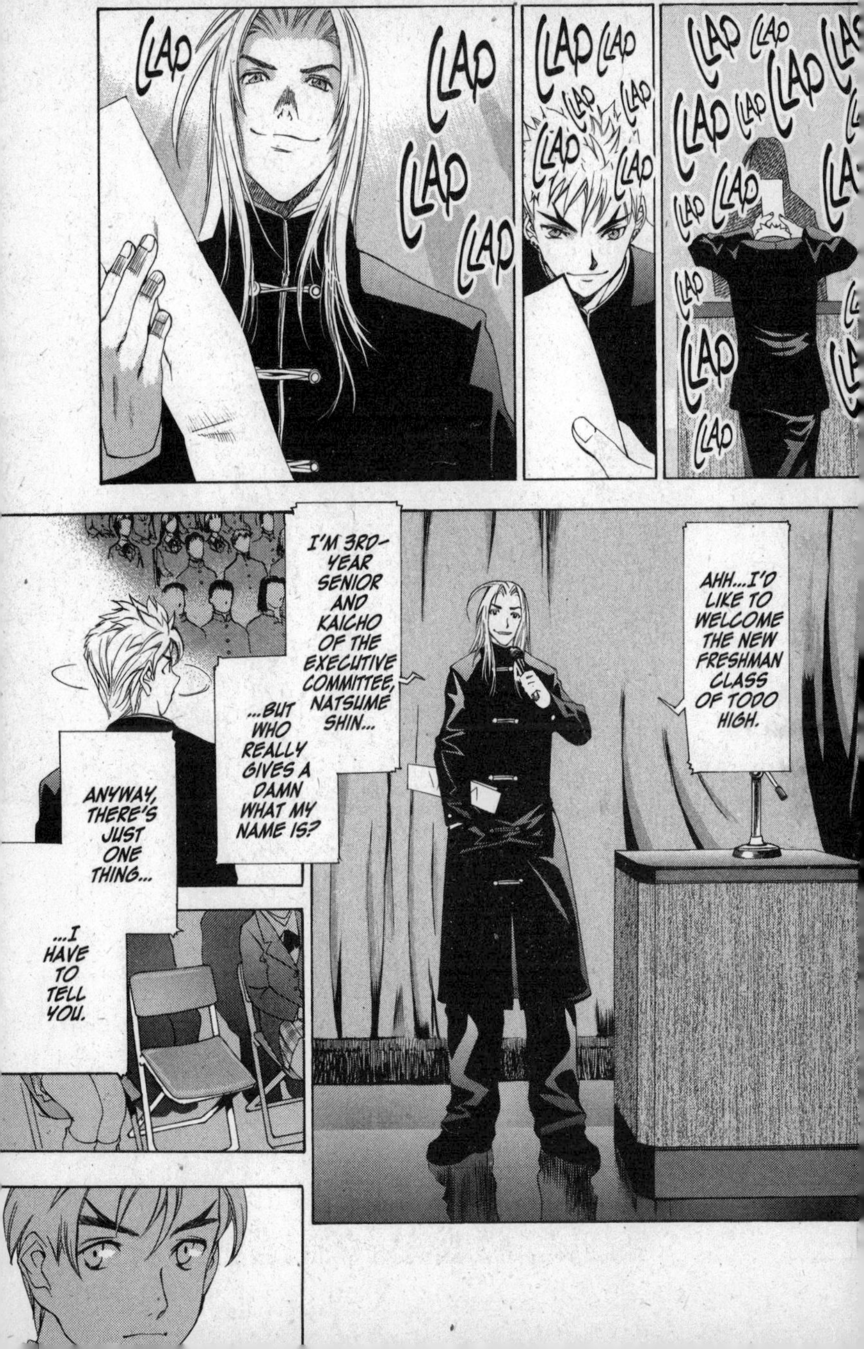

CLAP CLAP CLAP CLAP
CLAP CLAP CLAP CLAP
CLAP CLAP CLAP CLAP
CLAP CLAP CLAP CLAP
CLAP CLAP CLAP
CLAP CLAP CLAP
CLAP CLAP
AHH...I'D LIKE TO WELCOME THE NEW FRESHMAN CLASS OF TODO HIGH.
I'M 3RD-YEAR SENIOR AND KAICHO OF THE EXECUTIVE COMMITTEE, NATSUME SHIN...
...BUT WHO REALLY GIVES A DAMN WHAT MY NAME IS?
ANYWAY, THERE'S JUST ONE THING...
...I HAVE TO TELL YOU.

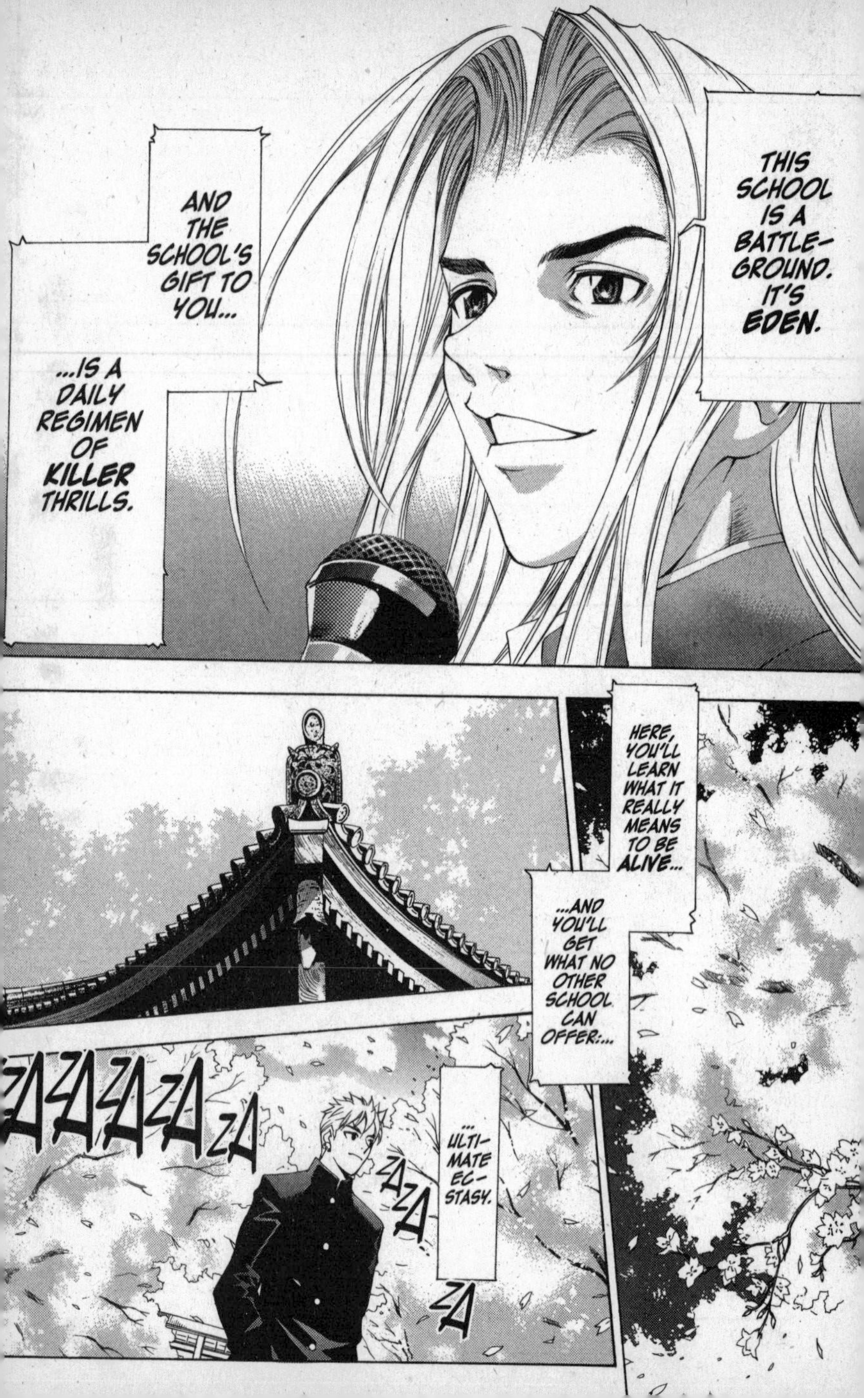
THIS SCHOOL IS A BATTLE-GROUND. IT'S EDEN.
AND THE SCHOOL'S GIFT TO YOU...
...IS A DAILY REGIMEN OF KILLER THRILLS.
HERE, YOU'LL LEARN WHAT IT REALLY MEANS TO BE ALIVE...
...AND YOU'LL GET WHAT NO OTHER SCHOOL CAN OFFER:...
...ULTI-MATE EC-STASY.
ZAZA ZA
ZA
ZAZAZAZAZA ZA

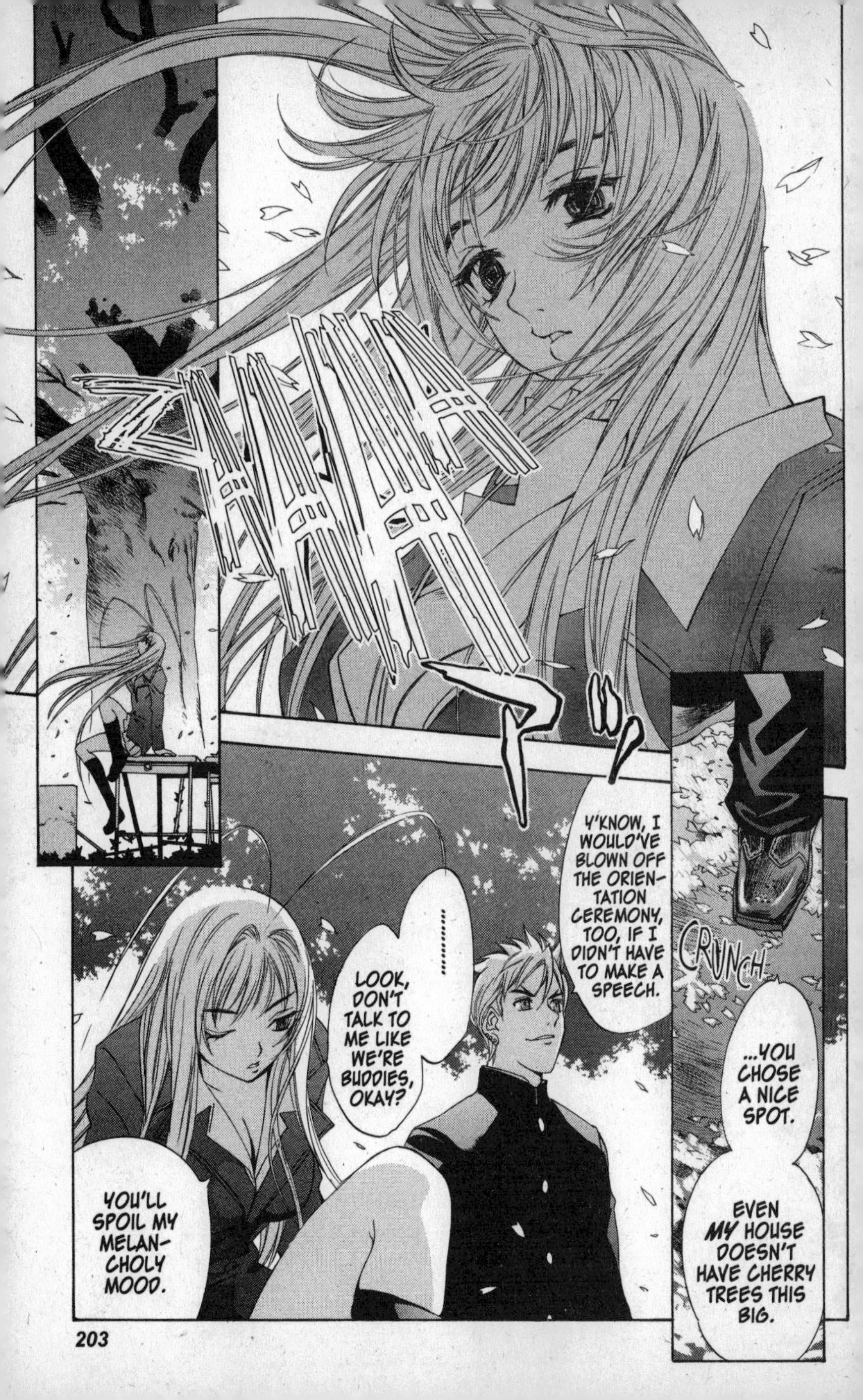
CRUNCH
...YOU CHOSE A NICE SPOT.
EVEN MY HOUSE DOESN'T HAVE CHERRY TREES THIS BIG.
Y'KNOW, I WOULD'VE BLOWN OFF THE ORIENTATION CEREMONY, TOO, IF I DIDN'T HAVE TO MAKE A SPEECH.
......
LOOK, DON'T TALK TO ME LIKE WE'RE BUDDIES, OKAY?
YOU'LL SPOIL MY MELANCHOLY MOOD.

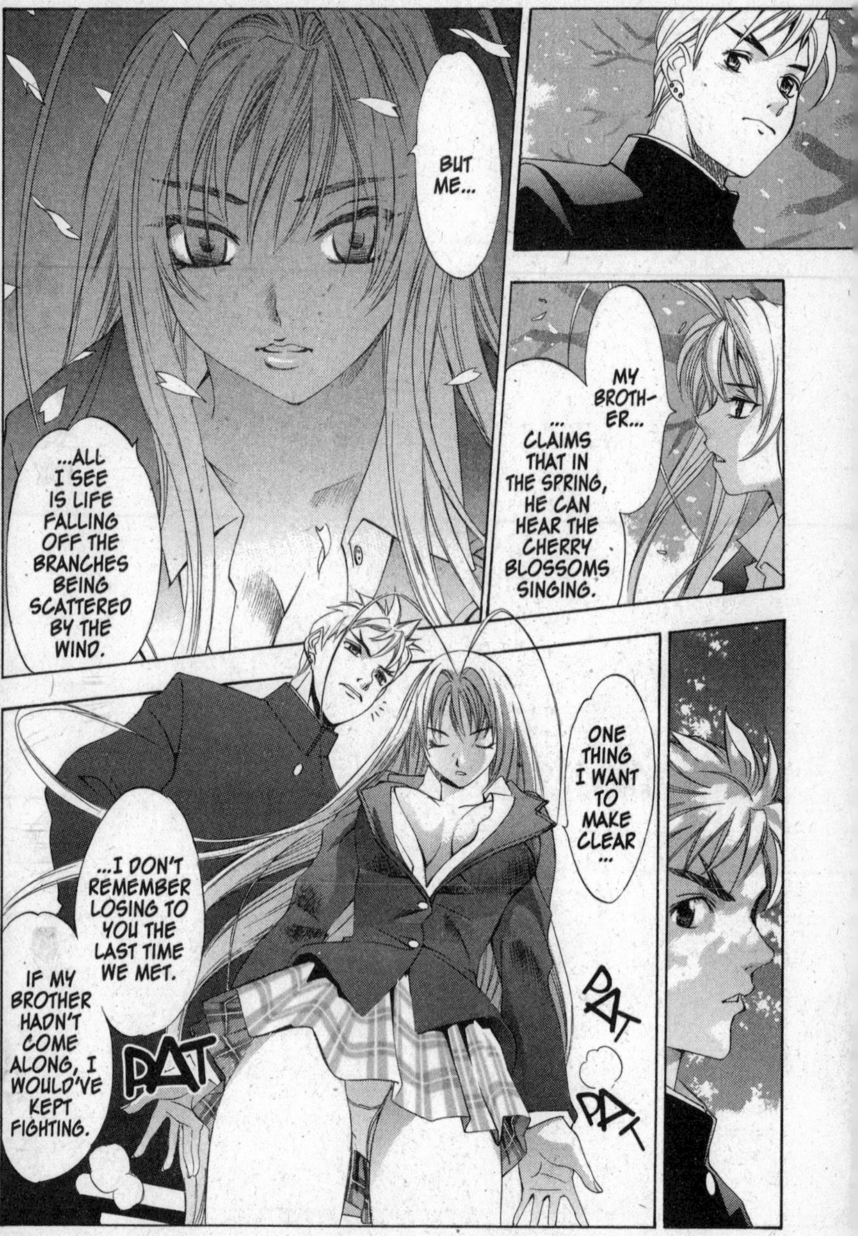
MY BROTHER...
... CLAIMS THAT IN THE SPRING, HE CAN HEAR THE CHERRY BLOSSOMS SINGING.
BUT ME...
...ALL I SEE IS LIFE FALLING OFF THE BRANCHES BEING SCATTERED BY THE WIND.
ONE THING I WANT TO MAKE CLEAR ...
PAT
PAT
...I DON'T REMEMBER LOSING TO YOU THE LAST TIME WE MET.
IF MY BROTHER HADN'T COME ALONG, I WOULD'VE KEPT FIGHTING.
PAT

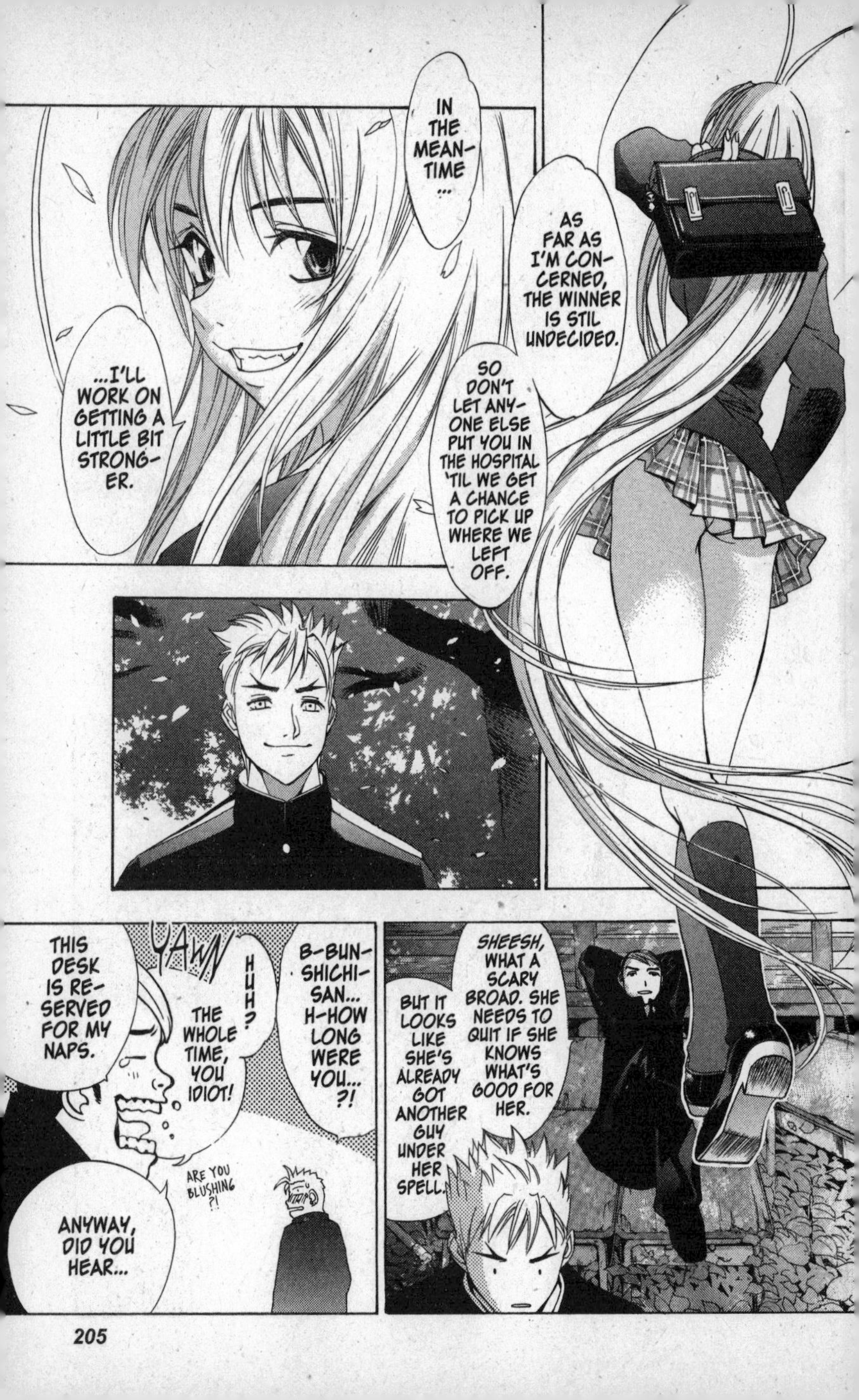
AS FAR AS I'M CONCERNED, THE WINNER IS STIL UNDECIDED.
SO DON'T LET ANYONE ELSE PUT YOU IN THE HOSPITAL 'TIL WE GET A CHANCE TO PICK UP WHERE WE LEFT OFF.
IN THE MEANTIME...
...I'LL WORK ON GETTING A LITTLE BIT STRONGER.
SHEESH, WHAT A SCARY BROAD. SHE NEEDS TO QUIT IF SHE KNOWS WHAT'S GOOD FOR HER.
BUT IT LOOKS LIKE SHE'S ALREADY GOT ANOTHER GUY UNDER HER SPELL.
B-BUNSHICHI-SAN... H-HOW LONG WERE YOU...?!
HUH?
YAWN
THE WHOLE TIME, YOU IDIOT!
THIS DESK IS RESERVED FOR MY NAPS.
ARE YOU BLUSHING ?!
ANYWAY, DID YOU HEAR...

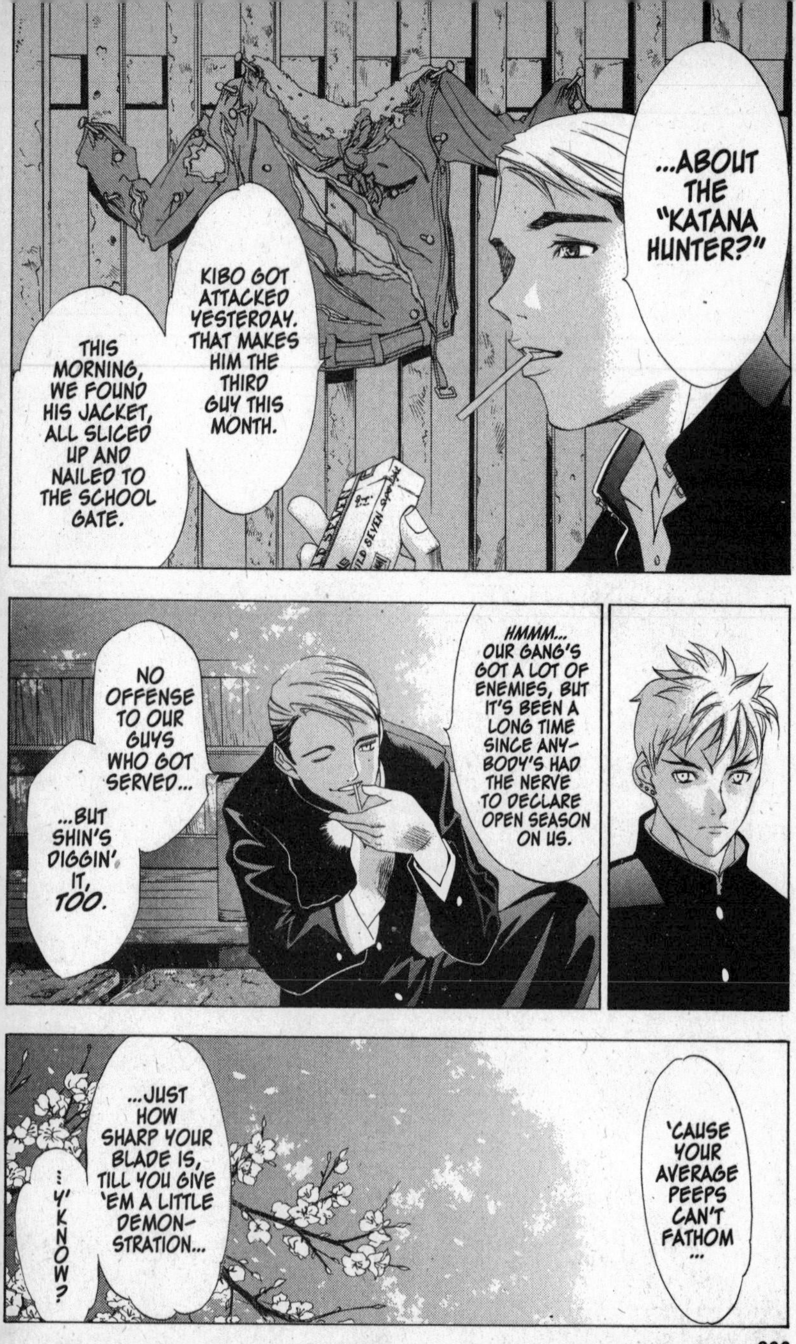
...ABOUT THE "KATANA HUNTER?"
KIBO GOT ATTACKED YESTERDAY. THAT MAKES HIM THE THIRD GUY THIS MONTH.
THIS MORNING, WE FOUND HIS JACKET, ALL SLICED UP AND NAILED TO THE SCHOOL GATE.
HMMM... OUR GANG'S GOT A LOT OF ENEMIES, BUT IT'S BEEN A LONG TIME SINCE ANY-BODY'S HAD THE NERVE TO DECLARE OPEN SEASON ON US.
NO OFFENSE TO OUR GUYS WHO GOT SERVED...
...BUT SHIN'S DIGGIN' IT, *TOO.*
'CAUSE YOUR AVERAGE PEEPS CAN'T FATHOM ...
...JUST HOW SHARP YOUR BLADE IS, TILL YOU GIVE 'EM A LITTLE DEMON-STRATION...
...Y'KNOW?

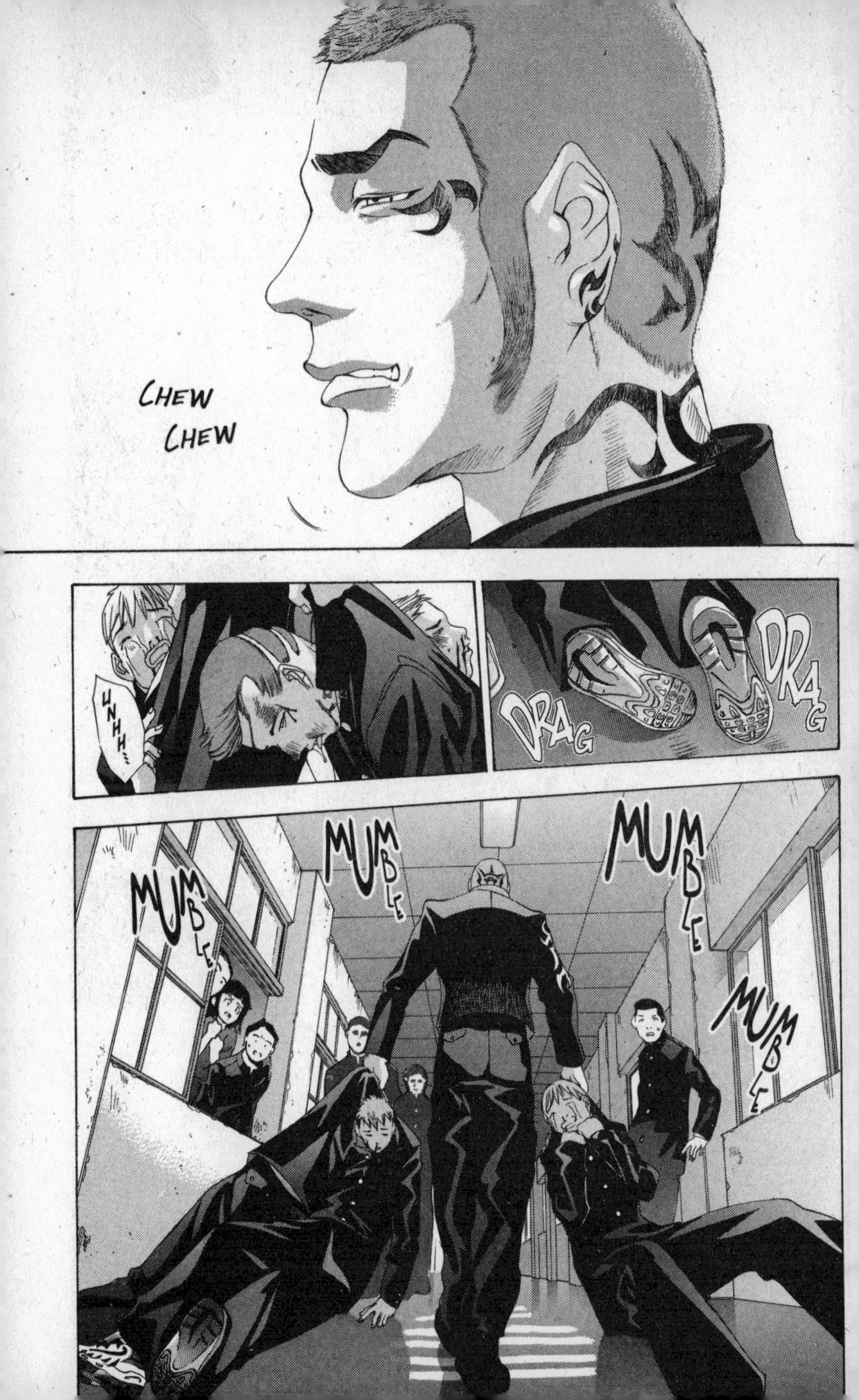
CHEW CHEW
DRAG
DRAG
UNHH...
MUMBLE
MUMBLE
MUMBLE
MUMBLE

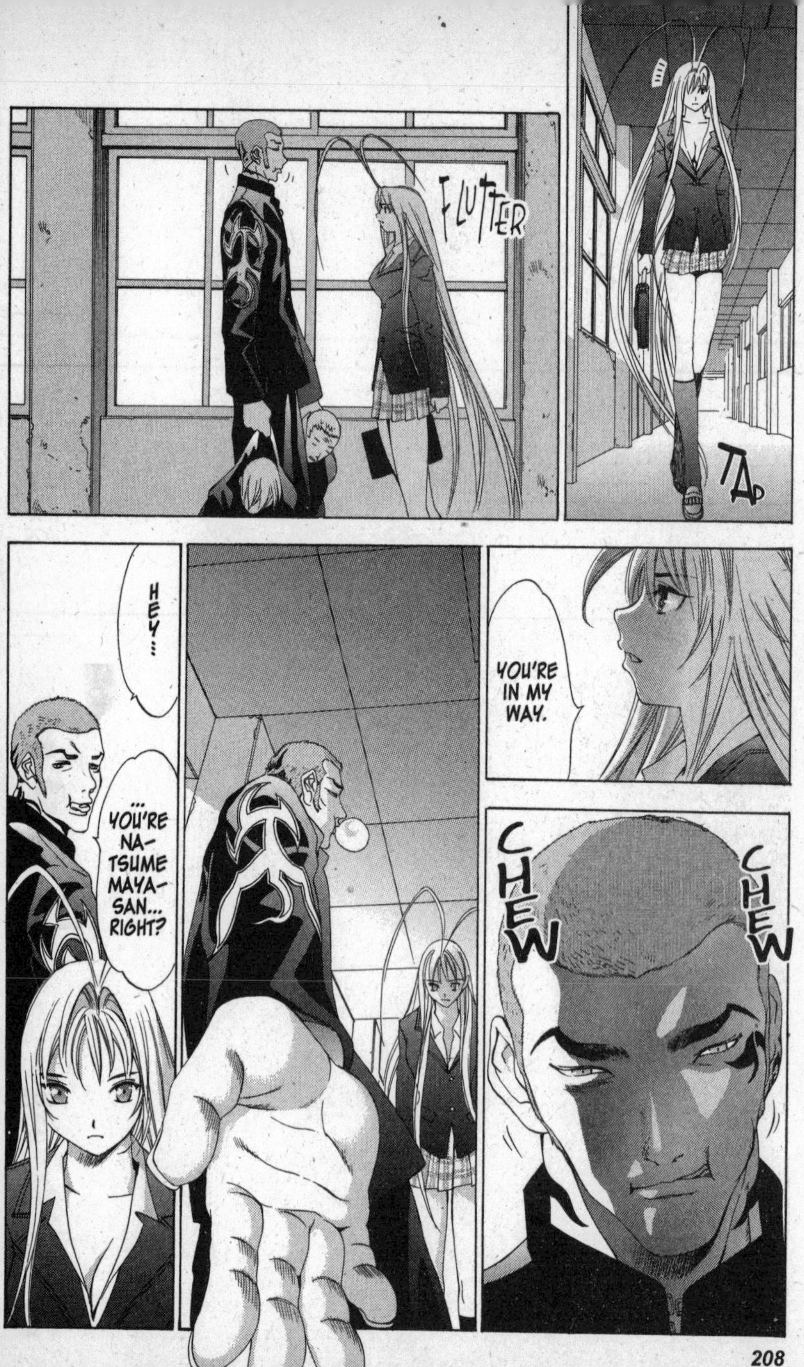

TAP
FLUTTER
YOU'RE IN MY WAY.
CHEW CHEW
HEY...
... YOU'RE NATSUME MAYA-SAN... RIGHT?

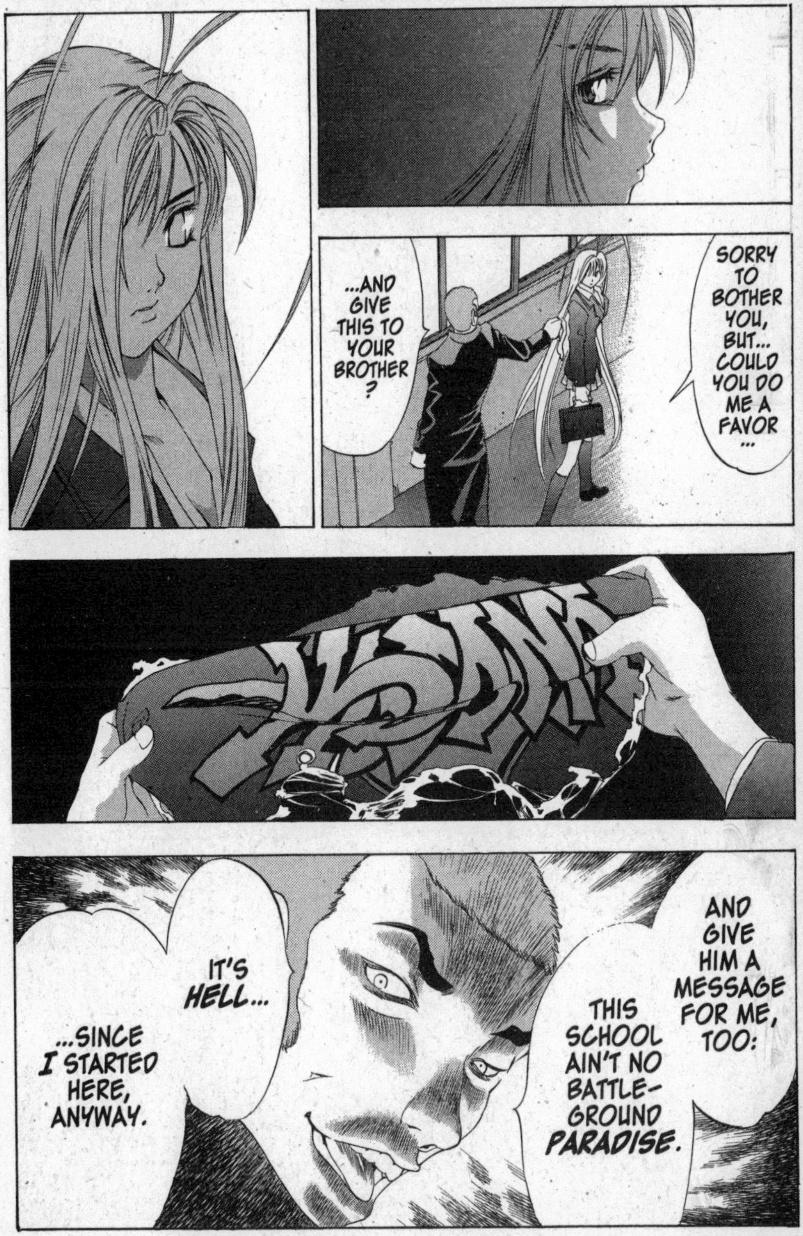
SORRY TO BOTHER YOU, BUT... COULD YOU DO ME A FAVOR...
...AND GIVE THIS TO YOUR BROTHER?
AND GIVE HIM A MESSAGE FOR ME, TOO:
THIS SCHOOL AIN'T NO BATTLE-GROUND PARADISE.
IT'S HELL...
...SINCE I STARTED HERE, ANYWAY.

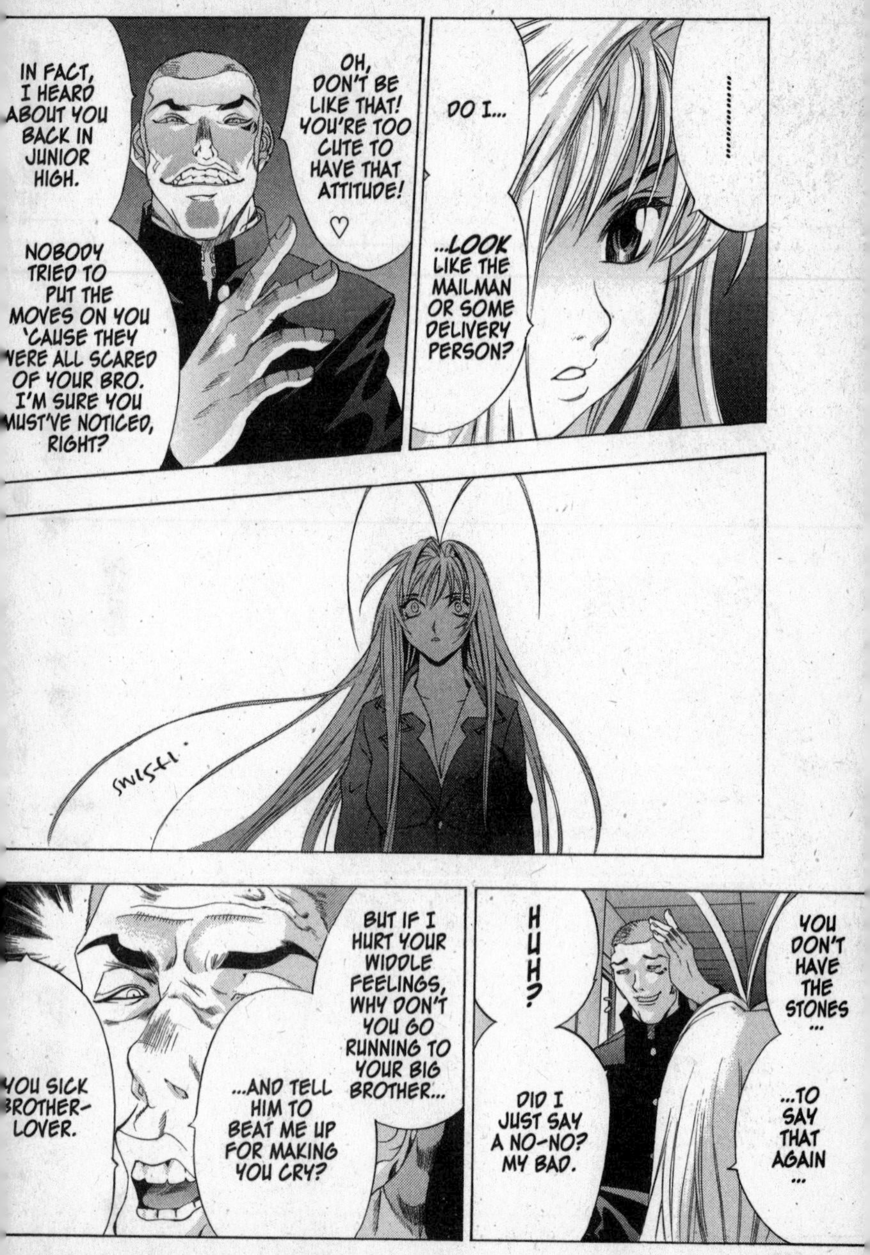

....
DO I...
...LOOK LIKE THE MAILMAN OR SOME DELIVERY PERSON?
OH, DON'T BE LIKE THAT! YOU'RE TOO CUTE TO HAVE THAT ATTITUDE! ♡
IN FACT, I HEARD ABOUT YOU BACK IN JUNIOR HIGH.
NOBODY TRIED TO PUT THE MOVES ON YOU 'CAUSE THEY WERE ALL SCARED OF YOUR BRO. I'M SURE YOU MUST'VE NOTICED, RIGHT?
SWISH
YOU DON'T HAVE THE STONES ...
...TO SAY THAT AGAIN ...
HUH?
DID I JUST SAY A NO-NO? MY BAD.
BUT IF I HURT YOUR WIDDLE FEELINGS, WHY DON'T YOU GO RUNNING TO YOUR BIG BROTHER...
...AND TELL HIM TO BEAT ME UP FOR MAKING YOU CRY?
YOU SICK BROTHER-LOVER.

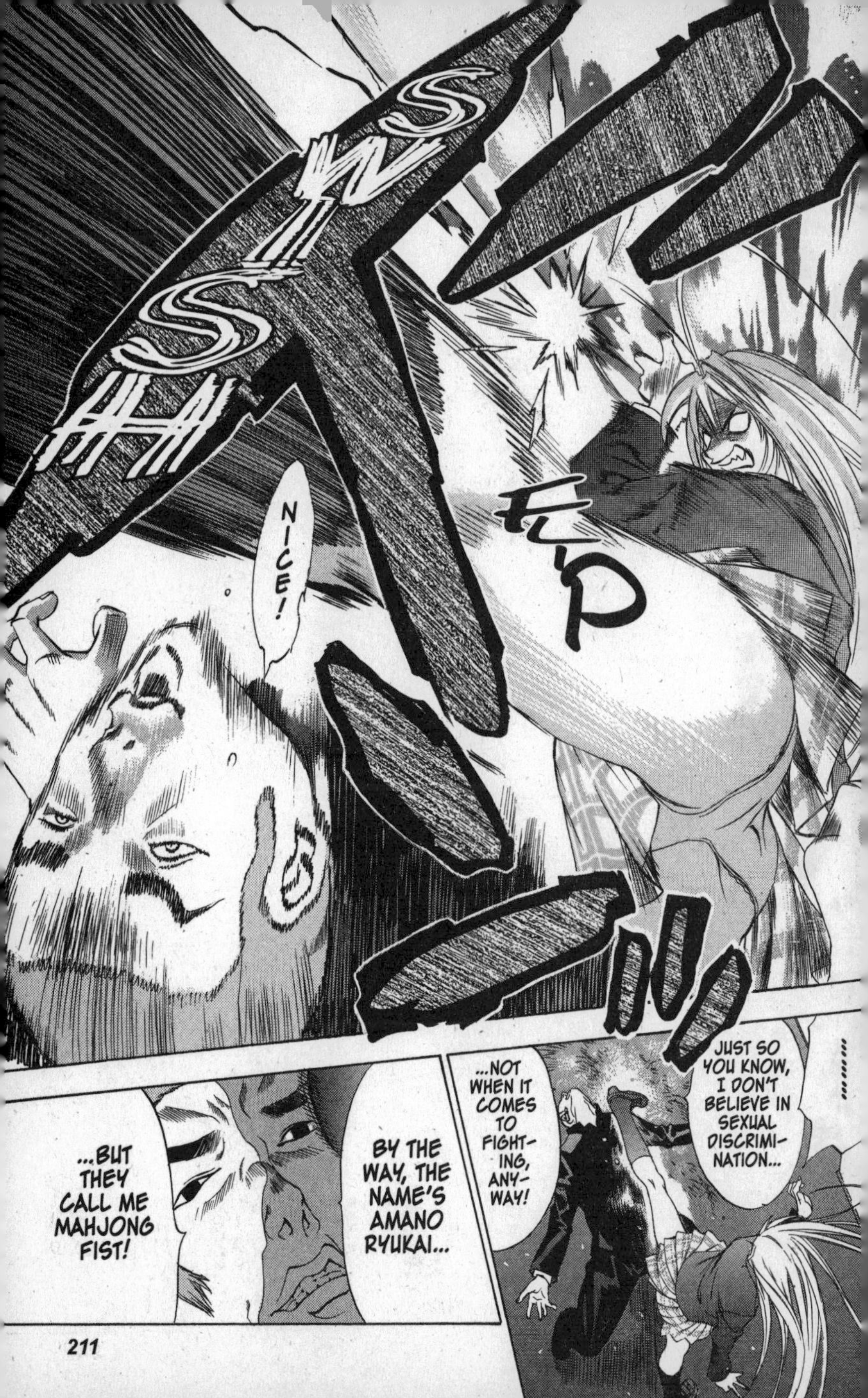
SWISH
FLIP
NICE!
......
JUST SO YOU KNOW, I DON'T BELIEVE IN SEXUAL DISCRIMINATION...
...NOT WHEN IT COMES TO FIGHTING, ANYWAY!
BY THE WAY, THE NAME'S AMANO RYUKAI...
...BUT THEY CALL ME MAHJONG FIST!

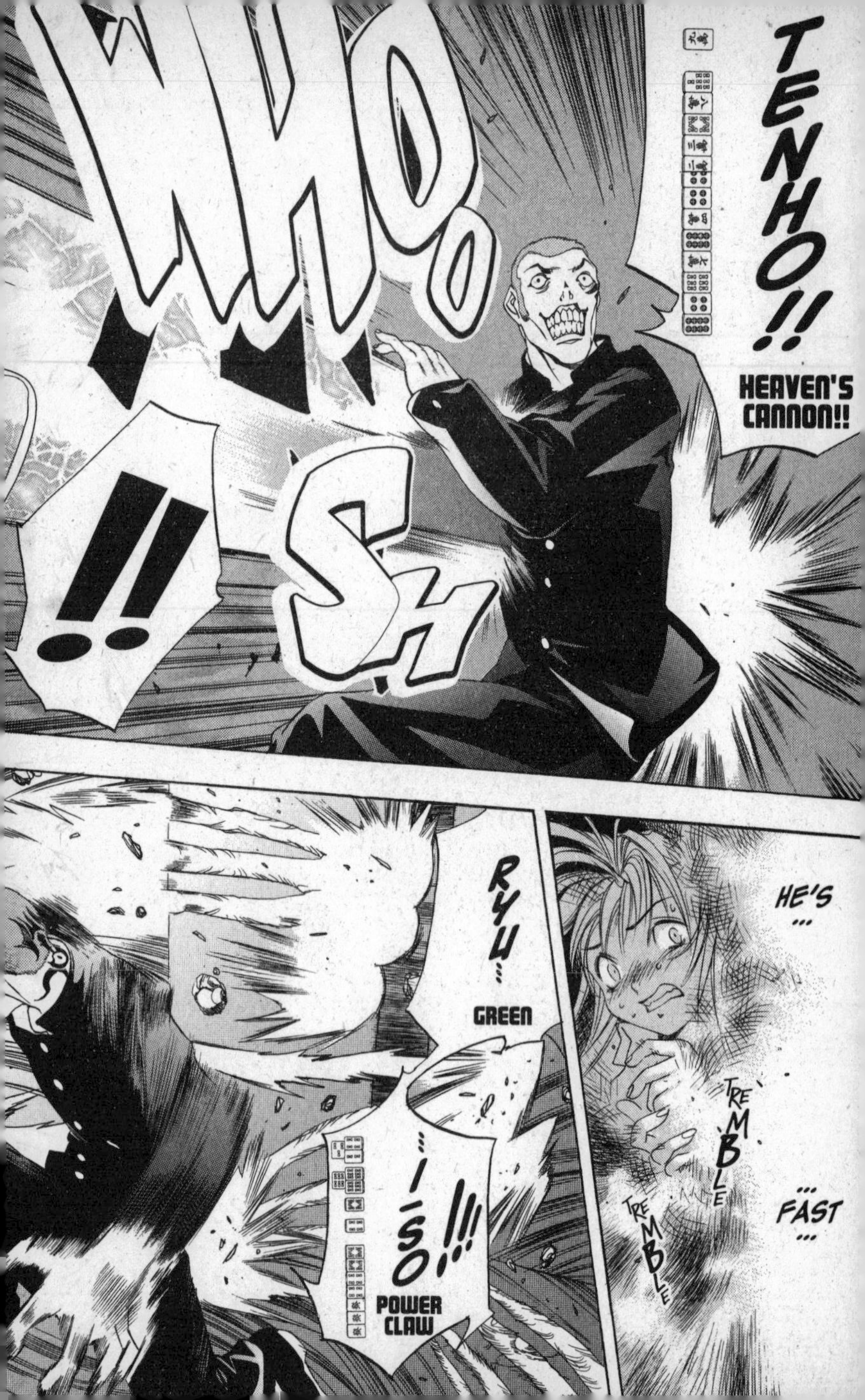
TENHO!!
HEAVEN'S CANNON!!
WHOOSH!!
HE'S...
...FAST...
TREMBLE
TREMBLE
RYU...
GREEN
...I-SO!!!!
POWER CLAW

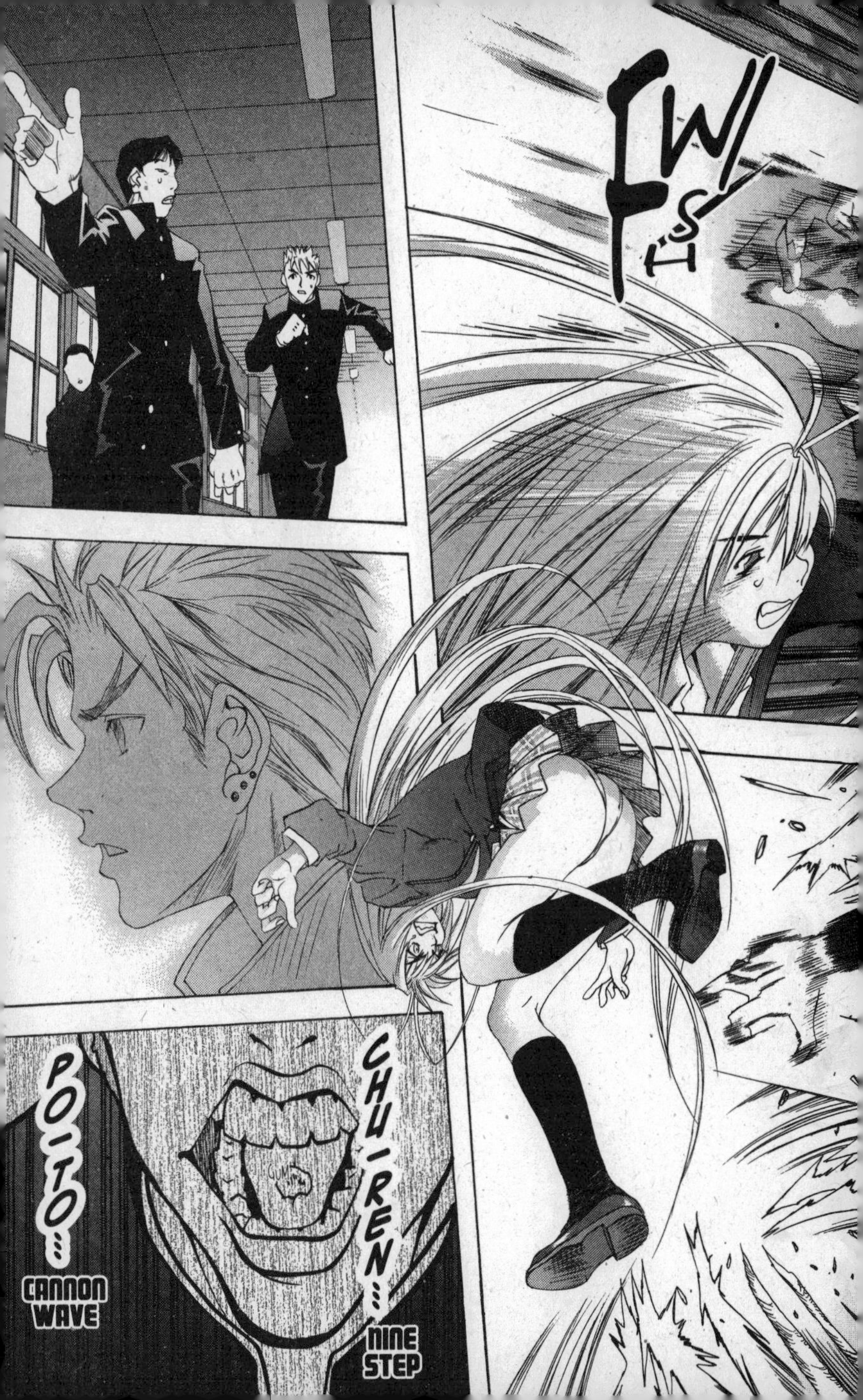
FWISH
CHU-REN...
NINE STEP
PO-TO...
CANNON WAVE

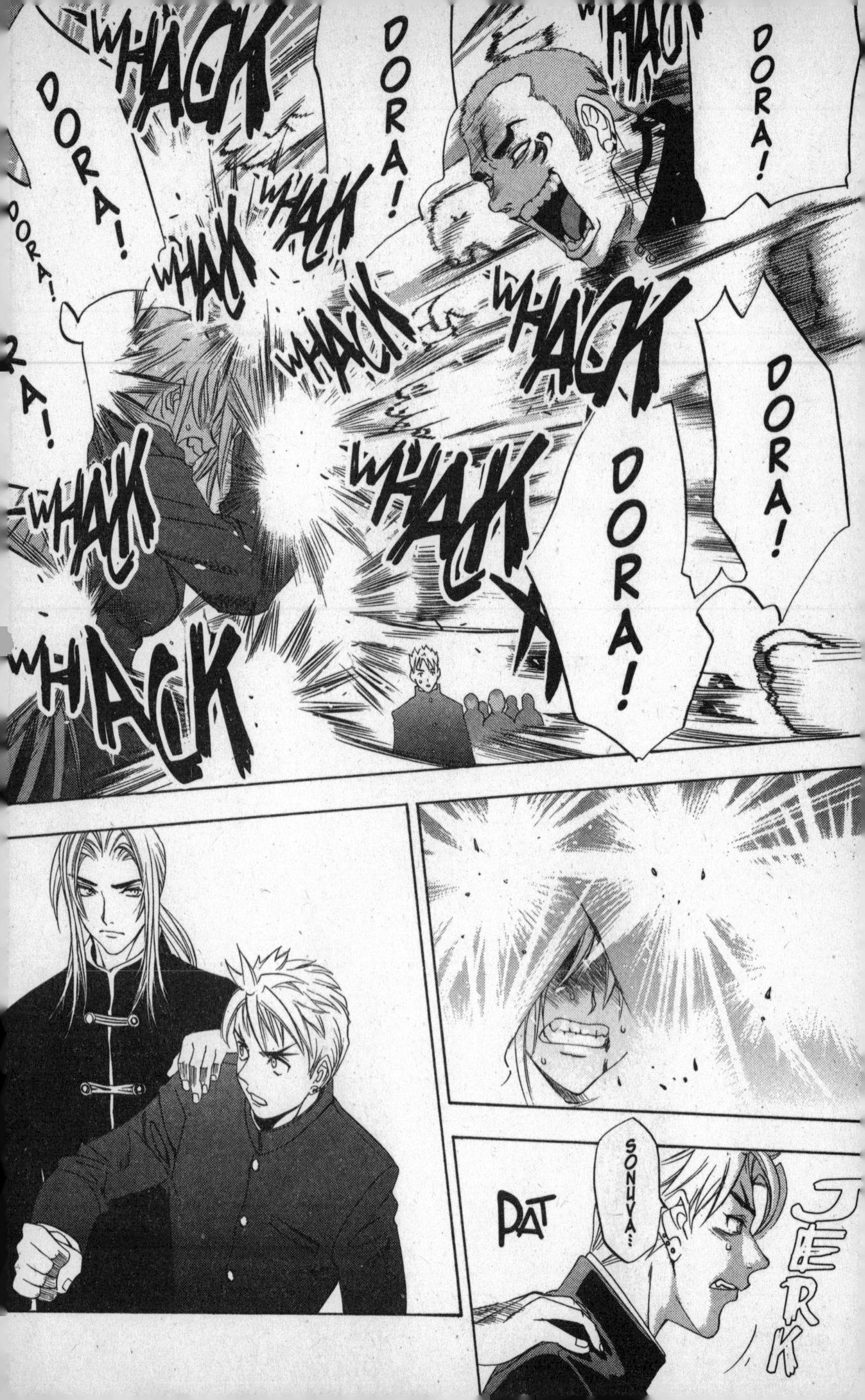
WHACK
DORA!
DORA!
DORA!
WHACK
DORA!
WHACK
WHACK
WHACK
WHACK
DORA!
DORA!
RA!
WHACK
WHACK
JERK
SONUVA...
PAT

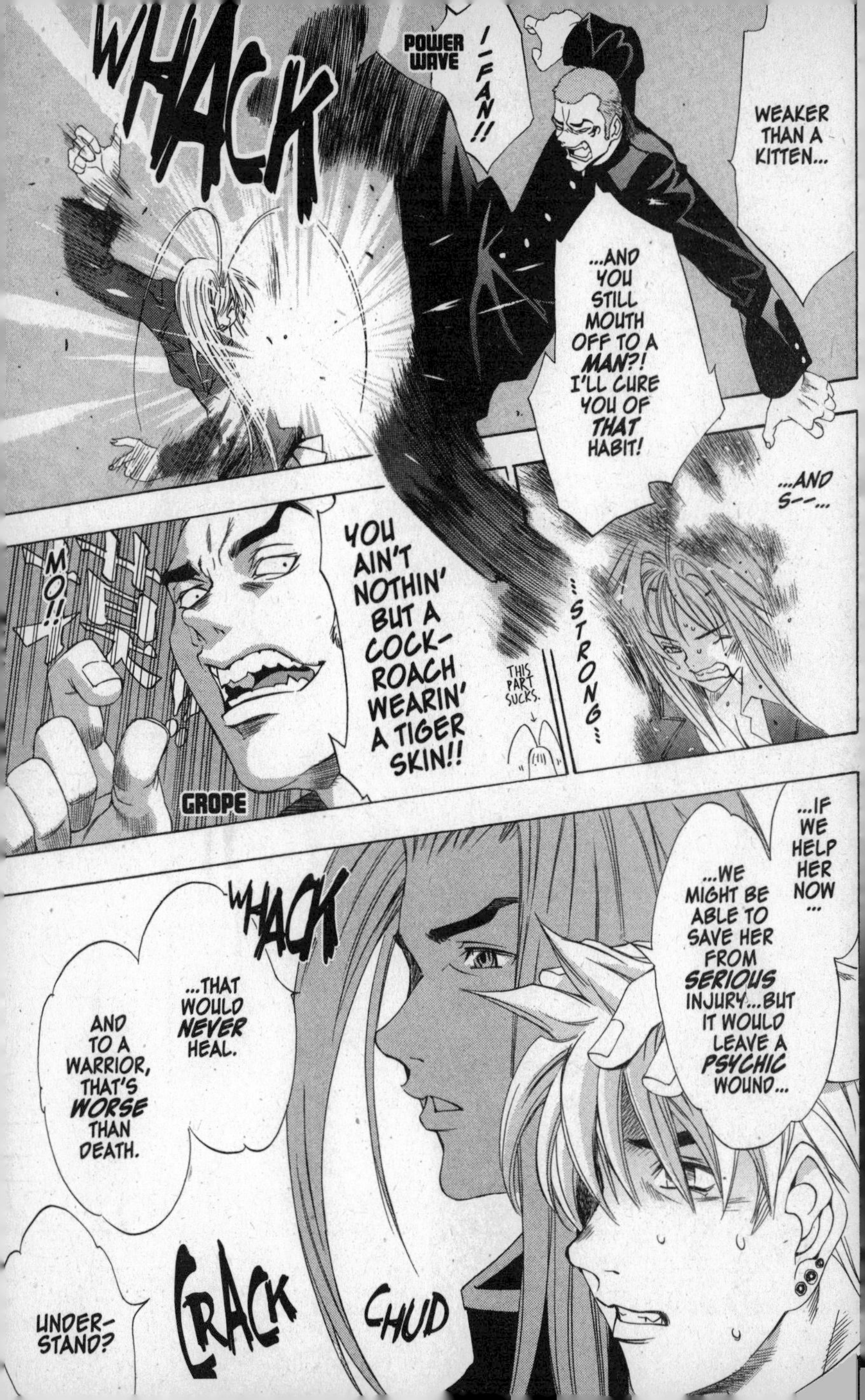
WEAKER THAN A KITTEN...
...AND YOU STILL MOUTH OFF TO A *MAN*?! I'LL CURE YOU OF *THAT* HABIT!
I—FAN!!
POWER WAVE
WHACK
...AND S--...
...STRONG...
THIS PART SUCKS.
YOU AIN'T NOTHIN' BUT A COCK-ROACH WEARIN' A TIGER SKIN!!
MO!!
GROPE
...IF WE HELP HER NOW...
...WE MIGHT BE ABLE TO SAVE HER FROM *SERIOUS* INJURY...BUT IT WOULD LEAVE A *PSYCHIC* WOUND...
WHACK
...THAT WOULD *NEVER* HEAL.
AND TO A WARRIOR, THAT'S *WORSE* THAN DEATH.
CHUD
CRACK
UNDER-STAND?

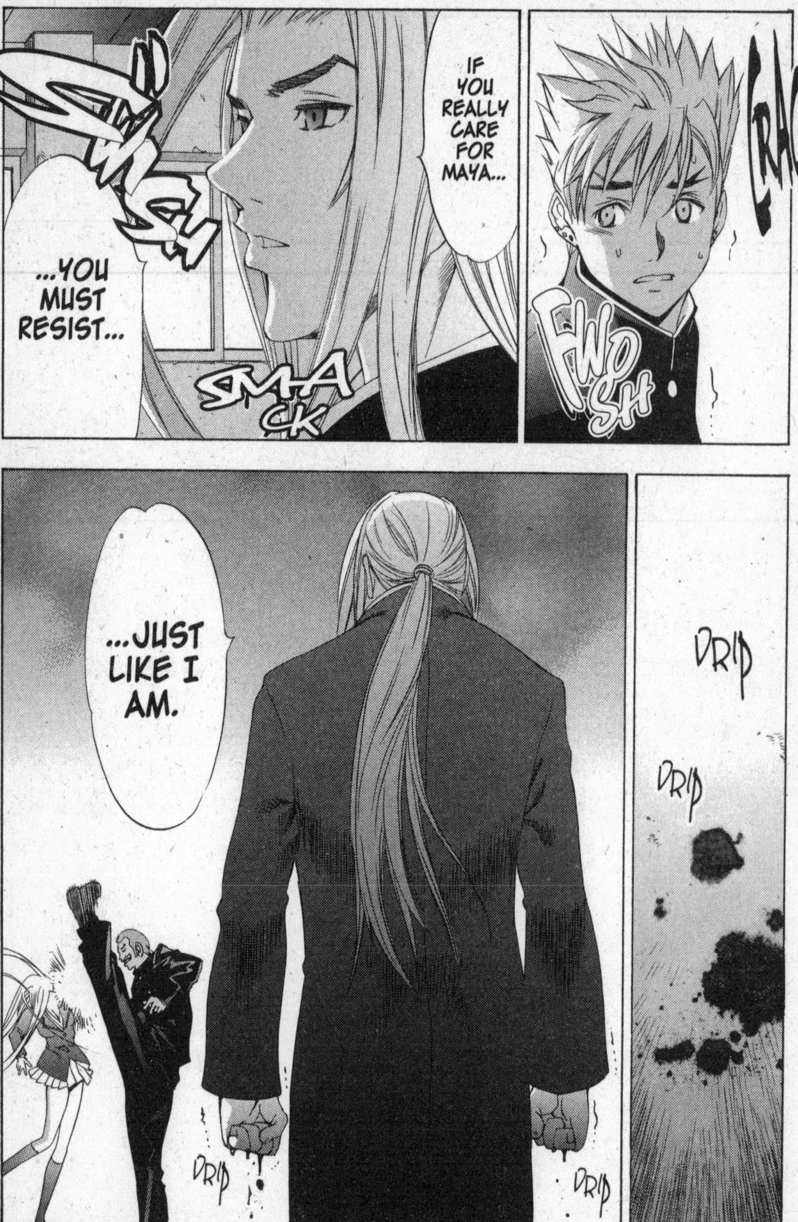
CRACK
FWOSH
IF YOU REALLY CARE FOR MAYA...
SWISH
...YOU MUST RESIST...
SMACK
DRIP
DRIP
...JUST LIKE I AM.
DRIP
DRIP

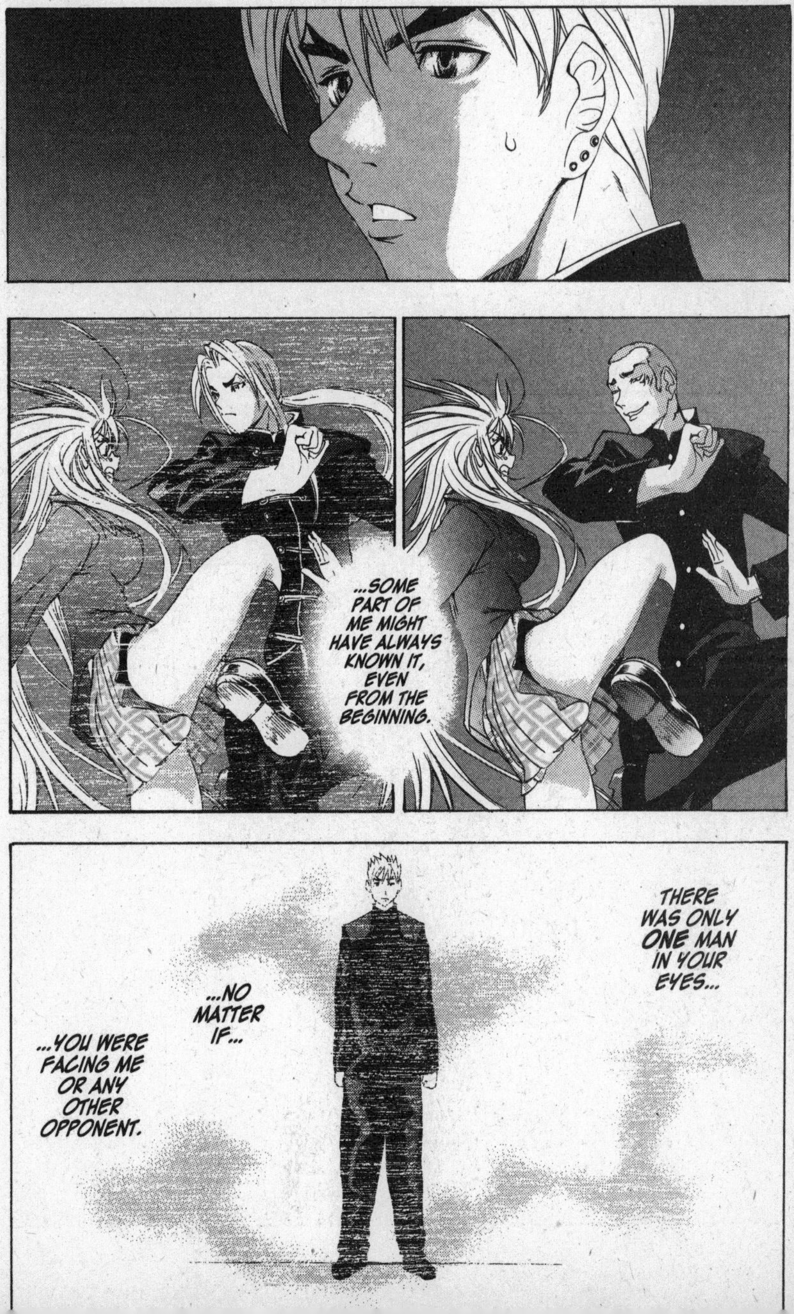
...SOME PART OF ME MIGHT HAVE ALWAYS KNOWN IT, EVEN FROM THE BEGINNING.
THERE WAS ONLY ONE MAN IN YOUR EYES...
...NO MATTER IF...
...YOU WERE FACING ME OR ANY OTHER OPPONENT.

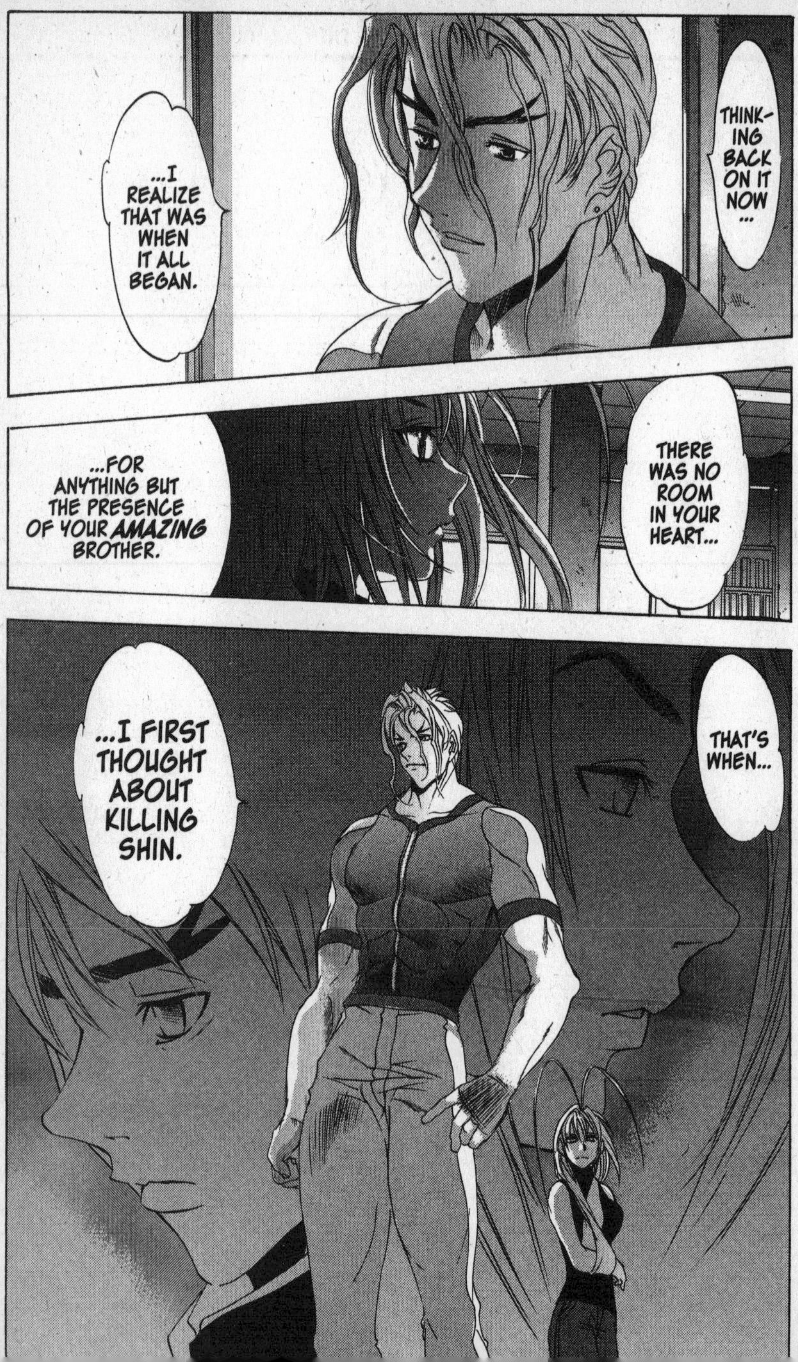
THINKING BACK ON IT NOW...
...I REALIZE THAT WAS WHEN IT ALL BEGAN.
THERE WAS NO ROOM IN YOUR HEART...
...FOR ANYTHING BUT THE PRESENCE OF YOUR AMAZING BROTHER.
THAT'S WHEN...
...I FIRST THOUGHT ABOUT KILLING SHIN.

Tenjho Tenge Volume 4: THE END

BONUS MANGA
GUREKICHI-KUN "SORRY FOR ONLY HAVING ONE PAGE THIS TIME OUT!"

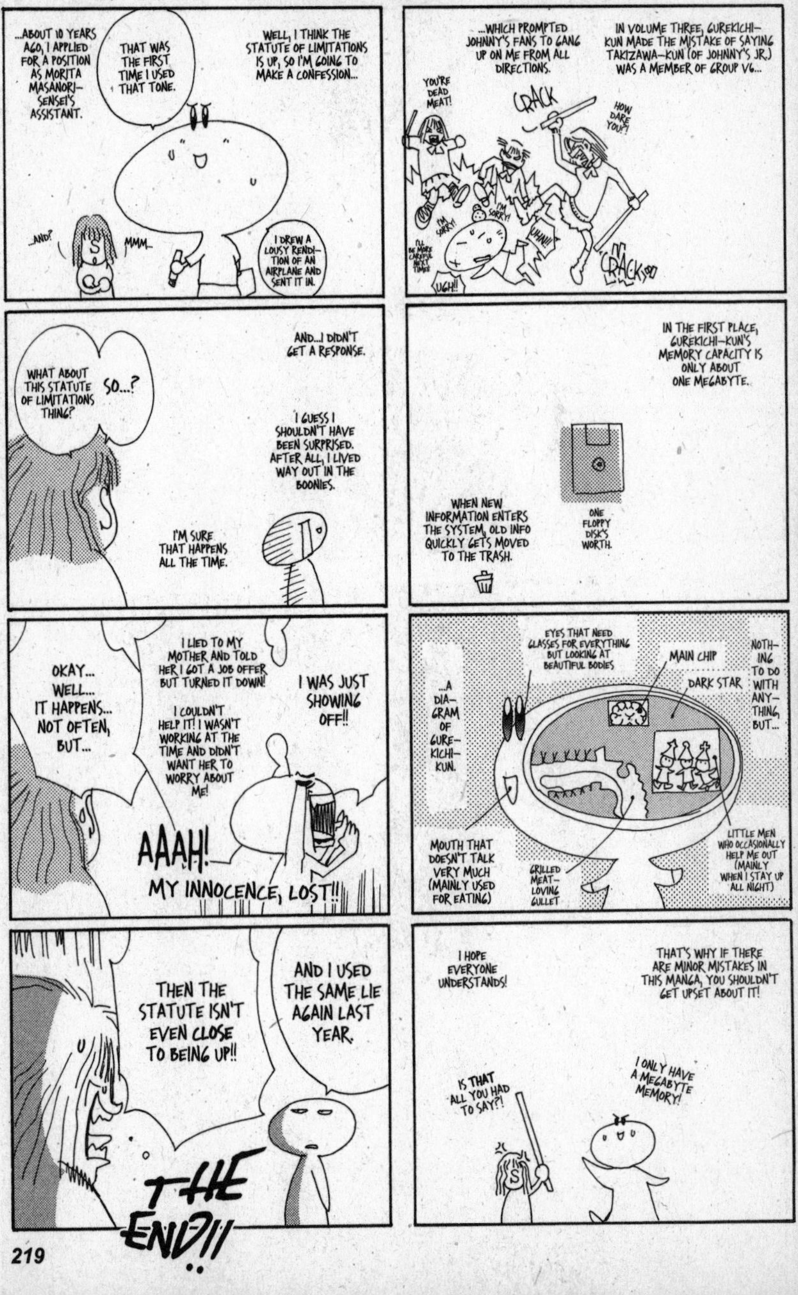
IN VOLUME THREE, GUREKICHI-KUN MADE THE MISTAKE OF SAYING TAKIZAWA-KUN (OF JOHNNY'S JR.) WAS A MEMBER OF GROUP V6...
...WHICH PROMPTED JOHNNY'S FANS TO GANG UP ON ME FROM ALL DIRECTIONS.
HOW DARE YOU!?
CRACK
YOU'RE DEAD MEAT!
I'M SORRY!
UHN!!
CRACK
I'M SORRY!
I'LL BE MORE CAREFUL NEXT TIME!
UGH!!
WELL, I THINK THE STATUTE OF LIMITATIONS IS UP, SO I'M GOING TO MAKE A CONFESSION...
THAT WAS THE FIRST TIME I USED THAT TONE.
...ABOUT 10 YEARS AGO, I APPLIED FOR A POSITION AS MORITA MASANORI-SENSEI'S ASSISTANT.
I DREW A LOUSY RENDITION OF AN AIRPLANE AND SENT IT IN.
MMM...
...AND?
IN THE FIRST PLACE, GUREKICHI-KUN'S MEMORY CAPACITY IS ONLY ABOUT ONE MEGABYTE.
ONE FLOPPY DISK'S WORTH.
WHEN NEW INFORMATION ENTERS THE SYSTEM, OLD INFO QUICKLY GETS MOVED TO THE TRASH.
AND...I DIDN'T GET A RESPONSE.
I GUESS I SHOULDN'T HAVE BEEN SURPRISED. AFTER ALL, I LIVED WAY OUT IN THE BOONIES.
SO...?
WHAT ABOUT THIS STATUTE OF LIMITATIONS THING?
I'M SURE THAT HAPPENS ALL THE TIME.
NOTHING TO DO WITH ANYTHING, BUT...
MAIN CHIP
DARK STAR
EYES THAT NEED GLASSES FOR EVERYTHING BUT LOOKING AT BEAUTIFUL BODIES
...A DIAGRAM OF GUREKICHI-KUN.
LITTLE MEN WHO OCCASIONALLY HELP ME OUT (MAINLY WHEN I STAY UP ALL NIGHT)
GRILLED MEAT-LOVING GULLET
MOUTH THAT DOESN'T TALK VERY MUCH (MAINLY USED FOR EATING)
I WAS JUST SHOWING OFF!!
I LIED TO MY MOTHER AND TOLD HER I GOT A JOB OFFER BUT TURNED IT DOWN!
I COULDN'T HELP IT! I WASN'T WORKING AT THE TIME AND DIDN'T WANT HER TO WORRY ABOUT ME!
OKAY... WELL... IT HAPPENS... NOT OFTEN, BUT...
AAAH!
MY INNOCENCE, LOST!!
THAT'S WHY IF THERE ARE MINOR MISTAKES IN THIS MANGA, YOU SHOULDN'T GET UPSET ABOUT IT!
I HOPE EVERYONE UNDERSTANDS!
I ONLY HAVE A MEGABYTE MEMORY!
IS THAT ALL YOU HAD TO SAY?!
AND I USED THE SAME LIE AGAIN LAST YEAR.
THEN THE STATUTE ISN'T EVEN CLOSE TO BEING UP!!
THE END!!

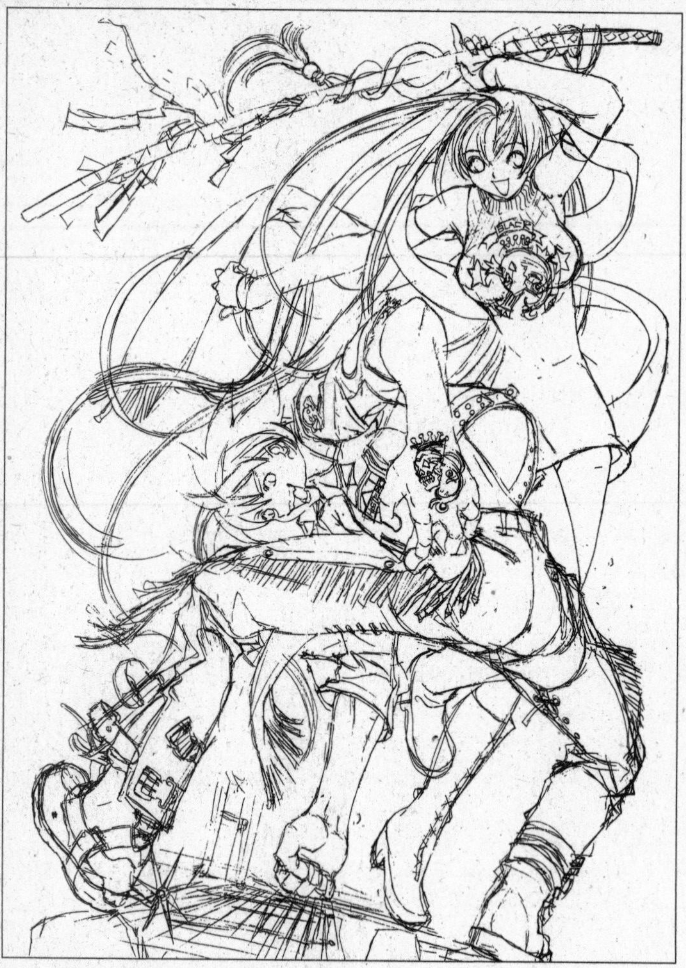

Editor Tomita Kenzo
Chief Editor Sakurada Ayami
Binding Abiko Yoshitake
With thanks to: Tatsumi Masahiro, Pacific, Takei Shin, Oririn, Nishizawa Fujiroku, Maruyama Masaharu, and Sasaki Akino

The stories in this volume were published originally in “UltraJump” 31-Feb 2001 edition (2000-2001).

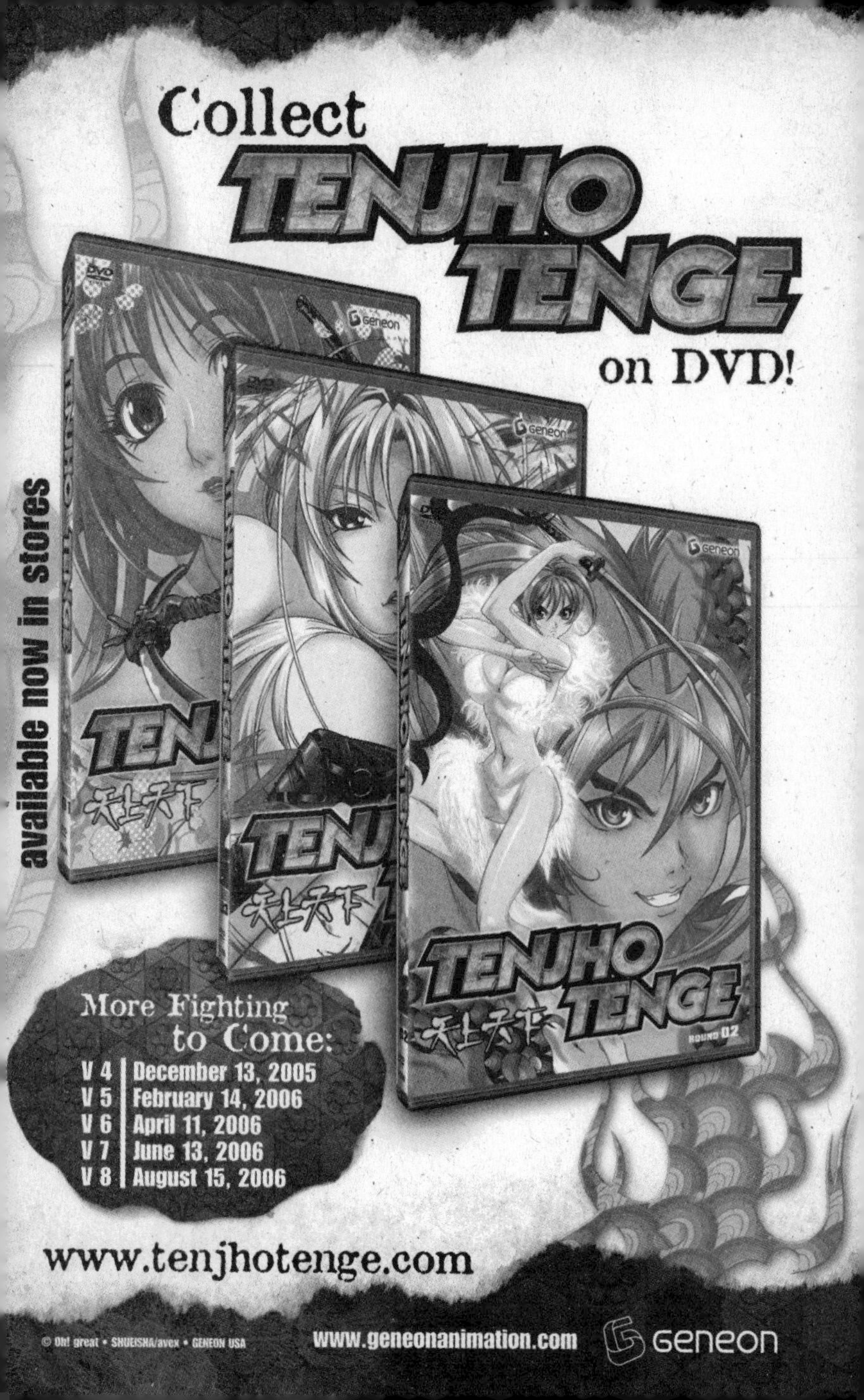
Collect
TENJHO TENGE
on DVD!
available now in stores
TENJHO TENGE
天上天下
ROUND 02
More Fighting to Come:
V 4 | December 13, 2005
V 5 | February 14, 2006
V 6 | April 11, 2006
V 7 | June 13, 2006
V 8 | August 15, 2006
www.tenjhotenge.com
© Oh! great • SHUEISHA/avex • GENEON USA
www.geneonanimation.com
geneon

the **DEVIL**
DOES EXIST

By TAKANASHI
Mitsuba

VOLUME 3

On sale now!

Kayano attempts to make sense of her feelings, but is always left confused. Just when she thinks she has seen the good side of Takeru, he does something completely infuriating. Then there is Yuichi, who was always so sweet to Kayano—lately, he is showing a much darker side. Will Kayano survive this bizarre love triangle...and who will she ultimately choose?

FROM **EROICA** WITH **LOVE**

By Aoike Yasuko

5 volumes available

EROICA YORI AI WO KOMETE
© 1976 Yasuko Aoike/AKITASHOTEN.

CHIKYU MISAKI

By Iwahara Yuji

1 volume available

CHIKYU MISAKI © 2001 Yuji
Iwahara/KADOKAWA SHOTEN.

Land of the **Blindfolded**

By Tsukuba Sakura

5 volumes available

MEKAKUSHI NO KUNI © 1998 Sakura Tsukuba/HAKUSENSHA, INC.

BACKLIST

CMX

MUSASHI #9

By Takahashi Miyuki

5 volumes available

KYUBANME NO MUSASHI © 1996
Miyuki Takahashi/AKITASHOTEN.

TENRYU
THE DRAGON CYCLE

By Matoh Sanami

3 volumes available

THE DRAGON CYCLE (TENRYU) © 1999
Sanami Matoh/AKITASHOTEN.

SEIMADEN

By Higuri You

2 volumes availa

SEIMADEN © 1994
You Higuri/KADOKAWA
SHOTEN.

CMX
Rating System

EVERYONE

Titles with this rating are appropriate for all age readers. They contain no offensive material. They may contain mild violence and/or some comic mischief.

TEEN

Titles with this rating are appropriate for a teen audience and older. They may contain some violent content, language, and/or suggestive themes.

MATURE

Titles with this rating are appropriate for mature readers. They may contain graphic violence, nudity, sex and content suitable only for older readers.

Jim Lee
Editorial Director
John Nee
VP—Business Development
Hank Kanalz
VP—General Manager, WildStorm
Paul Levitz
President & Publisher
Georg Brewer
VP—Design & DC Direct Creative
Richard Bruning
Senior VP—Creative Director
Patrick Caldon
Senior VP—Finance & Operations
Chris Caramalis
VP—Finance
Terri Cunningham
VP—Managing Editor
Stephanie Fierman
Senior VP—Sales & Marketing
Alison Gill
VP—Manufacturing
Rich Johnson
VP—Book Trade Sales
Lillian Laserson
Senior VP & General Counsel
Paula Lowitt
Senior VP—Business & Legal Affairs
David McKillips
VP—Advertising & Custom Publishing
Gregory Noveck
Senior VP—Creative Affairs
Cheryl Rubin
Senior VP—Brand Management
Jeff Trojan
VP—Business Development, DC Direct
Bob Wayne
VP—Sales

DC Comics, a Warner Bros. Entertainment Company.

Translation and Adaptation by
Sheldon Drzka

Saida Temofonte — Lettering
Larry Berry — Design
Alex Sinclair — Editor

ISBN: 1-4012-0563-1

FLIP IT!!

All the pages in this book were created—and are printed here—in Japanese RIGHT-to-LEFT format. No artwork has been reversed, so you can read the stories the way the creators meant for them to be read.

A note from the editors:
We have worked closely with the author and original publisher to prepare this American edition according to Oh! great's wishes. The author approved limited revisions in order to make his work more accessible to a wider American audience.

RIGHT TO LEFT?!

Traditional Japanese manga starts at the upper right-hand corner, and moves right-to-left as it goes down the page. Follow this guide for an easy understanding.

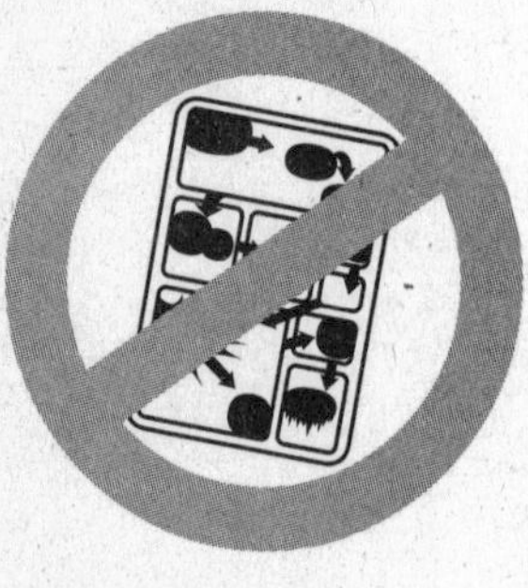

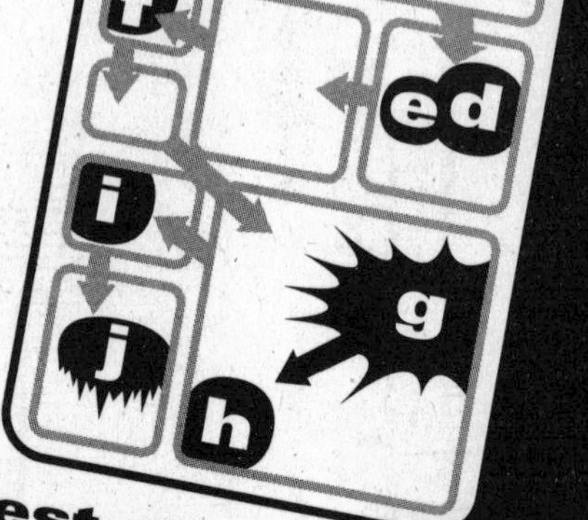
a
b
c
d
e
f
g
h
i
j

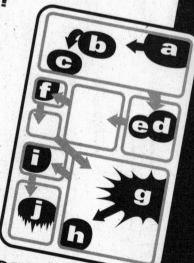

Catch the latest at cmxmanga.com!